SEXUAL SELECTION AND THE DESCENT OF MAN

SEXUAL SELECTION AND THE DESCENT OF MAN 1871-1971

edited by
BERNARD CAMPBELL
UNIVERSITY OF CALIFORNIA LOS ANGELES

ALDINE PUBLISHING COMPANY / Chicago

First published 1972 by
Aldine Publishing Company
529 South Wabash Avenue
Chicago, Illinois 60605

ISBN 0-202-02005-3
Library of Congress Catalog Number 70-169510

Printed in the United States of America

Preface

When Charles Darwin published his book *The Descent of Man and Selection in Relation to Sex* in 1871, he wrote in the introduction:

> During many years I collected notes on the origin or descent of man, without any intention of publishing on the subject, but rather with the determination not to publish, as I thought that I should thus only add to the prejudices against my views. It seemed to me sufficient to indicate, in the first edition of my "Origin of Species," that by this work "light would be thrown on the origin of man and his history"; and this implies that man must be included with other organic beings in any general conclusion respecting his manner of appearance on this earth.

When the climate of opinion became less prejudicial to the theory of evolution, Darwin gathered together his notes and prepared them for publication in book form. He states that his observations began in 1838 and from then on he "occasionally attended to the subject."

When prepared for publication, the notes were voluminous and fell into three groups: those pertaining to man's descent, those relating to sexual selection, and those relating to the expression of the emotions in man and animals. The first two topics formed the two parts of his 1871 book, and his observations on the evolution of human expressions followed in 1872.

Darwin's chapters on the descent of man are based on a review of general comparative anatomy and psychology. They do not depend on the evidence of any "missing link" in man's genealogy. On this basis, which today we would consider very limited, Darwin reached surprisingly accurate conclusions as to man's ancestor (an early Catarrhine, allied to the gorilla and chimpanzee), his birthplace (a hot country, probably Africa), and the time of his origin (between the Eocene and Miocene). His views were close to those of Ernst Haeckel, published in 1868 under the title *Natürliche Schöpfungsgeschichte,* although they were developed independently. Human evolution had been discussed by Huxley (*Man's Place in Nature*) in

1863, so that by 1871, Darwin's publication was assured a limited public, for the subject had acquired a certain respectability.

However, to suppose that even today, one hundred years later, the fact and implications of human evolution are widely accepted is quite erroneous. Even among scientists of the Judaeo-Christian tradition, there are many who stop short of full acceptance on religious grounds. And among those who do accept the theory of evolution by natural selection, many stop short when it comes to a consideration of human prehistory. The fact is that the evolution of man from a nonhuman primate was a continuous and not a discontinuous process. Many writers still postulate discontinuous saltations in certain aspects of the human evolutionary process (for example, language). But the readers of this book will not need convincing of the validity of Darwin's thought. As for the others, I recall a comment of Max Planck, who cynically remarked that "a new scientific truth does not triumph by convincing its opponents, but rather because its opponents die, and a new generation grows up that is familiar with it." At least one further generation will be required before the implications of man's place in nature are widely understood.

The idea of selection is as old as history—nearly as old as the domestication of animals. There is a passage in Plato's *Republic* (Book V) in which Socrates discusses the subject with Glaucon:

> "And do you breed from them all indifferently or do you take care to breed from the best only?"
>
> "From the best."
>
> "And do you take the oldest or the youngest, or only those of ripe age?"
>
> "I choose only those of ripe age."
>
> "And if care was not taken in breeding, your dogs and birds would greatly deteriorate?"
>
> "Certainly."
>
> "And the same of horses and animals in general?"
>
> "Undoubtedly."
>
> "Good heavens! My dear friend," I said, "what consummate skill will our rulers need if the same principle holds of the human species."
>
> "Certainly, the same principle holds. . . ."

This is interesting in light of the fact that in Ancient Greece male choice would certainly have been an overriding factor in the mating pattern.

Charles Darwin's grandfather, Erasmus, discussed sexual selection in his *Zoonomia,* and Charles alluded to it in his *Origin of Species.* When Darwin came to consider the problem of the differentiation of the human races, he found it indispensable to treat the subject of sexual selection in detail. The only author who had previously discussed the matter at any length was Ernst Haeckel (*Generelle Morphologie,* 1866, and *Natürliche Schöpfungsgeschichte,* 1868).

Charles Darwin was the first to examine and document the concept at length, and we owe him much for his remarkable observations and theoretical discussion. The subject is complex and very closely related to the more general concept of natural selection. In the years following 1871, biologists struggled to understand and document natural selection, and it is not surprising that the difficult case of sexual selection was neglected. Julian Huxley was one of the first to discuss it with authority in this century in his papers of 1914 and 1938 (see Chapter 8). After the war, interest was renewed by Bateman who did excellent genetic work on sexual selection in *Drosophila* in 1948 (see Chapter 7). In the next years a few more publications followed.

Darwin's ideas on the part played by sexual selection in human evolution would fascinate any student. Today we can begin to understand the adaptive significance of a good deal of human racial variability, but the function of many external features of men and women is obscure (some of these are discussed in Chapter 9). Our conclusions on this subject are clear, if disappointing; they emphasize our ignorance, even if they also suggest areas for future research. The fact of the matter is that we know very little about sexual differences in man, his sexual behavior, or the extent and kind of sexual selection that affects him. The subject has been taboo for too long, and we remain extremely ignorant in this whole area.

Darwin's interest in behavior always injected his biology with a unique liveliness. His work on the expression of the emotions in man and animals should be considered as part of his writing on the descent of man. Only today are we beginning to consider the behavior of a species as an integral and central part of its biology. The history of human evolution is meaningless without its behavioral dimension, and it has taken nearly 100 years to see this as clearly as Darwin did. In the ninety years since Darwin died, we have unlearned a lot that he can teach us. Today, in an age of specialization, it is doubly hard for us to take the eclectic approach that Darwin so ably espoused. But if we are to understand our past, that is indeed what we must attempt to do.

In this volume, we have attempted to look again briefly at some of the problems discussed by Darwin in 1871. In Chapter 1, Loren Eiseley considers the intellectual antecedents of evolution theory and the place of Charles Darwin in the history of human thought. In Chapters 2 and 3, ideas of human evolution are discussed by George Gaylord Simpson and Bernard Campbell, and in Chapter 4, Theodosius Dobzhansky reviews the meaning of race in man. Aspects of sexual selection are reviewed in Chapters 5 to 9. Here the authors have courageously undertaken the difficult task of hard thinking on old subjects coupled with original observations. This section of the book forms a valuable review of our understanding of sexual selection. In Chapters 10 and 11, a still more difficult task has been undertaken: to apply ideas of sexual selection to man. Here we can read the views of a social anthropologist (Robin Fox) and a biologist (Ernst Caspari). We can well see the problems and rewards when these two disciplines, which have been too long divorced, come together. Ernst Caspari summarizes our attempts to apply these ideas to man, and his chapter serves as an epilogue.

This book is therefore an attempt to broaden the scope of evolutionary biology by looking again at a long neglected concept. Let us hope it will contribute to a better understanding of the mechanisms of evolution, and eventually a better knowledge of ourselves.

Contents

SEXUAL SELECTION AND THE DESCENT OF MAN

1

LOREN EISELEY
UNIVERSITY OF PENNSYLVANIA

The Intellectual Antecedents of *The Descent of Man*

Introduction

To assess the significance of *The Descent of Man* one hundred years after its publication is not easy. In the first place, the book cannot really be viewed in isolation; rather it is a natural continuation of Darwin's "big book" of which the published *Origin of Species* was intended to be only an abstract. Later, as it became apparent that the *Origin* would survive and triumph, Darwin, at the urging of his friend Charles Lyell and his publisher, Murray, decided to diversify his endeavors and bring out his masses of accumulated evolutionary data in separate volumes. For the sake of his health he was "determined to . . . work slowly." This was in 1859. Man was designated by Darwin as the "greatest subject," but it is indicative of his caution that not until 12 years later did he assemble and publish his files of human material. By then Lyell had written on human antiquity (1861); Thomas Huxley had expressed himself forcefully on *Man's Place in Nature* (1863); and Carl Vogt had contributed his *Lectures On Man* (1864). By 1871 the subject was scarcely new; in fact, it could not have been new since the time of *Origin,* the implications of which were perfectly plain. Nevertheless, the world wanted to hear what the author of *Origin* had to say on the evolution of man. St. George Mivart observed in *Nature* the year *Descent* was published that "already there is a perceptible increase in the visitors to the monkey house" (Mivart 1871).

The Descent of Man is not nearly so carefully organized around a central theme as most of Darwin's individual studies. Critics, including his colleague, Alfred Russel Wallace, have remarked that *Descent* is two books, two subjects, mixed together. Some two-thirds of the work deals with sexual selection, and only a small proportion of the latter material has a bearing on man.

Charles Darwin was understandably weary by the time this volume was produced. He was too wise not to know that the world was fascinated by the human aspect of evolution just as earlier in the century it had been concerned by the overthrow of Biblical time. He had written *Origin* and in doing so became the first spokesman of the evolutionists. Inevitably he had to voice his views on man, but reticent as he was, the task was arduous. The worlds of the human paleontologist and the cultural anthropologist were scarcely cleared of morning mist. Powerful though his influence upon them was to be, it was too late for the great naturalist to pursue field work in either area. He preferred the solitude of Down, his earthworms, orchids, and the carnivorous sundew plant *Drosera.* These subjects could be exposed to personal experiment; they did not require the use of anecdotal literature.

In the preface to the second edition of *Descent,* Darwin speaks of its first "fiery ordeal." That it would receive criticism from some quarters was inevitable, but by 1871 Darwin was famous and his classic work, *The Origin of Species,* was reasonably secure. I suspect that the "fiery ordeal" lay to a certain extent in Darwin's mind. Man is a unique and troubling expression of the evolutionary forces. In nineteenth-century terms it was easier to explain his rise anatomically than to account for some of his distinctly human traits such as language and culture. *The Descent of Man* was bound to be both provocative and premature—premature in the sense that it raised certain questions that at the time could only be answered by slipping into dubious ambiguities and unconscious evasions.

Darwin was too sensitive a scholar not to comprehend this fact which accounts in some measure for his feeling of "ordeal." Once evolution is established on a really firm basis few will argue the details of the process in orchids, but if one writes about man every literate individual will figuratively peer over the author's shoulder and express his own views on the subject. It was under such pressures that Darwin began to speak of the "great weight [to be] attributed to the inherited effects of use and disuse." As for sexual selection, Darwin was attempting to analyze an extremely confusing subject, as is clear from a recent comment by Ernst Mayr: "How much of Darwin's sexual selection falls under the heading of 'mere reproductive success' can be determined only after a complete reevaluation of his material" (Mayr 1963, p. 201).

The tools for the precise examination of the human story were yet to be forged. Some remain elusive even to the minds of this century, some are just appearing in the new primatology and ethology. But the world awaited Darwin's word on man; the author of *Origin* could scarcely be expected to escape what, after all, was the heart of the controversy he had precipitated. Tired and shakey, he dipped his pen and wrote as though the last sentence of *Origin* still lingered in his mind: "We are not here concerned with hopes and fears, only with the truth as far as our reason allows us to discover it." It was well that he added the *caveat.* He had never been a truculent writer like some of his younger followers. Unlike them he had come too far alone.

There is the story of a visit, a last visit, that he paid to his boyhood home in Shrewesbury while he was engaged upon *The Descent of Man.* The later owner was gracious but untactful. He paced, talking expansively, from room to room with his weary visitor who wanted only silence and dreams. As Darwin descended the steep slope towards the town he remarked uncomfortably to his sister Henrietta: "If I had been left alone in that greenhouse for five minutes, I know I should have been able to see my father in his wheel chair. . . ."

In a way the little episode epitomizes Darwin's role in the intellectual life of the century. He was the dreamer destined to destroy simple belief, yet looking nostaligically backward into empty rooms and hearing silenced voices. Perhaps this aspect of his personality played a role in his long procrastination before publishing *Origin,* even his occasional hopes that others might be persuaded to assume the work. Charles Darwin never moved with the competitive expedition of a modern twentieth-century scientist such as J. D. Watson has revealed to us in *The Double Helix.* Darwin was compulsively drawn to subjects he could not abandon but, equally, he persisted in lingering alone upon some unseen threshold as if secretly indulgent to human weakness, willing to let man enjoy himself a trifle longer under the autumn sun of a declining day.

Through his mind were passing, all to be transformed and rejuvenated as in some great enchantment, the ideas of the early century. In him thought would concentrate and be reworked only to radiate beyond him to other minds. Perhaps no man in science heard more echoing voices or listened longer at the doorways of the past. "What an enormous sum Darwin availed himself of and reinvested," once exclaimed John Burroughs (1886). The literary naturalist had been greatly perceptive, but few of Darwin's contemporaries had observed the reluctance with which the fate-scarred man pursued his destiny. He appears a figure of Delphic ambiguity, an ambiguity that occasionally erupts in his own phrases. In short, Charles Darwin was haunted, and one of the subjects by which he was unconsciously haunted was something that the nineteenth century called "natural law."

The Providential Clock

The late physicist Max Born once remarked that science progresses through a series of intersecting and confusing alleys rather than down the broad and ever-widening highway that is the illusion fostered by our technological successes. Through these obscure alleys slip elusive shadows of thought that sometimes vanish only to reappear in a succeeding century. Other similar shadows grow large, as though incorporating the thought substance of an entire generation, but then undergo transmutations never envisaged when they first appeared. Darwin's world, the world of the Victorian era, like all centuries, had its roots in the metaphysics of the past. It was the inheritor of Galileo's thought and that of the great intervening mathematicians and astronomers, culminating in Sir Isaac Newton in the seventeenth century. The thought of these discoverers, devout though they were, was to give rise to a conception of natural law that would, by degrees, dismiss the Deity to whom they avowed allegiance and fix upon western man a determinism so severe that it gave rise to a literature of enormous melancholy, of which Hardy's epic poem *The Dynasts* is perhaps the last grand example:

> "Things mechanized
> By coils and pivots set to foreframed codes . . ."

Natural law has a history extending into antiquity but, like the word *nature* itself, it has assumed more than one meaning in the course of time. Only in the sixteenth and seventeenth centures, and paralleling the rise of science, did the term come to assume supreme importance in western thinking. Prior to that time God's reign over nature did not hamper Him from making miraculous exceptions, staying the sun, sending warning comets attesting great events, or otherwise participating actively in His world. Whether, as some have contended, the rise of immutable natural law has some correlation with the growth of centralized authority in the capitalist state (Needham 1952, pp. 21–22) or whether its rise merely represents a growing scientific sophistication is difficult to analyze. As in all complex historical situations, precisely identifiable causes may be difficult to distinguish from accidental but correlated events. To attribute the recognition of unvarying rules of nature purely to the emergence of state authority seems a somewhat simplistic Marxist invention.

The deterministic machine did not arise immediately among the natural philosophers; instead it evolved. Newton, whose mathematical triumphs clinched the direction of science for the next two centuries, was himself a religious man. He drew his conception of God as a nonmaterial being extended throughout space and time largely from Robert Boyle, who in turn had been influenced by the Cambridge Platonist Henry More. Newton, indeed, remarked that "a god without dominion, providence, and final causes is nothing else but Fate and Nature." To that position certain of the eighteenth-century materialists would paradoxically proceed, dropping along the way the three Newtonian attributes of Divinity. In the meantime, it may be well to inquire just how the unquestionably devout Newton had succeeded in creating a world machine that, in other hands, would negate the necessity of Providential control.

First of all, Newton possessed a strong empirical bent linked with mathematical genius of a very high order. He moved in a point world of primary qualities from which the organic world had been largely abstracted. Moreover, the Newtonian system of nature treats of the existent world, not the emergent world of novelty then unglimpsed. It is essentially a world of masses of varying distance and size affecting other masses in a calculable, if invisible, way.

Galileo distinguished between primary qualities such as the laws governing the movement of bodies and those secondary qualities such as light, color, and sound received by the human senses. This honest attempt to refine our conceptions produced by degrees a scientific distrust in anything at all subjective or unmeasurable by mathematical formulae. Galileo had termed the subjective, secondary qualities "mere words." Philosophers enraptured by the night sky no longer were stirred by the light and color of the living world. They had come to mistrust every sense but the mathematical. To obtain an ordered universe subject to one unifying system of law, they were willing to enter the cold, dark, soundless world of the void and remain there mentally. Not for nothing has Basil Willey commented that when the Romantic movement began a hundred years after Newton, "several of the leading poets attacked science for having killed the universe and turned man into a reasoning machine" (1951, p. 96).

The word *machine,* with God cast in the role of the Great Mechanic, epitomized seventeenth-century science, until Newton's feats of pure reasoning subjected the entire universe to one unifying system of law. There remained no longer a divine Empyrean, a celestial sphere beyond human ability to penetrate. Instead, earth and sky had been drawn into the same sustaining web of mathematics. Like Darwin, however, Newton was more cautious than some of his associates. In his *Universal Arithmetic* he expressed doubts that some problems could be handled mathematically at all—a heresy, says Burtt, to men like Galileo or Descartes (Burtt 1951, p. 210). Nevertheless, it is the world of the great clock that took precedence in seventeenth-century thinking: a world of absolute law, of silently spinning wheels set into operation by a remote cosmic intelligence no longer concerned to intervene directly in the workings of the world. Providence loses its original interpretation; at best it is confined, one might say, to swinging the pendulum that started the clock. Or again, it may occasionally be needed to make slight corrections in the cosmic machinery. Man exists, in essence, merely to worship the machine—a gigantic version of Boyle's Strasbourg clock, which, once started, requires no artificer. The world of the secondary qualities, the world of color, of organic activity, no longer mattered. At best the latter came to be treated as a world of smaller machines marching to the laws of the greater.

The providence so long believed in by the Christian world, the providence of personal divine intervention on behalf of individuals, the concern for the falling sparrow, was slowly being abandoned for a realm of unchanging, inflexible law laid down by an awe-inspiring but inconceivably distant deity. Providence had become merely a concealed name for the existent universe, its preservation and suspension in time. Newton and most of his colleagues were religious men imbued with wonder at the regularities of the cosmos. Where the worship of this regularity was to lead would become manifest only in another century.

The Satanic Machine

Observing the course of that great instrument, the Providential Clock, elaborated in the mind of Newton and more particularly in that of his less restrained eighteenth-century followers, one is struck by the rapidity with which over two centuries the role of Deity recedes and is replaced by causal law, a law so strict that a mind capable of positioning all the particles in the universe could foretell their movements and predict the entire future.

The bright world of secondary qualities was fading like an illusion. In the cold and darkness an irrelevant spectator, man, wandered among the flickering fires of the new industrialism. He had entered that *City of Dreadful Night* which James Thomson was to describe so graphically:

> I find no hint throughout the Universe
> Of good or ill, of blessing or of curse,
> I find alone Necessity Supreme;
> With infinite Mystery, abysmal, dark
> Unlighted ever by the faintest spark
> For us the flittering shadows of a dream.

As early as 1883 Carlyle wrote of the cosmos as a "steam engine rolling on in its dead indifference, to grind me limb from limb." Haeckel spoke of the "absolute dominion of the eternal iron laws of the universe." W. K. Clifford mourned with simple sadness that "the Great Companion is dead." Finally, as an epitome of this thinking Kingsley had protested "tell us not that the world is governed by universal Law; the news is not comfortable, but simply horrible" (Houghton 1957, pp. 74–75). Science, in breaking out of the closed world of the past, had made an orphan of humanity, an orphan in whom free will was well-nigh extinguished in favor of total mechanism. What might be called the providential machine of Newton, the machine governed and sustained by an increasingly remote divinity, had been insensibly altered by the nineteenth century into a world of inflexible law, of Calvinistic gloom and necessity. It constituted the intellectual world into which Charles Darwin was born.

Yet in observing major trends of thought one must take care to allow for the loose ends and diverse tendencies that constitute the thinking of any century. It is all too easy in retrospect to schematize beyond reality. No satisfactory study of what natural law meant to the nineteenth century exists in the literature. The era, however, contains harsh expressions of its significance, expressions which, in some instances, conceal a lurking religiosity. This trend is illustrated by attacks on the early evolutionists. John Herschel, for example, employed some rather dubious reasoning with which to castigate Robert Chambers (Millhauser 1959, p. 125). Here the reign of natural law is obviously used as a bulwark against any acceptance of emergent novelty.

Law and *Baconian induction* are the conservative catchwords of the early part of the nineteenth century. The one rigidly determines the possible, as if man had received a full revelation on law; the second, induction, is frequently called upon to combat uncomfortable speculation. The offender was accused of failing to accumulate sufficient facts to document his hypothesis. The conservative critic was thus placed in a strong position behind a great name. It is he who constitutes the sole judge of "fact." It is obvious that Darwin felt the weight of this academic subterfuge when he protested ingenuously, "I worked by true Baconian induction. . . ." It was dangerous to suggest one might have entertained an insight or a supposition before one examined "facts." Robert Chambers had been so heavily bombarded by critics of this persuasion that Darwin's wariness was greatly heightened. He had studied both Chambers and his critics. Thus Darwin had the advantage of observing what was liable to be a preview of his own later experience. It led him, no doubt, into some further procrastination, but it doubtless increased his determination to avoid hasty generalization, fond though he might privately be of speculation.

The full scope of the history of natural selection affords an entertaining example of how, in biology, the balanced, Newtonian world machine was later to give rise to a new conception of the struggle for existence. Historians of science have largely neglected the fact that, like the opposed faces on a coin, natural selection is actually made up of two superficially contradictory theorems, one of which was adopted before the other. The earlier theorem bore different appellations than natural selection. When the latter phrase was introduced by Darwin, the earlier usages faded away almost entirely without recognition that they bore an historical connection to Darwin's newly introduced terminology. The whole episode is revelatory of the importance of semantics in the shifts and permutations of scientific thought.

By the late eighteenth century the struggle for existence had been recognized by a number of writers, the great majority of whom were not evolutionists. They observed in *struggle* a providentially imposed system, a *machine,* as it were, for controlling animal numbers. Terms such as *pruning, policing,* and *natural government* indicate a recognition of population control and stabilization within particular environments. The cutting edge of selection is fully delineated in expressions such as *keeping the species up to par. Natural government* is seen by most of these writers as a completely conservative mechanism balancing one species off against another in a system of checks and balances whose aberrations are, in the long run, as correctable as the Newtonian scheme of the heavens. Nature, in short, is still *existent* nature. It contains no room for emergent novelty; it does not promote change.

Or does it? In the late eighteenth and early nineteenth centuries a curious and at first unnoted dynamism began to be observed in the organic world. The period, it must be remembered, was marked by the rise of the new industrial cities, and of expanding urban populations that had to be fed and clothed from the countryside. To meet this demand, a class of animal inventors or innovators arose who introduced new and highly successful breeds of sheep and cattle. One of the more successful of these rule-of-thumb breeders was Robert Bakewell, whose career attracted the later attention of Darwin.

The significance of these events that took place originally outside the domain of theoretical science lay in the fact that the farm breeder, practicing artificial selection, was drawing out of his living plants or animals changes in form or texture that had existed as mere potential within the species. Latent perfection, seemingly only to be realized by human effort, lurked concealed in the bodies of the most ordinary barnyard animals that had been dozing unremarked through rural centuries. Selection, in other words, had begun to be practiced before the appearance of the geneticist and before the realization in theoretical terms of where the existence of hidden novelty in the animal body might lead.

This novelty was all directed to practical ends by practical men. That nature might have provided such hidden variability for other than human aims went unremarked. The standard interpretation of the Christian time-scale was too short to allow for such massive transformations of life as those that occupy the modern evolutionist. Nevertheless, from the time of eighteenth-century Newtonian natural government to Darwin's recognition of natural selection as an effective explanation of organic diversity and change, a slow philosophical shift had been in progress. A purely conservative organic paradigm was in the process of giving way to one that could embrace, in the term *natural selection,* both the conservative and novel aspects of the struggle for existence.

It is even more remarkable that in the multitudinous reviews of *The Origin of Species* following its appearance in 1859, only one solitary commentator, H. B. Tristram, to my knowledge, ever glimpsed the relation of the earlier paradigm to the later. He wrote, piercing the semantic barrier that by 1866 enclosed the new biology: "As to the struggle for existence, the facts adduced by Mr. Darwin would equally harmonize with the theory that the struggle tends to *conserve* the type, as with that which maintains that it tends to *change* the type" (1866, p. 120).

In these words Tristram had correctly indicated the seeming paradox of the two major facets of natural selection. Both are true. As to which prevails on any given occasion, only the contingencies locked in the genes and the opportunities presented by the outside environment may determine whether a given phyletic response will partake of static or novel elements. The emergent world of change that had arisen like a phanton between the fingers of the gardener and stock breeder, the world glimpsed by Darwin in the Galapagos and in equally long meditations over the pages of agricultural books, was about to overthrow the conception of eternal balance.

Immediate nature was about to be replaced with something more intangible, a nature having to do with the latent and the possible. Such a nature of pure lurking potential was beginning to hover like a mist around what had previously been understood to be a single creative act of divine will. Statistical probability, later to be called Darwin's "empire of accident," threatened to overthrow the iron causality embedded in nineteenth-century physics. It is perhaps little cause for surprise that, on the whole, physicists like Lord Kelvin and astronomers like Herschel viewed the new movement with distaste.

Indeed there is some evidence that Darwin himself, brought up within the world of the great engine as he was, felt some hesitation over how to interpret his discoveries in terms that would not offend his readers. Ironically, natural selection, by displacing man from the center of cosmic attention, would readily enhance the gloom that already lingered over a world from which personal providence was departing. William Blake's "Satanic mill" of the industrial city was beginning to merge with the Satanic machine that had become the universe.

The Probability Machine

Darwin was born in a century which regarded the "laws" of nature as imbued with a kind of structural finality, an integral determinism, which it was the scientists' duty to describe. Biology and geology were still occupied largely in the classification and description of facts. Fossils, mountain building and erosion, animal and plant distributions, were beginning to tell man something of the earth's antiquity but only in the face of much emotional bias. It was not easy to perceive, behind the well-ordered world of the present, an extended and coalescing chain of phylogenies all pointing downward into unspeakable gulfs of time.

More germane to the issue, perhaps, was the strain that this whole achievement placed upon existing regularities. To dig into the past and discover immanence, to examine the present and find it laden with a novel organic future, meant that if one were to avoid charges of violating the persisting uniformity of the world one had better be prepared to elucidate the laws governing these strange phenomena. It is to Darwin's credit that he made the attempt, but it is also evident from his language and his hesitations that he was sore beset as to how to describe the world of contingency into which he had wandered.

Variation was a fact of nature; that he knew, as had the plant and animal experimenters before him. He lacked all knowledge of its cause but clearly recognized that it supplied the raw materials upon which selection operated. If we go back to the earliest years of Darwin's efforts we find that in a letter addressed to the geologist Lyell in 1837 when, as we know, he was first finding his way into the subject of natural selection, he speaks as follows: "Notebook after notebook has been filled with facts which begin to group themselves *clearly* under sub-laws" (F. Darwin, 1887 Vol. I, p. 298).

Sub-laws is the key word. It reveals Darwin dealing with an unruly and emergent novelty, seeking, after the manner of the period, to fit it into the inflexible natural law of his contemporary world.

Again, writing privately to Hooker in 1849, he reiterated his concern with the unpredictable variability which in some slight degree is everywhere to be found in the organic world (F. Darwin, 1887 Vol. II, p. 37). "What the devil," he puzzles as late as 1859, "determines each particular variation? What makes a tuft of feathers come on a cock's head, or moss on a moss rose?" Darwin is here struggling with two separate but related problems, the first of which (the frequency of variability) he chose to underplay in the first edition of *The Origin of Species*. It was difficult to see how one captured under "natural law" what seemed to leap into existence with a fine disregard of anything but pure chance. In the same year he confesses, baffled, to Joseph Hooker, "I believe . . . perhaps a dozen distinct laws are all struggling against each other in every variation which ever arises" (F. Darwin, 1903 Vol. I, p. 120). Laws Darwin seemed determined to pursue, but they continued to elude his best efforts. To explain coordinated evolutionary structures he was forced to fall back upon "mysterious laws" of correlation. Again, he maintained to Lyell that species formation "has hitherto been viewed as beyond law. . . ." (F. Darwin, 1903 Vol. I p. 194), the implication being that for the first time he is bringing scientific law into a subject previously confined to a "theological phase of development" (F. Darwin, 1903 Vol. I. p. 194).

Robert Chambers in the eighteen-forties had been taken severely to task for proposing in the *Vestiges* a "law of Development," which had received the scornful attention of Sir John Herschel, the astronomer. Darwin had, very obviously, taken note of this assault, and was determined, both logically and diplomatically, not to fall into the astronomical trap of equating his discovery, mathematically so indefinable, with a law like that which Newton had applied to gravity.

It is apparent from Darwin's correspondence that he continued to regard the analogy with gravity in a slightly wistful manner (F. Darwin 1903,

Vol. I, p. 184) but, in the end, he was content to term natural selection as, at various times, a hypothesis, a theory, or a broad metaphor. Writing to Asa Gray in 1859 he ventured to explain it "as a geologist does the word denudation—for an agent, expressing the result of several combined actions" (F. Darwin 1903, Vol. I, p. 126). Similarly, Darwin elsewhere indicated that the fall of a handful of feathers to the ground under the pull of natural law, that is, gravity, was easier to chart than the actions and reactions of the innumerable creatures and plants determining the mode of change among themselves. Darwin's caution, while it does credit to his philosophic sense, was to prove hopeless in terms of evading the sharp tongued Herschel, who promptly accused him of promulgating "the law of higgledy-piggledy."

With that phrase the Empire of Accident, in spite of Darwin's wish to abide by the nineteenth century's conception of order, had indeed arrived. In the first edition of the *Origin,* Darwin observed diffidently that "variations useful in some way to each being in the great and complex battle of life should sometimes occur in the course of *thousands of generations*" (emphasis added). His colleague Wallace was quick to observe that in making this remark, Darwin was playing into the hands of his opponents. Variation, in Wallace's view, was omnipresent, and favorable mutations by no means confined to distantly isolated and rare episodes (F. Darwin 1903, Vol. I, p. 270).

In later editions of the *Origin* Darwin quietly accepted Wallace's criticism and incorporated it into his work. The world of universal law, whether that ordered by a remote impersonal providence, or maintained by the "dreaming dark dumb thing" of Hardy's despair, was slowly giving way to something else. The Satanic Machine was about to be replaced by the novelties of the probability machine to which, later on, even nineteenth-century physics was to succumb. Somewhere a connection had to be made between mathematical chance as it was conceived by the great gamesmen and gamblers and *visible* biological novelty. Had the idea lurked hidden in the work of the eighteenth-century breeders? Perhaps it had.

Long ago when Darwin was still a youth aboard the *Beagle,* the naturalist Robert Mudie, faithful to his century, had written: "There is a law that maintains the species." Scarcely had he made this assertion before he was busy explaining that all cultivated plants or animals were more or less monsters and that of the appearance of their parentage we knew little or nothing. Even of wild forms he ends by hinting ambiguously of the emergence of species "altogether new." Finally he verges on complete heresy. "There is something," he almost whispers, "of the same kind in human beings" (Mudie 1832, pp. 366–371).

It may thus be seen that the wild, the fortuitous, the gambler's throw invisible in the germ cell, did not go entirely unnoted by perceptive naturalists prior to Darwin. In fact, it was upon their observations that he was to draw. Yearn as he might for law, for order, attribute as he would to unknown causes the tuft on a cock's head or the variant pattern on a turtle's shell, the secret escaped him. His contemporary, Mendel, who discovered a vital part of the key to change, would die unrecognized. The laws that Darwin sought would never be laws in the sense he had dreamed. They would turn at best into statistical regularities, descriptions sometimes as elusive and difficult to master as the feathers he had described rocking downward under the unknown force of gravity. The prescriptive power of the Newtonian machine was imperceptibly fading.

"If science is an account of the lawfulness of nature," Spencer Brown, the mathematician, once observed, "then history is an account of its chaos" (1957, p. 11). In penetrating the past of the organic realm, Darwin and Wallace had been forced to sacrifice existent nature, nineteenth-century nature, and indeed man himself, for a wilderness of subjective possibilities which, in turn, led out of the present into a world of "indefinite departure." Nature, the twentieth century was to discover, would no longer be the old visible "lawful" nature of field and forest, the nature which many Victorians regarded as the direct expression of God's will (Ellegard 1957, p. 565). Even the physicist, toward the end of the century, was to discover that his supposedly stable elements were capable of ghostly transmutation. The world beneath the atom did not follow the order of the macroscopic universe in which life moved and had its being. As Schneer puts it, "the natural law that prevails on the level of classical physics is simply an expression of the probabilities that prevail on this deeper, more fundamental level of experience" (1960, p. 359). In the words of Bronowski, chance is given a kind of order—the order with which probability theory operates (1953, p. 88).

Darwin's critics, who frequently misunderstood him as believing that *any* living thing, moss or carrot or cabbage, could be transformed into anything else—the law of higgledy-piggledy—were quite wrong. Darwin, though he had no word for it, was dealing with what now could be called historical probability, a phylogenetic course which might wander within limits but which had a set of limiting parameters determined by past mutation and selection. Historical probability, in other words chance-accumulated and selected variation, will determine the viability of new mutations.

Nevertheless, if we allow for this stricture, we must still accept Heisenberg's observation that "these may be biological processes . . . in which large scale events are set off by processes in individual atoms; this would appear to be the case particularly in the mutation of genes during hereditary processes" (1958, p. 42). Thus the prescriptive law as to what may be finally attenuates, thins and tends to vanish. Darwin, to a degree, yearned wistfully for the kind of law that would satisfy the men of his century. He did not find it. Perhaps in the end, however, we of this generation can look upon his efforts and admit as modern physics has had to admit, in the words of Chesterton, that "a thing cannot be completely wonderful so long as it remains sensible." Perhaps this was what kept Darwin at his interminable labors even when he strove wistfully to produce a law that would satisfy his antagonist, Lord Kelvin, whose truly Satanic mathematics would have allowed life and the sun but a fleeting moment of existence. For in nineteenth-century terms, he could prove, as Darwin could not, the mathematical reality of his conclusions.

Conclusion

We intimated in the introduction to this study something of Darwin's original dilemma: namely, the problem of how organic evolution and, above all, human transmutation, could be interjected into a scheme of natural law which concerned only the existing Newtonian world. By force of logic and the geological time extensions afforded by the work of Hutton, Lyell, and others, his views triumphed. It is equally clear, however, that the philosophical world which surrounded him and whose tenets he embraced haunted his studies to the end. "I am inclined," he wrote to Asa Gray in 1860, "to look at everything as resulting from designed laws, with the details, whether good or bad, left to the working out of chance. Not," he adds significantly, "that this notion *at all* satisfies me." Darwin's mind, troubled and insecure to the end, was wavering and rocking like autumn thistledown in its descent.

By 1865 Francis Galton, Darwin's cousin and an early worker in mathematical psychology, was intrigued with the concept that the moral and religious sentiments had been evolved through natural selection from the herd instincts of man's forerunners (Gantz 1939, p. 185). Huxley had perhaps been the first person to emphasize a relation between natural selection and morality in one of his lectures to working men in 1862 (Gantz 1939, p. 184). It is very evident from Gantz's useful and too little known survey, as well as the equally valuable account of James Tufts (1909) that once man had been stripped of his place in the Biblical conception of creation, the question of his moral nature and its origins was bound to become an object of debate. Some would point to man's powers of speech and his ethical nature as evidence that, whatever might be true of the rest of creation, man's role and origin upon the world stage must be different from that of his animal associates. Others accepted the concept of man's rise from the brute world with such enthusiasm that they rather forgot that man had risen at all.

The ancient quarrel that could be said to have arisen outside of Eden's gate, between Cain and his brother Abel, simply continued, as it continues today, in an evolutionary guise. As Tufts observed over fifty years ago:

> The striking thing . . . is the discredit which has now fallen upon the natural. One school of writers, indeed, maintains the rational and social nature of man, and the rational laws of cosmic nature, but the most striking evolu-

> tionary theories . . . conceive nature as the realm where force and the instinct for self-preservation hold sway. This was doubtless due largely to the theological dualism between the "natural" man born in sin, totally depraved with no good instincts, and the spiritual man who must needs be "born again," regenerated by special divine grace, before he would be just or good (1909, p. 198).

This ancient quarrel persists today in the clash between Robert Ardrey and his opponents. It might be observed, in turn, that, although neither party realizes it, the controversy reflects the two opposing facets of natural selection as I have earlier described them in this paper. The conservative paradigm might be said to contain the party of "natural" man, while the liberal or emergent paradigm may well reflect the faith of others in man's possible perfectability and potential mastery of his baser nature. The reductionist school here opposes the party of the future. The latter group, of course, have the history of man's rise to adduce as hopeful evidence, but the conservatives confront our optimism with the challenge that man clings to his midnight past. There the argument must rest in a time still so close to the forest and the ice. It might even be argued that the conservative school of thought has a lingering affection for the deterministic machine of nineteenth-century law and that their opponents place greater faith in the continued operations of the probability machine that called man into being.

Speculation about man's place in the natural world became a worldwide concern after 1859. Had Darwin never written again, books and periodicals would have continued to pursue the subject of man's moral nature as well as the evolutionary patchwork revealed in his body. It was regarded as right and appropriate that the first spokesman of evolution should speak about man. By 1871 ten years of accumulated data was available from a variety of sources, including Edward Tylor's *Researches into the Early History of Mankind.* Darwin drew heavily upon this literature as well as upon his own store of knowledge. Sexual selection, the subject which comprises so much of *The Descent of Man,* I will not touch upon because others will treat of it in this volume. In the sections of the book treating of man, Darwin compressed a sizeable amount of scattered speculation into a theory of naturalistic ethics.

One can state with surety about the body of Darwin's work that he thrice maintained continuities where the world had seen discontinuities; once in the origin of species, once in ethics, and once in language. The last two propositions he had defended in *The Descent of Man.* For these seeming great breaks he had argued the reality of multitudinous minute discontinuities, variations in the place of the great *saltus.* To a discriminating eye the little quantum jumps that accumulate by degrees into enormous novelties such as man in no way detract from the almost miraculous quality of the living world.

It would be foolish to expect, in a day when even Darwin made uses of anecdotal literature relating to these matters, that, in the anxiety to demonstrate continuities of development, parrots might not speak a trifle too intelligently, or use inheritance promote speech or other cultural habits in a way no longer acceptable to the anthropologist. These are small matters which do not basically affect the greater achievement: the great dream and the realization of the human pathway through time.

Philosophically Darwin may have removed us from a privileged position in the universe but he brought us, at the same time, back into the web of life. He showed us by implication our relationship and dependence upon other organic beings and thus contributed indirectly to the rise of the modern conservation movement. Old maids and cats and bees and clover prepared us as children for the interlinked net we are now struggling to preserve.

Darwin did not realize as did Freud the vestigial remnants still lurking below the conscious mind, nor, on the other hand, did he fully grasp that if ethics in some fashion arose from original primate sociality, it has been lifted beyond the purely utilitarian. In an excellent study of evolutionary moral theory, Quillian observes that though one may start with herd instinct one ends with a value, a value that expresses a spirituality which is an end in itself (Quillian 1945, p. 136). The moral sentiments have therefore passed, or are passing, beyond the possibility of being totally formulated in organic terms. A dialogue with ourselves has begun. Man, as Darwin intimated, is a self-examining creature.

The final step was made by the master himself: man partook of the rest of creation. In A. E. Housman's words, he had blown hither "from the twelve-winded sky," tumbled about in organs and in mind by the working forces of elemental chaos, prodded onward by a "law" which, if it was a law, provided no sure direction, a "law" which to Darwin's mind brooded over the desolate landscape of accident. But the parameters were there, narrowing upon man for the next possible leap either to oblivion or glory. Man had become self-conscious, self-measuring, perhaps the only creature in the cosmos to be so. In some strange sense the creature is already transcendent. Perhaps some few of his kind have already surpassed him. Did not Einstein, with his twentieth-century mind that ranged as far into the universe as Darwin's, once remark perceptively, "It is far from right to say that nature always plays the same game."

References

Bronowski, J. 1953. *The common sense of science.* Cambridge: Harvard University Press.

Brown, E. S. 1957. *Probability and scientific inference.* London: Longmans, Green and Co.

Burroughs, J. 1886. The literary value of science. *Macmillan's Magazine* 54: 184–191.

Burtt, E. A. 1951. *The metaphysical foundations of modern physical science.* 2nd revised ed. New York: The Humanities Press.

Chambers, R. 1845. *Vestiges of the natural history of creation.* 3rd ed. London: John Churchill.

Darwin, F., ed. 1887. *Life and letters of Charles Darwin.* 3 vols. London: John Murray.

———. 1903. *More letters of Charles Darwin.* 2 vols. London: John Murray.

Ellegard, A. 1957. Darwin's theory and nineteenth century philosophies of science. In *Roots of scientific thought: a cultural perspective,* ed. Philip Wiener & Aaron Noland. New York: Basic Books.

Gantz, K. F. 1939. The beginning of Darwinian ethics 1859–1871. In *The University of Texas Studies in English.* Austin: The University of Texas Press.

Heisenberg, W. 1958. *The physicist's conception of nature.* London: Hutchinson.

Houghton, W. E. 1957. *The Victorian frame of mind.* New Haven: Yale University Press.

Mayr, E. 1963. *Animal species and evolution.* Cambridge: Harvard University Press.

Millhauser, M. 1959. *Just before Darwin: Robert Chambers and the vestiges.* Middletown, Conn.: Wesleyan University Press.

Mivart, St. G. 1871. Ape resemblances to man. *Nature* 3: 481.

Mudie, R. 1832. *A popular guide to the observation of nature.* London: Whittaker, Treacher and Co.

Needham, J. 1952. Human law and the laws of nature in China and the West. *Hobhouse Memorial Lectures 1941–1950.* Oxford University Press.

Quillian, W. S., Jr. 1945. *The moral theory of evolutionary naturalism.* New Haven: Yale University Press.

Tristram, H. B. 1866. Recent geographical and historical progress in zoology. *The Contemporary Review* 2: 103–125.

Tufts, J. H. 1909. Darwin and evolutionary ethics. *Psychological Review* 16: 195–206.

Schneer, C. J. 1960. *The search for order.* New York: Harper and Row.

Willey, B. 1951. How the scientific revolution of the seventeenth century affected other branches of thought. In *The history of science.* Glencoe, Illinois: The Free Press.

2

GEORGE GAYLORD SIMPSON
UNIVERSITY OF ARIZONA AND
SIMROE FOUNDATION

The Evolutionary Concept of Man

Much light will be thrown on the origin of man and his history.
CHARLES DARWIN, 1859

Introduction

The Darwinian revolution had many diffierent aspects. It permeated all the life sciences and provided a new philosophical basis even for sciences in which its implications were not immediately obvious. Nevertheless its greatest impact, its most truly revolutionary effect, has been on man's concept of himself. If man were excepted from the evolutionary generalization, evolution might be considered a technical theory of little importance to nonbiologists. Darwin was well aware, indeed one might say all *too* well aware, of that probability. Thence, in *The Origin* (1859), he limited himself to the famous statement quoted at the head of this section, a remark that is almost coy at best, pusillianimous at worst. Darwin further resolved that he himself would not attempt to throw any light on the subject, excusing that resolution as tactical avoidance of inciting prejudice against his views on evolution in general.

The tactics were in vain. Darwin's purposely inconclusive remark was perfectly well understood, and the prejudices he thought to avoid were immediately and amply incited. Yet not all was prejudice. Others treated what Darwin feared to discuss, and soon learned men were supporting a Darwinian view of man that Darwin himself had not yet supported. There were many others, but perhaps Thomas Henry Huxley was most noteworthy. He published *Evidence of Man's Place in Nature* in 1863, an unequivocal and, to the open-minded, completely convincing demonstration of man's kinship with the apes. With that and much other support, Darwin finally abandoned his resolution and wrote a short book on the subject, *The Descent or Origin of Man,* published in 1871. It was issued in the same two volumes as *Sexual Selection,* under the combined title *The Descent of Man and Selection in Relation to Sex.* A third work, *The Expression of the Emotions in Man and Animals,* was to have been included but became too bulky and was issued separately in the following year (1872). The three topics are related, but each is an independent study despite the fact that the first two were published together. (It is unfortunate that this has led Ghiselin (1969), one of the most important recent students of Darwin's work, to neglect *The Descent of Man,* strictly speaking, and to discuss that work, which mentions sex only in passing, as if it were not on man but on sex.)

In *The Descent or Origin of Man,* Darwin's whole purpose was to demonstrate the plausibility of the following conclusion and to show that no conflicting view is plausible: with all his specific peculiarities, man has originated by evolution involving just the same principles and processes as the origin of any other species of organisms. Considerably enriched and somewhat altered in detail, that statement is the core of the evolutionary concept of man, and that is what has so revolutionized man's ideas of himself and his universe.

Although there was and is much opposition to evolution as a generalization, such opposition long since ceased to be intellectually respectable. Even in the 1870's it was no longer sustained by many whose qualifications merited attention. However, it was not the generalization that so widely disturbed trends of thought. It was the particularization of application to man, and even to the present time there are evolutionists who are—I am tempted to say "otherwise"—qualified to hold opinions who insist that man is in some way an exception to the generalization. From a certain point of view, *every* species is a special case. The opinions to be briefly considered here have in common that they hold man to be a special case in a way different in principle from all the other special cases.

It is particularly interesting that Wallace, the famed independent discoverer of natural selection, was among the first to express a definitely Darwinian view of the origin of man (Wallace 1864; see also Wilma George's interesting biography of Wallace, coincidentally centennial, 1964). In 1871 when Darwin listed some of those who had already espoused the views on human origins at which he had only hinted, he put Wallace at the head of the list, even before Huxley, although in fact Huxley had priority of publication on this subject. It is both curious and symptomatic that in the meantime Wallace had radically changed his views. Briefly in 1869 and fully in 1870 he adhered to Darwinian concepts of general evolution but made a unique exception for man, concluding that "a superior intelligence has guided the development of man in a definite direction, and for a special purpose."

That idea has not become a mere historical curiosity. Its essence has been retained in various external forms by several modern biologists. For example Eiseley, certainly a respectable authority, has summarized Wallace's views with great sympathy and on this subject questions those of Darwin (especially Eiseley 1958). Eiseley maintains—on what evidence I cannot imagine—that "a brain a little better than that of a gorilla would have sufficed for man." He seems to suggest that human evolution has involved something (What?) quite different *in principle* from the evolution of any other species.

More widespread among the views that hold man in some way outside the commonalty of evolution are those that consider our species in some sense not only the acme (so far, at least), but also the purpose and intention of the evolutionary process. That metaphysical and usually also theological concept has been held by some ever since, and even in less clear form before, Darwin. Today probably its best known exponent is the late Jesuit Father Teilhard de Chardin (especially 1959; discussed in Simpson 1964).

Those ideas on evolutionary man, which will not be further pursued here, have been mentioned in order to bring out a sometimes difficult but always essential distinction. A sound evolutionary concept of man requires not only knowledge of evolutionary processes but also judgment of their results in this particular species.

The evidence so overwhelmingly supports certain basic conclusions that they will be taken as established in the following discussion:

> The human species, *Homo sapiens,* is an outcome of the same natural processes that have produced all other species of organisms during the history of life on the earth.
>
> Man is related in varying degree to all other organisms, living and extinct; the degree and nature of the various relationships are to be investigated by comparisons of the species in question, interpreted by reasonably established evolutionary principles.
>
> The human species, like all others, has species-specific characteristics also to be interpreted in evolutionary terms.

Man Becomes a Zoological Specimen

> Human beings have a right to be human in the same sense as cats have a right to be cats.
>
> —A. H. Maslow, 1970

Pre-evolutionary biologists could treat mankind as, in a sense, *hors concours,* neither requiring nor permitting consideration in the same way as other animals, although it is interesting that Linnaeus and other antedarwinians did classify *Homo sapiens* as a species in the animal kingdom. The evolutionary concept is that man is a species in the same sense that *Felis lybica,* or any other comparable taxon of organisms, is a species. To begin with quite elementary zoology, this statement involves two special points. First, there is the concept of species. What is it that makes mankind a species, not several species and not one part of a larger species? Second, what are the specific characteristics of this species; how does one define and distinguish it? These were, in fact, pre-evolutionary questions, which now become significant in the evolutionary context.

The pre-evolutionary concept of a species, still anomalously encountered in some studies, was that a species is a group of essentially similar organisms, variations on a type different from that of other species. A more sophisticated biological concept, inspired by evolutionary principles but oddly nonevolutionary in itself, followed. In the first sense, which is typological, "The species may be defined strictly on morphological grounds as a group of individuals that resemble each other in most of their visible characters" (Linsley & Usinger 1961; their citation of authority for this definition is incorrect). In the second, nontypological but also nonevolutionary, sense, "Species are groups of actually or potentially interbreeding natural populations, which are reproductively isolated from other such groups" (Mayr 1940; see also Mayr 1963; he has made it clear that reproductive isolation is not necessarily absolute). The evolutionary concept is that, "An evolutionary species is a lineage (an ancestral-descendant sequence of populations) evolving separately from others and with its own unitary evolutionary role and tendencies" (Simpson 1961; first proposed in slightly different form in Simpson 1951).

On the premises here adopted, the strictly typological definition is unworthy of further notice. By both the other definitions mankind unquestionably belongs to a single species and comprises the whole of that species. That statement has profound implications, biological, technological (for example, medical), sociological, philosophical, ethical, and religious. Some will now be followed up, although not all can be. After mentioning the most important implication, that *in fact* all men are brothers, let us begin with the relatively simple point of zoological characterization.

For practical reasons, most zoological diagnoses, those designed simply for the recognition of taxa, are based on anatomy. Even when man is under consideration from a strictly zoological point of view, anatomical diagnosis is not really important if taken only for its own sake. No one, from the cradle onward and however naive in zoology, has any problem in recognizing a specimen of *Homo sapiens* as such. To diagnose the species as a "naked ape" is claptrap, not only because that is unnecessary for recognition but also because it is flatly false. Man is not an ape, naked or otherwise, any more than an ape is a man, hairy or otherwise. That is bad zoology, for a start. It is one of man's lesser distinctions that most men have less hair than most other primates. The interest of such differential characters is, first, that taken altogether they afford evidence on the affinities and ancestry of our species, and, second, that their evolutionary origins and possible functions afford insights into the nature of this species. It is, then, worthwhile to list a few of the most striking anatomical features of *Homo sapiens,* even though they are well-known to all and unnecessary for diagnosis:

Cranium globular, brain large relative to body size
Face short, almost vertical
Orbits directed anteriorly, fields widely overlapping
Dentition modally $\frac{2 \cdot 1 \cdot 2 \cdot 3}{2 \cdot 1 \cdot 2 \cdot 3}$, brachydont, series closed, canines small, cheek teeth bunodont, molars subquadrate
Posture erect, spinal column sigmoid
Arms shorter than legs
Thumbs well-developed, opposable
Ilium short craniocaudally, expanded dorsoventrally
Foot plantigrade at rest or in slow locomotion
Great toe (pedal digit I) not opposable, modally nearly or quite as long as second toe (II)

I have listed characters of the hard anatomy, especially useful for comparison with fossils and museum specimens. There are numerous additions in the soft anatomy (see, among many others, Sonntag 1924; Grassé 1955; Young 1957; Smith 1960; Campbell 1966). Darwin (1871) noted a number of these: reduction of the *panniculus* (used as a general term for subcutaneous skin-twitching sheets of muscle); immobile, unpointed ears; comparatively feeble sense of smell; small and useless caecum (appendix). Darwin's point was that these and the other human anatomical distinctions do not oppose and that many indeed support the theory of human evolution from early monkeys and apes. For example, some, such as the appendix, were considered useless or even harmful characters in man explicable only as vestiges of ancestrally functional organs. (In earlier usage, opposite to that of today, Darwin called them "rudimentary" rather than "vestigial.")

In making the point that human distinctions are not absolute but only evolutionary modifications of characters of other animals, Darwin noted that they vary, which is both a mark of evolution and a prerequisite for it. In spite of the quite incomplete knowledge of heredity at that time, he concluded that they are transmitted "in accordance with the laws which prevail with the lower animals." Knowledge of heredity is still not complete, but it is enormously more advanced and it accords fully with Darwin's conclusion. The same can be said for Darwin's conclusion that human characters have the same general causes and governing "laws" (we would now prefer to say "principles") as those of other animals.

It was already clear to Darwin and Huxley and is evident even from the gross anatomy of the various species that man's closest living relatives are gorillas and chimpanzees. Those two groups of apes are themselves so closely related that it is difficult to say and is not important whether man is more closely related to one or the other. The probable answer is that man's relationship to them is through their common ancestry and not to either one of them more than to the other. Much further evidence has now been acquired, especially: karyology (number, shape, and structure of chromosomes), serology (immune reactions of blood proteins), molecular biology (composition of complex molecules, such as hemoglobins). (For some examples see Washburn 1963, especially articles by Goodman, Klinger et al., and Zuckerkandl in that volume.) These have all completely confirmed the conclusion that our closest living relatives are chimpanzees and gorillas, indeed so strongly that a few researchers would remove those two groups from close association with the other apes and place them in the human family Hominidae (for example, Goodman in Washburn 1963, but the other participants in that symposium did not agree).

The evidence is thus distinctly opposed to the view that there was a basal dichotomy between a lineage ancestral to all the apes, Pongidae in a usual broad sense, and one ancestral to all members of the human family, Hominidae in the usual sense. If we are more closely related to gorillas and chimpanzees than to orangutans and gibbons, then our ancestry split off from the gorilla-chimpanzee lineage after the ancestral Pongidae as a whole had already arisen and diverged into ancestors of at least three groups of living apes and a number of extinct ones. Beyond (that is, before) that, our whole ape ancestry emerged from that of the Old World monkeys, and thence on backward very much as Darwin had already outlined it in 1871.

That is as far as the zoological comparison of living species takes us regarding the affinites and ancestry of *Homo sapiens*. Another approach, and the most direct one as regards ancestry, is through the fossil record. That record is notoriously incomplete, and has been particularly so in just this, the most passionately interesting part for us humans. Our clever ancestors were probably rather better than most in avoiding situations where they were likely to become embedded in sediments and fossilized. It also seems that most of them in early times lived in areas and ecological situations for which the fossil record is particularly patchy. Nevertheless many pertinent fossils are now known and, although all are fragmentary and their interpretation is by no means indisputable, the general trend is clear enough.

A number of apes, usually grouped in a subfamily Dryopithecinae of the ape family Pongidae, are known from the Miocene of Africa, Europe, and

Asia. In the early to middle Miocene, perhaps 15 to 25 million years ago, none of those known are positively identifiable as in a separate human lineage, and indeed according to some authorities such a lineage probably had not yet then separated from the gorilla-chimpanzee ancestry. In the late Miocene and early Pliocene, around 10 million years ago with a few million years each way, there lived in southern Asia and East Africa (and probably elsewhere in the Old World) *Ramapithecus,* which may well have belonged to the distinctly hominid lineage after it separated from that of the living apes. (The African form is sometimes called *Kenyapithecus.*) Unfortunately only fragments of upper and lower jaws and parts of the dentition are yet known (Simons 1968, and references there), and although these are hominid in appearance they do not suffice to convince everyone.

The oldest known fossils now generally agreed to belong to the family Hominidae are the australopithecines, known from over two million years ago and for several hundred thousand years thereafter. There were at least two partly contemporaneous groups: one heavier, less manlike, and probably divergent from the human ancestry, *Australopithecus* (or *Paranthropus*) *robustus;* and the other, *Australopithecus africanus,* more gracile, near or possibly in the direct ancestry of *Homo sapiens.* Another group, generally known as *"Homo habilis,"* as originally described was apparently a mélange of an earlier *A. africanus*-like form and a later form similar to *Homo erectus.* Opinions about the earlier form differ as to whether it should be referred to as *A. africanus,* considered a phyletic intermediate between *A. africanus* and *H. erectus,* or considered representative of a human ancestral lineage separate from and partly contemporaneous with *Australopithecus.* That difference of opinion is not as fundamental as it may sound. In any case there is agreement that *Homo* evolved from something very like *Australopithecus africanus* if not formally referable to that species, and the older specimens of *"Homo habilis"* (which include the type of that name) are good added evidence to that effect. There is an enormous literature on all these fossils, much of it rather more polemic than seems strictly necessary. For lists of the specimens actually known (except a few discovered quite recently) see Oakley & Campbell (1967). For examples of divergent views on their nomenclature and interpretation see Robinson (1967), Simons (1967), and Tobias (1968).

The most interesting and unexpected thing revealed by these immediate forerunners of *Homo* is that they had already closely approached the stance and limb characters of *Homo* while their absolute brain size was still within the ape range, although somewhat larger than the ape average in proportion to body size. Intelligence depends on more than gross size of the brain, but the australopithecines cannot have been as intelligent as normal *Homo sapiens.* They may have been still on a level with some apes in general capacity, although undoubtedly different in the structural quality of the brain. The australopithecine physiognomy must have been quite apelike.

All definitely identified australopithecines are from East and South Africa, although some poorly known Asiatic fossils may belong to this group. In view of the facts that possibly ancestral earlier forms are common to Asia and Africa and that a number of animals associated with the australopithecines also occurred in Asia, it would be quite surprising if the australopithecines were really confined to Africa.

Fossils of the next named stage in the human ancestry are definitely identified in Asia and Africa and probably also in Europe. These are the creatures long famous as *Pithecanthropus,* now technically called *Homo erectus.* They flourished around five hundred thousand years ago, with an incompletely known long transition from *Australopithecus* before that and a shorter transition to *Homo sapiens* thereafter. Their most obvious differences from *Homo sapiens* are the presence of larger brow ridges than is usual in the living species and especially a smaller average brain size. As would be expected, the varying brain sizes of *H. erectus* in its long and geographically wide history overlap at one end with *Australopithecus* and at the other with *H. sapiens,* but the mean size is neatly almost exactly midway between the two.

The frequent question "How old is man?" has no acceptable answer and would not have even if we knew the entire history in detail, which we don't and probably never will. It depends on what is meant by "man." If the species *Homo sapiens* is intended, the age is indefinite, because transition from *Homo erectus* was gradual and in the last analysis where we choose to draw a line between them must be purely arbitrary. We could say that most investigators would choose to draw the line somewhere between twenty thousand and five hundred thousand years ago, which is not a very satisfactory reply to the question. If the genus *Homo* is meant, the same sort of problem arises on an even grander scale. If the time of dichotomy between Hominidae and some lineage of Pongidae were taken as the origin of man, that event would in principle be more precisely datable, but in fact we do not yet know when it occurred within tens of millions of years, and if we did know, calling the very first hominids "men" would be confusing, because they were certainly much more like apes than like *Homo sapiens.*

Another zoological consideration of the bodily characteristics of our species is functional. Although there are some exceptions, apparent or real, we know that most of the characteristics of any organism are adaptive; that is, they are correlated with its way of life and its relationships with the environment. *Homo sapiens* is no exception. Examples are richly supplied by the list of outstanding characteristics of the hard parts previously given.

The large globular cranium is a correlate of brain size and thus of intelligence. Human intelligence, both quantitatively and qualitatively, is not merely adaptive, it is *the* fundamental human adaptation.

Facial structure is part of an adaptive complex involving among other things the large head, erect posture, increased reliance on stereoscopic vision, and changed dental adaptation.

The dentition has become adapted to an essentially omnivorous diet and to the fact that, unlike most apes and monkeys, man no longer needs to use his teeth as weapons or for display.

The peculiarities of spinal column, pelvis, thorax, arms, legs, hands, and feet are all parts of an adaptive complex involving upright posture, raising eyes to maximum height, bipedal locomotion, elimination of use of forelimbs in locomotion and their constant availability and high suitability for manipulation. This complex is man's most distinctive strictly anatomical characteristic. There is nothing like it in any other animal, not even in those that are also bipedal. Nevertheless it clearly arose from apelike structure, being in a sense imposed on or molded into that ancestral form, and that form set limits to the direction and extent of man's divergent adaptation.

Some Systematics

I. HOMO nosce Te ipsum (*)

(*) Nosse Se Ipsum gradus est primus sapientiae, dictumque *Solonis,* quondam scriptum litteris aureis supra *Dianae* Templum. Mus. ADOLPH. FRID. *Praefat.*

Sapiens. 1. H. diurnus *varians cultura, loco.*

Ferus. tetrapus, mutus, hirsutus. . . .

Americanus. α rufus, cholericus, rectus. . . .

Europaeus. β albus, sanguineus, torosus. . . .

Asiaticus. γ luridus, melancholicus, rigidus. . . .

Afer. δ niger, phlegmaticus, laxus. . . .

Montrosus. ε . . . .

—Carolus Linnaeus, 1758

Thus was the name *Homo sapiens* conferred in the great work that is the starting point for all zoological nomenclature. After the classic admonition that to know thyself is the first step to wisdom, the species was subdivided into four races or subspecies defined by color, "humor" (in the old sense of temperament), and carriage or build, plus a wild, dumb, hairy form and a catchall of monsters such as big, sluggish Patagonians ("*Patagonici* magni, segnes") and pointy-headed Chinese ("*Macrocephali* capite conica: Chinenses").

We still use the Linnaean system of nomenclature with only slight modification, although our evolutionary understanding of it is quite different from Linnaeus' static, typological understanding. Its fixed categories are not well adapted to an evolutionary continuum, but no one has come up with a more suitable and equally practical system of names, and names we must have. For us, exactly as for Linnaeus, we belong to the Kingdom Animalia, Class Mammalia, Order Primates, Genus *Homo,* and Species *Homo sapiens.* With a great many more organisms to deal with, we now use more categories so that a full classification has become:

Kingdom Animalia
 Phylum Chordata
  Subphylum Vertebrata
   Class Mammalia
    Subclass Theria
     Infraclass Eutheria
      Order Primates
       Suborder Anthropoidea
        Superfamily Hominoidea
         Family Hominidae
          Genus *Homo*
           Species *Homo sapiens*

Some authorities use even more subdivisions.

Each step up the hierarchy of categories takes in more organisms, and therefore includes more distantly related species than those at lower steps. Generally speaking, too, as the categories and the taxa referred to them become more inclusive, the implied common ancestry of all the taxa becomes more remote in time. The Hominoidea include the great apes as well as man, and while the time of last common ancestry is not yet closely determined, it was evidently within the last 40,000,000 years and perhaps considerably less. The Mammalia include not only all those forms but also such distant relatives as kangaroos. Again, the time of last common ancestry has not yet been placed exactly, but it was almost certainly not less than 100,000,000 years ago, and probably nearer 125,000,000. The Animalia include such greatly more distant relatives as ants, corals, and clams, and the latest common ancestor certainly lived considerably more than 600,000,000 years ago. Thus the system of classification now not only serves for pigeon holing and naming, as it did for Linnaeus, but also embodies and symbolizes the great sweep of evolutionary events so that it has a meaning that far transcends the original Linnaean system.

That significance and its usefulness are not always clear, even to some systematists. There are not just as many levels of affinity as there are categories in the hierarchy. To express all degrees of relationship, these would have to be determined between the species in question, here *Homo sapiens,* and *each* other species, of which there are millions. That is impossible, and a hierarchy with millions of categories would be useless even if attainable. It is also sometimes imagined that each step up the hierarchy does or should bring in species equally related to the taxon at the next lower level. That also is entirely impractical. For example, the step from Hominidae to Hominoidea brings in the ape family Pongidae, but the Hominidae are not equally or even similarly related to all pongids.

A good classification has an evolutionary meaning. If it is well constructed with adequate knowledge, it is consistent with the phylogenetic history of the group in question and it provides a conceptualization and a nomenclature for studying and expressing that history. It cannot in itself be an expression of the history. (On principles of classification and nomenclature see Simpson 1961, 1963; for an interesting and here relevant example of classification see that of the living Primates by Napier & Napier 1967.)

Some notice should now be taken of infraspecific systematic categories. Linnaeus' taxon *Homo sapiens monstrosus,* logical on his premises, is simply absurd on ours. His subtaxa *americanus, europaeus, asiaticus,* and *afer* are not absurd on any premises. Those are real populations within the species *Homo sapiens.* They exist and can be defined and recognized, even though Linnaeus' differential characters for them have indeed become absurd. American aborigines are no more uniformly "red, choleric, and upright" than European aborigines are uniformly "white, sanguine, and hefty," but they do have different even though quite variable characteristics and we do not mistake one for the other if both are fairly near the conditions modal for their groups.

The phenomenon here involved is biological and evolutionary, and it is well-known in a multitude of organisms of all kinds. Widespread species always have local populations that differ to greater or less degree in their characteristics and in the underlying genetic factors determining the ranges of those characteristics and passing them on through the generations. If the differences are fairly clear and tend to occur in rather large populations over considerable geographic areas, systematists often designate these subdivisions within a species as subspecies and give them names for convenience of reference and discussion. They normally originate in different geographic areas and with some probable exceptions their differences are adaptive to different environmental features of those areas. ("Environment" means the whole of a community, including the species in question itself, and not only the physical surroundings.) The subspecies and other different local populations not considered sufficiently definable or important enough to name are not discrete units. They grade into one another through the process of interbreeding that goes on throughout a whole species but may be less common between than within adjacent subspecies. Thus the number of species in a community is generally clear and definite, but the number of subspecies in a species is generally arbitrary to a large extent and may involve such biologically irrelevant factors as the preference of the investigator.

The evolutionary dynamics of the origin of such more or less differentiated infraspecific populations are now fairly well understood. Included in a great mass of evidence and innumerable studies are some examples of evolutionary changes so rapid that their natural progress has been followed scientifically while actually under way. The most famous and most completely understood is the British moth, originally gray, which has become predominantly black only in especially sooty areas where the black color tends to protect it from predation and hence is favored by natural selection (Kettlewell 1956). Another example also bearing on the interesting character of color, equally clear as to fact but less well understood as to cause, is that of European hamsters, also mostly gray, among which black individuals have become particularly frequent in certain environments with mixed forest and steppe vegetation (Gershenson 1945). Other examples are given and the evolutionary processes are discussed for instance by Dobzhansky (1951) and Grant (1963).

There are certain exceptions of a minor nature, extraneous rather than contradictory, but it is clear that such subspecies and analogous infraspecific groups normally evolve by natural selection in adaptation to conditions in the particular area where they live and at the particular time when in fact they do become differentiated. It makes sense to say that black moths were better adapted than their grey (or might we say "white"?) brothers near Birmingham in the 1950's. It would make no sense to conclude that because black was better there and then the black moths were superior in any other respect, even there and then, let alone in general. Even less sense would be made by supposing that they might be either superior or inferior in any other respect if transported to any other place or living at any other time. Moreover, if the original selection pressure were eliminated, the difference in color would become irrelevant, and in any sense at all the use of words like "better" or "worse" would become biologically absurd. In that particular example the selection pressure came from predation, but such selection can take an enormous number of different forms even when it bears on pigmentation, and so can its elimination.

Now I need hardly say that the point of the preceding three paragraphs was to discuss races without the emotional bias almost inevitably involved, in one direction or the other, when the human races are explicitly in question. In their evolutionary origin, the races of *Homo sapiens* were certainly no different from those of myriads of other animal species. Everything said about infraspecific systematics above applies equally well to the origin and basic evolutionary nature of the races of mankind. Nevertheless as regards the later history and the present situation of the human races there are three special factors, the first not uncommon, the second quite rare, and the third unknown in any other species. First: many members of infraspecific groups of *Homo sapiens* now live in areas and under environmental conditions quite different from those in which the groups originated. Second: in many, indeed most, places individuals still clearly recognizable as of different subspecific or racial origin now are associated in the same communities. Third: the development of human cultures has nowhere eliminated natural selection, but almost everywhere it has changed the intensity of such selection and greatly, even totally, altered its directions from those under which the races originated. Many of the issues commonly raised in current discussions about race are spurious from a strictly biological point of view. However, these special features of the condition of our species do entail new, poorly appreciated biological problems and have not exactly caused but have permitted and exacerbated all too real psychological and sociological problems.

In the seemingly endless flood of publications on race, one by Dobzhansky (1962, Chapter 10) seems to me the most competent, most nearly adequate, and most sensible single statement available. Although not in the same class on at least two of the three counts, I also mention one by me (Simpson 1969, Chapter 7).

As the present discussion is related to the centenary of Darwin's *The Descent of Man and Selection in Relation to Sex,* note may be taken of an apparent contradiction that arises from the generation gap, more than three generations now, between Darwin and us. In the first part of that book Darwin concluded that the origin of human races could not be ascribed to natural selection. It was just for that reason that Darwin devoted the second part of the book, much the longer part and really a separate work, to sexual selection, which he believed could account for not all but the greater part of the differences between races. Today we ascribe not all but the greater part to natural selection. In the main there are three reasons for this, none prejudicial to Darwin. First, Darwin, using somewhat different words, had little evidence that racial distinctions were adaptive, but now with vastly greater knowledge of human functions and history we know for many and have reason to suspect for many more racial traits that in fact they were adaptive under the conditions in which they actually originated. Second, Darwin at that point conceived of natural selection only as a factor promoting or opposing individual survival, whereas now, following a broader concept also (but less clearly) to be found in Darwin's works, we define natural selection as genetically correlated differential reproduction over a sequence of generations. By this broader but not anti-Darwinian definition, sexual selection, to the extent that it does occur, is not an alternative to natural selection but a special case of it. Third, Darwin was evidently right in believing that some differences among human populations have not evolved by natural selection (including the special case of sexual selection). Some of these can now be explained, at least in principle and in a general way (for example, by genetic drift or the founder principle; see Grant 1963), but they seem to be relatively unimportant as regards the major races.

Culture: A Biological Adaptation

> Mankind is unique in the living world in possessing culture. Culture is a store of information and a set of behavior patterns, transmitted by instruction and learning, by example and imitation. The central role in the transmission of culture belongs not to genes but to human symbolic languages. . . . Ability to acquire and to transmit culture is a function of human genes, although an evolutionist likes to stress that rudiments of his ability are also found scattered in non-human animals.
>
> —Theodosius Dobzhansky, 1969

Up to this point the reader may not be and indeed should not be satisfied with the characterization of himself. He knows that he is more than a curved backbone, a prehensile thumb, or even a large brain. He is not defined among the alternatives of *Homo sapiens europaeus* "albus, sanguineus, torosus," *Homo sapiens africanus* "niger, phlegmaticus, laxus," or the rest, even if the diagnosis be updated to the present. He, the real person, is the one who gets out of bed in the morning, puts on clothes, breakfasts with food from restaurant or grocer, reads a newspaper, discusses things with kin, wife, or friends, acquires and spends money, listens to music, looks at art objects, judges the state of his world, approves or protests as to him seems fit, and so on and on. If the evolutionary concept of man had nothing to do with those things, it would have a low relevance quotient, to borrow (or perhaps invent?) a bit of jargon.

In fact those things are just as much results of evolution—of biological or organic evolution—as the curved backbone, prehensile thumb, and other characteristics. Charles Darwin, who did not miss much, did not miss this when he finally got to human evolution a century ago. In his short book within a book, *The Descent and Origin of Man* (Darwin 1871, Part I), three of the seven chapters are devoted to mental, behavioral, and cultural aspects of mankind, and these subjects also recur here and there in the other four chapters.

Here, as with human physical traits, Darwin's main purpose was to demonstrate the plausibility that human characteristics evolved from those of "lower" animals, that is, from a generally apelike and before that generally early mammal-like ancestry. He averred that, "the lower animals, like man, manifestly feel pleasure and pain, happiness and misery." Some behaviorists consider that statement unscientific, but it is a commonsense interpretation of thousands of observations and I, for one, do not think that common sense needs to be banished from science. Darwin further gave evidence that "most of the more complex emotions" and many of "the more intellectual emotions and faculties" "are common to the higher animals and ourselves." (I have rearranged his phrases without distorting the sense; incidentally, by "lower animals" Darwin meant all nonhuman animals and his "higher animals" were the more advanced among the "lower animals," such as dogs and monkeys.) Love, pride, jealousy, shame, magnanimity, rage, excitement, ennui, dread, imitation, attention, memory, imagination, reason, and, extraordinarily, the use (but not manufacture) of tools are among the "emotions and faculties" specified. Even more important, Darwin maintained that the basis for social organization and the rudiments of culture (though these are not his words) could be found in "lower animals."

Although one item or another of Darwin's evidence may be questioned, its general import is now accepted by all knowledgeable biologists, psychologists, and anthropologists. It is believed that comparative studies of nonhumans not only establish the fact that human faculties and cultures evolved, but also provide clues at least to how they evolved, to their historical course and its significance. That is the rationale for the current great extension of behavioral studies of nonhuman primates, partly by experimentation, but lately especially by observations of noncaptive populations (for example, DeVore 1965), and to more extended studies of mammals in general (especially well summarized by Ewer 1968).

Those studies have tremendous interest and value, but they have limitations that are not always sufficiently noted. Some studies suffer from what may be called "the naked ape fallacy." As I have already pointed out, man is *not* a naked ape; he is a different species (and genus, and family) altogether. He has become adapted to environments and ways of life most radically different from those of any ape. It is not likely that any real human ancestor was behaviorally adapted just like any now living ape. Evidently apes have retained some traits also still present in man and probably they retain some now lost in man but present in our ancestors, but that is what has to be established by research. It is not, though it is sometimes taken as, a valid axiom or premise for research. The fallacy becomes more obvious when white rats are considered in their role of experimental animals studied not for their own sake but in hope of learning something about ourselves. Our relationship to white rats is distant indeed, and nothing like a white rat ever occurred in our ancestry. A number of physiological traits are similar in white rats and men and perhaps a few behavioral traits are, too, but that has to be demonstrated before the cross-species comparison or generalization merits any confidence.

Within the field of most likely relevance to human evolution, that of primate behavior, it has to be emphasized that the living species have not simply evolved one beyond the next. It is true that some have departed more and others less from a probable ancestral state, and that fact is a basis for valid comparative evolutionary methodology, but in every instance the species have also diverged one from another, and *Homo sapiens* has diverged the most of any. There are many characters that are qualitatively present in *Homo sapiens* and absent in all living Pongidae, such as the facts that man's anterior lower premolar is bicuspid and that men habitually communicate by true language. Characters of this sort present special biological problems and they have been used to support two unacceptable hypotheses: (1) that mankind was divinely created as a separate and distinct species, and (2) that these apparent discontinuities in fact arose discontinuously, overnight, or from one generation to the next by some weird form of mutation. It is sufficiently clear that what these characters really indicate is that they arose gradually in ancestors that no longer exist, that are extinct just in the special sense that the whole lineage, the whole species, was transformed into *Homo sapiens*. Some of the evidence is that many of these characters are still quite variable in man and that a rudiment of some of them or a basis for their origin occurs in some other animals.

It will occasion no surprise that Darwin was also well aware of these points and that he specified the major human mental, behavioral, and cultural peculiarities that are still most discussed. Man not only uses tools, he also makes them. But by stretching the point one might say that some chimpanzees, and even some still "lower" animals, have the barest rudiments of tool making (for example, Goodall in DeVore 1965). Man is self-conscious, and he reflects on past and future, birth and death. But self-recognition has been observed in a chimpanzee (Gallup 1970), and extensive evidence of memory and goal-directed activity in many animals entails some rudiments of past-future orientation. Man is a cultural and social animal with cultures and societies of unparalleled complexity. But here, as Darwin already discussed in some detail, it is just the complexity and not the existence of these characteristics that is peculiar to man. There are many social nonhumans, and whether they have a culture or not is only a matter of definition: it is part of some human cultures to live in houses, build dams, and dig canals, just as beavers do. Man has a sense of beauty. But some men apparently do not, and some people believe that chimpanzees have the rudiments of esthetics (for example, Morris 1962). Man believes in gods or a god. But, as Darwin had already noted, the superstitions of comparatively primitive peoples commonly lack one that would meet a theological definition of Omnipotent God, and so do the views of innumerable highly cultured men, such as Darwin himself. There is also some reason to believe that nonhumans may sometimes have an inchoate sense of uncomprehending awe that might be considered religious in a less definite and more rudimentary sense.

Among man's biological acquisitions the most important of the human faculties involved in the whole of his mental, social, and cultural life is undoubtedly language. Because the particular language we speak is learned and not inherited, there is some tendency not to consider it as a biological adaptation genetically determined and the result of organic evolution. However, we are born with a nervous system and other anatomical and physiological characters that are determined by heredity and that have evolved from ultimate ancestors who had no language. As this complex matures, it makes speech possible and, under usual circumstances, inevitable. That capacity is an extremely basic biological adaptation. So, incidentally, is the whole of our capacity for acquiring a culture, and the fact that we do not all acquire just the same culture is not relevant to this point. It is well to add that although all members of the species who can be considered normal have certain basic capacities such as the ability to learn a language and to acquire a culture, it does not follow that all are genetically equal even in those respects, let alone in numerous particulars of behavior. That is one of the many vitally important points that cannot be pursued in a single essay. Some concept of it can be gathered from a symposium edited by Spuhler (1967; see also Hirsch 1967).

The vital importance of language pervades virtually all of the most truly human aspects of the human species. It is far from the only but probably the most important means of conceptualization and thought. Its symbolic capacity carries over into other modes not obviously linguistic. It is by far our most important means of communication and of social organization and intercourse. It is a time-binding mechanism by which we record the past and anticipate the future. The species could not possibly have reached its present status without language, and language, in one way or another, will be a main determinant of its possible fate. It is no wonder that this subject has an extremely large and extremely confusing literature at all levels from the sublime to the ridiculous.

Problems have arisen in the use of language to discuss language. The very word "language" has been used so indiscriminately as to become almost hopelessly ambiguous. For example, the Beadles (1966), in an otherwise superb book with the significant title *The Language of Life,* speak of the molecular "language" of DNA, the chemical "language" of blood, and so on (see p. 207). They have no other word to use when in the same book (p. 44) they speak of "language" as totally confined to man. Less obviously distorted and on that account probably even more misleading is the frequent designation of all forms of animal communications as "language," for example the famous "language" of bees best known in English by the book called *The Dance Language and Orientation of Bees* (Frisch 1967). Here (although doubts have been raised) it is at least true that communication occurs; that is, information is emitted by one individual as coded signals received and reacted to appropriately by another individual (Gould, Henerey, & MacLeod 1970). The word "communication," although properly broader than "language," has also suffered devaluation by usage too broad to denote anything exactly. In such circumstances scientists have little choice but to turn to jargon, and for communication in the more precise sense suggested in the last sentence the seventeenth-century term "semiotics" was resurrected (Sebeok, Hayes, & Bateson 1964) and later more specifically tagged as "zoosemiotics" (by Sebeok first in 1963; see his extensive discussion in Sebeok 1965; on semiotics and the situation of linguistics among the sciences generally, see also Jakobson 1969). Sebeok extends the term "zoosemiotics" to include instances in which sender and receiver ("encoder" and "decoder") are the same individual.

Here there is neither the space nor the will to pursue most of the intricacies of this subject further. (They were pursued somewhat further in Simpson 1969, Chapters 6 and 8.) The essential point for present purposes is this: human language in general, as abstracted from any one language in particular, has essential characteristics that have never been observed in any natural nonhuman animal communication. Like every statement about language and communication, that one has been disputed, but it is accepted by such an overwhelming informed consensus that it really should be indisputable. Nevertheless two quite recent developments demand some further consideration of the significance of what still seems to be a valid and important generalization about the evolutionary distinction of *Homo sapiens*.

It appears that apes in general are anatomically incapable of producing just the sounds that are used in spoken human language (for example, see Du Brul 1958). Since the essential characteristics of human language do not require that it be spoken, it has occurred to several enquirers that chimps might acquire nonspoken language. Gardner & Gardner (1969) have worked with a chimp, Washoe, using gestures for signals. When reported (the full and continuing record is not yet published), Washoe had learned to communicate by gestures with many of the special characteristics of human linguistic communication. It still appears, however, that the system is more primitive than true human language and does not quite have all the latter's essential features (Bronowski & Bellugi 1970; Roger Brown, personal communication). Premack (1971) and his associates have taught another chimp, Sarah, to use manipulable visual symbols for communication similar to human language. That communication admittedly does not have all the detailed characteristics of human language, and whether it qualifies as language in a reasonably limited sense of the term is a matter of definition.

These fascinating developments require thought and suggest further experimentation and consideration. I shall just mention two of the many queries that come to mind. The use of acoustic signals, as in human spoken language, does not require the sounds (phonemes) of any particular human language, but only the capacity to emit *some* sound and to perceive it. All apes can do that. Why then have attempts to teach apes (or any other animals) a true acoustic language uniformly failed? Still more important, the failure of apes to evolve language on their own cannot be imputed to their inability to produce humanlike phonemes. They can at least learn something close to human language with visual signals, but no such language-like communication has ever been observed except in two captive (or domesticated) chimpanzees taught at length by humans.

It still appears that language is a unique and very basic evolutionary adaptation in the human species.

The Difference It Makes

Γνωθι σεαυτον (know thyself).

—Attributed to Thales (ca. 640–546 B.C.)

Γνωθι τους αλλους (know others).

—Attributed to Menander (343–291 B.C.)

Knowledge and human power are synonymous, since the ignorance of the cause frustrates the effect.

—Francis Bacon, 1620

It is all too easy to enumerate terrible ills and menaces that afflict the human species: overpopulation, wars, nuclear annihilation, racial and class strife, malnutrition, environmental pollution, political oppression, just for a start. This is not the first crisis the species has faced, but it may well turn out to be the worst, and it is the one that we who are living now must try to meet. In these dire straits some have felt that the study of evolution is beside the point or, at best, not particularly urgent. That is a serious error. Every one of the problems of mankind in some way involves the nature of man and man's concept of himself. Understanding these correctly will not forthwith solve all problems, but we can be quite sure that the problems will not be solved unless these factors are understood correctly and taken into account. I will close by pointing out as briefly as possible why that is true.

The greatest impact of the Darwinian revolution in thought was that it finally completed the liberation from superstition and fear that began in the physical sciences a few centuries before. Man, too, is a natural phenomenon. He has evolved into a self-responsible being, and for his own sake he must understand the nature of his world and his place in it. Among aspects of the crisis and indeed among its multiple, intricately interacting causes are certain tendencies to shrink from responsibility by reverting to superstition (astrology, mysticism) or by gross evasion (drugs, copping out) or to react to problems by childish tantrums made horrible by adult power. Those devices will not solve the problems. Learning and applying more about ourselves is the only hope.

Mankind is a single species and a unique species. For better or for worse, we are all in this together, whatever our characteristics may be and wherever we may live. This species did not evolve on a noncooperative dog-in-the-manger basis. Aggression and territorialism are not ineradicable parts of human biological nature. They are maladaptive, and we must use an evolutionary adaptability to counteract or readjust them where they occur harmfully among us.

Human races arose as evolutionary subspecies, not in any meaningful way "better" or "worse," "lower" or "higher," but simply adapted, by and large, to different conditions. Those primitive adaptations have become almost completely irrelevant. But man is probably also the most adaptable of all species. The problem now is for the whole species to adapt to conditions not met by any of the ancient racial adaptations.

Man's most powerful present means of adaptation are sociocultural, but the ability to adapt in those ways is both provided and circumscribed by our biological heritage. That heritage is still subject to change. Evolution is still going on not only socioculturally but also biologically. In some societies negative individual selection (the concept evoked by "the survival of the fittest") is lessened or almost eliminated, but natural selection by sustained group fecundity tends to become stronger everywhere, perhaps especially in societies with low mortality selection. We do not know just what differential fecundity is now doing to the species—the subject is almost taboo among some of those who should be most concerned with it—but that can be learned, and it certainly behooves us to find out. If mankind persists, obviously it will do so in biological form. If we are to have a desirable biological future, we must know our biological natures, which are evolutionary, and act on that concept.

No species lives alone. All species live in communities with other species in environments that include all those species, and all interact with their environments, affecting them and being affected by them. This situation is and has always been true of *Homo sapiens*. Man's history has included ways of coping with the environment by evading its unwanted impacts. He rarely worried about his impact on the environment. Now all at once large numbers of us have suddenly realized that our environment is, in a sense, striking back for what we have done to it. We are on the verge of making it unfit for us to live in. We are becoming maladapted in an evolutionary sense, and the usual outcome of maladaptation for a species is extinction.

It comes down to this: we are a uniquely evolved species that must form a true concept of itself and must learn to cope with its own nature if it is to survive. We must value the members of our species, all of them, and seek conditions in which all can attain their potential values, a concept that includes controlling our density and our destructive activities. Another word from the late Abraham Maslow (1970) is an appropriate close:

> The sheer fact of membership in the human species constitutes ipso facto a right to become fully human, i.e. to actualize all the human potentials possible.

References

Beadle, G. & M. Beadle. 1966. *The language of life: An introduction to the science of genetics.* Garden City: Doubleday.

Bronowski, J., & U. Bellugi. 1970. Language, name, and concept. *Science* 168: 669–673.

Campbell, B. 1966. *Human evolution: An introduction to man's adaptions.* Chicago: Aldine.

Darwin, C. 1859. *On the origin of species by means of natural selection, or the preservation of favoured races in the struggle for life.* London: Murray.

———. 1871. *The descent of man and selection in relation to sex.* London: Murray.

———. 1872. *The expression of the emotions in man and animals.* London: Murray.

DeVore, I., ed. 1965. *Primate behavior: Field studies of monkeys and apes.* New York: Holt, Rinehart, and Winston.

Dobzhansky, T. 1951. *Genetics and the origin of species.* Third edition, revised. New York: Columbia Univ. Press.

———. 1962. *Mankind evolving: The evolution of the human species.* New Haven and London: Yale Univ. Press.

———. 1969. Evolution of mankind in the light of population genetics. *Proc. XII Intern. Congr. Genetics* 3: 281–292.

DuBrul, E. L. 1958. *Evolution of the speech apparatus.* Springfield: Thomas.

Eiseley, L. 1958. *Darwin's century: Evolution and the men who discovered it.* Garden City: Doubleday.

Ewer, R. F. 1968. *Ethology of mammals.* London: Logos Press; New York: Plenum Press.

Frisch, K. von. 1967. *The dance language and orientation of bees.* Cambridge: Harvard Univ. Press.

Gallup, G. G., Jr. 1970. Chimpanzees: Self-recognition. *Science* 167: 86–87.

Gardner, R. A., & B. T. Gardner. 1969. Teaching sign language to a chimpanzee. *Science* 165: 664–672.

George, W. 1964. *Biologist philosopher: A study of the life and writings of Alfred Russell Wallace.* London, Toronto, New York: Abelard-Schuman.

Gershenson, S. 1945. Evolutionary studies on the distribution and dynamics of melanism in the hamster (*Cricetus cricetus L.*). *Genetics* 30: 207–251.

Ghiselin, M. T. 1969. *The triumph of the Darwinian method.* Berkeley and Los Angeles: Univ. of California Press.

Gould, J. L., M. Henerey, & M. C. MacLeod. 1970. Communication of direction by the honey bee. *Science* 169: 544–554.

Grant, V. 1963. *The origin of adaptations.* New York and London: Columbia Univ. Press.

Grassé, P.-P., ed. 1955. *Traité de zoologie.* Tome XVII, Mammifères. 2 vols. Paris: Masson.

Hirsch, J. 1967. Behavior-genetic, or "experimental," analysis: The challenge of science versus the lure of technology. *Amer. Psych.* 22: 118–130.

Huxley, T. H. 1863. *Evidence of man's place in nature.* London: Williams and Norgate.

Jakobson, R. 1969. Linguistics in its relation to other sciences. *Actes X Congrés Internat. Linguistes* 1: 75–111 (and discussion by others, 111–122).

Kettlewell, H. B. D. 1956. Further selection experiments on industrial melanism in Lepidoptera. *Heredity* 10: 287–301.

Linnaeus, C. 1758. *Systema naturae per regna tria naturae secundum classes, ordines, genera, species, cum characteribus differentiis synonymis, locis.* Editio decima, reformata. Laurentii Salvii, Holmiae.

Linsley, E. G., & R. L. Usinger. 1961. Taxonomy. *The encyclopedia of biological sciences,* ed. P. Gray, pp. 992–997. New York: Reinhold.

Maslow, A. M. 1970. *Motivation and Personality.* Rev. Ed. New York: Harper & Row.

Mayr, E. 1940. Speciation phenomena in birds. *Amer. Nat.* 74: 249–278.

————. 1963. *Animal species and evolution.* Cambridge: Belknap Press.

Morris, D. 1962. *The biology of art.* London: Methuen.

Napier, J. R., & P. H. Napier. 1967. *A handbook of living primates: Morphology, ecology and behaviour of nonhuman primates.* London and New York: Academic Press.

Oakley, K. P., & B. G. Campbell. 1967. *Catalogue of fossil hominids. Part I: Africa.* London: British Museum (Natural History).

Premack, D. 1971. Language in chimpanzee? *Science* 172: 808–822.

Robinson, J. T. 1967. Variation and the taxonomy of the early hominids. *Evolutionary Biol.* 1: 69–100.

Sebeok, T. A. 1965. Animal communication. *Science* 147: 1006–1014.

Sebeok, T. A., A. S. Hayes, & M. C. Bateson, eds. 1964. *Approaches to semiotics.* The Hague: Mouton.

Simons, E. L. 1967. The significance of primate paleontology for anthropological studies. *Amer. Jour. Phys. Anthrop.* n.s., 27; 307–332.

————. 1968. A source for dental comparison of *Ramapithecus* with *Australopithecus* and *Homo. South African Jour. Sci.* 64: 92–112.

Simpson, G. G. 1951. The species concept. *Evolution* 5: 285–298.

————. 1961. *Principles of animal taxonomy.* New York: Columbia Univ. Press.

————. 1963. The meaning of taxonomic statements. In *Classification and human evolution,* ed. S. L. Washburn, pp. 1–31. Chicago: Aldine.

————. 1964. *This view of life.* New York: Harcourt Brace Jovanovitch.

————. 1969. *Biology and man.* New York: Harcourt Brace Jovanovitch.

Smith, H. M. 1960. *Evolution of chordate structure.* New York: Holt, Rinehart and Winston.

Sonntag, C. F. 1924. *The morphology and evolution of the apes and man.* London: John Bale, Sons and Danielson.

Spuhler, J. N. 1967. *Genetic diversity and human behavior.* Chicago: Aldine.

Teilhard de Chardin, P. 1959. *The phenomenon of man.* New York: Harper and Row.

Tobias, P. V. 1968. The taxonomy and phylogeny of the australopithecines. In *Taxonomy and phylogeny of Old World primates with reference to the origin of man,* ed. B. Chiarelli, pp. 277–315. Turin: Rosenberg and Sellier.

Wallace, A. R. 1864. Origin of the human races and the antiquity of man deduced from natural selection. *Anthrop. Rev.* 2: clviii-clxxxvci.

———. 1870. *Contributions to the theory of natural selection.* London: Macmillan.

Washburn, S. L., ed. 1963. *Classification and human evolution.* Chicago: Aldine.

Young, J. Z. 1957. *The life of mammals.* New York and Oxford: Oxford Univ. Press.

3

BERNARD CAMPBELL
UNIVERSITY OF CALIFORNIA,
LOS ANGELES

Man for All Seasons

> In each great region of the world the living mammals are closely related to the extinct species of the same region. It is, therefore, probable that Africa was formerly inhabited by extinct apes closely allied to the gorilla and chimpanzee; and as these two species are now man's nearest allies, it is somewhat more probable that our early progenitors lived on the African continent than elsewhere.
>
> Charles Darwin, *The Descent of Man,* 1871

Introduction

When Darwin wrote *The Descent of Man,* his object was to consider first "whether man, like every other species, is descended from some pre-existing form; secondly, the manner of his development; and thirdly, the value of the differences between the so-called races of man" (1871). Today, there is no need to argue that man is descended from some pre-existing form; this is a well-founded theory that finds wide acceptance.

The manner of man's evolution is the aspect of the descent of man to which Darwin was least able to address himself. In 1871 he was not in a position to cite any fossil men which could be considered intermediate links in the lineage of man's ancestors. The Neandertal skull, one of the first found[1] and most famous fossil men of the time, had been described by Huxley (1863) as "the extreme term of a series leading gradually from it to the highest and best developed of human crania." The large cranial capacity, among other features, led Huxley to conclude that the skull did not fall far enough outside the normal range of variation of modern man to justify regarding it as a "missing link." Darwin followed Huxley in this conclusion, and it was in a sense correct, insofar as we now recognize that

1. At the time of writing *Descent,* two further fossils of the Neandertal race had in fact been found, that from Engis (a child's skull) and that from Gibraltar (for details see Oakley & Campbell 1971).

West European Neandertal man was in the relationship of cousin rather than ancestor to modern man.

Darwin did not appear perturbed by the absence of fossil evidence. Breaks in the fossil record were common, and the discovery of vertebrate fossils had been, until that time, a very slow and fortuitous process. Darwin (1871) added that "our progenitors, no doubt, were arboreal in their habits, and frequented some warm, forest-clad land" suggesting Africa to be the more probable. Thus the regions most likely to afford fossils had not at that time been searched by geologists. During the past one hundred years, however, the fossil evidence for human evolution has accumulated at an accelerating pace. We now have not only the direct evidence of the evolutionary process, but enough detail to consider in a limited way the manner of man's descent: his successive adaptations.

Following Simpson (1953), we may define adaptations as those characteristics of an organism advantageous to it or to the conspecific group in which it lives. Obviously such characteristics are evolved and accumulated during evolution, and the word could be applied to any characteristic of a successful species. What we are concerned with here are those characteristics that man evolved since his separation from a common lineage with the apes and that gave him success in the new environments he entered during his evolution. They include a vast range of anatomical, behavioral, and cultural structures and traits that could not be described in detail in a large book, let alone a short paper. We therefore need to consider them as a whole and in limited aspect.

The aspect I have chosen, classical ecology, is one that would have appealed to Darwin. In short, I wish to consider how man managed to tap an increasing proportion of energy from his ecosystem and how this was done in the different climatic zones he successively entered. Since all organic life depends on solar energy as the ultimate source of its food, evolutionary success can be seen as the proportion of the total solar energy that any species can tap and incorporate into its own biomass. Since the quantity of energy is finite, and the conversion rate more or less fixed by the process of photosynthesis (in the region of 1 per cent), gains by one organism will usually be at the expense of another—a generalization that is particularly true in the case of man.

My view of man, then, is to be economic. Economics seem always to have controlled our destiny, as they do today. I will review the series of adaptations which man has undergone and devised to increase the extraction rate from his environment: the extraction of energy in the form of food, and later fuel and power. To this end I shall briefly review man's biological and cultural adaptations to the tropical, temperate and arctic biomes, and attempt to summarize an overall pattern of successive adaptation in human evolution.

Forest and Savanna: The First Phase

The detailed fossil evidence for human evolution has reduced theories of the origin of the Hominidae from a large number to just two, and these two have a great deal in common. Both state that the earliest Hominids split from the apes in tropical Africa, and both would accept that this split occurred about the same time as the apes themselves divided into the two species chimpanzee and gorilla. In one theory (for example, Campbell 1966, Pilbeam 1970, Simons 1967) the split is believed to have occurred more than 15 and probably nearer 25 million years ago. In the second (Washburn 1968, Wilson & Sarich 1969) the split is believed to have occurred less than 10 million years ago.

The differences involved in these two theories are of degree rather than of kind, and the degree is mainly a matter of timing. The evolutionary process would have been broadly the same in each case, but while in the first theory the split would have occurred among apes which were primarily adapted for arm swinging as a mode of locomotion, in the second theory the split would have occurred among knuckle-walking apes. There is therefore an important difference in the locomotor adaptation that we should attribute to the earliest Hominids. The difference of opinion is based on a wide range of indirect evidence, but in the end we should be able to elucidate which hypothesis is correct by the collection and evaluation of the fossil evidence. In particular, we should ask if there are any fossil Hominidae of 10 or more million years of age. The record of *Australopithecus* goes back in a very clear and satisfactory series to 5.5 million years (at Lothagam; see Patterson et al. 1971), but before that time we have no *certain* fossil evidence.

From an earlier date we have specimens of the genus *Ramapithecus* (=*Kenyapithecus*) from India and East Africa which have been described as early hominids. The Indian fossils are more than 8 million years of age, and the Fort Ternan fossils (Kenya) carry a date of 14 million years BP (Evernden & Curtis 1965). The Kenyan specimen is of great interest: in its anatomy it seems to fall neatly between the later hominids and the early Dryopithecines. Particularly striking is the first lower premolar tooth, which is halfway between the sectorial ape tooth and the bicuspid human tooth. Anatomically these fragments fulfill our expectations to a remarkable degree (Simons 1968, Andrews 1971).

The status of these fossils is, however, not a foregone conclusion. As we pass back in time, the fossil record becomes less well documented, and bones of *Ramapithecus* are rare and fragmentary. At the same time, the nearer we come to the split, the more difficult it will be to distinguish the bases of the two diverging families; the fossils will carry more characters of common inheritance and fewer characters of independent acquisition. It may therefore take some time before the matter is resolved. We urgently need evidence of the skull and limb bones of *Ramapithecus.* Extensive fossil evidence may well prove necessary to elucidate the status of these early and closely related groups of hominoid primates.

The faunal context of *Ramapithecus,* in both India and Kenya, implies riverine forest and possibly more open woodland (perhaps bordering on savanna). The climate was warm and moist, and it looks as though ecologically, *Ramapithecus* was not very different from the chimpanzee. The evidence further indicates that there was an ecological corridor between Eurasia and East Africa, and many of the fauna of the Fort Ternan site are from Eurasia (Simons 1969a). Therefore it is possible that *Ramapithecus* came from Eurasia and evolved from an early Eurasian *Dryopithecus* ape. It is equally possible that the movement of *Ramapithecus* was in the opposite direction, and in this case it is probable that the ancestral form was chimpanzeelike, perhaps close to *Dryopithecus* (*Proconsul*) *africanus* (Pilbeam 1969). Alternatively, the early hominids may have evolved over a wide area of the tropical and subtropical regions of the Old World. But the similarity of man to the chimpanzee, which has been demonstrated by Wilson & Sarich (1969) through biochemical traits as well as by classical comparative anatomy, strongly suggests that we are right to look for man's origin in Africa.

If *Ramapithecus* is a hominid in its total morphological pattern, then we can be fairly sure that the split occurred sometime earlier, at least 15 million years BP. If *Ramapithecus* is not an early hominid, the opinion of Sarich and Washburn that the split occurred less than 10 million years ago may hold. It will still be necessary to find intermediate fossils from the Pliocene as positive evidence for this theory.[2] Whatever the date of the split, the evidence at present strongly supports Darwin's prediction that our progenitors lived in "some warm, forest-clad land," and it is likely that this land was indeed Africa.

Evidence of the changes in climate in prehistoric Africa are not yet so well understood as those of prehistoric Europe. The faunal evidence suggests a reduction in rainfall toward the end of the Miocene and an accompanying reduction in the area of tropical rain forest. The forest was in part replaced by woodland, tree savanna, and open grassland savanna, though the actual area of ecotone between forest and savanna may not have been materially altered. By the early Pleistocene, evidence from the fauna and sediments at the base of Olduvai Gorge and in the Transvaal cave deposits suggests that the climate was not very dissimilar to that of today, though some variation in rainfall was not uncommon.

2. The biochemical evidence available at present does not give either direct or convincing evidence of the late date of the split between Pongid and Hominid. All it does is to emphasize their close relationship. In consideration of the work of Wilson & Sarich (1969), the reader should consult Read & Lestrel (1970), Bauer (1970) and Simons (1969b).

A visitor to the Serengeti and Kenya Rift Valley today, however, will find a great predominance of open grassland, which in some places has degenerated to a scrubby woody vegetation as a result of overgrazing. The grassland savanna is largely maintained by periodic fires set by pastoral tribes such as the Masai to encourage grazing for their cattle and to kill tsetse fly and ticks. Fire allows the growth of grasses but kills most trees and tree seedlings. Such open conditions are therefore recent. It seems probable that in Pleistocene times the extensive plains of East Africa that lie at an elevation of between 4,000 and 6,000 feet carried perennial grassland, sometimes open, but more usually with scattered trees (such as species of *Acacia*) in most areas. There are still today limited regions of montane and riverine forest, and in the past these were probably more extensive. The use of fire to maintain pasture in East Africa has certainly changed the ecology of the tropical savanna.

These considerations are important in developing our ideas about the adaptations of the early hominids. They evolved from an arboreal apelike species and would have depended on trees as an escape from predators and a safe sleeping place. The first and most significant phase in human evolution almost certainly took place in forest fringe woodland where water was available, an ecotone that offered the safety and familiarity of the forest together with the richness of the savanna fauna. This development was not so much a change in habitat as an expansion into and exploitation of an ecotone with greater diversity of species. Undefended by size or large canines, these small hominids must have survived by cunning and an effective escape route from predators.

Reliance on meat would have developed slowly. From a diet containing very little meat (such as that of a chimpanzee), the proportion would have increased, especially in the dry season, or when vegetable foods were scarce. That meat would ever have composed more than 50 per cent of the diet of early hominids seems extremely improbable; a far smaller percentage is a more likely figure. Today the Bushmen of the Central Kalahari desert survive in much more arid regions, and when game is absent during the dry season they survive for long periods on vegetable foods. High meat diets are a recent adaptation to winter arctic desert conditions where there is no vegetation whatsoever. The dentition of the Hominids at all known stages is oriented toward chewing and grinding rather than cutting and slicing and carries clear evidence of a preponderantly vegetable diet.

We can therefore suppose that the early hominids came to exploit a range of fauna as a subsidiary food resource, with the adaptations of the bipedal stance and run and, later, the use of the cutting tool. There is no convincing evidence at this early stage of the use of weapons to kill game, but it is quite possible that sticks and bones would have been used as clubs (Wolberg 1970). Sticks are thrown in agonistic display by apes (Hall 1963) and would almost certainly have been used as clubs by hominids.

Techniques of killing must have been developed that did not involve the use of sharp canine teeth.

There is little doubt that during this period of adaptation the social structure of the hominids underwent some modification. Even among living chimpanzees we see a tighter social structure in savanna woodland than in forest areas (Nishida 1968), and this pattern was undoubtedly followed by early hominids (Campbell 1966). The relationship between social structure and ecology has been clearly demonstrated among primates (Crook 1970, and Chapter 9). This relationship is important for our consideration of early hominid adaptations, because the social group sets the scene for social hunting. (Compare the baboons described in Oakley 1951.)

By the time of the deposition of Bed I, Olduvai Gorge, above the 1.8 million-year-old larva flow, a stable adaptation to woodland savanna was almost certainly achieved. Food remains on the living floors at many sites testify to successful hunting as well as scavenging. The move to the savanna was completed. We know, however, that the Olduvai sites were on a lake shore (Hay 1970), and it seems certain that the hominids were dependent on both a constant supply of fresh water and the presence of trees (Figure 3.1). Arid areas without fresh water but with saline lakes would not have been satisfactory sites for hominid occupation, as Bed III, Olduvai, testifies.

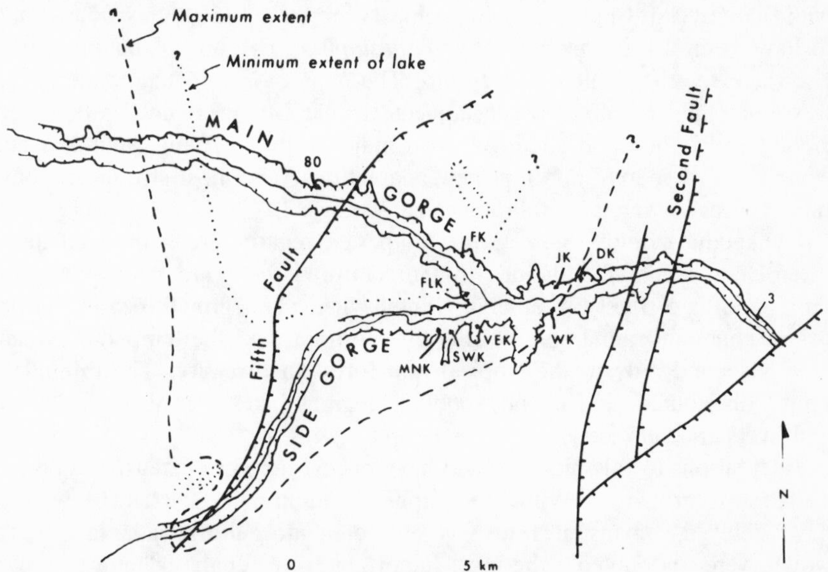

Figure 3.1. Olduvai Gorge, showing the shorelines of a lake that existed in this region during Bed I times, about 1.8 million years ago. All the sites bearing hominid fossils (indicated by capital letters) lie in this region of the gorge (from Hay 1970).

Further adaptations to arid savanna regions must have appeared by Olduvai times. We know that the stone tool kit was by now quite extensive (Leakey 1971), and probably included tools for making implements of wood and bone. Large stones suitable for tool making were collected from point sources as much as eight miles from the lake shore. Animal products such as skins and ligaments would probably have been used and prepared with stone tools. The site at DK carries evidence that has been interpreted as indicating some sort of shelter from rain or wind. The relative size of the brain compared with body size of the australopithecines had increased over that of the apes, and the pelvis was manlike in many features. Their hunting skills were quite well developed. Their survival indicates that these hominids were successful until more advanced hominids had evolved by the Middle Pleistocene. We do not yet know whether this took place in Africa or further north, but the fossil and archeological remains suggest that adaptation to cold winters was an important factor in the evolution of man.

Temperate Adaptations: A Critical Advance

It now seems possible that the expansion of the hominid populations into temperate zones was the most significant step in the evolution of *Homo*. While it was previously thought that the appearance of *Homo* coincided with the successful hunting of big game (Campbell 1966), this now seems to have been an art mastered by *Australopithecus,* and we have to look elsewhere for the hallmark of *Homo*. The expansion into temperate zones was more than a shift between adjacent tropical biomes such as occurred among earlier hominids; it involved a major climatic change and was accompanied by many important new adaptations. The most striking adaptations, however, were cultural rather than biological.

Unlike the tropical biomes, the temperate regions are subject to quite extensive seasonal fluctuations in temperature: there are usually two or three months of frosty weather in winter when plant growth ceases. There is also abundant fauna and a richly diverse flora, and the temperate woodland is second only to the tropical rain forest in diversity. The rainfall is evenly distributed, and in the woodland regions lakes, permanent streams, and rivers are common.

Adaptations to this biome would have opened up very extensive food resources to early man. While geographical (mountain) barriers may well have delayed expansion into this environment, cultural adaptations to winter were undoubtedly the most important factor enabling man to move north.

From the period from two to one million years BP we have tropical fossil hominids from Java which seem to be somewhat similar to the later *Australopithecus* (=*Homo habilis*) fossils from East Africa. These populations could have entered Southeast Asia via a tropical woodland and savanna corridor at this time if not earlier. They are usually classified as *Homo erectus.*

Perhaps the earliest occupation of a temperate zone is that recorded at the Vallonet Cave in southern France (Alpes-Maritime), which is believed to be of Günz age (Howell 1966). There is evidence of hearths in the Escale Cave in the nearby region of Bouches-de-Rhone; these deposits date from a period which is at least early Mindel. Neither of these sites, however, is so convincing as the inter-Mindel site at Vértesszöllös in Hungary (Kretzoi & Vertés 1965), where there are hearths with burnt bones and numerous broken and split bones of a substantial mammalian fauna, particularly rodent bones but also those of bear, deer, rhino, lion, and canid. There are several hundred artifacts of chert and quartz, mainly choppers and chopping tools, flake tools, and side scrapers.

The great cave of Choukoutien, near Peking, is another important site of about the same age (though Chinese workers now claim a Mindel-Riss date; see Hsu Jen 1966). It has very extensive deposits containing numerous hearths with food remains of 45 different species, including sheep, zebra, pigs, buffalo and rhinoceros, together with deer, which form about 70 per cent of the total. The tool kit has much in common with that of Vértesszöllös and indeed with the "developed Oldowan" from Olduvai Gorge.

Dating from the late Mindel we have two other important European sites, and both show the use of fire. At Torralba and Ambrona in Spain (two contemporary sites, three kilometers apart) we have evidence of extensive butchery by bands of *Homo erectus* who appear to have been trapping elephants in a bog and butchering them on the spot. Bones of more than 20 elephants have been found in a small area together with remains of horses, cervids, aurochs, rhinoceros, and smaller animals: evidently extensive slaughter took place at this site from time to time. There is also evidence of shaped and polished tools of wood and bone (Howell 1966) and there is a rich Early Acheulian industry.

At Terra Amata, in present-day Nice, we have evidence of seasonal habitations on coastal dunes. There are ovoid arrangements of stones with regularly spaced post holes. Within the shelters these represent, the floors were covered with pebbles or animal hides (imprints are preserved). Hearths occur in holes or on stone slabs sheltered by low stone walls. Food residues include elephant, deer, boar, ibex, rhinoceros, small mammals, and marine shells and fish. The industry is of Early Acheulian type, and includes a few bone artifacts (Howell 1967).

Although he probably entered this latitude during the preceding warm interglacial, on the basis of the present evidence man seems to have become well established in north temperate zones during the Mindel glaciation. By Mindel times (variously dated between 700,000 and 400,000 BP), highly efficient and productive hunting techniques were employed; and it appears that no animal was too large or too dangerous to be killed by hunting bands. The product of the hunt would have served to support an increased population through an improved food supply and other animal products, such as skins, that could be used in an advancing technology.

Because at most times of the year vegetable foods in the temperate regions would have been fairly plentiful, systematic hunting was primarily a means of supplementing a diverse vegetable diet. Mammal meat would have become a primary food resource only during late winter and early spring. Berries and seeds would have been eaten by this time, and the new succulent vegetation would not yet be grown. Even the game would have dispersed to find food. Because this limiting period of the temperate year would have kept hunting populations fairly sparse, both gene flow and the transmission of cultural traits would have been restricted. New developments in human evolution were in future to be tied to adaptations which increased man's extraction rate by the exploitation of additional food resources and by food storage techniques.

THE SIGNIFICANCE OF WINTER

There is very limited evidence of biological adaptation to cold in modern man. Biologically suited to the tropics as he was, his survival through the cold winters of the temperate zone required extensive cultural adaptations unmatched by the evidence from Africa.

Whether in a grass hut shelter (such as those found at Terra Amata) or cave site, fire would have been maintained not only for warmth but as essential protection against giant carnivores such as cave bears and brown bears which were dangerous competitors for life space in cave sites. Archeological evidence strongly supports the notion that fire was used in temperate biomes for a very long period in human evolution. The earliest evidence of fire in Africa is from the Cave of Hearths and is dated about 55,000 BP.

Cold winters also necessitated considerable development in social behavior. It seems inescapable that there would have been a fairly complete division of labor by this time: the men hunting and the women minding the babies and gathering vegetable foods, water (in skins), and fuel. Perhaps for the first time babies were put down and left in charge of siblings or aunts at the base camp. The division of labor and separation of the sexes must have increased the need to communicate abstract ideas by the development of language, and the vocabulary expanded (Campbell 1971). Perhaps the expression of the emotions (which language could replace) was first inhibited in a closely knit cave-dwelling band, and this emotional inhibition was to become increasingly important. It may prove to have been one of the most fundamental social developments which has shaped the psychology of modern man.

From the skeletal evidence at Choukoutien we can deduce that more than 50 per cent of the population died before the age of 14, before they reached full reproductive age. This suggests that it would have been necessary to produce four children per family simply to maintain the population level, and it is probable that more than four children were born in each family. The impossibility for hunter-gatherers of carrying and nursing more than one child at a time indicates that a cultural adaptation such as infanticide was possibly quite common.

The cold made demands on man's ingenuity to devise protective facilities such as clothing and tents. It was surely an important factor in the evolution of human intelligence. All the necessary adaptations had their anatomical correlates in the brain, the skeleton, and the soft parts of the body. The people of Choukoutien show a great advance over *Australopithecus*. Their endocranial capacity is twice that of *Australopithecus* and falls into the range of modern man. At Choukoutien the cranial capacity varies between 915 and 1,225 cc, while at the Vértesszöllös site in Hungary (which is at least half a million years old), the cranial capacity has been estimated to be about 1,550 cc. This is three times the mean for *Australopithecus* and above the mean for modern man (1,325 cc). The only well preserved cranium from Africa of *Homo erectus* is the skull from site LLK II at Olduvai Gorge, which has a cranial capacity of 1,000 cc. Such is the variability of cranial capacity in man that samples of one individual have little significance, but they are suggestive.

The people at Choukoutien were also anatomically more advanced than *Australopithecus;* they were of greater stature and more sturdily built, with a well-developed bipedalism. Yet they still carried a heavily built masticatory apparatus that clearly distinguished them from modern man.

The cultural adaptations man developed to survive in temperate and arctic biomes were an extraordinary achievement, and northern winters were undoubtedly a factor of great importance in the evolution of *Homo sapiens.*

Arctic Adaptations

None of the sites discussed so far carry evidence of permanent cold, but only of seasonal frost. The fauna and pollen data suggest a cool climate becoming either colder (as at Vértesszöllös) or warmer (as at Torralba). The climate at Terra Amata near the sea was certainly mild, and that at Choukoutien was of interstadial or interglacial type.

Man at this time survived cold temperate winters, but there is no evidence that he had yet adapted to the arctic conditions of the Mindel glaciation. Following the Mindel period, we have more northerly fossils of late Riss-Würm interglacial date (Swanscombe and Steinheim) which represent the expansion of human populations northward during warm temperate spells. In view of the extreme difficulty of survival in northern coniferous forest and arctic tundra, it is not to be expected that man would have entered these zones at a very early date. Today it is hard to see how early man could possibly have adapted to arctic conditions without domesticated animals such as reindeer or dogs. The presence of Neandertal man in the first Würm glaciation of western Europe is a surprising fact. It suggests an advanced use of both tools and facilities.

Though the present evidence suggests that Neandertal man did not survive throughout the first major advance of the Würm glaciation, it does clearly demonstrate that he could survive extreme cold and must have lived some thousands of years under arctic conditions. This Würm advance of the northern ice sheets brought a cold moist climate characterized by animals such as mammoth, woolly rhinoceros, reindeer, musk-ox, ibex, blue fox and marmot. All these were hunted, together with the formidable cave bear.

Neandertal man was well established in southern and central Europe before the colder weather descended, and he survived the cold to a great extent by using caves and rock shelters. Judging by the extent of their cultural remains the Neandertal people adapted successfully to the climate and were able to exploit the huge herds of reindeer and other animals. In some areas such as the Dordogne, the local topography must have offset the very extreme conditions. The Dordogne river and its tributaries dissect deeply into a limestone plateau and offer a number of sheltered valleys. Possibly the vast herds of animals which must have undertaken regular seasonal migrations used these valleys as migratory routes. It seems possible that here, as in southwest Asia (Binford 1968b), these people came to rely on harvesting migratory animals. Many temperate animals, and more particularly arctic species, migrate regularly in the spring and autumn between coastal plain and mountain pasture. These people were thus not only able to harvest "earned" resources (which gain their food within the local habitat where they live), but to tap "unearned" resources—animals which pass through or spend some portion of their annual life cycle in one biome and yet gain most of their food (energy) in another biome. To settle along the migration routes of herd mammals such as reindeer, musk-ox or ibex and intercept them between their summer and winter feeding grounds is a sophisticated adaptation that we can fairly safely attribute to late Neandertal man. It was a simple step to allow autumn-killed meat to dry and freeze for use during the winter, as many Eskimo do today. We can also deduce that the game was sufficient for their needs, for they must have relied to a great extent on meat during the winter.

An interesting clue is provided by the teeth of the man from La Ferrassie (see Boule & Vallois 1954). They show a particular type of extreme wear also found today among the Eskimo and some other hunters caused by chewing animal skins to soften them for clothing. It is indeed highly probable that Neandertal man had exploited the whole range of animal products, and especially skins, to develop a well-differentiated material culture. He could well have made the kind of clothing that we find among the Eskimo, though the ready-made shelter of rocks and caves would probably have stood in place of the warm and intimate family igloo.

Probably the most difficult problem facing these arctic people was transport. Without dogs or sleds, they would be confined to a small area during the winter months, and their movements would have been limited to the valleys in which they lived. This restriction shows how successfully they had been able to exploit the local food resources of the region.

The successors of Neandertal man in western Europe, the Aurignacian and Magdelenian peoples, have left us a far more detailed picture of their adaptations than their predecessors. Migratory herds of reindeer were harvested in very large numbers, and often formed 85 to 90 per cent of the faunal assemblage. (Other animals hunted include mammoth, bison and horse.) When climatic conditions became severe again, as they did toward the end of this period, the later Magdelenians (14,000–12,000 BP) began the systematic hunting of new kinds of unearned resources: migratory birds, aquatic mammals, and fish. The significance of these additions to their food supply can scarcely be overstated. Migratory fish and fowl appear in early spring, a time of maximum food shortage, and make possible the survival of a much larger population throughout the year. At the same time, it is probably important that fish oils (unlike terrestrial animal fats) contain vitamin D, and this may have been an essential vitamin source to people living in areas where insolation was low and clothing essential at all times. Evidence of rickets is present among Neandertal skeletal remains; as far as we know, these people were unable to catch fish and complement their own low vitamin D production. Shortage of this vitamin may indeed have been one of the factors that mitigated against their survival (Mayr & Campbell 1971).

This extensive exploitation of migratory animals, which must have arisen slowly through the later stages of human evolution, was to have a profound effect on the evolution of man's social life. The most obvious result was that it allowed a more sedentary way of life to develop. Home bases could be occupied for longer periods of time during migrations and the ensuing winter, and there was no longer such a premium on the mobility of hunting bands. During the early phases of hunting and gathering (a way of life which Bushmen and Australians still follow) possessions and infants were limited by the need for mobility. A mother with a baby or a small child who must break camp frequently and transport her baby as well as her household gear will not welcome a second infant to care for and carry or a mass of material possessions. She will have few compunctions about taking any means necessary to limit family size. Today, hunter-gatherers practice infanticide, abortion, and other means of birth control to retain their essential mobility.

Sedentism changed all this. As soon as a band could remain more or less permanently in one place, an increase in possessions and in population densities was possible. The limitation on numbers was removed, and population could now expand to a level related to that dictated by the increased food supply. When we compare the sites of the earlier Magdelenian to those of the later period (since 14,000 BP), we find that the living sites are more numerous, larger, and more often situated low on river banks, frequently at places where the river narrows. Many of these sites have yielded evidence that they were inhabited throughout the year. Thus we find these permanent settlements associated with an increase in density and in group size. These profound changes have been discussed elsewhere (Binford 1968a, Binford & Campbell 1973). It is also clear that these developments may have required a much greater complexity of social structure, compared with the essentially egalitarian local bands that characterize most hunter-gatherer groups. It opened the way to the developments that characterize the Neolithic period.

Alteration of the Ecosystem

In his adaptations as a hunter-gatherer, man remained part of a more or less stable natural ecosystem, as he adapted to the particular conditions of each biome and each region. Because food supplies were not the limiting factor in population growth, except perhaps at certain very critical periods, we do not find evidence of overkill or of any serious instability following the appearance of man in a region. As a hunter he was competing with carnivores for herbivores, but the ecosystem is characterized by a functional dynamism that allows it to equilibrate in the face of climatic and other minor changes, especially if it is diverse in species.

Farming is the protection of food plants and animals at the expense of wild forms of less nutritive value to man. It also involves domestication, which is the selective breeding of certain species for their tameness and their value as food. The overall effect of the practice is a reduction in the diversity of organisms in an area, which is balanced by an increase in the domestic species, and a larger proportion of the solar energy in the area is turned into human food, either as plants or meat. Pastoralism can be a surprisingly effective adaptation in this respect, especially when more than one animal species is herded in a single area. Where field agriculture results in whole areas of the ground being covered in one or two food species, the conversion rate of solar energy into human food is even higher. Although we only cultivate 10 per cent of the earth's land surface today, it has been estimated that the human population has increased from a potential maximum of about 10 million hunter-gatherers to its present size: some 3½ billion (many of whom suffer from malnutrition and starvation). But the ecological cost of the introduction of pastoralism and agriculture is high; it implies the destruction of the natural ecosystem and of the diversity of species which assure its stability. The Neolithic was the start of the destruction of man's natural environment, and as the rate of population increase grew, the rate of destruction increased.

In the past 5,000 years man has altered the ecosystem in many parts of the world and destroyed the natural balance. Pastoralism itself has been one of the most destructive forces; it is clear that wherever it has been carried out in semi-arid regions, whether in Australia, Asia, Africa, the Americas, or in limited areas in the Mediterranean regions of Europe, there has been degradation of the grasslands and the threat or reality of soil erosion. The local fauna has been destroyed and the existing ecosystem degraded beyond the point where it can naturally equilibrate. Where soils are eroded, the loss is irrevocable. The displacement of game and the destruction of their natural environment has done far more damage to natural life than all the hunting of the Pleistocene. In the same way agriculture and deforestation for timber have involved the destruction of vast areas of forest (areas of naturally high rainfall), and we have lost both the forest with its associated flora and the forest animals (which often have a very limited distribution). All these developments, though they may eventually prove to endanger his survival, have enabled man to increase his extraction rate from his environment and place himself increasingly at the top of the energy food chain of the biosphere.

Trends of Human Ecology and Adaptation

During his evolution man has occupied an increasing series of subsystems within the world ecosystem. From his beginning in the forest/savanna ecotone of Africa (and possibly Asia) he spread northward into temperate and arctic biomes. The evolution of man through this climatic spectrum shows a number of trends.

FLEXIBILITY AND RANGE OF BEHAVIOR

Man's relatively large brain is a reflection of a particular kind of progressive evolution that has been described by Herrick (1946) as "change in the direction of increase in range and variety of adjustments of the organism to its environment." An increased dependence on learning as a basis for appropriate response to environmental stimuli has allowed a much greater flexibility in that response. Innate mechanisms form the basis for learning, rather than for programming, the actual behavior. Behavioral flexibility allows the evolution of complex social behavior, which is facilitated by language, a novel behavior pattern unique to man. The flexibility and range of human behavior is man's primary biological adaptation, which has made possible his unique mode of cultural adaptation. The evolution of increasing cranial capacity began to accelerate about one million years ago and has continued throughout man's adaptation to temperate regions. The correlation may well be significant.

CULTURAL ADAPTATIONS

Throughout his evolution man's behavioral development takes the form of a material culture. From an early use of very simple tools, complexity developed. Adaptations to temperate climates in particular involved dependence not only on tools but on facilities, defined by Wagner (1960) as objects that restrict or prevent motion or energy exchanges (such as dams or insulation), so that anything that retains heat is included (tents, houses, or clothing). Containers of various sorts—skins for carrying water, pots or boats, fences or even cords—fall into this category. Temperate adaptation requires far more facilities than tropical adaptation; and their most important aspect is the extent to which they enabled man to become even marginally independent from certain limiting factors in the environment.

Much later in human evolution during the Neolithic, the first machines were invented. The atl-atl, bow and arrow, firedrill, and eventually the wheeled cart enabled man to carry out tasks previously beyond his power. His advancing technology gave him enormous power over his environment and the food resources it contained.

INCREASE IN TROPHIC SPAN

Advances in material culture allowed man to increase his trophic span. From a mainly vegetarian diet in the forest, man spread onto the savanna to become a part-time hunter. In this way he came to tap a second trophic level in a very diverse environment. Evidence was found at Choukoutien that man was obtaining food from three trophic levels by killing and eating carnivores as well as herbivores. The Eskimo today (as perhaps the Magdelenians in their time) kill carnivorous sea mammals in the next trophic level, and this gives them an even greater trophic span. As man moved north, he moved up the food chain; his original dependence on a single trophic level was spread to four tropic levels. This gave him a much more reliable food supply in northern regions of low diversity, where oscillations in populations of animals are common and where vegetable foods may be almost unobtainable during the winter and early spring. This adaptation to a very varied diet is probably unique to man and allows his survival in a wide range of habitats. However, owing to the inefficiency of energy transfer from one trophic level to the next (which lies in the region of 10 per cent), the transfer of solar energy into human beings is most efficiently achieved at the first trophic level. During the present period of overpopulation more and more people are having to live on a vegetable diet as meat becomes a scarcity. In this way the world population is fed, though limitations in variety of vegetable foods may result in serious protein deficiency.

EXPLOITATION OF UNEARNED RESOURCES

The use of unearned resources of food (and later fuel and minerals) had a far-reaching effect on the balance of man's ecosystem: sedentism followed and then the expansion of populations. Sites that were favorable for the exploitation of terrestrial and aquatic unearned resources were settled, and social organization became more complex. Many groups budded off from parent populations and were forced into less favored semi-arid regions. It was under these circumstances that the harvesting of seeds became adaptive. The first documented attempts at agriculture in both Old and New Worlds appear in semi-arid zones bordering established riverine settlements. With the development of agriculture and its associated stored surplus, there was a further expansion of population and an increased dependence on other kinds of unearned resources, such as water for irrigation, and the grain crops themselves, as they were transported over long distances into growing villages and towns.

EXPLOITATION OF ENERGY SOURCES OTHER THAN FOOD

Nearly a million years ago man may have learned to capture and maintain fire both for protection and warmth. The use of timber for fuel and eventually for smelting made possible important cultural developments and resulted in the deforestation of vast areas. The use of fossil fuels in the past 300 years has in turn made possible our western civilization, and these limited energy sources will need replacement by nuclear, solar, or tidal energy in the near future. Following the development of field agriculture the use of draft animals was another important energy source: ploughing was developed and heavy transportation was facilitated. Eventually man learned to harvest the energy of the wind and rivers.

URBANIZATION

The appearance of agricultural surplus brought technological specialization and more complex social organization. The development of storage and transport facilities that made possible trade was a basic adaptation that brought the interdependence of human groups. As settlements increased in size and density, the effects of disease (which perhaps were not so important in the earlier stages of human evolution) would have become evident and a significant factor in population growth. After the development of agriculture, when population levels again came to stability, far more people would have died prematurely of disease (including malnutrition) than were ever killed by hunter-gatherers as newborn infants.

THE MEDICAL REVOLUTION: REDUCING THE DEATH RATE

As a constant factor in man's evolution, endemic disease would have had little impact on human consciousness. But with increasing population density and mobility, epidemics would have become significant factors in human selection and survival. The horror of this natural check on population growth was well-known in cities such as Paris and London that suffered the plague and black death. Toward the end of the nineteenth century, new discoveries in medicine (such as Pasteur's discovery of germs) brought about a further increase in human populations (and later in domestic herds), not by increasing the effective birth rate but by reducing the death rate. Today lives are preserved to suffer malnutrition and starvation, which the doctors cannot treat.

ONE ECOSYSTEM

All these trends have interacted in such a way as to produce an accelerating development of human biomass and culture. From a series of self-supporting social units of perhaps 25 to 50 individuals, each adapted to a particular region, we now find cities of many millions of people living under artificial circumstances in the sense that they are totally dependent on others for their survival, and their environment is totally man-made. Dependence on unearned resources has reached a new level. The city of Los Angeles is an extreme example: it receives 90 per cent of its water from watersheds other than its own, some sources hundreds of miles away where otherwise fertile valleys have been robbed. The United Kingdom imports approximately half its food requirements from all parts of the world. Such dependence on foreign resources and the necessary transport of materials and food from one biome to another have brought the different ecosystems of early man together, so that they form today one great system with much-reduced differentiation. Although outposts of wilderness (the name we give the natural world) do survive, all are becoming caught in man's unbalanced ecosystem.

I thought, We have geared the machines and locked all
together into interdependence; we have built the
great cities; now
There is no escape. We have gathered vast populations
incapable of free survival, insulated
From the strong earth, each person in himself helpless, on
all dependent. The circle is closed, and the net
Is being hauled in. . . .

—Robinson Jeffers, "The Purse-Seine", 1937

References

Andrews, P. 1971. *Ramapithecus wickeri* mandible from Fort Ternan, Kenya. *Nature,* 231: 192–194.

Bauer, K. 1970. An immunological time scale for primate evolution consistent with fossil evidence. *Humangenetik* 10: 344–350.

Binford, L. R. 1968a. Post-Pleistocene adaptions. In *New perspectives in archaeology,* ed. S. R. Binford & L. R. Binford, pp. 313–341. Chicago: Aldine.

Binford, S. R. 1968b. Early Upper Pleistocene adaptations in the Levant. *Amer. Anthrop.* 70: 707–717.

Binford, S. R., & B. G. Campbell. 1973. *Human ecology.* London: Heinemann.

Boule, M., & H. V. Vallois. 1954. *Fossil man.* New York: Dryden Press.

Campbell, B. G. 1966. *Human evolution: an introduction to man's adaptations.* Chicago: Aldine.

————. 1971. The roots of language. In *Psycholinguistics,* ed. J. Morton. London: Logos Press.

Crook, J. H. 1970. Socio-ecology of primates. In *Social behaviour of birds and mammals,* ed. J. H. Crook. London and New York: Academic Press.

Darwin, C. R. 1871. *The descent of man and selection in relation to sex.* London: John Murray.

Evernden, J. F. & G. H. Curtis. 1965. The Potassium-argon dating of Late Cenozoic rocks in East Africa and Italy. *Current Anthrop.* 6: 343–85.

Hall, K. R. L. 1963. Tool using performances as indicators of behavioral adaptability. *Current Anthrop.* 4: 479–94.

Hay, R. L. 1970. Silicate reactions in three Lithofacies of a semi-arid Basin, Olduvai Gorge, Tanzania. *Mineral. Soc. Amer. Spec. Pap.* 3: 237–255.

Herrick, C. J. 1946. Progressive evolution. *Science, N. Y.* 104: 469.

Howell, F. C. 1966. Observations on the earlier phases of the European Lower Paleolithic. *Amer. Anthrop.* 68: 88–201.

————. 1967. Recent advances in human evolutionary studies. *Quart. Rev. Biol.* 42: 471–513.

Hsu Jen. 1966. The climatic condition in North China during the time of Sinanthropus. *Scientia sinica* 15: 410–414.

Huxley, T. H. 1863. *Evidence of man's place in nature.* London: Williams & Norgate.

Leakey, M. D. 1971. *Olduvai Gorge.* Vol 3. Cambridge: Cambridge University Press.

Kretzoi, M., & L. Vertés. 1965. Upper Biharian (Intermindel) pebble-industry occupation site in Western Hungary. *Current Anthrop.* 6: 74–87.

Mayr, E. & B. G. Campbell. 1971. Was Virchow right about Neandertal? *Nature,* 229: 253–4.

Nishida, T. 1968. The social group of Wild Chimpanzees in the Mahali Mountains. *Primates* 9: 167–224.

Oakley, K. P. 1962, first published 1951. A definition of man. In *Culture and the evolution of man,* ed. M. F. Ashley Montagu, pp. 3–12. New York: Oxford University Press.

Oakley, K. P. & B. G. Campbell. 1971. *Catalogue of fossil hominids, Part 2, Europe.* London: British Museum (Natural History).

Pilbeam, D. R. 1969. The Tertiary Pongidae of East Africa: evolutionary relationships and taxonomy. *Bull. Peabody Mus.,* 31.

————. 1970. *The evolution of man.* London: Thames & Hudson.

Patterson, B., A. K. Behrensmeyer, & W. D. Sill. 1971. Geology and fauna of a new Pliocene locality in North-Western Kenya. *Nature,* 22: 918–921.

Read, D. W. & P. Lestrel. 1970. Hominid phylogeny and immunology: a critical appraisal. *Science,* 168: 578–580.

Simons, E. L. 1967. The earliest apes. *Scientific American* 217: 28–35.

————. 1968. A source for dental Comparison of Ramapithecus with Australopithecus and Homo. *South Afr. J. Sci.* 64: 92–112.

————. 1969a. Late Miocene Hominid from Fort Ternan, Kenya. *Nature,* 221: 448–451.

————. 1969b. The origin and radiation of the primates. *Ann. N. Y. Acad. Sci.* 167: 319–331.

Simpson, G. G. 1953. *The major features of evolution.* New York: Columbia University Press.

Wagner, P. 1960. *The human use of the earth.* Glencoe, Ill.: Free Press.

Washburn, S. L. 1968. *The study of human evolution.* The Condon Lectures, Oregon State System of Higher Education.

Wilson, A. C., & V. M. Sarich. 1969. A molecular time scale for human evolution. *Proc. Nat. Acad. Sci.* 63: 1088–1093.

Wolberg, D. L. 1970. The hypothesized Osteodontokeratic culture of the Australopithecinae: A look at the evidence and the opinions. *Current Anthrop.* 11: 23–37.

4

THEODOSIUS DOBZHANSKY
UNIVERSITY OF CALIFORNIA, DAVIS

Genetics and the Races of Man

Introduction

"It is not my intention here to describe the several so-called races of men; but to inquire what is the value of the differences between them under a classificatory point of view and how they have originated." The above is the opening sentence of Darwin's chapter "On The Races of Man" in *The Descent of Man.* A century later, it remains appropriate to open with the same sentence a discussion of the races of man in the light of genetics. For despite the enormous growth of the information concerning racial variation both in man and in other organisms, the problems that occupied Darwin are still at issue. In a sense, the uncertainties have increased. It is the contention of a small but vociferous group of students that mankind is not differentiated into races. But even if this contention were justified, our discussion would not lose its point. If mankind has no races, it is surely not homogeneous or uniform. The diversity would still have to be described, studied, and explained. Two kinds of diversity can be distinguished: that of individuals and that of populations.

Diversity of Individuals

"What is man," asks the Psalmist, "that Thou art mindful of him, and the son of man, that Thou visitest him?" The contribution of biology toward answering this question is the assertion of irreducible singularity of every man as individual, unprecedented, and nonrecurring. Monozygotic, or so-called identical, twins bear the greatest resemblance to one another; barring mutations, they have the same genetic endowment; and yet even they have nonidentical life experiences, which make them different individuals. The appearance and the behavior of an individual is called his phenotype. Though changing with age and even from one moment to the next, the phenotype is always a product of the interactions of the heredity, the genotype, and the environment. What we observe directly, or with the aid of instruments and laboratory tests, are the phenotypes of individuals.

Good or bad health, beauty or ugliness, goodness and honesty or wickedness and evil, are phenotype characteristics. It is the phenotype which lets some individuals survive and others die, some to leave offspring and others to remain childless. The statement found in some biological writings, that only the genetic endowment, the genotype, is important is wide of the mark. The genotype is important inasmuch as it engenders some phenotypes and not others. The quality of a genotype is appraised through the phenotypes which it produces in the environments that exist or can be devised by our technology. Analysis of the evolutionary process deals nevertheless largely with genotypes. Natural and artificial selection are powerless if the materials at their disposal are genotypically uniform. Biological evolution can be defined as sustained genetic change. Without genetic changes the phenotype would be at the mercy of environmental fluctuations. Genetic change confers at least a relative stability and irreversibility on evolutionary alterations.

It is now logical to inquire how extensive are the genetic differences between individuals of the same species, particularly of the human species. This problem has long been, and to some extent still is, a subject of controversy. Classical geneticists, beginning with De Vries and Morgan, assumed, as often implicitly as explicitly, that most genes are held in homozygous condition in most individuals of a species. De Vries believed that new species arise through single mutational events. *Drosophila* geneticists were bedeviled by the concept of the normal or wild type. A vast majority of the flies of a given species of *Drosophila* found in their natural habitats are rather uniform in appearance. Bred in laboratories, these wild-type flies throw occasional mutants, some of them sharply, even dramatically, differing from the wild type in structure, color, or other characteristics. Mutant and wild-type flies can be crossed, and show segregation of normal and mutant traits as single entities.

Further and more penetrating genetic studies gradually disclosed a more complex but interesting situation. In *Drosophila,* it was found rather early that, in addition to the major mutants, there exist also less spectacular modifiers, polygenes in modern terminology, which are responsible for minor variations in sundry traits of the flies. In many species, the wild-type concept is patently inapplicable. What would one choose to designate the "normal" or wild-type man? More and more species, including man, were shown to be polymorphic, that is, to have two or more clearly distinguishable genetic forms in their populations. The many blood group polymorphisms, in addition to such traits as eye colors, are examples of human polymorphisms. The external uniformity of natural populations of *Dro-*

sophila proved to be deceptive; it conceals polymorphisms in the chromosome structures, owing chiefly to the occurrence of inversions of blocks of genes. As stated above, the term "polymorphism" is usually applied to situations where the genetic variants in the populations are clearly distinguishable by phenotype. Distinguishability is, however, a function of the refinement of the methods of study. The genotypes giving rise to different blood groups are accurately identifiable, but those responsible for the infinite variety of facial features are not. Yet at the gene level, human populations are doubtless polymorphic for many more genetic variants than we are able to diagnose precisely.

Classical and Balance Theories

The prevalence of polymorphisms raises a thorny problem. What maintains the polymorphisms in human and other populations? One school of thought, upheld steadfastly by the late H. J. Muller and his followers, cleaves as closely as possible to the classical view that most genes in populations are invariant. Moreover, and this point is crucial, they hold that the variable genes are represented by two or more variant states, alleles, one of which is normal and beneficial and the others more or less deleterious. The deleterious alleles are maintained by recurrent mutations. Except for dominant lethal changes, a certain number of generations is likely to elapse between the mutational origin of the deleterious variant and its elimination by normalizing natural selection. The yet uneliminated deleterious variants constitute the genetic load, or the genetic burden, of the population. A conclusion that logically follows is that, if we were able to stop mutation and eliminate the genetic load, the optimal or "normal" man, homozygous for all good genes, would emerge. Most adherents of the classical theory blandly refuse to draw this conclusion.

Another theory, elaborated in great detail by Michael Lerner (1954) and Bruce Wallace (1968), is that a large proportion (presumably different in different species) of the genes are held in populations in polymorphic condition by balancing natural selection. There are several kinds of balancing selection. The best known, or at least most frequently discussed, is heterotic balance. This occurs when two or more alternative alleles, such as A_1 and A_2, form heterozygous combinations, A_1 A_2, which are superior in Darwinian fitness to both homozygotes A_1 A_1 and A_2 A_2. Less well-known, but possibly even more important in nature, is diversifying selection. The environments inhabited by populations of most or even of all species, including mankind, vary in space and in time. A polymorphic population is likely to include a collection of genotypes that are optimally adapted in different subenvironments. A polymorphic species can then exploit the resources of its habitat more fully or efficiently than can a monomorphic population. None of these genotypic polymorphs need be unconditionally better than the others. "Normal" man or "Normal" *Drosophila* are fictions (Dobzhansky, 1970).

In recent years, the balance theory has received strong support from studies by Lewontin & Hubby (1966), Harris (1967), and others on enzyme polymorphisms in populations of *Drosophila* and of man. The approach used in these studies is novel and brilliant. A geneticist can normally detect only those genes which undergo mutational changes, are represented in his materials by two or more variants, and are carried in individuals that can be crossed and produce fertile hybrids. If all humans had brown, or all had blue, eyes, we would not be aware of the existence of genes changing the eye color. This awareness creates a bias: we detect genes that are polymorphic or otherwise variable in the populations. Techniques of electrophoresis on starch or on other gels detect enzymes which are alike in all individuals studied, as well as those represented by two or more variants (allozymes). On the assumption that the enzymes studied represent a random sample of the genetic traits of the species, one obtains an estimate of what proportion of all genes are polymorphic or monomorphic, and what percentage of the genes are carried in heterozygous condition in an average individual.

The estimates obtained are that about 40 per cent of genes are polymorphic in the populations of *Drosophila pseudoobscura,* and that an average individual is heterozygous for some 12 per cent of its genes. The estimates for man are surprisingly similar: 40 per cent of the genes are polymorphic, and the average heterozygosity per individual is about 16 per cent. It should be noted that these figures are low since the electrophoretic techniques distinguish only those enzyme variants which differ in the electric charges on their molecules. But even with these underestimates, the genetic variety present in human and other populations appears to be prodigious. A minimum estimate of the number of genes in a human sex cell is something like 20,000. With this number, at least 8000 genes will be polymorphic in human populations and an individual will be heterozygous on the average for some 3200 genes. With these figures, the potentially possible human diversity is immense. A heterozygote for n genes can form 2^n kinds of gametes with different gene complements; two parents heterozygous for the same n genes can give 3^n different genotypes in the progeny, and if heterozygous for n different genes can give 4^n different genotypes. With n being 3200 or greater, the potentially possible number of human genotypes is between 3^{3200} and 4^{3200}. Either figure is vastly greater than the number of atomic particles in the universe. What these figures mean is only that the variety of human constitutions that can ever be realized is vanishingly small compared to the potentially possible variety.

Taking into consideration any two variable genes, the genotype of an individual can be represented by a point in two-dimensional space; with three genes, the space is three-dimensional. With n variable genes, every genotype is symbolically represented as a point in an n-dimensional space. Except for monozygotic twins, every individual now alive, having lived, and to live in the future is symbolized by a point different from all others. The array of points for all these individuals comes nowhere near filling the space: a vast majority of possible points have no individuals corresponding to them.

Is any one of the virtual infinity of actually existing or potentially possible human genotypes in any meaningful sense normal or optimal? It is doubtful, to say the least. It is no longer reasonable to maintain that, for every one of the thousands of variable genes, one allele is always beneficial and the rest belong to the genetic load. The partisans of the classical theory of genetic population structure have retreated to a less easily assailable position: most genetic variants found in populations of the human and other species are neither useful nor harmful. They are adaptively neutral. Natural selection neither promotes nor inhibits their spread. We shall consider this possibility below, together with the problem of adaptive significance of human racial traits. Here we may conclude our discussion of the diversity of human individuals by a negative statement: the Normal Man does not exist. Normal men, if one wishes to retain this rather equivocal designation, are a great array of individuals, no two of whom (excepting monozygotic twins) are either phenotypically or genotypically alike. The sole, though obviously important, characteristic which these persons share in common is satisfactory physical and mental health, which permits them to survive and to function in their environments. In man, the key features of the environments are those created by human cultures. The array of genotypes which compose the adaptive norm of the human species allow their carriers to function at least passably well as members of human societies.

Diversity of Populations

Immanuel Kant, who was a naturalist before he became the prince of philosophers, wrote in 1775 the following remarkably perceptive lines:

> Negroes and whites are not different species of humans (they belong presumably to one stock), but they are different races, for each perpetuates itself in every area, and they generate between them children that are necessarily hybrid, or blending (mulattoes). On the other hand, blonds and brunettes are not different races of whites, for a blond man can also get from a brunette woman, altogether blond children, even though each of these deviations maintains itself throughout protracted generations under any and all transplantations.

Kant understood the distinction between individual (intrapopulational) and group (interpopulational) variability better than do some modern authors.

The make-up of group variability is a function of the reproductive biology of the organism. It is quite distinct under sexual and asexual reproduction. Consider first organisms, chiefly though not exclusively plants, in which the prevalent or obligatory method of reproduction is asexual fission, budding, diploid parthenogenesis, or self-pollination. Thousands or even millions of individuals of such organisms belong to the same clone or pure line, and have the same genotype. These are, indeed, "pure races." The inhabitants of a territory can be described by listing which pure races occur there, and specifying their relative frequencies. To cite a single example, Allard and Kannenberg (1968) found in central California at least eight pure lines of the grass *Festuca microstachys;* the relative frequencies of these lines differ from locality to locality, apparently depending on which lines are best adapted to the environments of the particular locality.

Mankind is a sexually reproducing species. Excepting monozygotic multiple births, it has no clones, pure lines, or pure races. And yet anthropologists have long been under the spell of the notion of pure race. This notion is, in turn, one of the protean manifestations of the typological way of thought, the roots of which go back at least to Plato's eternal Ideas. Human populations are polymorphic for eye and hair colors, blood groups, and many other traits. Could one declare blue-eyed persons to constitute one race and brown-eyed another? Or may one race include the possessers of blood group O, another of A, and the third of B? These divisions would be ludicrous; parents and children, as well as siblings, would often find themselves belonging to different races. Nevertheless, "races," almost equally meaningless, the dolichocephalics and the brachycephalics, have been copiously discussed and written about. The genetics of the human head shape is not well known; several pairs of genes are probably involved, and all gradations from extreme longheadedness to roundheadedness can be observed.

The notions of pure races and of Platonic types or ideas are lurking in the background of various taxonomies of constitutional types. Kretschmer's pyknic, athletic and asthenic body builds and associated psychological types are admittedly rare in their extreme or pure forms. Nevertheless, they can be somehow perceived among the manifold products of the general miscegenation in which mankind has been engaged for millennia. Sheldon's 88 somatotypes are combinations of graded series of three supposedly independent variables: endomorphy, mesomorphy, and ectomorphy. The genetics of these variables is obscure. If there existed series of multiple alleles in each of the three genes, for endomorphy, mesomorphy and ectomorphy, the 88 somatotypes could be interpreted as an elaborate instance of intrapopulational polymorphism. This hypothesis, however, remains to be demonstrated.

For more than half a century, the Polish school of anthropology consistently adhered to strictly typological assumptions (see the reviews by Czekanowski 1962, the venerable dean of this school, and also Wiercinski 1962 and Bielicki 1962). Populations are described in terms of the incidence in them of racial "types," which are "distinguished by diagnosing the racial affinities of individuals independently of their ethnic origins." European populations are composed of Nordic, Mediterranean, Armenoid and Lapponoid races or racial types. The frequencies of these types in each population are given with precision to one-tenth of one per cent, as though men belonged to one or another clone or pure line, like *Festuca microstachys* grasses. Mediterranean individuals in the Polish, Swiss, and Italian populations are assumed to be more alike than any of these are to their Nordic or Armenoid neighbors or brothers. Michalski and Wiercinski can identify as many as 16 "racial elements" of which mankind is a composite. Each of these races or types or elements is recognized by a constellation of chiefly morphological traits, such as stature, eye and hair colors, hair form, cephalic, orbital, facial and nasal indices. A set of mathematical techniques has been devised to identify to which racial type every individual belongs. Can this identification really be accomplished? As with biological mathematics generally, the results of even the most precise and elaborate calculations do no more than give numerical expressions of the biological assumptions put at the base of the mathematical model. The assumptions used in the present case, insofar as they have been stated at all, are untenable. The crucial assumption is that the trait constellations which supposedly identify the racial types, such as Nordic, Armenoid, Lapponoid, are inherited as alleles of a single gene, somewhat like those giving O, A, and B blood groups. This assumption is in flat contradiction with all that is known about the genetics of these traits, scanty as this knowledge admittedly is. Wiercinski (1962) gives an example of a family in which the father is diagnosed as Alpine, the mother Nordic, and their two children Lapponoid and Nordic. This classification stretches one's credulity to the breaking point.

Mendelian Populations

A person has two parents, four grandparents, eight greatgrandparents, and so on. Continued for some 32 generations, the number of ancestors would turn out greater than the total world population. Of course, this description is not so. Notwithstanding the universality of incest taboos, all our ancestors were more or less distant relatives. Though it cannot be documented, all humans are relatives. If one could construct a complete pedigree of all mankind, it would be a complex network in which every individual is multiply related to every other. Mankind is a Mendelian population, a reproductive community all members of which are connected by ties of mating and parentage. A Mendelian population may be said to have a common gene pool. The genes of every individual are derived from, and unless he dies childless some of them return to, this pool.

In theory, mankind could be described by listing its gene loci, and indicating the frequencies in the gene pool of the different alleles at each locus. Such a description, even if it were possible to carry out in practice, would not be entirely satisfactory. Mankind is not a panmictic population, in which every individual would have an equal probability of mating with every individual of the opposite sex and of the appropriate age. The chance that a boy born in Canada will marry a Canadian girl is greater than that he will marry a girl from China or Uganda. In common with many sexually reproducing animal and plant species, mankind is differentiated geographically into subordinate Mendelian populations; the intermarriage within these subordinate populations is more frequent than between them. There are also specifically human agencies which cause further discontinuities in the intermarriage patterns: these agencies are economic, social class, linguistic, religious, and other subdivisions.

Mankind, the biological species, is the inclusive Mendelian population. Within it there is a hierarchy of subordinate Mendelian populations, geographically or socially partially isolated from each other. Only the smallest subdivisions, inhabitants of some villages, groups of equal social status in small towns and the like, may be regarded as approximately panmictic. Races are Mendelian populations within a species. They are not Platonic or statistical types, not collections of genetically identical individuals, and not subdivisions of primordial mankind submerged by long-continued miscegenation. They are Mendelian populations which differ in the incidence of some genes in their gene pools.

The delimitation of the Mendelian population of the human species presents no difficulty. At our time level there is no gene exchange between the gene pool of the human species and those of even its closest biological relatives, pongids. It is sometimes asked how one defines a human being. Biologically, the answer is simple: any individual is human whose genes are derived from the gene pool of the human species. By contrast, the delimitation of the Mendelian populations which are called races is always to some extent vague, because their gene pools are not wholly disjunct. This is a restatement in modern terms of Darwin's conclusion that "The most weighty of all arguments against treating the races of man as distinct species, is that they graduate into each other, independently in many cases, as far as we can judge, of their having intercrossed."

The subordinate, intraspecific, Mendelian populations, in man as well as in other sexual organisms, are as a rule not fully discrete. Because of gene exchange, they merge into each other. Very often one cannot tell where one ends and the other begins. This fact is disconcerting to some orderly minds. How can one make something so ill-defined the basic unit of biological and antropological study? Two observations can be made in this connection. First, the complexities of nature should not be evaded. Second, the only way to simplify nature is to study it as it is, not as we would have liked it to be.

Gene Exchange, Gradients, and Clines

Biologically basic, and until the advent of culture the only factor maintaining (though not in itself producing) the genetic differentiation of intraspecific Mendelian populations, is isolation by distance.[1] The phenomenon is very complex, and still far from adequately understood. Probably the most penetrating analyses thus far are those of Wright (a detailed summary and review of the literature is in Wright 1969). Three models have been suggested. Mathematically the most tractable is the "island" model; the other two are isolation by distance over a uniform inhabited area, and the "stepping-stone" model. The island model assumes that the species consists of discrete colonies within which panmixia prevails, but which receive the proportion, m, of immigrants drawn at random from the rest of the species. The isolation of the islands may vary in space and in time, the value of m ranging from zero (complete isolation) to one (no isolation). If the immigrants come (as they usually do) from the neighboring colonies, rather than from the species at large, we have the stepping-stone model. This merges into the situation where the distribution area of the species is inhabited continuously and uniformly, but the mobility of individuals is limited, so that the parents come from a more or less small fraction of the total area.

Situations conforming to all three models, as well as intermediate states, are found in man. Cavalli-Sforza (1959) studied the "matrimonial migration" among towns and villages of the Parma diocese in northern Italy, and Harrison (1967) among villages in Oxfordshire in England. The bride and the groom may be inhabitants of the same village, or the mates may be from different villages. Both authors found that the probability of marriage is a negative exponential function of the distance between the villages in which the potential mates reside. It is also a function of the numbers of the inhabitants in the villages; the greater the population of a village the more

1. Isolation by distance, or geographical isolation, should not be confused with reproductive isolating mechanisms, which act as barriers against gene exchange between incipient or full species. Reproductive isolation is by definition genetic. For example, ethological isolation, lack of sexual attraction between females of one and males of another species, is conditioned by some of the gene differences between these species. So is hybrid inviability and hybrid sterility. By contrast, geographically isolated populations, such as those inhabiting different islands, may, in principle, be genetically identical. Even if they are not genetically identical, the differences between them need not be responsible for their geographic separation. Ecological isolation, genetically conditioned preference for different habitats, is in a sense intermediate between geographic and reproductive isolation.

potential mates it contains. Figure 4.1 summarizes Harrison's data for the marriage distances in population of the parish of Charlton, according to the statistics of 1861. Places within one mile distance from Charlton contributed some 55 mates per 1000 inhabitants, while places 4 or more miles away contributed 5 mates or fewer.

An important factor in matrimonial migration, and consequently in the gene flow between Mendelian populations, is not only physical distance but also the facility of travel. Cavalli-Sforza found the following distribution of marriage distances among the inhabitants of level and mountainous parts of the Parma diocese in Italy (Table 4.1).

The mobility among the inhabitants of the plain is greater, except perhaps at distances of more than 42 units, than among the mountaineers. Cavalli-Sforza (1969 and references therein) has correlated this greater mobility, and also the greater population density on the plain than in the mountains, with genetic differentiation of the village populations. Common genetic markers, OAB, MN, and Rh blood types, have been recorded for the populations. No significant differences between the villages on the plain were found, while an appreciable heterogeneity was brought to light

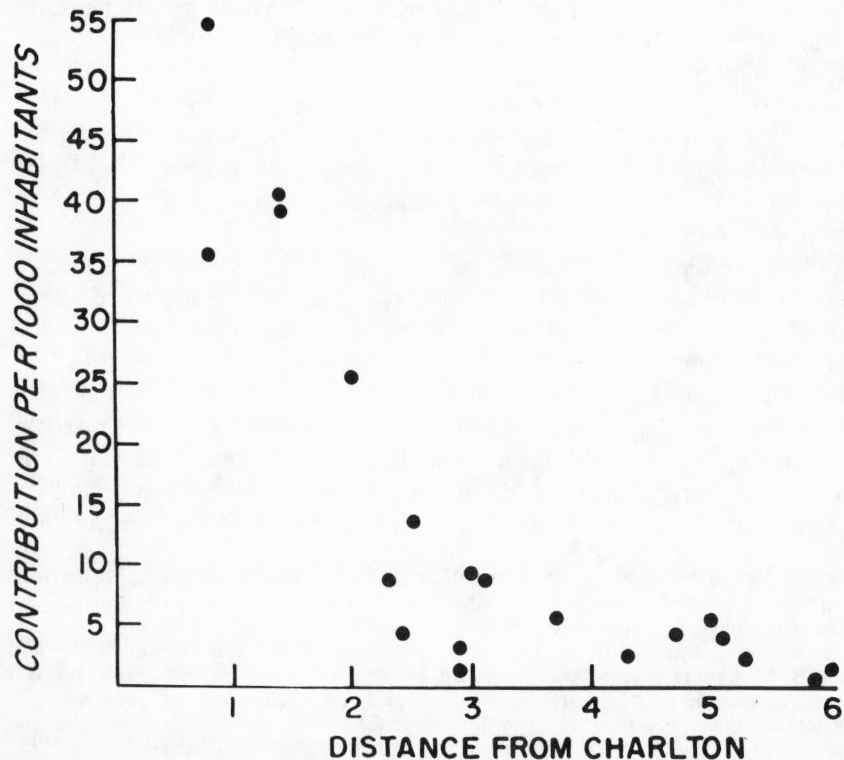

Figure 4.1. Comparative contributions of the surrounding villages to the breeding population of Charlton in 1861 (from Harrison 1967).

Table 4.1. Matrimonial distances in percents among the inhabitants of the plain (P) and mountainous (M) parts of the Parma diocese. A unit distance is 0.625 km (after Cavalli-Sforza 1959).

Distance	*P*	*M*
0– 2.5	51.3	64.2
2.5– 6.5	9.9	9.9
6.5–12.5	15.2	6.6
12.5–20.5	9.9	6.3
20.5–30.5	6.0	3.9
30.5–42.5	3.7	1.8
>42.5	3.7	6.7

among the mountain villages. The highest heterogeneity was observed in the parishes ("comunes") with lowest population densities. Neel (1969) and his collaborators carried out gene frequency studies of 25 different gene loci in 39 villages of the Yanomama tribe of American Indians on the Upper Orinoco in Venezuela. Very appreciable diversities have been recorded for several loci (R^2 from 0 to 0.11, MS from 0 to 0.21, P^1 from 0.34 to 0.70, Jk^a from 0.38 to 0.84). Cavalli-Sforza ascribes the heterogeneities to random genetic drift rather than to local differences in natural selection. Neel interprets these differences "as primarily reflecting the manner in which new villages originate." However that may be, the role of the gene exchange between local populations as a genetically leveling factor is quite apparent.

The above are examples of microgeographic differentiation of Mendelian populations of the human species. Man is a social animal; his settlement patterns and the reproductive biology of human populations sometimes permit genetic differences to arise among geographically adjacent population nuclei. We now turn to macrogeographic differentiation, which is quantitatively but probably not qualitatively distinct from microgeographic. For some tens of thousands of years, mankind has been a nearly cosmopolitan species. Human populations live under a variety of physical and cultural environments. Although man has always been a wanderer, and his traveling ability has increased enormously owing to the progress of his technology, some populations are separated by distances so great that the gene exchange between them is limited. Populations that inhabit different continents and parts of the same continent often differ in many genes; as a consequence, they differ in many morphological, physiological, and perhaps psychological characteristics. In other words, mankind is an aggregate of racially distinct populations.

The genetic nature of race differences is only beginning to be understood. The classical race concept, in anthropology as well as in biology, was typological. Every individual of the negroid, mongoloid, caucasoid, and even Jewish and Nordic "races" was a variant of a quasi-mythical type of his race, and "never the twain shall meet." Operationally, this concept led to characterization of the racial types by systems of average values of measurements and observations made on samples of populations living in or descended from ancestors who resided in different territories, belonging to different castes, speaking different languages, and the like. The more separate measurements or traits went into the construction of a racial type, the more valid and reliable it was supposed to be. This typological approach reached its extreme, almost a reductio ad absurdum, in the above discussed attempts to find different racial types among individuals of the same population, and even among members of the same family.

Genetics has gradually made the ineptitude of typological approaches evident to an increasing majority of anthropologists. Mendelian populations should be described in terms of the incidence in them of separate characteristics, and ideally of the alleles of variant genes. Boyd's (1950) pioneering attempt to carry out such a description using the then known blood genes met a sceptical reception, although the race classification he arrived at was little different from some current typological ones. The two decades since then greatly increased the information available, and also revealed complexities that were not so clearly apparent before.

When the frequencies of gene alleles or of separate phenotypic traits are plotted on maps (see examples in Mourant 1954, Mourant et al. 1958, Lundman 1967), one finds as a rule gradients (clines) of increasing or decreasing frequencies toward or away from some centers. Thus, the allele I^B of the OAB blood group system reaches frequencies between 25 and 30 per cent in Central Asia and northern India. Its frequencies decline westward to 15–20 per cent in European Russia, 5–10 per cent in western Europe, and even lower in parts of Spain and France. The frequencies decline also southeastward, practically to zero among Australian Aborigines, and northeastward, to below 10 per cent among the Eskimos and to zero in unmixed Amerindians. The center of light skin and eye pigmentation is northwestern Europe; the pigmentation becomes darker eastward and especially southward, reaching maximum in subsaharan Africa, southern India, and Melanesia. Rohrer's index (body weight divided by the height cubed) reaches its highest values among the Eskimos, and its lowest in southern Asia, Australia, and Africa.

Are any genetic differences between human populations qualitative, in the sense that some gene alleles are absent in some and reach one hundred per cent frequencies in other populations? As noted by Darwin, "Of all the differences between the races of man, the color of the skin is the most conspicuous and one of the best marked." Indeed, cases of albinism excepted, no native of subsaharan Africa is born as lightly pigmented as the natives of Europe, and no European develops as dark a pigmentation as an African. However, this skin color difference is due to the additive effects of at least three pairs of genes without dominance. Heritable color variations are found among Europeans as well as among Africans. One can well imagine that skin color could be darkened considerably by selective breeding in a population of European descent and lightened in a population of African descent. Whether or not the intraracial pigment variations are due to the same gene loci which are responsible for the interracial differences is uncertain. One of the alleles of the Rh system (cDe) reaches frequencies above 50 per cent in African populations, but it occurs with low frequencies, generally below 5 per cent, in individuals without known African ancestry elsewhere in the world. An allele of the Diego locus seems to be lacking among Europeans and frequent among Amerindians, not reaching however one hundred per cent frequencies among the latter. An allele of the Duffy system has frequencies above 90 per cent among Negroes in western Africa, and is also found but with low frequencies among Europeans.

Our tentative conclusion, subject to modification by future findings, must be that qualitative differences, in the above defined sense, are absent among human populations. This conclusion is in no way contradicted by our ability to distinguish any individual native of (for example) Congo or Ghana from any Scandinavian, and both of these from any native of eastern Asia. The reason is, of course, that the populations native in these countries differ in frequencies not of a single but of many genes. What is important is that typological race concepts must be replaced by populational ones. Individuals are not accidental departures from their racial types. On the contrary, the interpopulational, racial, differences are compounded of the same genetic variants which are responsible for the genetic differences among individuals within a population (Dobzhansky 1970).

Racial Differences and Nomenclature

The apparently endless variety of living beings is as fascinating as it is perplexing. There are no two identical humans, as there are no two identical pine trees or *Drosophila* flies or infusoria. The runaway diversity of our perceptions is made manageable by means of human language. Classifying and giving names to classes of things is perhaps the "primordial" scientific activity. It may antedate the appearance of *Homo sapiens,* and it is bound to continue as long as symbol-forming animals exist. Biologists and anthropologists describe and name the complexes of organisms which they study in order to identify for themselves, and let others know, what they are talking and writing about.

Human beings whom we meet, and about whose existence we learn from others, are numerous and diversified. We have to classify them and attach recognition labels to the classes. So, we distinguish the speakers of English, Russian, Swahili, and other languages; college students, industrial workers, and farmers; intellectuals and the "silent majority." Those who study physical, physiological, and genetic variations among men, find it convenient to name races. Races are arrays of Mendelian populations which belong to the same biological species, but which differ from each other in the incidence of some genetic variants.

The question is often posed: Are races objectively ascertainable phenomena of nature, or are they mere group concepts invented by biologists and anthropologists for their convenience? Here we must make unequivocally clear the duality of the race concept. First, it refers to objectively ascertainable genetic differences between Mendelian populations. Second, it is a category of classification which must serve the pragmatic function of facilitating communication. One can specify the operational procedures whereby any two populations can be shown to be racially different or racially identical. The populations may contain different arrays of genotypes or similar arrays.

Racial differences exist between populations "out there," regardless of whether or not somebody is studying them. Yet this does not mean that any two genetically different populations must receive different race names. For example, Cavalli-Sforza has found no significant genetic differentiation between inhabitants of the villages on the densely settled Parma plain; he did find such a differentiation between the villages in the more sparsely settled mountains. Racial differences are, therefore, ascertained among the latter but not among the former. It would nevertheless not occur to anyone to give race names to the populations of every mountain village. This nomenclature is uncalled for, because the village names are adequate labels for the populations that live in them.

How many arrays of populations in the human species should be provided with race names is a matter of expediency. Already Darwin noted that "Man has been studied more carefully than any other organic being, and yet there is the greatest possible diversity among capable judges" concerning the number of races recognized and named. Different authors referred to by Darwin named from two to as many as sixty-three races. The incertitude is undiminished today. Hardly any two independently working classifiers have proposed identical sets of races. This lack of unanimity has driven some modern "capable judges" to desperation. They claim that mankind has no races. Furthermore, they say the very word "race" should be expunged from the lexicon. This proposal is often motivated by a laudable desire to counteract racist propaganda. But will this be achieved by denying the existence of races? Or will such denials only impair the credibility of the scientists making them? Is it not better to make people understand the nature of race differences rather than pretend that such differences are nonexistent?

To give an example of a race classification by an author fully conversant with modern biology and anthropology, Garn (1965) recognizes 9 "geographical races" and 32 "local races," some of the latter being subdivisions of the former. The geographical races are as follow:

1. Amerindian
2. Polynesian
3. Micronesian
4. Australian
5. Melanesian-Papuan
6. Asiatic
7. Indian
8. European
9. African

Among the local races not included in his major geographical groups, Garn distinguishes three interesting categories: Ainu and Bushmen are "long-isolated marginal"; Lapps, Pacific Negritos, African Pygmies, and Eskimos are "puzzling, isolated, numerically small"; and American Negroes, Cape Colored, Ladinos, and Neo-Hawaiians are "hybrid local races of recent origin." On the other hand, Lundman (1967) recognizes only 4 main races: white, yellow, red (Amerindian), and black; his 16 subraces correspond in part, but only in part, to Garn's local races. If one of these classifications be accepted as correct, must the other necessarily be incorrect? This, I believe, is a wrong way to judge race classifications; we should rather ask which classification is more convenient, and for what purpose.

In sexually reproducing and outbreeding organisms, every individual can usually be recognized as a member of one and only one species. Adherents of the typological race concepts believed that the same should be true of races, that every individual, excepting only the progenies of interracial crosses, should be classifiable as belonging to a certain race. This classification is not possible. Species are genetically closed, while races are genetically open systems. There is no individual whose membership in the species man or the species chimpanzee could be called in question. These species do not exchange genes. There are however many local populations in northwestern Asia intermediate between the white and the yellow, and in northern Africa intermediate between the white and the black races. Moreover, individual members of these intermediate populations do not necessarily have two parents belonging to "pure" white, black, or yellow races. Whole populations are intermediate. Sometimes this situation is due to secondary intergradation (Mayr 1963), that is, to interbreeding of genetically distinct populations in the near or remote past. The gene exchange is, in fact, the origin of Garn's "hybrid local races." More often the intermediate populations are autochthonous; primary intergradation is a result of gene diffusion taking place while the racial divergence of the populations is increasing, as well as after the populations have diverged. The gene gradients or clines result from both primary and secondary intergradation.

Gene gradients make it only rarely possible to draw a line on the map on the two sides of which live different races. Race boundaries are more often blurred than sharp. Worse still, the gradients of the frequencies of different genes and traits may be only weakly or not at all correlated. This can easily be seen on maps that show the frequencies of various traits in human populations, such as different blood antigens, pigmentation, stature, etc. (see, for example, the maps in Lundman 1967). Human races are not the discrete units imagined by typologists. Some disappointed typologists have seen fit to draw the radical conclusion: races do not exist.

But let us take a closer look at the situation. If gene or character gradients are uniform, the gene frequencies increase or decrease regularly by so many percentages per so many miles travelled in a given direction. With uniform gradients, race boundaries can only be arbitrary. However, often the gradients are steeper in some places and are more gentle or absent elsewhere. Consider two gene alleles, A_1 and A_2, in a species with a distribution area 2100 miles across. Suppose that for 1000 miles the frequency of A_1 declines from 100 to 90 per cent; for the next 100 miles from 90 to 10 per cent; and for the remaining 1000 miles from 10 to 0 per cent. It is then reasonable and convenient to divide the species in two races, characterized by the predominance of A_1 and A_2 respectively, and to draw the geographic boundary between the races where the cline is steep.

Why are the gene frequency gradients gentle in some places and steep in others? The steepening of the gradients usually coincides with geographic and environmental barriers that make travel difficult. Barriers to travel are also barriers to gene diffusion. Newman (1963) has analyzed human racial taxonomy in a very thoughtful article. His general conclusion is "that there are valid races among men, but that biology is only beginning to properly discover and define them. . . . I consider some of Garn's races probably valid, others probably invalid, with still others in the 'suspense' category for lack of adequate data." He validates Garn's Asiatic, African, and Amerindian races as showing good trait correlations in such visible traits as pigmentation, hair form and quantity, nose and lip form, cheek bone prominence, eyelid form, and general body shape. European, Indian, and Australian are "unwarranted abstractions," on account of the high variability and discordance (lack of correlation) in the geographic distribution of many traits. Melanesian, Polynesian, and Micronesian are in the "suspense" category.

The adherents of the "no races" school argue that one should study the geographic distributions of genes and character frequencies, rather than attempt to delimit races. The truth is that both kinds of studies are necessary. Gene and character geography is the basis of the biological phenomenon of racial variation; classification and naming are indispensable for information storage and communication. The fact that races are not always or even not usually discrete, and that they are connected by transitional populations, is in itself biologically meaningful. It is evidence that gene flow between races is not only potentially possible but actually taking place. Gene flow between species, however, is limited or prevented altogether. To hold that because races are not rigidly fixed units they do not exist is a throwback to typological thinking of the most misleading kind. It is about as logical as to say that towns and cities do not exist because the country intervening between them is not totally uninhabited.

Race Differences as Products of Natural and Sexual Selection

A century ago Darwin felt "baffled in all our attempts to account for the differences between the races of man." In particular natural selection could hardly be invoked, because "we are at once met by the objection that beneficial variations alone can be thus preserved; and as far as we are enabled to judge (although always liable to error on this head) not one of the external differences between the races of man are of any direct or special services to him." He put more faith in sexual selection: "For my own part I conclude that of all the causes which have led to the differences in external appearance between the races of man, and to a certain extent between man and the lower animals, sexual selection has been by far the most efficient." Of the 828 pages of the first edition of *The Descent of Man and Selection in Relation to Sex,* Part I, "On the Descent of Man," takes 250 pages, and part II, "Sexual Selection," more than twice as many (Darwin 1871).

It is almost incredible that, a century after Darwin, the problem of the origin of racial differences in the human species remains about as baffling as it was in his time. Several circumstances have conspired to make it so. The chief one was that until less than a generation ago, the leading anthropologists believed race differences to be mostly adaptively neutral, and consequently made little effort to discover their selective values. Radical changes in human environments brought about by cultural developments made the problem particularly difficult to approach; a genetic trait may have played a role a million years ago which was quite different from its role ten thousand years ago, and that again different from what it is at present. And finally, by a curious twist of reasoning, the doctrine of human equality seemed to exclude the possibility of differential genetic adaptedness.

The adaptive significance of even so obvious a trait as skin pigmentation has not been fully clarified. The notion that dark pigmentation is protective against sunburn is very old. It is made plausible by the fact that dark-skinned races are (or were) inhabitants of the tropics, and light-skinned ones of temperate and cold countries. This rule is however not free of exceptions; the Indians of equatorial South America are not particularly dark, and some of the natives of northeastern Siberia are at least as dark as those of Mediterranean Europe. These exceptions have been "explained" by assuming that the relatively light people in the hot countries and the relatively dark ones in cold countries are recent immigrants, or that they live mostly in forest shade rather than in the open. It has also been supposed that light skins facilitate the synthesis of vitamin D in countries with little sunshine, while dark pigmentation protects against excessive amounts of this vitamin where sunshine is abundant. There is good evidence that light skins are more prone to develop skin cancers owing to sun exposure than are dark skins. Still another surmise is that dark skin pigmentation may facilitate absorption of solar radiation "where energy must be expended to maintain body temperature, as at dawn and dusk in otherwise hot climates" (Hamilton & Heppner 1967). A dark skin may give protective coloration to a hunter stalking game or escaping from predators.

The above hypotheses concerning the adaptive significance of pigmentation are not mutually contradictory or exclusive. And yet their multiplicity attests to the inadequacy of our understanding of the most conspicuous of all human racial differences. A considerable amount of careful study has been devoted to the physiology of human populations adapted to certain particularly rigorous environments, such as Indians of the Andean Altiplano (cold, low oxygen supply) and Eskimos of the Arctic (Baker & Weiner 1966, Baker et al. 1967). Riggs & Sargent (1964) and others compared the reactions of young negro and white males to exertion under humid heat condition. Some statistically assured differences in the expected directions have been found, but it is not ruled out that part of these differences may be the product of physiological adaptation to the environments in which the persons grew up.

The racial differences in the incidence of various blood groups have long been a challenge to those who believe that all racial differences must be established by natural selection. There is no doubt that certain pathological conditions (for example, duodenal ulcers) occur more often in carriers of some blood antigens than in others, but it is questionable whether these correlations are even in small part responsible for the racial differences. Attempts to correlate the blood groups with resistance to some infectious diseases, such as plague, smallpox, and syphilis, have thus far been unconvincing (see a review in Otten 1967).

Sexual selection "depends on the advantage which certain individuals have over other individuals of the same sex and species, in exclusive relation to reproduction" (Darwin 1871, Vol. I, p. 256). In our present view, the difference between natural and sexual selection is not fundamental. The selection coefficient, that is, the difference between the Darwinian fitnesses of different genotypes, measures the relative rates of transmission of certain components of these genotypes from generation to generation. It is of lesser consequence, though certainly not immaterial, that differential gene transmission is in some instances due to greater success in mating, while in others it is caused by differential mortality, or fertility, or greater speed of development, or anything else. Genetic variants which are favored by the balance of all these causes will increase, and those disfavored will diminish in frequency in the populations. Lessened success in mating may be compensated by a greater viability or fertility, or vice versa.

That sexual selection, in the classical Darwinian sense, occurs in man is clear enough. Although almost everybody in tribal societies has an opportunity to mate and produce offspring, socially more influential and more prosperous individuals may not only have access to more mates but be able to provide better conditions, which increase the probability of survival of their offspring to maturity. Good evidence of this has been provided, for example, by Salzano, Neel & Maybury-Lewis (1967) and Chagnon et al. (1970) for Xavantes and Yanomamas, two of the surviving primitive tribes of South American Indians. In both tribes, "Whereas women are uniformly exposed to the risk of pregnancy and rarely fail to reproduce, men, on the other hand, are characterized by an appreciably higher variance in their reproductive performance." In one of the villages studied two head men sired approximately one-fourth of the total population.

Some forms of physiological sterility of females as well as of males are genetic. The genetic basis of the psychological variables which predispose individuals to spinsterhood, bachelorhood, or prolificity in technologically advanced societies is another matter, reliable data on which are almost totally lacking. It is, for example, an open question whether homosexuality has an appreciable genetic component. However, if the existence of such a genetic predisposition were proven, its bearing on race differentiation would still be in doubt. Genetically caused partial or complete sterility, better known in Drosophila than in human populations (see Marinkovic 1967), is part of the concealed genetic load; when the components of this load become overt, they come under control of normalizing natural selection. Normalizing selection can hardly bring about appreciable racial differentiation. What interests us rather is to what extent the racial divergence of populations is brought about by directional selection, of either the sexual or the natural kind. In other words, one wishes to know not only whether a given genetic trait is influenced by selection, but also, and this is a more difficult problem, why different variants of this trait are favored in different populations. The present state of knowledge in this field is quite unsatisfactory.

Race Differences and Random Genetic Drift

The genes of the two Xavante chiefs mentioned above, who sired about one-quarter of their village population, became more frequent in that population than the genes of the less prestigious male inhabitants. Let it be noted that this is true of the genes which might have facilitated their access to chieftainship, as well as genes quite irrelevant in this respect.

Every chief, like any other individual, has a constellation of genes somewhat different from other chiefs or other individuals. The populations of villages containing exceptionally prolific individuals become, for that reason, genetically differentiated from one another. This situation has, indeed, been observed among the Xavantes and Yanomamas by the authors cited above and among hordes of aboriginal Australians by Birdsell (1950). Nor is such differentiation found only among primitive tribes. Glass (1954) and Steinberg et al. (1967) observed it among certain religious isolates in America; although the people involved presumably adhere to strict monogamy, variations in the numbers of children per family inevitably occur. In the course of time, these variations add up to diversification of the gene frequencies, that is, to incipient racial diversity. In contrast to selection, which is a directional and deterministic process, here we are dealing with stochastic or random genetic processes. Random genetic drift, random walk, founder principle, and non-Darwinian evolution are some of the names applied to these processes. Can they help to explain the origin of race differences in mankind and other species?

The roles ascribed to stochastic vs. deterministic processes in evolution have gone through an interesting cycle. It would be out of place to discuss the matter here in detail, but a brief account is in order. The prestige of natural selection as an evolutionary agent was at its lowest ebb during the early part of the current century, while genetics was groping for the formulation of its basic concepts. Between 1926 and 1932, Chetverikov, Fisher, Haldane, and Wright arrived, largely independently, at the biological or synthetic theory of evolution. In this theory, the deterministic processes of selection are regarded as fundamental. However, Wright recognized also the importance of random genetic drift, sometimes called "the Sewall Wright principle." He did not, as he was erroneously accused by some writers, regard this principle as an alternative or a substitute for natural selection, but as an agency the interactions of which with natural selection have important evolutionary consequences.

True enough, some authors, mostly nongeneticists, sought to utilize random genetic drift as an explanation of the origin of differences between organisms to which they could not readily attribute survival value. Race differences in man are in this category. Heuristically, this is a tactical error. To investigate the effects of a trait on the Darwinian fitness of its carriers, one should entertain as a working hypothesis that this trait may have such effects. A reaction against this error was strong in the forties, fifties, and the early sixties. Although the theoretical possibility of random drift could not be denied, its role in natural populations, and hence in evolution, was declared negligible. The pendulum has swung back since King & Jukes (1969) published their provocative paper on "Non-Darwinian Evolution," and Kimura & Crow (1969) and Kimura and Ohta (1969) have for quite different reasons urged that most mutational changes have no effects on fitness, and hence must be engaged in random walk in the population gene pool. Non-Darwinian evolution is now in fashion, especially among molecular biologists.

King & Jukes (1969) named their theory "non-Darwinian" because it postulates that many, if not most, evolutionary changes are not the products of natural selection. This name disregards more than a century and a half of the history of biology, which saw several non-Darwinian, non-selectionist, theories of evolution. To mention some of them: the Lamarckisms of Lamarck and of the turn-of-the-century Lamarckians (which are not the same theory), orthogenesis of Eimer, nomogenesis of Berg, aristogenesis of Osborn, as well as several frankly vitalistic notions. Furthermore, Darwin was himself in part a non-Darwinian, since he credited (mistakenly, we believe) the inheritance of acquired modifications as an important adjunct to natural selection. Moreover, in *The Origin of Species* he wrote: "Variations neither useful nor injurious would not be affected by natural selection, and would be left a fluctuating element, as perhaps we see in the species called polymorphic." Excepting the reference to polymorphic species, this sentence is as good an anticipation of the modern non-Darwinism as could be imagined.

Naming apart, what are the arguments in favor of the random walk as an important source of evolutionary change? Briefly, King and Jukes argue that because of the degeneracy (redundancy) of the genetic code, about a quarter of the base substitutions in the DNA-RNA chains will give the same amino acid and thus leave the protein coded by the gene unchanged. The relative incidence of the twenty amino acids in diverse proteins of diverse organisms agrees, with the conspicuous exception of arginine, with statistical expectations based on the assumption of random permutations of the nucleotides in DNA. Comparison of homologous proteins in different organisms shows different numbers of amino acid substitutions, the numbers being allegedly proportional to the time elapsed since the separation of the phyletic lines leading to the organisms in paleontological history. This is interpreted to signify that the amino acid and nucleotide substitutions occur at uniform rates in time, as might be expected if they occurred at random.

Unfortunately for this theory, the rates are distinctly different for different proteins; some proteins conserve their amino acid sequences more tenaciously than others. This may mean that the nucleotide sequences in some genes are inherently more mutable than in others. Far more plausible is that natural selection discriminates rigorously against most changes in some genes, but is more permissive with other genes. More detailed comparisons of homologous proteins, such as cytochrome-c or hemoglobins, show that some parts of the molecules are constant in most diverse organisms, presumably because they are essential for whatever physiological functions these proteins perform. Interesting attempts have been made to fit the numbers of changes in other parts of the same molecules to expectations based on the Poisson series, that is, on the assumption that these changes are fixed at random, uncontrolled by natural selection. The results obtained have been interpreted as confirming the hypothesis of random fixation, but the possibility that they are due to selection has not, in my opinion, been ruled out. There may be all degrees of likelihood that the substitutions of the amino acids at different positions will be accepted and promoted by natural selection. Since the changes that obviously do not fit the Poisson series are deliberately left out of consideration, the fit of the remainder may be spurious.

Gene changes which become racial characteristics are those which produce at least some phenotypically detectable effects. Changes that do not alter the gene products are scarcely relevant to the present issue, however interesting they may be in other contexts. Of course, some phenotypically detectable changes may also be neutral with respect to fitness, and will represent the "fluctuating element" postulated by Darwin. Their frequencies will, then, be subject to random genetic drift. Given very long time and very many generations, some of the changes will be lost in some populations, fixed in others, and remain fluctuating in still others. The question is whether the time intervals which must be assumed are not prohibitively long. Kimura & Ohta (1969) have shown that the average number of generations intervening between the origin and fixation of an adaptively neutral mutant gene is close to $4N_e$, where N_e is the genetically effective population size.

To evaluate the possibility that random genetic drift may have been responsible for racial differences, one would need to know at least the orders of magnitude of the N_e's at different stages of human evolution. Reliable data are unfortunately lacking. Hordes, tribes, clans, and even nations may well have suffered from time to time reductions to small numbers of individuals owing to starvation, epidemics, warfare, and other calamities, and then expanded again when circumstances became propitious. A tribe may undergo fission, or may bud off a small group of founders who move away and found a new tribe. The absolute as well as effective sizes of the founder populations may occasionally be of the order of tens or even fewer. The founder variety of the genetic drift (that is, unique or repeated reductions, rather than continuously small effective populations) may well be responsible for the intertribal genetic differences, of which examples have already been given.

It does not seem at all likely that the 9 major races, or for that matter, the 32 "local races" in Garn's classification, could have arisen through the operation of the founder principle. Although qualitative differences seem to be few, gene frequency differences are often considerable, and, what is more important, occur at numerous gene loci. Even if the Amerindian, Asiatic, European, African and other races be supposed to have descended from single pairs of progenitors, these racial Adams and Eves could not have been sampled from the same population.

The genetic divergence of the races must have been a gradual process; inasmuch as the developing races lived on different continents and under different environments, natural selection had ample opportunities to promote genes which fitted them to different conditions of life. How much differentiation in neutral genetic traits could have occurred at that stage? The effective populations of the primordial races must have been in hundreds of thousands or in millions, and the average length of a generation hardly less than 20 years. The time intervening between the origin and fixation of a neutral genetic variant would then be, 80 N_e years, in millions or tens of millions of years. Any gene exchange between the diverging races would greatly lengthen the time, or make it infinite. These are, as indicated above, time estimates from the origin of a genetic variant to its fixation in a population. If races differ merely in the relative frequencies of certain gene alleles, neutral with respect to fitness, such differences might arise more rapidly. In sum, the genetic mechanisms which caused the origin and the differentiation of the races of mankind remain almost as uncertain now as they were in Darwin's time.

Do Races Differ in Genetic Capacity for Mental Development?

This is a "sensitive" issue, arousing violent emotional reactions in many people. Yet a discussion of the genetics of race would be gravely incomplete if this issue were sidestepped, as it so often is. In my previous writings (for example, Dobzhansky 1964 and elsewhere) I have tried to point out that some of the emotional reactions are due to sheer misunderstanding. Equality is confused with identity, and diversity with inequality. Even some eminent biologists who should have known better wrote that biology showed that men are unequal! Human equality and inequality are not statements of observable biological conditions. They are policies adopted by societies, ethical principles, and religious commandments.

People can be made equal before the law, equality of opportunity may be promoted or guaranteed, human dignity equally recognized, and human beings can be regarded as equally God's sons and daughters. To have equality, people need not be identical twins; they need not be genetically alike. And vice versa: Individuals can be treated unequally, as social superiors and inferiors, masters and servants, elite and plebeian. There is no reason why monozygotic twins must necessarily be social equals, even though they are genetically as nearly identical as two individuals can be. People can be made equal or unequal by the societies in which they live; they cannot be made genetically or biologically identical, even if this were desirable, which it surely is not. In principle, human diversity is compatible with equality and with inequality.

Any two human individuals, identical twins excepted, carry different sets of genes. This fact has traditionally been stressed by partisans of social inequality and soft-pedaled by champions of equality. It should be the other way round: equality is meaningful only because people are not identical. Like illness, the genetic lottery is no respecter of the social position or rank of the parents. Owing to gene recombination in the progeny of highly heterozygous individuals, genetically well- and poorly-endowed children can be born to parents of either kind. This does not deny the existence of some positive correlations between the genetic endowments of parents and offspring. The fact that these correlations are far from complete is socially and ethically no less important than that the correlations are there.

The above is a necessary preamble to the substantive issue: how great is the genetic diversity among individuals and among populations, such as races, in their capacities for mental development? This issue is entangled with the perennial arguments about nature vs. nurture, heredity vs. environment. Some sophistication has been achieved in the approach to this problem: no informed person now dichotomizes human mental abilities into those due to heredity and those due to environment. It is rather a question of heritability, of partitioning the observed variance into its genetic (additive, dominance, epistatic) and environmental components. Most extensive, though far from sufficient, data have been accumulated on the heritability of the intelligence quotient (reviews are in Shields 1962, Erlenmeyer-Kimling & Jarvik 1963, and Jensen 1969). Despite some weaknesses, the technique of comparison of monozygotic and dizygotic twins remains the best source of information. Having reviewed all twin data reported in the literature, Jensen has arrived at an average heritability figure of 80 per cent for the intelligence test scores. Taking into consideration also the correlations between relatives other than twins, Jensen obtains an only slightly lower estimate of 77 per cent.

The meaning of the intelligence quotient continues to be in dispute. It is fairly generally admitted that the IQ does not measure a single faculty, but rather a battery of at least six aptitudes: verbal ability, word fluency, numerical, spatial, and reasoning abilities, and memory. These six abilities are not very strongly correlated, and may well be independent in their genetic conditioning. Some progress has been achieved toward their independent measurability. A person who is top-flight in one or more of them may be mediocre or deficient in others. On the other hand, defenders of IQ usability point out that the IQ ratings have vindicated themselves by their predictive power of probable scholastic achievement. There is an appreciable correlation, between 0.4 and 0.7, of IQ rating and the occupational status achieved or likely to be achieved.

Statistical differences in mean IQ's have been demonstrated again and again between representatives of different racial groups, especially in the United States. The means are highest for persons of European descent and lowest for those of African and Amerindian origin. But what is the significance of these means? Racists have seized upon them as proof of racial superiorities and inferiorities. By egregious miscomprehension or deceitfulness, they argue that since the heritability of the IQ has been shown to be high, race differences in the IQ averages are genetically fixed and irremediable. This argument is certainly unproven and unconvincing. It is obvious that the environments in which the racial groups live in the same country are appreciably and often drastically different, and furthermore the environmental differences are most pronounced precisely in those aspects which are most relevant to intellectual development. Heritability is not a fixed parameter; under an ideally uniform environment it would be 100 per cent, and it is reduced more or less strongly by environmental heterogeneity; it will be zero in genotypically uniform populations, and increased by genetic heterogeneity. One can only conclude that the degree to which the differences in the IQ arrays between races are due to genetic predisposition is at present an unsolved problem.

The differences between the mean IQ's of white and black populations in the United States amount to about one standard deviation in the white population, or less. In other words, the distributions of the IQ scores of these two races or castes broadly overlap. There are numerous, not merely exceptional, blacks whose IQ's are higher than the white mean, and numerous whites below the black mean. There is every reason to think, although the data are scanty and unreliable, that the same is generally true of all race differences within the human species. The practical consequences of this are evident. Individuals should be judged by what they are, not by what race or subrace they come from. Equality of opportunity means that everybody must be given equal chance to develop and demonstrate his abilities; it does not mean that everybody should be forced into the same position or profession, or given the same role to play in economic or intellectual life. Moreover, however excellent may be the genetic potential, it can be frustrated and defeated by lack of environmental and educational opportunity. Conversely, nobody, short of gross pathology, can be wholly impervious to environmental improvement.

Finally, consideration must be given to an argument which is the more misleading since it is superficially so plausible. It runs approximately as follows. Races of animal and plant species develop adaptedness to their respective environments. Breeds of domestic animals and plants are made to serve different purposes or to live under different conditions. These racial characteristics are very largely genetically fixed. Why, then, suppose that man's races are a singular exception? Modern technologically advanced societies have been constructed chiefly by a minority of human breeds. It is likely that at least some of the "lesser" breeds do not possess aptitude sufficient to create, manage, or even to live in these societies.

The above argument must be honestly and squarely faced. Yes, mankind is a product of a unique evolutionary pattern. The cardinal distinction between mankind and all other forms of life is that man's adaptedness depends more on his cultural than on his genetic inheritance. Culture is acquired by each individual by learning, and transmitted by instruction, chiefly, though not exclusively, by means of a language consisting of socially agreed-upon symbols. To adapt to new environments, mankind changes mainly its cultural inheritance, rather than its genes, as other organisms do. Genes and culture are not independent but interdependent. It is man's genetic endowment which makes him able to think in symbols, abstractions, and generalizations. The potentiality of cultural evolution, which is uniquely human, has developed through the evolution of his gene pool. But the contents of his gene pool do not determine the contents of his culture. The genes give man his ability to speak, but do not decide what he shall say.

The basic and unique capacity of man is his genetically established educability by means of symbolic language. This educability is a species trait, common to all races and all nonpathological individuals. Its universality is no more surprising than that all people have a body temperature and blood pH which varies within narrow limits. Educability and symbolic language became universal human traits because existence in man-made environments depended on the possession of these traits. Nothing of the sort happened to any other animal species, wild or domesticated. Genetically fixed specializations in both morphology and behavior have often been deliberately built into different domestic breeds.

The foregoing remarks should not be taken as denying that the variability of human behavior in general, and of educability in particular, has a considerable genetic component. Suppose, for the sake of argument, that it can be established that some fraction of the mean difference in the IQ scores of whites and blacks is indeed genetic. Would that be a vindication of the racists in Alabama, South Africa, and elsewhere? Certainly not. Two basic facts refute the racists; first, the broad overlap of the variation curves for IQ's and other human abilities; second, universal educability, and hence a capacity for "improvement," however this last term be defined. We may accordingly agree with Darwin (1871) that

> Although the existing races of man differ in many respects. . . . yet if their whole organization be taken into consideration they are found to resemble each other closely in a multitude of points. . . . The same remark holds good with equal or greater force with respect to the numerous points of mental similarity between the most distinct races of man. The American aborigines, negroes and europeans differ as much from each other in mind as any three races that can be named; yet I was incessantly struck, whilst living with the Fuegians on board the "Beagle," with the many little traits of character, shewing how similar their minds were to ours; and so it was with a full-blooded negro with whom I happened once to be intimate.

References

Allard, R. W., & L. W. Kannenberg. 1968. Population studies in predominantly self-pollinating species. *Evolution* 22: 517–528.

Baker, P. T., E. R. Buskirk, J. Kollias, & R. B. Mazess. 1967. Temperature regulation at high altitude: Quechua Indians and U. S. whites during total body cold exposure. *Human Biol.* 39: 155–169.

Baker, P. T., & J. Weiner. 1966. *Biology of human adaptability.* New York and Oxford: Oxford Univ. Press.

Bielicki, T. 1962. Some possibilities for estimating interpopulation relationship on the basis of continuous traits. *Current Anthrop.* 3: 3–8.

Birdsell, J. B. 1950. Some implications of the genetical concept of race in terms of spatial analysis. *Cold Spring Harbor Symp. Quant. Biol.* 15: 259–314.

Boyd, W. C. 1950. *Genetics and the races of man.* Boston: Little Brown.

Cavalli-Sforza, L. L. 1959. Some data on the genetic structure of human populations. *Proc. X Internat. Congr. Genetics* 1: 389–407.

————. 1969. Human diversity. *Proc. XII Internat. Cong. Genetics* 3: 405–416.

Chagnon, N. A., J. V. Neel, L. Weitkamp, H. Gershowitz, & M. Ayres. 1970. The influence of cultural factors on the demography and pattern of gene flow from the Makiritare to the Yanomama Indians. *Amer. J. Phys. Anthrop.* 32: 339–350.

Czekanowski, J. 1962. The theoretical assumptions of Polish anthropology. *Current Anthrop.* 3: 481–494.

Darwin, C. 1871. *The descent of man, and selection in relation to sex.* 2 vols. London: John Murray.

Dobzhansky, T. 1964. *Heredity and the nature of man.* New York: Harcourt Brace Jovanovitch.

————. 1970. *Genetics of the evolutionary process.* New York: Columbia Univ. Press.

Erlenmeyer-Kimling, L., & L. F. Jarvik. 1963. Genetics and intelligence, a review. *Science* 142: 1477–1479.

Garn, S. M. 1965. *Human races.* Springfield: Charles Thomas.

Glass, B. 1954. Genetic changes in human populations, especially those due to gene flow and genetic drift. *Adv. Genetics* 6: 95–139.

Hamilton, W. J., & F. Heppner. 1967. Radiant solar energy and the function of black homeotherm pigmentation; an hypothesis. *Science* 155: 196–197.

Harris, H. 1967. Enzyme variation in man: Some general aspects. *Proc. 3rd Internat. Congr. Human Genetics,* pp. 207–214.

Harrison, G. A. 1967. Human evolution and ecology. *Proc. 3rd Internat. Congr. Human Genetics,* pp. 351–359.

Jensen, A. R. 1969. How much can we boost IQ and scholastic achievement? *Harvard Educ. Rev.* 39: 1–123.

Kant, I. 1775. *Von den verschiedenen Racen der Menschen.* Königsberg: Hartung.

Kimura, M. & J. F. Crow. 1969. Natural selection and gene substitution. *Gen. Research* 13: 127–141.

Kimura, M. & T. Ohta. 1969. The average number of generations until fixation of a mutant gene in a finite population. *Genetics* 61: 763–771.

King, J. L., & T. H. Jukes. 1969. Non-Darwinian evolution. *Science* 164: 788–798.

Lerner, I. M. 1954. *Genetic homeostasis.* Edinburgh: Oliver & Boyd.

Lewontin, R. C., & J. L. Hubby. 1966. A molecular approach to the study of genetic heterozygosity in natural populations. II. *Genetics* 54: 595–609.

Lundman, B. 1967. *Geographische Anthropologie.* Stuttgart: Gustav Fischer.

Marinkovic, D. 1967. Genetic loads affecting fertility in natural populations of *Drosophila pseudoobscura. Genetics* 57: 701–709.

Mayr, E. 1963. *Animal species and evolution.* Cambridge: Belknap.

Mourant, A. E. 1954. *The distribution of human blood groups.* Oxford: Blackwell.

Mourant, A. E., A. C. Kopec, & K. Domaniewska-Sobczak. 1958. *The ABO blood groups: comprehensive tables and maps of world distribution.* Oxford: Blackwell.

Neel, J. V. 1969. Some changing constraints on the human evolutionary process. *Proc. XII Internat. Congr. Genetics* 3: 389–403.

Newman, M. T. 1963. Geographic and microgeographic races. *Current Anthropol.* 4: 189–191, 204–205.

Otten, C. M. 1967. On pestilence, diet, natural selection, and the distribution of microbial and human blood group antigens and antibodies. *Current Anthropol.* 8: 209–226.

Prakash, S., & R. C. Lewontin. 1968. A molecular approach to the study of heterozygosity in natural populations. III. *Proc. Nat. Acad. Sci.* 59: 398–405.

Riggs, S. K. & F. Sargent. 1964. Physiological regulation in moist heat by young American negro and white males. *Human Biol.* 36: 339–353.

Salzano, F. M., J. V. Neel, & D. Maybury-Lewis. 1967. Further studies on the Xavante Indians. *Amer. J. Human Genetics* 19: 463–489.

Shields, J. 1962. *Monozygotic twins brought up apart and brought up together.* New York and Oxford: Oxford Univ. Press.

Steinberg, A. G., H. K. Bleibtreu, T. W. Kurczynski, A. O. Martin, & A. M. Kurczynski. 1967. Genetic studies in an inbred human isolate. *Proc. 3rd Internat. Congr. Human Genetics,* pp. 267–289.

Wallace, B. 1968. *Topics in population genetics.* New York: Norton.

Wiercinski, A. 1962. The racial analysis of human populations in relation to their ethnogenesis. *Current Anthropol.* 3: 2, 9–20.

Wright, S. 1969. *Evolution and the genetics of populations: The theory of gene frequencies.* Chicago: Univ. Chicago Press.

5

ERNST MAYR
MUSEUM OF COMPARATIVE ZOOLOGY
HARVARD UNIVERSITY

Sexual Selection and Natural Selection

Introduction

Julian Huxley (1938b) remarked quite rightly, "None of Darwin's theories has been so heavily attacked as that of sexual selection." The reasons for this widespread criticism are manifold, and some of them will be analyzed in the present paper. Even though some of the criticism was justified, it is now clear that Darwin was right in principle and that the label "sexual selection" has helped to bring together and organize a vast body of scattered observations (for a summary of Darwin's views, see *The Descent of Man,* pp. 613–617). The vitality of the principle is best documented by the large number of recent review papers or chapters in general books (for instance, Boesiger 1967, Ghiselin 1969, Huxley 1938abc, Maynard Smith 1958, and Montalenti 1959).

Darwin devoted two-thirds of his *Descent of Man* (1871) to the presentation and substantiation of his principle of sexual selection. This induced some of his critics to claim that he had invented this principle because he was unable to explain many attributes of man as due to natural selection. This insinuation is quite unfounded, as Darwin himself points out in the preface to the second edition (1874, p. vi) of *The Descent of Man.* Indeed, an entire section in chapter 4 of the first edition of *The Origin of Species* (1859, pp. 87–90) is devoted to this subject and headed "Sexual Selection." His principal ideas on the subject are clearly sketched out in this early treatment. *The Descent of Man* was, as Darwin said, his first opportunity for a full-length treatment of the subject of sexual selection.

Darwin introduced the concept of sexual selection to explain certain aspects of the reproductive biology of animals that he was unable to ascribe to natural selection. The sharp distinction that he thereby made between two different kinds of selection was one of the reasons for the attacks on him. The controversy was aggravated by repeated shifts in the meaning of key words such as *fitness, struggle,* and *female choice.*

In order not to run into the same difficulties, we must define our terms. We must begin by finding out how Darwin himself defined sexual selection. He writes that it "depends on the advantage which certain individuals have over others of the same sex and species solely in respect of reproduction" (p. 209). In all cases in which the males have acquired a particular structure, "not from being better fitted to survive in the struggle for existence, but from having gained an advantage over other males, and from having transmitted this advantage to their male offspring alone, sexual selection must here have come into action. It was the importance of this distinction which led me to designate this form of selection as Sexual Selection" (pp. 210). Darwin was fully aware that not all differences between the sexes are the result of sexual selection. Many are either sex associated aspects of reproduction (primary and accessory sex organs) or are correlated with niche specializations of the two sexes, and of these Darwin states expressly, "They have no doubt been modified through natural selection." (p. 209). Sexual selection, in contradistinction, deals only with those components of sexual dimorphism that were acquired as a result of mere reproductive advantage.

A separation of sexual and natural selection makes sense only if one adopts the same definition of fitness as Darwin, who employed the term in an uncomplicated, everyday sense. Fit, to him, meant well adapted, and anything that improved the chance for survival in the struggle for existence increased fitness. Fitness for Darwin was the property of a whole individual, or, as we might say, of an entire genotype. Subsequently, the mathematical geneticists (Haldane, Fisher, Wright) redefined fitness rather drastically when they introduced the concept of the fitness of single genes. This required defining fitness in terms of the "contribution to the gene pool of the next generation." Fitness under this new definition could be due either to superior fitness in the Darwinian sense or reproductive advantage that does not add to the adaptedness of the species. Sexual selection under this new definition merely becomes one of various forms of natural selection. To be sure, this new definition facilitates the mathematical treatment, and yet I have a feeling that something rather important was lost in the process. In questioning the usefulness of this redefinition of fitness I am not alone. Huxley, for instance, said:

> When we examine the problem more critically, we find that we must differentiate between two quite distinct modes of natural selection, leading to different types of evolutionary trend, which we may call survival selection and reproductive selection. . . . In the actual processes of biological evolution, survival selection is much the more important; selection exerts its effects mainly on individual phenotypes, and operates primarily by means of their

differential survival to maturity. This will produce evolutionary effects because, as Darwin saw, (a) the majority of individuals which survive to maturity will mate and leave offspring; (b) much of the phenotypic variance promoting survival has a genetic basis (1963, pp. xviii–xix).

The questions that need to be answered now begin to become apparent. There are two in particular: Is it possible to make such a sharp distinction between natural selection and sexual selection, as claimed by Darwin and Huxley? And if the existence of genuine sexual selection can be established, what different forms does it take in various groups of organisms and how widespread in the animal kingdom are biological characteristics that can be interpreted as due to sexual selection?

Sexual selection as envisioned by Darwin usually resulted in sexual dimorphism, that is, in a difference between males and females. However, not all of sexual dimorphism is the result of sexual selection. Most of the differences between the sexes are clearly the result of natural selection. Among these are accessory sexual characters (like claspers) which facilitate copulation and fertilization, as well as a wide range of characters having to do with parental care, such as the pouch of female marsupials, the mammae of female mammals, and the brood pouches of male sea horses and of many invertebrates. Females often show additional adaptations that have nothing to do with sexual selection. For instance, cryptic coloration is widespread among those species of birds in which females alone perform the duties of incubation, but in butterflies also the females are often more cryptically colored than the males. There is a strong selection pressure for reduced size in the females of the hole nesting species of ducks (only the females incubate!). Consequently, there is an increased size dimorphism in these species which, at least initially, had nothing to do with sexual selection. The same is true for the sexual size dimorphism of many other species of animals. Additional cases of sexual dimorphism resulting from natural selection pressures will be listed below. However, they do not refute the possibility of genuine sexual selection.

What Characters Are Due to Sexual Selection?

With so many components of sexual dimorphism explicable through natural selection, it is legitimate to ask whether any are left that can not be explained that way. Of this, Darwin was convinced:

> There are many other structures and instincts [of males] which must have been developed through sexual selection—such as the weapons of offence and the means of defence of the males for fighting with and driving away their rivals—their courage and pugnacity—their various ornaments—their contrivances for producing vocal or instrumental music—and their glands for emitting odors, most of these latter structures serving only to allure or excite

> the female. It is clear that these characters are the result of sexual and not of ordinary selection, since unarmed, unornamented, or unattractive males would succeed equally well in the battle for life and in leaving a numerous progeny, but for the presence of better endowed males. We may infer that this would be the case, because the females which are unarmed and unornamented, are able to survive and procreate their kind (pp. 210–211).

Darwin's supporters as well as his critics have pointed out that Darwin bracketed together in this statement a rather heterogeneous set of phenomena. In particular, two classes of phenomena must be dealt with separately. First there are the weapons and other characteristics of males displayed in fighting among themselves. The role of the females in these fights is strictly passive. Wallace and others denied that such characters qualify as products of sexual selection. Second, there are all those other characteristics by which males attempt to attract females and induce them to copulate. Let us begin with the discussion of this second category.

MALE ORNAMENTS AND ATTRACTANTS

There are numerous species of birds in which the males are brightly colored and adorned with special plumes, such as the birds of paradise or the peacocks. Such spectacular structures could never have evolved, says Darwin, unless females exercise a choice among various eligible males and, more than that, unless females have a sense for beauty.

There were two elements in Darwin's "female choice." First, a deliberate preference by the female for one particular male chosen from a group of available males. Second, an esthetic sense on the part of the female which resembles very much our human appreciation of beauty. Indeed, it was this deliberate choice of the female which suggested the term sexual selection to Darwin, as the equivalent to the conscious selection of the animal breeder:

> Just as man can give beauty according to his standard of taste, to his male poultry, or more strictly can modify the beauty originally acquired by the parent species . . . so it appears that female birds in a state of nature, have by a long selection of the more attractive males added to their beauty or other attractive qualities. No doubt this implies powers of discrimination and taste on the part of the female which will at first appear extremely improbable; but by the facts to be adduced hereafter, I hope to be able to shew that the females actually have these powers" (p. 211).

Alas, Darwin did not convince his contemporaries; their reaction was almost wholly negative. We must remember that Darwin published his theory of sexual selection during a period when even natural selection was rejected by most of his contemporaries. Not surprisingly, sexual selection had to face even rougher sledding. A. R. Wallace (1889) found it unacceptable, but, curiously, for the only time in his entire career he did not invoke natural selection in order to explain male beauty. He ascribed the brilliance of the male's plumage to excess vitality and found the cause "for the origin of ornamental appendages of birds and other animals in a surplus of vital energy leading to abnormal growth in those parts of the integument where muscular and nervous action are greatest" (p. 293). Wallace's almost "Lamarckian" explanation has been refuted often enough in the literature not to require any further attention. Yet it must be conceded to Wallace and other critics that Darwin's analysis was incomplete.

FEMALE DISCRIMINATION

On the basis of his own observations and of the abundant records of the naturalists, Darwin was convinced of the existence of "female choice" (however defined). The students of animal courtship have substantiated Darwin's assertion. They are now virtually unanimous in stating that the females are far more discriminating than the males. It is easy to observe that males tend to display not only to their own females, but also to females of related species, to males of their own or related species, and, in the absence of appropriate display partners, to even less appropriate objects. If the females were lacking discrimination to a similar extent, an enormous amount of hybridization would take place. Males are very easily stimulated to engage in courtship, while females are often inactive and respond to the overtures of the males not at all or only after long-continued male displays. The reasons for this "coyness" have been provided by Richards (1927), Bateman (1948), and other recent authors. (For a fuller treatment, see Chapter 7.) They point out that this difference in the behavior of the sexes is a result of the highly unequal investment of the two sexes in reproduction. The male produces millions of gametes, and his role in reproduction usually ends with copulation. This requires a negligible expenditure of physiological energy, while the female usually produces only a limited number of yolk-rich eggs and in addition devotes a large amount of time and energy to caring for eggs and young. The male has little to lose by courting numerous females and by attempting to fertilize as many of them as possible. Anything that enhances his success in courtship will be favored by selection. The situation is quite different in the case of the female. Any failure of mating with the right kind of male may mean total reproductive failure and a total loss of her genes from the genotype of the next generation.

> Failure for a female mammal may mean weeks or months of wasted time. The mechanical and nutritional burden of pregnancy may mean increased vulnerability to predators, decreased disease resistance, and other dangers for a long time. . . . Once she starts on her reproductive role, she commits herself to a certain high minimum of reproductive effort. Natural selection

> should regulate her reproductive behavior in such a way that she will assume the burdens of reproduction only when the probability of success is at some peak value that is not likely to be exceeded (Williams 1966, p. 183).

There is thus a high selective premium on the discrimination by females of the most appropriate mate. Assuming that there is some correlation between the vigor and the persistence of the male's courtship with his fitness, it will be of selective advantage for the female to have a prolonged refractory period in order to test the male's perseverance and coordination. That it is normally the female which exercises choice in mate selection is the direct consequence of the highly unequal energy expenditure of the two sexes.

In Darwin's time female choice was largely conjectured. Wallace (1889) emphasized that there was no observational evidence for it, and he, therefore, characterized Darwin's argument as speculative. This view was countered by Poulton (1890), one of the few naturalists who stood up for Darwin, and said that such a lack of evidence is not surprising "because the vast majority of those interested in nature are either anatomists, microscopists, systematists, or collectors. There are comparatively few true naturalists, men who would devote much time and the closest study to watching living animals amid their natural surroundings, and who would value a fresh observation more than a beautiful dissection or a rare specimen" (p. 287). The deficiency deplored by Poulton has since been largely repaired. There is now abundant observational evidence, to be reported upon in other chapters of this book, that most females are very fickle indeed and usually remain for a long time unimpressed by the displays of large numbers of suitors before finally accepting one of them. Furthermore, it has been clearly shown that very specific characteristics may determine this choice. This has been demonstrated for positive and negative imprinting, by the Petit principle (Petit 1958, Boesiger 1967) and by observations of pair formation in birds and the sexual success of communally displaying birds. Similar preferences have been described for mammals (for example, Beach & LeBoeuf 1967). All of this recent work is a vindication of Darwin's original assumption.

However, the question as to the nature of the criteria on which females base their choice is still open. Is it really true, as claimed by Darwin, that female animals appreciate "beauty"? The first evolutionist who had the courage to come out in favor of a well developed esthetic sense among females was Poulton (1890). To say, as had Darwin's critics, that the male characteristics are simply species recognition marks, does not explain why they appear beautiful to the human eye, says Poulton. "For the purposes of recognition, beauty is entirely superfluous and indeed undesirable; strongly marked and conspicuous differences are alone necessary" (p. 316). "The musical value of the song of birds can not be explained as a means of recognition between the sexes. The beauty of song is something more than its clearness, loudness and individuality" (p. 319). The existence of an esthetic sense in birds, he says, is clearly demonstrated by the bower-birds who decorate their bowers with flowers and other colorful objects. The subsequent discovery of bower painting (Marshall 1954) further strengthens this case.

Poulton finally summarizes additional evidence supporting Darwin:

> There are one or two general facts which seem to me to strongly support the theory of Sexual Selection and to oppose any theory which is not based on selective breeding.
>
> (1) Sexual colors only developed in species which court by day or twilight, or have probably done so at no distant date. [Compares butterflies and moths.]
>
> (2) Sexual colors are not developed on parts of the body which move so rapidly that they become invisible. [Wings of hummingbirds and rapidly flying moths.]
>
> (3) Colors are best seen from the direction which corresponds to the position from which the female would see them. [Examples among butterflies and pheasants] (p. 331).

Prerequisites for the Functioning of Sexual Selection

ONE-SIDED FEMALE PREFERENCE

Such extreme developments as the wings of the Argus pheasant, the train of the peacock, or the plumes of some of the birds of paradise are evidence for a long continued directional evolution. This could hardly have occurred if each female had a different taste. Fisher (1930) called attention to this problem and proposed a solution making use of an association (in the genotype) between high general fitness and certain types of ornamentation. If such an association exists, it would explain why certain bizarre ornamentations should have such a high fitness: those females which happen to have a preference for ornaments linked with a superior general genotype will be favored by selection and consequently their particular preference will spread in the female population. Females thus would be able to "recognize" highest fitness by certain ornamentations. O'Donald (1962) has calculated the magnitude of the effects of such selection and showed it to be feasible. The greater weight we now ascribe to linkage suggests that such co-selection is indeed a feasible mechanism.

A SURPLUS OF MALES

Darwin saw clearly that sexual selection, narrowly defined, can operate only if there is a considerable surplus of males. "When the sexes exist in exactly equal numbers, the worst endowed males will (except where polygamy prevails), ultimately find females, and leave as many offspring, as well fitted for their general habits of life, as the best endowed males" (1871, p. 213). This disturbed Darwin greatly because "after investigating, as far as possible, the numerical proportion of the sexes, I do not believe that any great inequality in number commonly exists" (*ibid.*, p. 213). Darwin's own attempts to escape this dilemma (for example, a large reservoir of unmated birds) were not successful and need not be discussed. It has now become obvious that different interpretations pertain to species with polygyny (or promiscuity) and to those with strict monogamy. In the former case there is a clear-cut competition among males, and this will be discussed below. The sexual dimorphism of monogamous species has little if anything to do with sexual selection and can be explained in terms of straight natural selection (Hamilton 1961; See below under epigamic selection and isolating mechanisms).

STRUGGLE AMONG MALES

Female choice was one half of sexual selection for Darwin, fighting among males was the other half. Here also Darwin used the term "struggle" which had already got him into a good deal of trouble with respect to natural selection. He does not inform us whether he uses it in a "metaphorical" (*Origin of Species,* p. 62) or literal sense. Actually, he seems to use the term in both senses. "It is certain that amongst almost all animals there is a struggle between the males for the possession of the female. This fact is so notorious that it would be superfluous to give instances. Hence, the females have the opportunity of selecting one out of several males, on the supposition that their mental capacity suffices for the exertion of a choice" (p. 212). The logic of this statement is not compelling. There is no evidence whatsoever that the choice of the females is influenced by the size or form of the weapons that help a particular male to be victorious over another male. It seems to me that if the outcome of the struggle between the males had been decisive, there would be little opportunity left for choice by the females. The victorious male would gather all the females of the neighborhood into a harem while the vanquished males would be driven out of bounds. This is the classical situation in many mammal societies. At best the females would have the choice of which harem of the victorious male they would join. Wallace is even more impressed than Darwin by the importance of fighting between males. He considers it "a form of natural selection which increases the vigor and fighting power of the male animal, since in every case the weaker are either killed, wounded or driven away. . . . It is evidently a real power in nature; and to it we must impute the development of the exceptional strength, size, and activity of the male, together with the possession of special offensive and defensive weapons" (pp. 282–3). The modern naturalist is far less impressed. Cases of actual fighting between males for the possession of females seem to be the exception. What males usually fight for are territories which serve either as mating stations or as the place where the animal expects to raise his family. In such cases what the female chooses is not necessarily the strongest or most beautiful male, but sometimes simply the male with the most attractive territory. There is not necessarily a close correlation between strength, beauty, and acquisition of the best territory.

In monogamous species of birds virtually all males acquire a territory, and most of them also acquire a mate. Under these circumstances there is little leeway for sexual selection. The situation is quite different in species of birds and mammals in which the mating system is either polygyny or promiscuity. I refer to the analyses of Verner (1964), Orians (1969), and Bartholomew (1970) for a more detailed discussion of these mating systems. What is becoming increasingly evident is that even in these polygynous mating systems the development of sexual dimorphism is far more due to natural selection than to sexual selection, at least in the species in which breeding takes place within the territory of the male. Although bitter fights sometimes occur between territory neighbors, particularly among the pinnipeds, the objective of the fights seems to be territory. The defense of such territories is largely carried out by threats and bluffing (Huxley 1938a). Warning colors, ruffs, and manes play an important role during these threat displays.

From several recent studies of birds as well as mammals it is highly probable that the choice of the female is largely determined by the quality of the territory and not by the particular appearance of the male territory holder. If this could be confirmed and if the males have a similar ability to discriminate between good and bad territories, then the fighting ability of males would indeed be closely correlated with the well-being of their offspring. It would be a matter of natural rather than of sexual selection.

Sexual Selection or Natural Selection?

In the preceding discussion of the fights among males for superior territories, it has become apparent that phenomena which at first had appeared to be clear-cut evidence for sexual selection ("struggle among males") were largely forms of natural selection. Darwin did not see this as clearly as later workers. Indeed, he classified not only fighting among males but also various other phenomena under sexual selection which we would now unhesitatingly designate as components of natural selection. Darwin was not unaware of these ultimate explanations (see below), but he chose to disregard them, perhaps for didactic reasons. Wallace went to the other extreme: "The term sexual selection must, therefore, be restricted to the direct result of male struggle and combat. This is really a form of natural selection, and is a matter of direct observation" (1889, p. 296). Hence, sexual selection did not really exist for him. In the ensuing years many attempts were made to draw a sharp line between characteristics that had been acquired through sexual selection and those due to natural selection. None of these attempts was particularly successful, although Richards (1927) was quite correct in saying, "A character that has been acquired or preserved by the action of Sexual Selection must either be displayed to the other sex in courtship or used to drive away rivals" (p. 300). However, as we shall presently see, many characters that owe their existence to natural selection are likewise employed in these two contexts, and Richards himself demonstrated this in his outstanding review of the subject. It is now evident, in part owing to the analyses of Richards and Huxley (1938), that there are three major, and presumably several minor, selection pressures which favor the development or enhancement of sexual dimorphism, without requiring sexual selection.

EPIGAMIC SELECTION

Copulation, in most species of animals, is only the last step in a long series of interactions between male and female. The first is the mutual finding of the sex partners. Here we generally find one of three possible situations. (1) The male may be stationary (often on a well-defended territory); in this case the male makes his station known by songs and calls, as among birds, frogs, cicadas, and many orthopterans. These signals are usually highly stereotypic (see below, under isolating mechanisms), and whatever difference between individual males may exist is limited to the loudness and persistence of these signals. Or (2) the female is stationary, as among many moths, and attracts the males by chemical means (scents). In these cases the female is usually ready to mate as soon as the first male arrives. Or (3) both male and female are mobile, as among many butterflies, and mating is usually preceded by rather protracted displays. It is only in the third alternative that discrimination of sex plays a role, because sex recognition is automatically given in case one (by the advertising song of the males) and case two (by the scent of the female). As Richards (1927) pointed out correctly (and so had Wallace and others before him), characteristics which facilitate the finding of one sex by the other will be favored by natural selection because their existence will reduce the length of time during which the sex partners are vulnerable to predation and other dangers during their search for each other.

Except in (2) above, the hormonal states and reproductive conditions of the two sex partners must first be synchronized before copulation can occur. For birds, Marshall (1936) has described the relationship between display and the physiological state of the female as follows:

> It has been shown that the gonad-stimulating hormone of the pituitary will cause ovarian development and ovulation in birds, and that sexual posturing or even the mere association of two individuals will initiate nest building

> and ovulation. There is a presumption, therefore, that sexual posturing produces exteroceptive stimuli which act upon the anterior pituitary through the hypothalamus, and so effects the necessary synchronization between the sexual processes of the male and female birds. Herein then, in all probability, lies the biological or race-survival value of sexual display and of the adornment which in many species is taken advantage of to render the display more effective. Those birds which have brighter colours, more elaborate ornamentation, and a greater power of display must be supposed to possess a superior capacity for effecting by pituitary stimulation a close degree of physiological adjustment between the two sexes so as to bring about ovulation and the related processes at the most appropriate time (pp. 445–46).

However, protracted displays serving to increase the physiological readiness of females have also been described for *Drosophila,* spiders, squid, lizards, and many other species. Courtship consists of an exchange of stimuli between male and female until both have reached a state of physiological readiness in which successful copulation can occur. The analysis of these signals is made difficult because they serve at least three independent functions: (1) to suppress fleeing or attacking tendencies in the sex partner (this has been particularly well described by the Peckhams (1890) for spiders); (2) to advertise the presence of a potential mate; and (3), as stated, to synchronize mating activity (for their role as isolating mechanisms, see below).

All these functions are important for natural selection, but the question is still open as to what extent these signals, particularly those of the more aggressive sex, also serve sexual selection. Darwin assumed rather naively that "the best armed males" were also the strongest and that "the more attractive" males were "at the same time more vigorous" (p. 220). As stated above, there is, however, no demonstration of an automatic correlation between the two characteristics. However, Fisher (1930) saw quite clearly that a plumage character of a male bird which had originally been acquired through natural selection for purely physiological reasons may "proceed, by reason of the advantage gained in sexual selection, even after it has passed the point in development at which its advantage in natural selection has ceased" (p. 152). The fact that display characters are most pronounced in species in which there is a surplus of males or a special mating system (such as promiscuity or polygyny) seems to confirm this inference. Indirectly, it is also confirmed by the fact that in monogamous species, such as herons (egrets) in which the pair bond is continuously tested and strengthened by mutual displays, there has been a "transference" of the display characters from the males to the females with the result that both sexes have elaborate display plumes.

We can summarize the findings on epigamic characters by saying that their development was probably favored originally by natural selection, to synchronize the physiological state of the two sexes, but that sexual selection is presumably superimposed in all cases in which a male may gain reproductive advantage owing to an extreme development of an epigamic character.

ISOLATING MECHANISMS

It is well known that the mating drive in the males of many species is so strong that they display not only to females of their own species, but also to females of related species. If the females were equally lacking in discrimination, an enormous amount of hybridization among closely related species would take place. Since hybrids are ordinarily of considerably lower fitness, natural selection will favor two developments: first, any genetic change that would make the females more discriminating, and second, any characteristics in the males that would reduce the probability that they be confused with the males of another species. Such characteristics are designated isolating mechanisms. Darwin, curiously, almost entirely ignored the role of species specific male characteristics as isolating mechanisms. Wallace was considerably more perceptive on this point. He was convinced that one of the chief meanings of sexual coloration is to enable "the sexes to recognize their kind [= species], and thus avoid the evils of infertile classes . . . . The wonderful diversity of color and of marking that prevails, especially in birds and insects, may be due to the fact that one of the first needs of a new species would be, to keep separate from its nearest allies, and this could be most readily done by some easily seen external mark of difference" (pp. 217–8). He continues: "Among insects the principle of distinctive coloration for recognition has probably been at work in the production of the wonderful diversity of color and marking we find everywhere, more especially among the butterflies and moths; and here its chief function may have been to secure the pairing together of individuals of the same species" (p. 226). Curiously, later writers on the subject, such as Poulton (1890), Richards (1927), and Huxley (1938b), although mentioning the role of species specific male characters as isolating mechanisms, paid very little attention to them. It was not until Dobzhansky (1937) emphasized the great evolutionary importance of isolating mechanisms that their role was fully appreciated. It has now become apparent that many male characteristics which Darwin had considered as products of sexual selection actually serve as isolating mechanisms and were acquired through natural selection or at least as by-products of speciation and subsequently reinforced by natural selection. Mayr (1942) gave one of the early summaries of the new viewpoint and called attention to the fact that the conspicuous male characteristics sometimes were lost in island birds when there were no other closely related species on the same island. The loss of these characters was apparently due to a relaxation of selection for the distinctive isolating mechanisms.

Behavioral isolating mechanisms and epigamic selection grade into each other imperceptibly. Considering that there will be a constant selection pressure on the females to respond as quickly and precisely as possible to the displays of males of their own species, such species specific isolating mechanisms function simultaneously as epigamic characters to facilitate the physiological coordination of the two display partners.

DIFFERENT NICHE UTILIZATION

In many species, particularly of birds, males and females differ from each other in niche utilization. This was fully appreciated by Darwin (1871, pp. 208–209) who recognized that sexual dimorphism associated with a difference in ecology had nothing to do with sexual selection. "When . . . the two sexes differ in structure in relation to habits of life, they have no doubt been modified through natural selection" (p. 209). Much of the literature on such ecological sexual dimorphism has been recently summarized by Selander (1966, 1969).

HETEROGAMY

The enormous genetic variability of populations that has recently been demonstrated suggests the possibility that there might be a selective premium on any mechanism that would favor the choice of an unlike mate (heterogamy). So far, all the search has been for evidence in favor of homogamy, particularly by authors interested in sympatric speciation. Consequently, no one has seriously looked for cases of heterogamy; and what little evidence exists has been found incidentally in other work.

The best evidence is the work of Ehrman & Petit (1968) on mating preference in Drosophila. In several species, females, when offered a mixture of a common and a rare genotype, prefer the rare one. Since, statistically, a female in nature is more likely to belong to the commoner genotype, such a mating preference will tend to increase (or at least preserve) the heterozygosity of the population (see Boesiger 1967 for a general summary).

Another interesting case was described by Jehl (1970). He found, in a species of Arctic sandpipers, that the greater the size differential, the more quickly pair formation took place. The largest males and smallest females were the first to mate, and their broods were the first to hatch. Owing to the shortness of the Arctic summer, there is undoubtedly a selective advantage in rapid pair formation. This, however, does not preclude the possibility of the presence of a tendency for heterogamy. Jehl was unable to discover any differences between males and females in food utilization.

Natural Fitness and Reproductive Advantage

Darwin in several statements implied that natural selection and sexual selection were mutually exclusive phenomena. For instance: "Sexual selection depends on the success of certain individuals over others of the same sex, in relation to the propagation of the species; while natural selection depends on the success of both sexes, at all ages, in relation to the general conditions of life" (1874, p. 614). And yet, throughout his discussions, he stresses how many of the secondary sex characters of males contribute to general fitness. Huxley (1938b) questions whether or not it is desirable to mark off sexual selection sharply from natural selection and whether the male secondary sexual characters involved with combat and display are clearly distinguishable from other male characters. He concludes that "display characters are inextricably entangled with those subserving threat and also sex recognition. . . . It is clear that Darwin's original contention will not hold. Many of the characters which he considered to owe their evolution to sexual selection do have value to the species in the general struggle for existence, and not merely in the struggle between males for reproduction" (pp. 33–34).

Both Darwin and Wallace, with virtually no tangible evidence, assumed that the males which won out in the struggle with other males would mate "with the most vigorous and best nourished females. . . . If such females select the more attractive, and at the same time vigorous males, they will rear a larger number of offspring" (Darwin, 1874, p. 220). In other words, they assumed that there was a correlation between general fitness and the kind of characters that would lead to victory in the struggle among males. Wallace likewise believed that reproductive success of males was the result of their "vigor and fighting power" and that reproductive success could all be explained in terms of natural selection. Now, eighty years later, there is still little tangible evidence that there really is such a correlation. However, in one study of *Drosophila melanogaster* it was found that the males with the highest sexual drive also produced the highest number of offspring (Fulker 1966).

The preceding discussion of epigamic selection, of the importance of superior male territories, and the role of isolating mechanisms all demonstrated that male secondary sexual characters, perhaps originally acquired through sexual selection, almost invariably also contribute to general fitness.

INCREASED FITNESS OR MERE REPRODUCTIVE ADVANTAGE?

The listing above of numerous situations in which sexual selection is accompanied by an unquestioned increase in fitness leads to the question whether there are any forms of sexual selection which result in the evolution of characters that are useless or deleterious to the species. The excessive plumes of birds of paradise and peacocks as well as the antlers of certain cervids (such as the Irish elk) will have to be mentioned until somebody proves that they are not deleterious. But even if we disregard such excesses, a belief in sexual selection forces us to ask this question: If the female chooses her mate primarily on the basis of esthetic criteria, how can this truly benefit the species? Or, to use Darwin's own words, how can it contribute to fitness when males have acquired a particular structure, "not from being better fitted to survive in the struggle for existence, but from having gained an advantage over other males" (1874, p. 210). It is distinctly conceivable that extreme courtship adaptations acquired as a result of sexual selection may actually reduce the ecological success, that is, the fitness, of a species.

This point raises once more the question of the definition of fitness and of modes of selection. It is quite possible, as suggested by Haldane (1932) and Huxley (1938b), that one should make a distinction between intrapopulation (intraspecies) and interspecies selection. As long as density dependent factors regulate population size, sexual selection for ornamental characters may not have any effect on the interspecific component of selection. If, as everyone seems to agree, the females have no difficulty in getting fertilized and producing offspring, a certain amount of selection for "useless male characters" may have no effect whatsoever on the fitness of the species in interspecific selection. Natural selection will surely come into play as soon as this sexual selection leads to the production of excesses that significantly lower the fitness of the species in interspecific encounters. I feel that here is an area that has not been thought out completely.

A BALANCE OF OPPOSING SELECTION PRESSURES

A number of genetic characters have been described in recent years which do not increase general viability but merely enhance reproductive success (Mayr 1963, pp. 199–201). The list includes homostyly in certain genera of plants, meiotic drive, and high fertility (*Microtus,* Man). In each case, however, the deleterious effects are somewhat reduced by an opposing pressure of natural selection.

The situation is particularly well illustrated by two recently described cases in which there is opposition between the response of females or males to releasing mechanisms and a selection pressure for cryptic (or mimetic) coloration. In *Papilio glaucus* Burns (1966) found that males of this butterfly mate less frequently with the mimetic female morph than with the nonmimetic morph. The males apparently show a preference for the ancestral color pattern of the species even though the new mimetic morph has presumably existed for thousands of generations. The female polymorphism in this species is maintained by a balance between the predator-induced selective advantage of the mimetic morph and the mating advantage of the ancestral morph. The selection against the establishment of a new color morph among the males, however, is so strong that polymorphism among males is a rarity. Predator selection, however, can occasionally override sexual selection. In a population of sticklebacks (*Gasterosteus aculeatus*) on the Olympic Peninsula in western North America, a blackish protective coloration has evolved in response to depredations by a black predatory fish. Male sticklebacks in nuptial plumage are black-bellied in this population, and females, in the absence of other color types, spawn normally in the nests of these black-bellied males. Even though this black-bellied population is four to eight thousand years old, females still show a five-to-one preference for red-bellied males in a double choice aquarium experiment (McPhail 1969). This case shows that natural selection may sometimes override the effects of sexual selection.

Conclusion

1. Darwin's assumption that the females in many species of animals (sometimes also the males) make a definite choice of their sex partner has been confirmed in numerous recent investigations.
2. Darwin was wrong, however, in assuming that most aspects of sexual dimorphism in animals are the result of sexual selection.
3. Nevertheless, a residue of male ornaments and attractants remains which can hardly be ascribed only to natural selection. A male can achieve an increased contribution to the gene pool of the next generation through features which do not contribute to the fitness of the species but merely to the reproductive success of the possessor of these characters.
4. Whenever such sex-limited features affect interspecific selection, the pressure of natural selection will tend to eliminate deleterious excesses.

Darwin's theory of sexual selection has been a most useful organizing principle, stimulating numerous investigations and leading to an intensive analysis of a highly complex set of phenomena.

References

Bartholomew, G. A. 1970. A model for the evolution of pinniped polygyny. *Evolution* 24: 546–559.

Bateman, A. J. 1948. Intra-sexual selection in *Drosophila. Heredity* 2: 349–368.

Beach, F. A., & B. J. LeBoeuf. 1967. Preferential mating in the bitch. *Animal Behavior* 15: 546–558.

Boesiger, E. 1967. La signification évolutive de la sélection sexuelle chez les animaux. *Scientia* 111: 1–17.

Burns, J. M. 1966. Preferential mating versus mimicry: Disruptive selection and sex-limited dimorphism in *Papilio glaucus. Science* 153: 551–553.

Darwin, C. 1859. *On the origin of species by means of natural selection, or the preservation of favoured races in the struggle for life*. London: John Murray.

———. 1871. *The descent of man, and selection in relation to sex.* 1st ed. London: John Murray.

———. 1874. *The descent of man, and selection in relation to sex.* 2nd ed. London: John Murray.

Dobzhansky, T. 1937. *Genetics and the origin of species.* New York: Columbia University Press.

Ehrman, L., & C. Petit. 1968. Genotype frequency and mating success in the *Willistoni* species group of *Drosophila. Evolution* 22: 649–658.

Fisher, R. A. 1930. *The genetical theory of natural selection.* Oxford: Clarendon Press.

Fulker, D. W. 1966. Mating speed in male *Drosophila melanogaster:* a psychogenetic analysis. *Science* 153: 203–205.

Ghiselin, M. T. 1969. *The triumph of the Darwinian method.* Berkeley and Los Angeles: Univ. of California Press.

Haldane, J. B. S. 1932. *The causes of evolution.* London: Longmans, Green and Co.

Hamilton, T. H. 1961. On the functions and causes of sexual dimorphism in breeding plumage characters of North American species of warblers and orioles. *The American Naturalist* 95: 121–123.

Huxley, J. 1938a. Threat and warning coloration in birds with a general discussion of the biological functions of colour. In *Proc. 8th Internat. Ornith. Cong.* (1934), pp. 430–455.

———. 1938b. Darwin's theory of sexual selection and the data subsumed by it, in the light of recent research. *The American Naturalist* 72: 416–433.

———. 1938c. The present standing of the theory of sexual selection. In *Evolution: Essays on aspects of evolutionary biology,* ed. G. R. deBeer. Oxford: Clarendon Press.

———. 1963. *Evolution: The modern synthesis.* London: Allen and Unwin.

Jehl, J. R., Jr. 1970. Sexual selection for size differences in two species of sandpipers. *Evolution* 24: 311–319.

Marshall, F. H. A. 1936. Sexual periodicity and the causes which determine it. *liminary statement.* Oxford: Clarendon Press.

Marshall, A. J. 1954. *Bower-birds: their displays and breeding cycles, a pre-Philosophical Trans. Roy. Soc.* B, 226: 423–456.

Maynard Smith, J. 1958. Sexual selection. In *A century of Darwin,* ed. S. A. Barnett. Cambridge: Harvard Univ. Press.

Mayr, E. 1942. *Systematics and the origin of species.* New York: Columbia Univ. Press.

———. 1963. *Animal species and evolution.* Cambridge: Belknap Press of Harvard Univ. Press.

McPhail, J. D. 1969. Predation and the evolution of a stickleback (Gasterosteus). *J. Fish. Res. Bd. Canada* 26: 3183–3208.

Montalenti, G. 1959. Il concetto di selezione sessuale da Darwin ai nostri giorni. *Convegno di Genetica 1957,* supplemento a La Ricerca Scientifica, Anno 29, pp. 3–18.

O'Donald, P. 1962. Theory of sexual selection. *Heredity* 17: 541.

Orians, G. H. 1969. On the evolution of mating systems in birds and mammals. *The American Naturalist* 103: 589–603.

Peckham, G. W., & E. G. Peckham. 1890. Additional observations on sexual selection in spiders of the family Attidae, with some remarks on Mr. Wallace's theory of sexual ornamentation. *Occas. Pap. Nat. Hist. Soc., Wisconsin,* 1: 117–151.

Petit, C. 1958. Le déterminisme génétique et psycho-physiologique de la compétition sexuelle chez *Drosophila melanogaster*. *Bull. Biol.* 92: 248–329.

Poulton, E. D. 1890. *The colours of animals: their meaning and use, especially considered in the case of insects*. London: Kegan Paul, Trench, Trübner, and Co.

Richards, O. W. 1927. Sexual selection and allied problems in the insects. *Biological Reviews* 2: 298–364.

Selander, R. K. 1966. Sexual dimorphism and differential niche utilization in birds. *The Condor* 68: 113–151.

————. 1969. The ecological aspects of the systematics of animals. In *Systematic Biology,* Nat. Acad. Sci. Publ. no. 1692: 213–247.

Tinbergen, N. 1954. The origin and evolution of courtship and threat display. In *Evolution as a Process,* ed. J. Huxley, A. C. Hardy, & E. B. Ford. London: Allen and Unwin.

Verner, J. 1964. Evolution of polygamy in the long-billed marsh wren. *Evolution* 18: 252–261.

Wallace, A. R. 1889. *Darwinism: an exposition of the theory of natural selection with some of its applications*. London: Macmillan and Co.

Williams, G. C. 1966. *Adaptation and natural selection: a critique of some current evolutionary thought*. Princeton: Princeton Univ. Press.

6

LEE EHRMAN

THE ROCKEFELLER UNIVERSITY AND
STATE UNIVERSITY OF NEW YORK, PURCHASE

Genetics and Sexual Selection

Introduction

The concept of sexual selection and its possible role in evolution is derived from Charles Darwin. He defined sexual selection as *"a struggle between individuals of one sex, generally the males, for the possession of the other sex. The result is not death to the unsuccessful competitor, but few or no offspring"* (1859, my italics).

Within many animal species the two sexes display characteristically different phenotypes, for example, in the distribution of hair and in the degree of development of the mammary glands. Darwin thought that the evolution of such sexual dimorphism was due to its positive correlation with greater mating success and fertility. Sexual selection, he said, was the " . . . advantage which certain individuals have over others of the same sex and species solely in respect of reproduction." Indeed, "the power to charm the females has been in some instances more important than the power to conquer in battle" (Darwin, 1871). Here Darwin was almost forced to invoke and to overestimate this concept of sexual selection because he was at an admitted loss as to how to explain the origin, consistency, and the maintenance of human racial differences. These phenotypic "external characteristic differences . . . cannot be accounted for in a satisfactory manner by the direct action of the conditions of life, nor by the effects of the continued use of parts, nor through the principle of correlation . . . but there remains one agency, namely Sexual Selection, which appears to have acted powerfully on man, as on many animals . . . It can further be shown that the dif-

I wish to thank those people who kindly read parts of this chapter: R. Alexander, L. Firschein, A. Lill, D. Sank, H. Spieth and H. Wiley. I also wish to thank Mrs. R. Yeshion, teacher of the deaf, for her assistance.

The author is the grateful recipient of United States Public Health Service Research Career Award 2K03 HD09033–07.

ference between the races of man, as in colour, hairness, form of features, etc. are of a kind which might have been expected to come under the influence of sexual selection." (See Huxley 1942 for further discussion of Darwin's predicament, and Dobzhansky, chapter 4.)

At present it seems best to simply define sexual selection as *all mechanisms which cause deviations from panmixia* (but see King's definition, 1968.) Then sexual isolation and assortative mating, as examples, become special instances of sexual selection, affecting both sexes. Regardless of which definition is adopted, however, sexual selection assumes greater importance when species with polygamous mating systems are considered. In these cases more sexually active, successful males may exclude others of their own sex from the reproductive process. In monogamous species, on the other hand, which pair for life or for a breeding season, almost all mature individuals find partners and reproduce themselves. Man is one such species, of course, and Kirk (1966) estimates that fewer than ten per cent of all adults in the United States pass through reproductive ages without marrying (seven per cent for women). And this figure, he claims, "will continue to go down in the near future." In 1960 only twelve per cent of U.S. women were still childless at age 35.

The functioning of sexual selection in monogamous species is then only plausible if certain secondary sexual traits confer upon their possessor a greater fertility, that is, if they produce more progeny than nonbearers. This sort of differential fertility is more correctly judged natural selection than sexual selection. George Williams (1966) points out the disproportionately greater burden of parenthood for females. This being so, a female "will assume the burdens only when the probability of success is at some peak that is not likely to be exceeded." Such selectivity is certainly also applicable to the choice of an inseminating male. Simply put, "fit" fathers are more likely to have "fit" offspring than "unfit" or less fit ones. And if a male is capable of advertising himself and his intentions properly, of occupying the proper territory at the proper time, and of catching a female either literally or figuratively, then he is not likely to be in poor health or even undernourished. One may even expect him to be genetically fit.

This idea is neither astounding nor new; it occurs repeatedly even in a fiction. Jonathan Swift had his noble, horselike Houyhnhnms practice not only sexual selection, but a type of birth control as well. As Captain Lemuel Gulliver explains,

> When the matron Houyhnhnms have produced one of each sex, they no longer accompany with their consorts, except they lose one of their issue by some casualty . . . This caution is necessary to prevent the country from being overburthened with numbers . . . In their marriages, they are exactly careful to chuse such colours as will not make any disagreeable mixture in the breed. *Strength* is chiefly valued in the male, and *comeliness* in the female, not upon the account of *love*, but to preserve the race from degenerating: for, where a

female happens to excel in *strength,* a consort is chosen with regard to *comeliness.*" (*Gulliver's Travels,* 1726; the italics are Swift's own.)

Drosophila, Genetics, and Sexual Selection

Drosophila is without doubt the organism about which most is known concerning the relationships between genetics and sexual selection. I shall therefore concentrate on *Drosophila* in this chapter. Already in 1911, Lutz had published experiments on selectivity in matings where some of the potential mates bore various kinds of lesions. He removed the so-called sex combs (rows of stout bristles located on a tarsal segment of the forelegs) of *D. melanogaster* males, and found their acceptability to females unaltered by this surgery. In 1915 Sturtevant wrote, "Much has been written on the subject of sexual selection since Darwin first developed the theory, and many remarkable observations have been recorded. There has, however, been very little experimental work in this field. Darwin and those who have followed him have obtained much of their evidence from the insects and within this group some of the most striking cases of elaborate mating habits have been reported in the Diptera." He then inquired if a single point mutation, detected by a change it produces in some visible morphological trait, can affect the sexual successes of its bearers. Table 6.1 records his results of tests of two eye color mutations, a body color mutation, and of one affecting the shape of the fly's wings. Wild-type *Drosophila melanogaster* have red eyes, grayish bodies, and wings that are not curved at all.

The numbers of observations are quite small, but the results are clear enough. They do show that only the *vermilion* male is not at a disadvantage, while the *yellow* and *white* males are below their wild-type competitors in mating successes compared to *curved* males. More data have been obtained by Merrell (1949, 1950, 1953), and Reed & Reed (1950):

Competing Males	Ratio of Mating Successes
yellow: wild type	11:130
cut: wild type	9:64
raspberry: wild type	39:79
forked: wild type	63:52
white: wild type	75:100

Yellow is the same body color mutant used originally by Sturtevant, and so is the *white* eye color. *Cut* alters the wing margins, *raspberry* the eye shape and surface, and *forked* bends the bristles all over the fly's body. Only with *forked* is there no significant difference between scores for the mutant and for the wild-type males (but *forked* males live only, on the average, two-thirds as long as nonforked ones). See the work of Rendel

Table 6.1. Sturtevant's Sexual Selection in Drosophila

"Chooser"	*"Chosen"*	*Number of cases*
Red vs. white eyes (Normal body color)		
Red ♂	Red ♀	54
	White ♀	82
White ♂	Red ♀	40
	White ♀	93
Red ♀	Red ♂	53
	White ♂	14
White ♀	Red ♂	62
	White ♂	19
Gray (normal) vs. yellow body color (Red eyes)		
Gray ♂	Gray ♀	25
	Yellow ♀	31
Yellow ♂	Gray ♀	12
	Yellow ♀	30
Gray ♀	Gray ♂	60
	Yellow ♂	12
Yellow ♀	Gray ♂	25
	Yellow ♂	8
Vermilion Black-yellow ♀	Red-gray ♂	13
	White-gray ♂	1
Gray and yellow body colors (White eyes)		
Gray ♂	Gray ♀	11
	Yellow ♀	4
Gray ♀	Gray ♂	21
	Yellow ♂	3
Red and white eyes (Yellow body color)		
Red ♂	Red ♀	3
	White ♀	4
White ♂	Red ♀	9
	White ♀	9
Red ♀	Red ♂	9
	White ♂	2
White ♀	Red ♂	21
	White ♂	1
Red and vermilion eyes (Gray body color)		
Red ♂	Red ♀	7
	Vermilion ♀	5
Vermilion ♂	Red ♀	4
	Vermilion ♀	4
Red ♀	Red ♂	11
	Vermilion ♂	14
Long and curved wings (Other characters normal)		
Long ♂	Long ♀	10
	Curved ♀	13
Curved ♂	Long ♀	5
	Curved ♀	3
Long ♀	Long ♂	14
	Curved ♂	4
Curved ♀	Long ♂	9
	Curved ♂	5

From Sturtevant, 1961, pp. 34 & 35.

(1945), Tan (1946), and Maynard Smith (1956) with other *Drosophila* species.

This sort of investigation, which pits mutant against nonmutant or one mutant versus a different kind, has been developed by Bösiger (1962, 1963ab). He scored the percentages of females inseminated by males taken from long-inbred mutant laboratory stocks and by hybrid males produced by reciprocal crosses between these strains of *D. melanogaster:*

Source of Males	Number of Males	Percentage of Fertilized Females
forked	267	23.8
sepia	302	28.3
F_1 (*sepia* ♀ × *forked* ♂)	227	74.3
F_1 (*forked* ♀ × *sepia* ♂)	237	78.4

Here, in addition to a study of the effects of point mutations on sexual selection, a demonstration is given of the influence of heterozygosity on the sexual vigor of the males. More extensive data can be found in Bösiger (1957, 1958, 1965, and 1967).

Working with some of the classical mutants of *Drosophila melanogaster,* Petit (1954, 1958) discovered that the mating success of male individuals may depend upon the frequency of a given type of male in a population. When, for example, wild-type and *Bar* (a mutant narrowing the shape of the eye) males and females are present together in the same container, the mean number of matings per male is greater if his kind is rare, and lower if it is common in the population. This same phenomenon was rediscovered in 1965 by Ehrman, Spassky, Pavlovsky, and Dobzhansky, using karyotypic variants in *Drosophila pseudoobscura.* Spiess (1968 and appendix to Ehrman 1966) recorded this *frequency-dependent sexual selection* in *D. persimilis,* and Ehrman & Petit (1968) found it to be part of the behavioral performance of freshly collected *D. equinoxialis, D. tropicalis,* and *D. willistoni.* (Also see Fraser & Burnell 1967, Kojima & Yarbrough 1967, Tobari & Kojima 1967, and Kojima & Tobari 1969.)

If, as seems probable (Ehrman 1970), this effect occurs in natural as well as in laboratory populations, its importance in the process of evolution may be considerable. Indeed, if rarity confers a selective advantage upon the carriers of a genotype, this genotype may increase in frequency until the advantage decreases and disappears. Balanced genetic polymorphism in natural populations may be maintained by this mechanism as well as by heterosis (Dobzhansky 1970).

The following excerpt from my data (1966, 1967, 1968ab) will serve as an illustration. Two genotypes of *D. pseudoobscura,* which we may symbolize simply as A and B, were introduced into observation chambers, and the matings that took place were recorded. The relative numbers of A and

B males present in the chambers, and the absolute numbers of matings in which A and B males participated are as follows:

Frequency in the Observation Chamber	*Numbers of Matings Observed*	
A : B	*A*	*B*
18:2	78	27
16:4	75	43
14:6	63	46
12:8	42	75
10:10	49	66
8:12	57	63
6:14	37	71
4:16	46	64
2:18	33	80

At intermediate frequencies (10A:10B to 6A:14B) the matings occur in about the proportions of the two kinds of males present; when B is rare (18A:2B to 12A:8B) it manages to mate more frequently than A, and when A is rare (4A:16B and 2A:18B) its success in mating is greater than that of B.

More data are presented (and the influence of heterozygosity also considered as was done with point mutations by Bösiger) in the data in Table 6.2. The chi-squares indicate the significance of the deviations observed from random matings, that is, from the numbers expected if the probability of an individual securing a mate is independent of the frequencies of the two genotypes in the chamber. These chi-squares have one degree of freedom and 3.84 is significant at the five per cent level, while 6.63 is significant at the one per cent level.

Table 6.2 shows that when AR/AR and AR/CH, AR/AR and CH/AR, or CH/CH and CH/AR are present in equal numbers (the 10:10 ratio), both kinds of males and females mate in proportion to their numbers. The highest, but still not significant, chi-square in these instances is only 2.33. When CH/CH males compete with equally numerous AR/CH males the heterozygote is more successful (giving a significant chi-square of 6.69). When CH/CH is made rare (the 2:18 ratio), this superiority of the heterozygote is lost, but is expressed again when AR/CH is rare. The other three combinations clearly give positive frequency-dependent results; males representing the rare genotype enjoy an advantage in mating. This genetically-determined and frequency-dependent sexual selection is conferred upon the rare type of male by the females, who do the "choosing" in this *Drosophila* material. These selective females have been aptly described as "discriminatingly passive" while the males are "indiscriminatingly eager" (Bateman 1948). Sexual recognition is a trial and error affair

Table 6.2. Matings observed with different proportions of homokaryotypic AR or CH and heterokaryotypic AR/CH (from an AR♀ × CH♂ cross) or CH/AR (from a CH♀ × AR♂ cross) Drosophila pseudoobscura *flies per observation chamber (from Ehrman 1968).*

	Runs	*Males*		χ^2	*Females*	
		Ho	*He*		*Ho*	*He*
AR/AR:AR/CH		AR/AR	AR/CH		AR/AR	AR/CH
1. 10:10	6	63	47	2·33	58	52
2. 18:2	6	83	17	5·44	89	11
3. 2:18	6	19	86	7·65	12	93
AR/AR:CH/AR		AR/AR	CH/AR		AR/AR	CH/AR
4. 10:10	6	50	53	0·09	49	54
5. 18:2	6	84	27	25·31	99	12
6. 2:18	7	25	85	19·80	14	96
CH/CH:AR/CH		CH/CH	AR/CH		CH/CH	AR/CH
7. 10:10	7	41	68	6·69	56	53
8. 18:2	8	75	26	27·81	87	14
9. 2:18	9	18	84	6·63	15	87
CH/CH:CH/AR		CH/CH	CH/AR		CH/CH	CH/AR
10. 10:10	7	49	53	1·75	55	57
11. 18:2	7	72	49	125·03	105	16
12. 2:18	7	16	97	2·17	13	100

ARrowhead and CHiricahua are two widely used autosomal inversions, located in the same autosomal pair of chromosomes. (Ho = homokaryotype; He = heterokaryotype).

among drosophilids. Males will generally court females of any species (or a dead fly, lumps of food, even other males) and will immediately repeat courtship and mounting (Ehrman & Strickberger 1960; Ehrman 1964). Table 6.2 and Table 6.3 show that there is no frequency-dependent sexual selection operating upon the females themselves. All of them eventually get inseminated. This control of sexual selection by one sex (usually the females), and its operation upon the other sex (the males) was, of course, clearly recognized by Darwin.

Experiments were then undertaken to discover the sensory basis for frequency-dependent sexual selection in Drosophila (Ehrman 1969). How does a *Drosophila* female know which males are rare? Olfactory and vibratory (airborne and substrate) cues can be considered; so was the influence of actual physical contact as opposed to distance stimuli between courting individuals. Data summarized in Table 6.3 indicate positive results in favor of olfactory signals. Actual physical contact between the flies was also important. Row 1 of Table 6.3 presents data on the pronounced mating advantage enjoyed by rare ARrowhead males when five pairs of these flies were confined in a simple observation chamber with twenty pairs of CHiricahua *Drosophila pseudoobscura,* all virgin at the start. (These are the same karyotypes designated in Table 6.2, but here they are

Table 6.3. Numbers of matings recorded in single observation chambers, in double chambers, and in double chambers with space between them and air currents flowing through them; 20 CH : 5 AR pairs present per run.

		Matings				
		Males			Females	
	Runs	AR	CH	χ_1^2	AR	CH
1. Single chamber	5	48	66	34.81	25	89
2. Double chamber	5	18	94	1.08	19	93
3. Current from "double chamber"	5	45	58	36.13	20	83
4. Current toward "double chamber"	5	27	83	1.42	24	86

χ_1^2 (0.05) = 3.84; χ_1^2 (0.01) = 6.64

wholly homozygous.) Entries in row 1 show the rare AR males to be definitely mating out of proportion to their numbers. For row 2 a double-decker observation chamber, so to speak, was fabricated. See Figure 6.1. Flies entirely of the type which were rare above (AR), were confined to the lower level so they would supply contaminating and perhaps confusing odors and noises. These easily filtered upward through the cheesecloth separation between the two levels, and flies from both levels came together at this barrier. There is no advantage of rare males indicated in row 2; their rarity was effectively obscured from the selecting females who did not then prefer them. Rows 3 and 4 involved the use of the gadget in Figure 6.2. For row 3 nothing actually contaminated the environment within the observation chamber and so row 3 duplicates the data in row 1. Row 4 is like row 2 in that no advantage of rare males in the process of sexual selection is demonstrated; this is so in row 4 because the rare males are not rare in the olfactory environment of the observation chamber—a

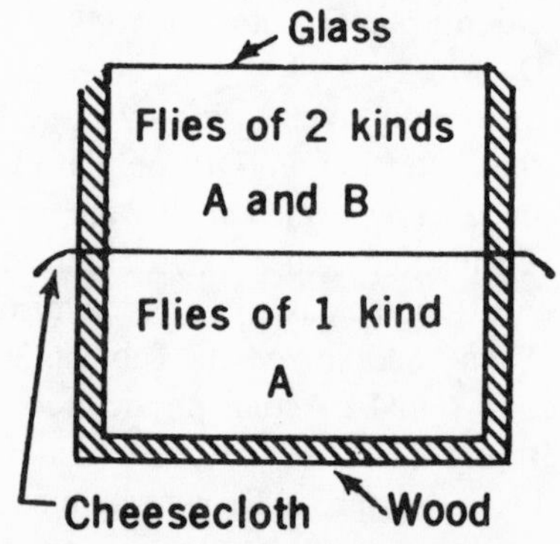

Figure 6.1. A double-decker observation chamber.

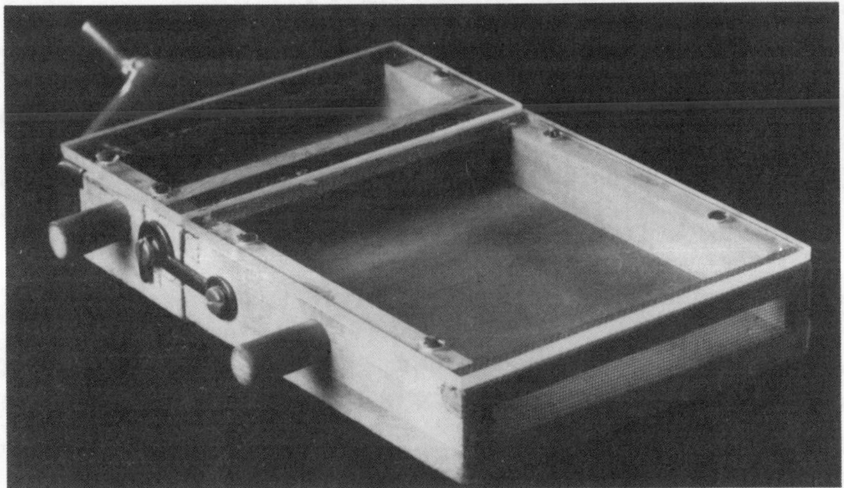

Figure 6.2. Double chamber for observation of Drosophila *matings. The matings taking place in the larger compartment are recorded. The smaller compartment contains the flies producing contaminating odors. A blower is attached by a rubber tube to the nozzle in the upper left corner.*

gentle current first passing over large numbers of courting rare type couples is delivered into the observation chamber in this instance. If the rare males do not actually "smell" rare, they are not treated as rare males, that is, they are not blessed by the females with any advantage in the competition that is sexual selection.

More recently (Ehrman 1970b), it has been found possible to artificially induce this sort of frequency-dependent mating advantage, even when there is no difference in the actual frequencies of the competing males. (These experiments again involve the use of the double chambers described above.)

As our final example (see Ehrman & Petit 1969 for more complete references) from the drosophilids, H. T. Spieth's recent (1968) and startling discovery of the existence of lek behavior in certain Hawaiian *Drosophila* can be mentioned. Lek behavior may be defined in terms of male performance and territoriality in order to attract females. "Ordinary" nonterritorial *Drosophila* court, mate, and even oviposit when and where they gather at sources of food. They meet each other in the places where they feed. Lek behavior introduces a "spatial separation of courtship from feeding and oviposition and intensifies sexual selection since the males must attract the females to the lek or mating sites. As in other organisms, the result of sexual selection is sexual dimorphism and this has been developed to an extraordinary degree in the Hawaiian males." *Drosophila* species exhibiting lek behavior generally display greater phenotypic differences between the two sexes than do other *Drosophila* which have not evolved this lek behavior.

Males of various species of *Drosophila,* whether or not they exhibit lek behavior, spend less time at feeding sites than do females. Females remain longer to lay eggs. But males who will later defend their leks are nonetheless tolerant of other males while feeding; their behavior toward one another is calm at this time. They will never display in the manner illustrated in Figures 6.3 and 6.4 while occupied at a food source. Yet they leave feeding sites even more quickly than "ordinary" *Drosophila* males to get to the defense of their territories. There they become belligerent; they are suitably equipped with sexually dimorphic structures (on wings, abdomen, antennae, forelegs, and the like) enabling them to posture aggressively and to repel intruding males or unreceptive females. Here they are anything but calm, cryptic, and tolerant of other individuals. The most vigorous or largest fly usually is the victor in all contests, and to him belong all the females attracted by his displays. These territorial *Drosophila* may then be said to contribute to the verification of Darwin's claim that "Sexual selection implies that the more attractive individuals are preferred by the opposite sex; and as with insects, when the sexes differ, it is the male which, with rare exception, is the most ornamental" (1871, Part II, Chapter XI). One only wishes to correct the Master by setting off the adjective "attractive" in either quotation marks or italics, so that it is not interpreted merely to mean beauty.

Acoustical Insects

A great part of *The Descent of Man and Selection in Relation to Sex* deals with organisms other than the human one; Darwin apparently found this necessary to explain and then defend his newly introduced theory of sexual selection. One chapter (the tenth of volume one) deals with the secondary sexual characteristics of insects. Darwin included the illustration below (Figure 6.5), showing the stridulatory apparatus of a male field cricket. It was accompanied by comments on the prodigious volume and duration of nocturnal cricket choruses, and the statement, "All observers agree that the sounds serve either to call or excite the mute females." (For one of the observers Darwin cites, see Bates 1863.) The correctness of Darwin's evaluation of, and emphasis upon, cricket stridulation as the acoustical basis of sexual selection in these animals has been confirmed by careful experiments based upon observations in the field.

Fulton (1933, 1937) has analyzed the chirping rates, i.e., the songs of two cricket subspecies, *Nemobius allardi* and *Nemobius tinnulus,* and of their hybrids. These are depicted in Figure 6.6, and described in item three below. These two subspecies have overlapping distributions, and it is in

Figure 6.3. A Drosophila grimshawi *male exhibiting lek display. Note the tip of the abdomen being dragged against the substrate (a leaf stem). This results in the depostion of a thin liquid film. The large pictured wings of the male enhance visual advertisement of his presence (from Spieth 1968).*

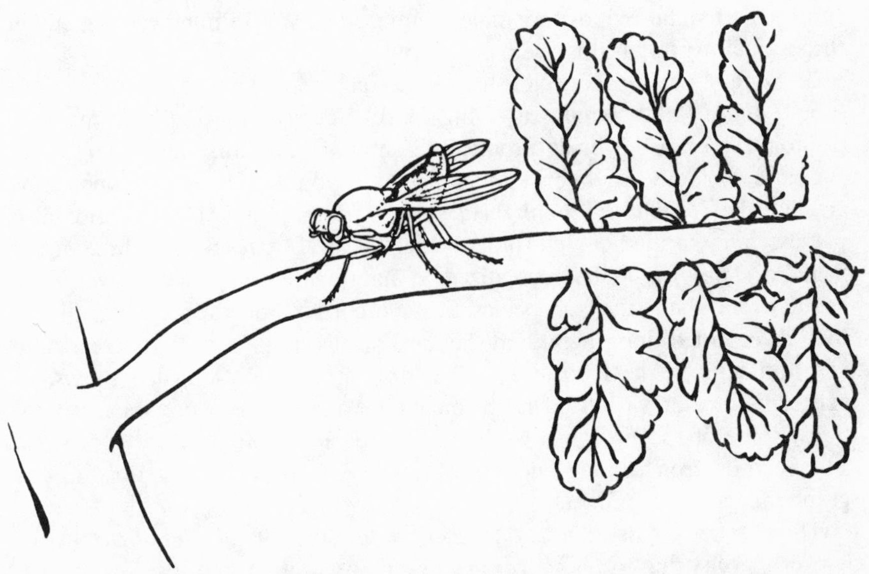

Figure 6.4. Drosophila comatifemora *male exhibiting lek display. Note the elevated tip of the abdomen. A bubble of fluid will be extruded and retracted repetitively from the anal papillae. This male is defending a limited area, his lek. Other suitable areas are single leaves, a fern pinna, a section of a fern stem, or part of a tree trunk in the Hawaiian rain forests (from Spieth 1968).*

their areas of sympatry that sexual selection for acoustical differentiation may be expected to be most intense. *Nemobius allardi* and *N. tinnulus* are compared as follows.

1. *Habitat. N. tinnulus* prefers open woodland, not dense forest, but will sometimes be located along forest borders or in shrubby areas, usually where there is a ground cover of fallen leaves. The type of open woodland preferred is developmental or subclimax, or occasionally, the edge of a climax forest. *N. allardi,* associated with grass, occurs in grass sod either in the open or under trees where enough sunlight has filtered through to permit grass to grow. This subspecies prefers either partial shade or constant moisture, and so is also found near streams. Both subspecies occur in the states of Ohio, Iowa, and North Carolina in North America. Both subspecies begin to mature in early August, and nymphs and adults may be collected in the late fall. The breeding season seems to continue as long as the weather permits.

2. *Color and Morphology. N. tinnulus* is brown with a reddish head. *N. allardi* varies in its coloration considerably, depending upon the locality; however, it is always darker than *N. tinnulus.* The color pattern of the nymphs of both subspecies are the same. These subspecies do differ slightly, however, in the shape of the male genitalia, the shape of the distal end of the female ovipositor, male tegmina, and in the number of teeth in the stridulatory apparatus (vein).

3. *Song.* "Each subspecies has a characteristic and easily recognized song. [*Allardi*] and *tinnulus* use single stroke chirps differing in frequency" (Fulton 1937). F_1 hybrids produce an intermediate chirping rate ("1" in Figure 6.6). Some F_1 hybrid songs are quite like the *N. allardi* one; none are like the *N. tinnulus* nonhybrid song. The majority of F_2 hybrids also possess an intermediate chirping rate ("•" in Figure 6.6). These intermediate songs would be recognized in nature, but they have never been heard even where the subspecies are sympatric. For this reason, all the hybrids reported upon here, and they are not many in number, were reared with difficulty in the laboratory. The F_2 hybrid generation also shows, as expected, greater variation in chirping rates than do the previous generations; some of the F_2 songs were consistently most rapid and others slow. The records from a few such individuals are connected by dots in the graph that is Figure 6.6.

The two backcross offspring to *N. tinnulus* sing like *N. tinnulus,* but the backcross offspring to *N. allardi* are like F_2 generation hybrids. The results are similar to what might be expected if there were two or more (most likely, more) gene determinants of song pattern in this material. Certainly the pattern of inheritance is not simple. There is no question of only one pair of alleles being involved nor of complete or even incomplete domi-

Figure 6.5. Gryllus campestris. *Right: the underside of part of the wing-nervure, much magnified, showing the teeth,* st. *Left: the upper surface of the wing-cover, with the projecting, smooth nervure,* r, *across which the teeth,* st, *are scraped (from Darwin 1871).*

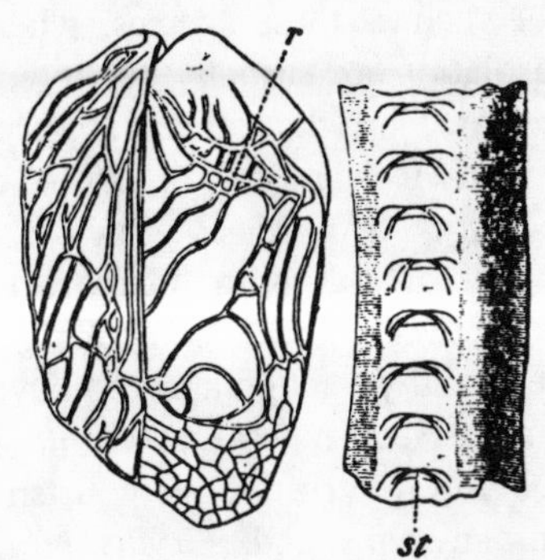

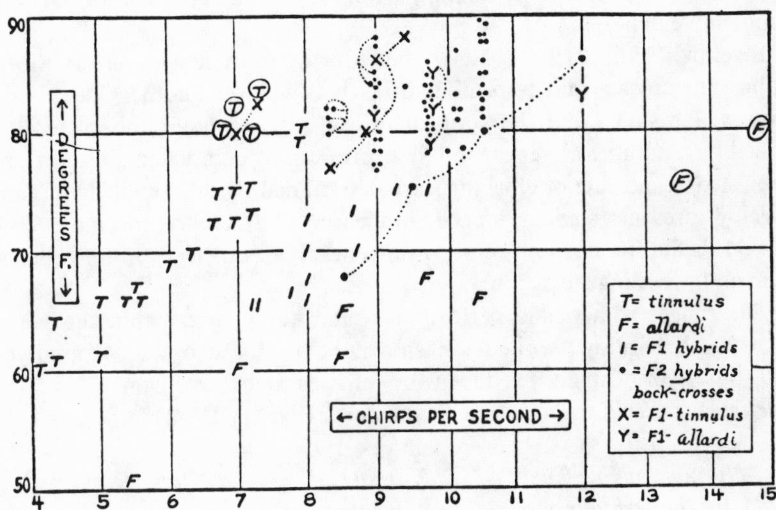

Figure 6.6. Chirping rates of Nemobius allardi *(F) and* N. tinnulus *(T) and their hybrids of the first (1) and second (dots) generation, and the progeny of back-crosses of the first generation hybrids with* allardi *(Y) and* tinnulus *(X). Records connected by dotted lines are from the same individual (from Fulton 1933).*

nance. The song of these two *Nemobius* species (Alexander & Thomas 1959) appears polygenic in its genetic architecture. This is often so with reproductive isolating barriers between Mendelian populations (Ehrman 1964) such as these species, where the polygenes fostering the reproductive isolation are usually scattered all over the genomes involved. All of these data, on the other hand, are unlike the single gene substitution Hörmann-Heck reports (1957) between *Gryllis campestris* and *Gryllis bimaculatus,* two species of field crickets. As a result of the production and testing of hybrids between these two species, she finds single gene differences between them controlling precourtship sounds (with no dominance), and postcopulatory behavior as well (complete dominance here). Hörmann-Heck notes that *Gryllis campestris* males raise their elytrae just once before the distinctive courtship song, and that this movement has no accompanying sound. *Gryllis bimaculatus* repeatedly raises its elytrae at the same point during the courtship sequence, and the movement is from a resting position to a stridulating one. The hybrids between these species behave in an intermediate manner. They produce but one sound. But here a *caveat:* Alexander (1968b, pp. 190–193) has been unable to verify Hörmann-Heck's data though he does validate Fulton's (on pp. 188–190 where he provides an interesting solution to the problem of *Nemobius* wing movement).

Bigelow (1960, 1964) has obtained results quite similar to those of Fulton, in crosses and tests of hybrids between yet another set of cricket species. He says "that the song of crickets is a complex character determined by a number of genes, and that certain song components (for example, wing stroke and rate of chirping) are determined by different sets of genes." Bigelow presents some evidence implicating the X chromosome (♀XX : ♂XO) as the site of some "chirp-rate genes," but this is, even now, no more than an interesting suspicion.

The ranges of acoustic performance and equipment within the material with which Bigelow worked are shown below for two sets of nonhybrids and the hybrid male produced by crosses between them (A = *Gryllis veletis;* B = *Gryllis rubens;* see Alexander & Bigelow 1960):

	Number of File Teeth on the Stridulatory Ridge	*Number of Wings Examined*	*Pulse Rate (Wing Stroke Rate) Per Second*
A	138 ± 10.0	21	24–29
AxB	118 ± 7.5	9	40–42
B	97 ± 8.3	36	60

This "A x B" hybrid produced 230–240 chirps per second like its A parent's 150–240 chirps per second range, and 5,000–6,500 tooth strikes on the file (stridulatory ridge) per minute. These song analyses were made from recordings by R. D. Alexander. He concludes as does Bigelow, that it is the wing stroke rate which is the single most important song characteristic in cricket species differentiation, and that this crucial pulse-setting factor is genetically controlled multifactorially, by polygenes.

Perdeck (1958) has studied the "isolating value," the specific distinctiveness of sounds making up the song patterns of two sibling grasshopper species, *Chorthippus brunneus* and *C. biguttulus*. Here, both males and females answer exclusively to the sounds of their conspecific partners, and certain aspects (note length and number of notes per phase) of the song pattern of hybrids between these species are intermediate to those of the parents. Other aspects (note rate) are not intermediate.

Crickets, katydids and grasshoppers lack acute vision as sexually mature individuals. They still manage to meet and to select between potential mates, and they accomplish this efficiently, acoustically. Acoustical variations, furthermore, within and between cricket species have in every case so far analyzed been shown to be the result of genetic differences. See Alexander (1968ab, and 1969) for comprehensive reviews of this point, as well as for a report of his as yet unpublished work with Shaw (but see Shaw 1966) on songs of the North American katydid genus *Pterophylla.* He has correctly noted (1967) that selective (sexual and/or natural) action on communicatory systems "ought to" maximize the effective range and directionality of signals, acoustical and otherwise. In accomplishing this, selection "ought to" minimize signal similarities between and maximize signal similarities within species repertoires, at least where the signals in question serve as part or all of a reproductive barrier.

The Genetics of Sexual Selection In Birds

"Those who have read Darwin's *Descent of Man* know what immense importance in the amelioration of the breed in birds this author ascribes to the mere fact of sexual selection. The sexual act is not performed until every condition of circumstance and sentiment is fulfilled until time, place, and partner are all fit." (James 1890).

But, two centuries before either Darwin or William James, William Harvey had written:

> Our common cock, whose pugnacious qualities are well known, as soon as he comes to his strength and is possessed of the faculty of engendering, is distinguished by his spurs, and ornamented with his comb and beautiful feathers, by which he charms his mates . . . and is furnished for the combat with other males, the subject of dispute being . . . the perpetuation of the stock in this line or in that; as if nature had intended that he who could best defend himself and his, could be preferred to others for the continuance of the kind (Harvey 1651).

Recently Lill & Wood-Gush (1965) have experimentally investigated assortative mating in the domestic chicken. Table 6.4 itemizes the patterns of display exhibited by courting males; it also documents differences in the

Table 6.4. Courtship of females of the three breeds by males of each breed (from Lill & Wood-Gush 1965).

Male group	*Total displays*	*Waltz*	*Wing flap*[3]	*Tidbit*[4]	*Feather ruffle*	*Head shake*	*Self-preen*	*Tail wag*	*Bill wipe*	*Corner-ing*	*Calls*	*High step*	*Rear approach*	*Strutt-ing*	
Brown Leghorn	1143	255	154	236	15	100	5	4	11	27[2]	374	—	6	5	To Brown Leghorn ♀♀
White Leghorn	184	14	15	32	10	36	5	—	4	—	68	—	—	—[1]	
Broiler Strain	1175	113	226	232	27	85	8	—	—	—[1]	502	—	—	—[1]	
Brown Leghorn	549	27	91	172	20	195	10	6	34	—	37	3	—	8	To White Leghorn ♀♀
White Leghorn	1623	296	113	583	73	110	12	1	21	1	561	2	—	—[1]	
Broiler Strain	1292	81	403	367	38	114	22	—	—	—[1]	266	2	—	—[1]	
Brown Leghorn	956	270	82	208	9	96	16	6	15	16	229	4	—	5	To Broiler ♀♀
White Leghorn	49	4	—	1	1	3	4	—	—	—	36	—	—	—[1]	
Broiler Strain	1287	144	174	314	21	81	8	—	—	—[1]	605	1	—	—[1]	

[1]These displays have *never* been observed in present material of these strains.
[2]Performed mostly by one male.
[3]There is also a sound component in wing flapping.
[4]Tidbitting may vary in duration and in intensity; the male pecks at litter or feathers, scrapes his feet and calls.

frequencies of these patterns as shown by two long-inbred commercial breeds, White Leghorn and Brown Leghorn, and a Broiler Strain. A brief characterization of these three types of birds would be: Brown Leghorn: colored black on the underside of its body and on its tail, a mosaic of brown colors above; White Leghorn: pure white plumage, slightly smaller in size than Brown Leghorns and "chunkier." White Leghorns produce calls at a higher pitch than do Brown ones. Broilers are multicolored and variable, with no two birds alike in coloration, but all Broilers are taller and heavier than both kinds of Leghorns. Broiler calls are deeper in pitch than those of Leghorns, too. With regard to the females, hens accept males by crouching to receive them. This deep crouch is sometimes referred to as "solicitation." In the courtship of the Brown Leghorn cock, for instance, the "waltz" and "rear approach" (see Table 6.4) were the two key displays which evoked the characteristic female solicitation response (See Figure 6.7). Three other displays: calling, wing-flapping, and high intensity tid-bitting (again in Table 6.4), appear to enhance the sexual arousal of courted hens. From this and other data such as that in Table 6.5 and its accompanying Figure 6.8, derived from phenotype modification experiments, these authors conclude that females discriminate between would-be mates primarily by means of comparative male appearance rather than quantitative differences in the courtship displays of these males themselves. Males, too, use primarily visual cues, especially that provided by female plumage color (Lill 1968ab). Plumage color and bodily outline

Figure 6.7. A Brown Leghorn cock avoids the cue White Leghorn hen and "waltzes" to the caged Brown Leghorn hen (from Lill & Wood-Gush 1965).

Table 6.5. Effects of plumage color and contour alteration of Brown Leghorn line males on solicitation behavior of homogamic females (from Lill 1968b).

Test no.	Modification of males	Area modified	*Percentage fluctuation in ♀♀ solicitation pre- and post-modification* To control ♂♂	To modified ♂♂
a	color: white feathers added to give mottled effect	whole plumage	54.5 increase	38.0* decrease
b	color: green feathers added to give mottled effect	hackles	17.8 increase	0.0 unchanged
c	color/contour: blue feathers added, rachis outward	hackles and crest	38.8 decrease	28.3 decrease
d	color/contour: blue feathers added, rachis outward	breast, back, saddle, hackles	12.5 increase	18.4 decrease
e	color: black dye applied	wings, back, upper saddle	0.0 unchanged	42.3† decrease
f	color: white feathers added to give mottled effect	breast, abdomen	75.0 increase	23.5† decrease

*5% levels of significant difference in solicitation behavior of hens to modified males (chi-square test).
†1% level of significance.

(contour) is dimorphic with regard to sex in these birds. Males reared with their own breed of females only, or in total isolation, court them significantly more frequently than they court alien females. Males reared with their own and other breeds of females exhibit this homogamic mating preference only weakly or not at all. In this instance, sexual selection could be invoked to explain the evolution of intraspecific, and even intrastrain, recognition cues and signals. Such prompt and efficient recognition facilitates "proper" matings and avoids or diminishes the number of "improper"

Figure 6.8. A Brown Leghorn cock with white feathers attached to alter neck color and contour (as in test c of Table 6.5) (from Lill 1968b).

ones. An "improper" mating may be defined as one producing relatively or actually inviable and/or sterile offspring, or no offspring at all.

Nonrandom mating was also recorded by these authors within a single inbred line (and by Lill 1966, in Burmese Red Jungle fowl). Some males, not females, are preferred over others of their own line. (No females appear to be preferred in this way. Apparently, all closely related females are equally suitable to the roosters.) Brown and White Leghorn females each prefer males of their own breed, but some Broiler Strain females preferred Brown Leghorn males. This heterogamic preference, the only one recorded in these studies, is interestingly enough directed in favor of those males bearing a close phenotypic (visual), resemblance to one of the generally assumed wild types, the Burmese Red Jungle fowl, *Gallus gallus spadiceus*. Even rearing these Broiler Strain females exclusively with their own breed of males did not produce homogamy in mating. Lill and Wood-Gush therefore suggest, "The possibility of a truly innate preference for 'wild type' cannot be entirely disregarded at this stage."

The results presented above, besides providing an example of the major role vision may play in sexual selection, in some species, indicate that genetic divergence of a minor sort, that is in relatively few characters, may suffice to effect a degree of assortative mating (Lill 1966). Though Darwin was surely correct in noting that "A hornless stag or spurless cock would have a poor chance of leaving numerous offspring" (1859), we may profitably inquire how this poor reproductive performance would be brought

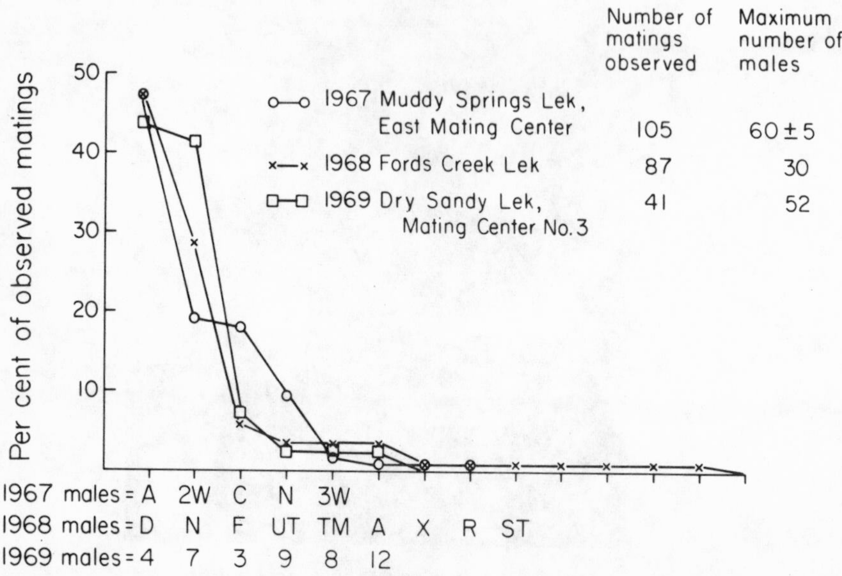

Figure 6.9. Distribution of matings among male Sage Grouse at three mating centers.

about. Would it be (1) via the loss of a battle by the handicapped male to a normal one (see Lill 1968c); or (2), according to the data of Lill & Wood-Gush (1965), because females perceive the altered male phenotype and reject it? They then select for and solicit only the normal males approaching them. In either case, however, each sex will be sexually selecting for the "best," the most nearly perfect available in the alternate sex, and in this way for the best in their joint progeny.

More recently, additional proof of the existence of sexual selection in birds has been provided by Wiley's excellent study (1970) of the sage grouse, *Centrocercus urophasianus.* Figure 6.9, compiled from his observations at three different leks on the prairie of western North America, demonstrates that seven per cent of the males present may perform eighty-five per cent or more of the matings. He points out that successful males in this instance are likely to be the older males and that most sage grouse males never manage to copulate at all.

Sexual Selection In Man

> We can base no conclusion about man on the habits of fighting cocks . . . we must not conclude from the combats of such animals for the enjoyment of the females that the case would be the same with mankind.
>
> —Rousseau, *A Discourse on the Origin of Inequality,* 1762

There is little reliable information on the genetic aspects of sexual selection in the human species. For this reason Maynard Smith's (1958) imaginary example of how sexual selection might operate in man will have to suffice. Imagine a society in which women prefer redheaded husbands, and assume that this preference is genetically determined. (Red hair is inherited. A redhaired individual is apparently either homo- or heterozygous for "red" genes supplemented by "blond" or "brown" ones. The effects of genes for red hair are masked by genes for very dark hair [Scheinfeld 1965].) Redhaired men will therefore have their choice in the selection of mates and are likely to marry early. Whether or not our imaginary society is monogamous or polygamous is the next question to be considered. These alternatives have very different effects on the outcome of sexual selection. Redheaded men, and genes for red hair, will increase in frequency only assuming that:

Strictly Monogamous Society	*Not Strictly Monogamous Society*
1) Earlier marriages result in the production of more offspring.	
2) The fertility of redheaded men is greater than that of nonredheaded men, or 3) Redheaded men pick more fertile	2) Redheaded men will have ample opportunity to marry more than once, and multiple marriages, even sequential ones, may produce more offspring than just a single marriage.

wives than do nonredheaded men who must choose from "leftovers,"

or

4) Women who marry redheaded men raise more offspring than women who do not marry redheads.

However, 2), 3), and 4) are not sexual selection but natural selection.

3) Redheaded men are more likely to engage in the production of illegitimate children than are nonredheaded men because the former are preferred by women. The sum of legitimate and illegitimate offspring is likely to be greater than the number of legitimate offspring alone.

Conclusion: Sexual selection exerts whatever effect it has genetically with greater magnitude within polygamous mating systems.

Parsons (1967) has discussed assortative mating in man. Assortative mating is the tendency for certain kinds of males and females to pair; it is nonrandom mating. Parsons points out that assortative mating can be demonstrated for stature and other physical traits (Pearson & Lee 1903), for intelligence, for psychological traits, (for example, neurotic tendencies and dominance), and even for musical ability (Spuhler 1962, Beckman 1962). Hatt & Parsons (1965) record nonrandom mating in an Australian city populated by different ethnic groups brought together by migration. Matings occur generally more often between individuals both carrying surnames of English, or Irish, or Scottish origin than do marriages between adults bearing surnames from two of these ethnic groups (see Table 6.6). More confusion, Parson cautions, may lie in possible imprinting, in the choice of one's spouse based upon traits of one's relatives, especially one's parents. See Schutz (1963, 1965) for experimental evidence about sexual imprinting in birds.

Psychological isolation, wherein there exists primarily psychological rather than physical barriers to mating, is also likely to be operative in human populations. For example, adults of quite different heights or intelligences or cultural values are less likely to be attracted to one another than to individuals sharing these same qualities or traits. Because of its genetic consequences, a sociological aspect of sexual selection should also be con-

Table 6.6. Frequencies of the six possible marriage classes from English (E), Scottish (S) and Irish (I) surnames with expectations based on random mating (from Hatt and Parsons 1965).

Marriage class	*Observed frequencies*	*Probability assuming random mating*	*Expected frequencies*	*Expected / Observed*
E × E	141	p^2	138.785	0.984
E × S	148	2pq	151.354	1.023
E × I	100	2pr.	101.077	1.011
S × S	50	q^2	41.265	0.825
S × I	41	2qr	55.116	1.344
I × I	26	r^2	18.404	0.708

sidered. One specific example is Galton's family histories of British peerages. He investigated the generally acknowledged fact that the families of great men tend to die out much more frequently than do individual families of the English population in general (1869). Galton noted that a considerable proportion of newly created English peers married heiresses. These wealthy women necessarily came from families producing few offspring themselves; many offspring result in more subdivisions of family wealth with end portions allowing none of the female offspring to be termed heiresses. Then their desirability as mates for ambitious new peers seemed to diminish proportionately.

Heiresses marrying peers in turn perform reproductively (that is, probably manage their use of birth control devices) as did their mothers before them. Fisher (1930) cites Pearson's (1899) table detailing the comparative number of children born to mothers and to daughters associated with the British peerage:

Number of children born to mother	*Number of cases*	*Total number of children born to daughters*	*Average children per daughter*
1	35	104	2.97
2	67	237	3.54
3	111	249	3.14
4	136	464	3.41
5	138	550	3.99
6	132	513	3.89
7	114	448	3.93
8	87	354	4.07
9	74	313	4.23
10	50	219	4.38
11	24	122	5.08
12	19 }	99 }	5.21 }
13	9 } 32	77 } 206	8.56 } 6.44
14	1 }	10 }	10.00 }
15	3 }	20 }	6.67 }

There is clearly a positive correlation between the number of children born to the daughters with the number of children born to their mothers. An increase of one child in the mother's brood is correlated with an increase of slightly more than two-tenths of a child in her daughter's. In this instance therefore, sexual selection has the result of coupling comparative infertility with high ability and achievement.

For more recent data on sexual selection in the human species and especially on assortative mating with respect to educational attainment and physical characteristics note the proceedings of The Fourth Princeton Conference, 1967, on Population Genetics and Demography. In this conference report Spuhler (1968) provides an extensive list of references on assortative mating with respect to physical characteristics as numerous and diverse as age, head circumference, and ear lobe length, for example. Kiser (1968) finds that, for both Caucasians and nonCaucasians, assortative mating, as it is currently practiced, tends to favor the fertility of those of lowest educational attainment. (Also see Reed 1965.)

Table 6.7, taken in part from Kiser (1968), contains data on assortative mating for educational attainment and its relation to subsequent fertility in marriages where the wife has already presumably reached the post-reproductive, menopausal stage of her life, aged 45–54. The two highest values for reproductive performance are for women with less than a total of eight years of schooling (3,231 offspring counted; 28.9 per cent more than expected, row 7) and for men with less than a total of eight years of schooling (3,046 offspring counted; 30.1 per cent more than expected, row 14, and last one.)

Finally, patterns of marriage participated in by handicapped people, if they wed at all, warrant attention. Most of us have vague general impressions that handicapped individuals marry other handicapped people. Sank (1963) has found that "the practice of assortative mating, i.e., the tendency of the deaf to marry the deaf is a striking feature of the social habits of the deaf." She presents data on 201 deaf x deaf marriages and the 491 resulting offspring, in her sample from the population of New York State; these are marriages between people who were deaf before their marriage took place:

Number Deaf × Deaf Marriages	*Hearing Offspring*	*Deaf Offspring*
147	294	—
40	106	57
14	—	34

Sank and Kallman estimated that in this population, some fifty per cent of all early total deafness is genetically determined, while the remaining fifty per cent is of essentially environmental origin. Rainer & Firschein (1959), who surveyed mating and fertility patterns in families with early total deafness, point out that although deafness is a severe defect, it need not interfere with survival to adulthood, marriage, and the production of children. They note that when a deaf adult has had two deaf parents, his or her rate of marriage is higher than that of a deaf adult with no deaf parents. With both parents deaf, the marriage rates are 83.3 per cent or 94.7 per cent depending upon the sex of the afflicted individual; with hearing parents equivalent values are 65.9 and 74.4 per cent respectively. "If this difference continues to prove significant, the trend may have negative selective value." Evidence that this trend is indeed a continuing one is pro-

Table 6.7. Estimate of impact of assortative mating by education on fertility rates in the white population of the United States by education of wife or husband, and by age of wife (after Kiser 1968).

	Wives 45–54			
			Observed Differs from Expected	
Education, and Spouse (Considered)	*Expected Fertility Rate*	*Observed Fertility Rate*	*Absolute*	*%*
Wife	.....	.....	.....	+10.7†
College				
4+	1,634	1,745	+111	+ 6.8
1–3	1,919	1,919	0	0
High school				
1–3	1,941	1,971	+ 30	+ 1.5
4	2,104	2,310	+206	+ 9.8
Elementary				
8	2,241	2,598	+357	+15.9
under 8	2,507	3,231	+724	+28.9
Husband	.....	.....	.....	+13.8†
College				
4+	1,921	1,915	− 6	− 0.3
1–3	1,905	1,900	− 5	− 0.3
High school				
4	1,953	1,952	− 1	0
1–3	1,795	2,184	+389	+21.7
Elementary				
8	2,207	2,497	+290	+13.1
under 8	2,342	3,046	+704	+30.1

vided by Fay's three-fourths of a century old (1898) observations on deaf American subjects. "Most of the statistics that have hitherto been published have indicated a tendency on the part of deaf people to marry one another rather than hearing persons. This tendency appears markedly in the marriages reported in the present collection of records, as is shown by the following table" (which gives the number and percentage of the marriages in which both partners were deaf, and the same information about unions in which one partner was deaf and the other hearing; see Table 6.8).

Table 6.8. Marriages of the deaf

	Number	*Percentage*
Both partners deaf	3,242	72.512
One partner deaf; the other hearing	894	19.995
One partner deaf; the other unreported whether deaf or hearing	335	7.493
Total	4,471	100.000

From Fay, 1898.

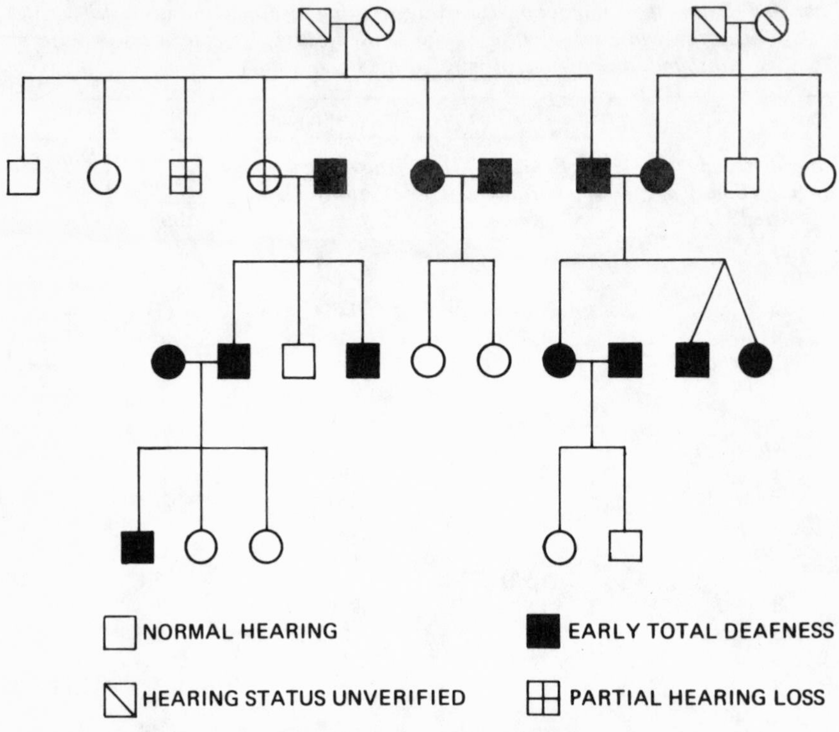

Figure 6.10. Family pedigree.

Furthermore, when Altshuler (1963) considered the *preferred* hearing status for the mates of deaf people, he finds that the vast majority, 86 per cent out of his sample of 453 persons, preferred a deaf spouse. Among deaf women, expressions of preferences for hearing spouses, occurred mainly among the least educated (incomplete grade school education, for instance.) It would seem that, in the case of deaf women, education helps to reconcile their spouse preference with existing possibilities. Among deaf men, however, the reverse is apparently so; fifty per cent of the deaf men who have completed higher education express a desire for a hearing wife. Altshuler notes that apart from speech being more likely to be practiced in this particular instance, "a hearing wife can be an asset to individual achievement by fostering identity and relationship with the hearing world."

We will conclude with an interesting pedigree (Figure 6.10) provided by Sank (1963) of a single family in which at least four nonconsanguineous deaf x deaf marriages have taken place plus one deaf x partially deaf union. (Two additional marriages in this family were between people of unverified hearing status.)

It is probably wisest to let Darwin (1871) summarize both this section and this chapter:

The reader who has taken the trouble to go through the several chapters devoted to sexual selection, will be able to judge how far the conclusions at which I have arrived are supported by sufficient evidence. If he accepts these conclusions, he may, I think, safely extend them to mankind.

Man scans with scrupulous care the character and pedigree of his horses, cattle, and dogs before he matches them; but when he comes to his own marriage he rarely, or never, takes any such care. He is impelled by nearly the same motives as are the lower animals when left to their own free choice, though he is in so far superior to them that he highly values mental charms and virtues. On the other hand he is strongly attracted by mere wealth or rank. Yet he might by selection do something not only for the bodily constitution and frame of his offspring, but for their intellectual and moral qualities. Both sexes ought to refrain from marriage if in any marked degree inferior in body or mind; but such hopes are Utopian and will never be even partially realised until the laws of inheritance are thoroughly known (pp. 402–403).

References

Alexander, R. D. 1967. Acoustical communication in arthropods. *Annual Review of Entomology* 12: 495–526.

————. 1968a. Life cycle origins, speciation, and related phenonema in crickets. *Quarterly Review of Biology* 43: 1–41.

————. 1968b. Arthropods. In *Animal Communication,* ed. T. A. Sebeok. Bloomington: Indiana University Press.

————. 1969. Comparative animal behavior and systematics. In *Systematic Zoology*. Washington, D. C.: National Academy of Sciences.

Alexander, R. D., & R. S. Bigelow. 1960. Allochronic speciation in field crickets, and a new species, *Acheta veletis. Evolution* 14: 334–346.

Alexander, R. D., & E. S. Thomas. 1959. Systematic and behavioral studies on the crickets of the *Nemobius fasciatus* group (Orthoptera: Cryllidae: Nemobiinae.) *Annals of the Entomological Society of America* 52: 591–605.

Altshuler, K. 1963. Sexual patterns and family relationships. In *Family and Mental Health Problems in a Deaf Population,* ed. J. D. Rainer, K. Z. Altshuler, & F. J. Kallmann, pp. 92–112. Dept. of Medical Genetics, New York State Psychiatric Institute, Columbia University.

Bateman, A. J. 1948. Intra-sexual selection in Drosophila. *Heredity* 2: 349–368.

Bates, H. W. 1863. *The Naturalist on the River Amazon.* London: John Murray.

Beckman, L. 1962. Assortative mating in man. *Eugenics Rev.* 54: 63–67.

Bigelow, R. S. 1960. Interspecific hybrids and speciation in the genus *Acheta* (*Orthoptera: Gryllidae*). *Canadian J. Zool.* 38: 509–524.

————. 1964. Song differences in closely related cricket species and their significance. *Australian J. of Science* 27: 99–102.

Bösiger, E. 1957. Sur l'activité sexuelle des mâles de plusieurs souches de *Drosophila melanogaster. C. R. Acad. Sc. Paris* 244: 1419–1422.

————. 1958. Influence de l'hétérosis sur la vigueur des mâles de *Drosophila melanogaster. C. R. Acad. Sc. Paris* 246: 489–491.

————. 1962. Sur le degré d'hétérozygotie des populations naturelles de *Drosophila melanogaster* et son maintien par la sélection sexuelle. *Bull. Biol. France et Belgique* 96: 3–122.

———. 1963a. On the evolutionary significance of heterozygosity in Drosophila populations. *Genetics Today, XI International Congress of Genetics* I: 157.

———. 1963b. Comparison du nombre de descendants engendrés par des mâles homozygotes et des mâles hétérozygotes de *Drosophila melanogaster. C. R. Acad. Sc. Paris* 257: 531–533.

———. 1965. L'influence du degré d'hétérozygotie sur la fertilité chez *Drosophila melanogaster. Atti dell V° Congress Internationale per la Riproduzione Animal e la Fecondazione Artificiale* 7: 349–351.

———. 1967. La signification évolutive de la sélection sexuelle chez les animaux. *Scientia* 102: 207–223.

Darwin, C. 1859. *The origin of species by means of natural selection.* London: John Murray.

———. 1871. *Descent of man and selection in relation to sex.* London: John Murray.

Dobzhansky, T. 1970. *The Genetics of the Evolutionary Process.* New York: Columbia University Press.

Ehrman, L. 1964. Courtship and mating behavior as a reproductive isolating mechanism in Drosophila. *American Zoologist* 4: 147–153.

———. 1966. Mating success and genotype frequency in *Drosophila. Animal Behaviour* 14: 332–339.

———. 1967. Further studies on genotype frequency and mating success in *Drosophila. American Naturalist* 101: 415–424.

———. 1968a. Frequency dependence of mating success in *Drosophila pseudoobscura. Genetic Research,* Cambridge 11: 135–140.

———. 1968b. Reproductive isolation in *Drosophilia.* In *Animal Behavior in Laboratory and Field,* ed. Allen W. Stokes, pp. 85–87. San Francisco: W. Freeman Co.

———. 1969. The sensory basis of mate selection in *Drosophila. Evolution,* 23: 59–64.

———. 1970a. A release experiment testing the mating advantage of rare Drosophila males. *Behavioral Science* 15: 363–365.

———. 1970b. Simulation of the mating advantage of rare Drosophila males. *Science* 167: 905–906.

Ehrman, L., & C. Petit. 1968. Genotype frequency and mating success in the *willistoni* species group of *Drosophila. Evolution* 22: 649–658.

Ehrman, L., B. Spassky, D. Pavlovsky, & T. Dobzhansky. 1965. Sexual selection, geotaxis, and chromosomal polymorphism in experimental populations of *Drosophila pseudoobscura. Evolution* 19: 337–346.

Ehrman, L. & M. Strickberger. 1960. Flies mating: a pictorial record. *Natural History* 69: 28–33.

Fay, E. A. 1898. *Marriages of the Deaf in America.* Washington, D. C.: Volta Bureau, Gibson Bros.

Fisher, R. A. 1930. *The Genetical Theory of Natural Selection.* Oxford: Clarendon Press.

Fraser, A. J. & D. Burnell. 1967. Simulation of genetic systems. XII. Models of inversion polymorphism. *Genetics* 57: 267–282.

Fulton, B. B. 1933. Inheritance of song in hybrids of two subspecies of *Nemobius fasciatus* (*Orthoptera*). *Annals Entomological Society of America* 26: 368–376.

———. 1937. Experimental crossing of subspecies in *Nemobius. Annals Entomological Society of America* 30: 201–206.

Galton, F. 1869. *Hereditary Genius*. London: Macmillan.

Harvey, William. 1651. *Anatomical Exercises on the Generation of Animals*. In *Great Books of the Western World*. Volume 28. Chicago: Encyclopaedia Britannica, Inc., 1952.

Hatt, D. & P. A. Parsons. 1965. Association between surnames and blood groups in the Australian population. *Acta Genetica* 15: 309–318.

Hörmann-Heck, S. von. 1957. Untersuchungen über den Erbgang emiger Verhaltensweisen bei Grillenbastarden (*Gryllus campestris* L. x *Gryllus bimaculatus* De Geer). *Zeitschr. Tierpsychol.* 14: 137–183.

Huxley, J. S. 1942. *Evolution, the Modern Synthesis*. New York: Harper.

James, W. 1890. *The Principles of Psychology*. In *Great Books of the Western World*. Volume 53. Chicago: Encyclopaedia Britannica, Inc., 1952.

King, R. C. 1968. *A Dictionary of Genetics*. London: Oxford University Press.

Kirk, D. 1966. Demographic factors affecting the opportunity for natural selection in the United States. *Eugenics Quarterly* 13: 270–273.

Kiser, C. V. 1968. Assortative mating by educational attainment in relation to fertility. *Eugenics Quarterly* 15: 98–112.

Kojima, K. & Y. Tobari. 1969. The pattern of viability changes associated with genotype frequency at the alcohol dehydrogenase locus in a population of *Drosophila melanogaster*. *Genetics* 61: 201–209.

Kojima, K. & K. Yarbrough. 1967. Frequency dependent selection at the Esterase 6 locus in *Drosophila melanogaster*. *Proc. Natl. Acad. Sc. U.S.A.* 57:645–649.

Lill, A. 1966. Some observations of social organization and non-random mating in captive Burmese Red Jungle fowl (*Gallus gallus spadiceus*). *Behaviour* 26: 228–242.

————. 1968a. An analysis of sexual isolation in the domestic fowl: I. The basis of homogamy in males. *Behaviour* 30: 8–126.

————. 1968b. An analysis of sexual isolation in the domestic fowl: II. The basis of homogamy in females. *Behaviour* 30: 127–145.

————. 1968c. Some observations on the isolating potential of aggressive behaviour in the domestic fowl. *Behaviour* 31: 127–143.

Lill, A., & D. G. M. Wood-Gush. 1965. Potential ethological isolating mechanisms and assortative mating in the domestic fowl. *Behaviour* 25: 16–44.

Lutz, F. E. 1911. Experiments with *Drosophila ampelophila* concerning evolution. *Carnegie Inst.: Wash. Publ.* 143: 1–60.

Maynard Smith, J. 1956. Fertility, mating behavior, and sexual selection in *Drosophila subobscura*. *J. Genet.* 54: 261–279.

————. 1958. *Sexual selection:* In *A Century of Darwin,* ed. S. A. Barnett, pp. 231–244. London: Heinemann.

Merrell, D. 1949. Selective mating in *Drosophila melanogaster*. *Genetics* 34: 370–389.

————. 1950. Measurement of sexual isolation and selective mating. *Evolution* 4: 326–331.

————. 1953. Selective mating as a cause of gene frequency changes in laboratory populations of *Drosophila melanogaster*. *Evolution* 7: 287–296.

Parsons, P. A. 1967. *Genetic Analysis of Behaviour*. Methuen Monograph. Suffolk: Chaucer Press.

Pearson, K. 1899. Mathematical studies in evolution; VI. Genetic reproductive) selection. *Phil. Trans. Roy. Soc. A* 192: 257.

Pearson, K. & A. Lee. 1903. On the laws of inheritance in man. I. Inheritance of physical characters. *Biometrika* 2: 357–462.

Perdeck, A. C. 1958. The isolating value of specific song patterns in two sibling species of grasshoppers. (*Chorthippus brunneus* Thunb. and *C. biguttulus* L.) *Behaviour* 12: 1–75.

Petit, C. 1954. L'isolement sexual chez *Drosophila melanogaster*. Etude du mutant *white* et de son allélomorphe *sauvage*. *Biol. Bull. France et Belgique* 88: 435–443.

———. 1958. Le déterminisme génétique et psychophysiologique de la compétition sexuelle chez *Drosophila melanogaster*. *Bull. Biol. France et Belgique* 92: 248–329.

Petit, C. & Lee Ehrman. 1969. Sexual selection in Drosophila. In *Evolutionary Biology,* ed. Dobzhansky, M. Hecht, & Wm. Steere, III, pp. 177–223. New York: Appleton-Century-Crofts.

Rainer, J. D. & I. L. Firschein. 1959. Mating and fertility patterns in families with early total deafness. *Eugenics Quarterly* 6: 117–127.

Reed, S. C. 1965. The evolution of human intelligence. *American Scientist* 53: 317–326.

Reed, S. C. & E. W. Reed. 1950. Natural selection in laboratory populations of *Drosophila.* II. Competition between a white eye gene and its white allele. *Evolution* 4: 34–42.

Rendel, J. M. 1945. Genetics and cytology of *Drosophila subobscura.* II. Normal and selective matings in *Drosophila subobscura. J. Genet.* 46: 287–302.

Rousseau, J. J. 1762. A discourse on the origin of inequality. In *Great Books of the Western World.* Vol. 38, p. 346. Chicago: Encyclopaedia Britannica, Inc. 1952.

Sank, D. 1963. Genetic aspects of early total deafness. In *Family and Mental Health Problems in a Deaf Population,* ed. J. D. Rainer, K. Z. Altshuler, F. J. Kallmann. New York State Psychiatric Institute, Columbia University.

Sank, D. & F. J. Kallmann. 1963. The role of heredity in early total deafness. *Volta Review* (November) 65: 461–470.

Scheinfeld, A. 1965. *Your Heredity and Environment.* Philadelphia: J. B. Lippincott.

Schutz, F. 1963. Objektfixierung geschlechtlicher Reaktionen bei Anatiden und Hühnern. *Natürwissenschaften* 19: 624–625.

———. 1965. Sexuelle Prägung bei Anatiden. *Zeitsch. Tierpsychol.* 22: 50–103.

Shaw, K. C. 1966. An analysis of the phonoresponse of males of the true katydid, *Pterophylla camellifolia* (Fabricus) (*Orthoptera: Tettigoniidae*). *Behaviour* 31: 203–260.

Spiess, E. 1968. Low frequency advantage in mating of *Drosophila pseudoobscura* karyotypes. *American Naturalist* 102: 363–379.

Spieth, H. T. 1968. Evolutionary implications of sexual behavior in *Drosophila. Evolutionary Biology* 2: 157–193.

Spuhler, J. N. 1962. Empirical studies on quantitative human genetics. *U.N./W.H.O. Seminar on The Use of Vital and Health Statistics for Genetic and Radiation Studies* pp. 241–252. 1960 Geneva: World Health Organization.

———. 1968. Assortative mating with respect to physical characteristics. *Eugenics Quarterly* 15: 128–140.

Sturtevant, A. H. 1915. Experiments on sex recognition and the problem of sexual selection. *Journal of Animal Behavior* 5: 351–366. (In *Selected Papers of A. H. Sturtevant: Genetics and Evolution,* ed. E. B. Lewis. San Francisco, W. H. Freeman Co., 1961.)

Swift, J. 1726. *Gulliver's Travels*. In *Great Books of the Western World*. vol. 36. Chicago: Encylopaedia Britannica, Inc., 1952.

Tan, C. C. 1946. Genetics of sexual isolation between *Drosophila pseudoobscura* and *Drosophila persimilis*. *Genetics* 31: 558–573.

Tobari, Y. & K. Kojima. 1967. Selective modes associated with inversion karotypes in *Drosophila ananassae*. I. Frequency-dependent selection. *Genetics* 57: 179–188.

Wiley, R. H. 1970. *Teritoriality and non-random mating in Sage Grouse Centrocercus urophasianus*. Ph. D. dissertation, New York, The Rockefeller University.

Williams, G. C. 1966. *Adaptation and Natural Selection*. Princeton: Princeton University Press.

7

ROBERT L. TRIVERS
HARVARD UNIVERSITY

Parental Investment and Sexual Selection

Introduction

Charles Darwin's (1871) treatment of the topic of sexual selection was sometimes confused because he lacked a general framework within which to relate the variables he perceived to be important: sex-linked inheritance, sex ratio at conception, differential mortality, parental care, and the form of the breeding system (monogamy, polygyny, polyandry, or promiscuity). This confusion permitted others to attempt to show that Darwin's terminology was imprecise, that he misinterpreted the function of some structures, and that the influence of sexual selection was greatly overrated. Huxley (1938), for example, dismisses the importance of female choice without evidence or theoretical argument, and he doubts the prevalence of adaptations in males that decrease their chances of surviving but are selected because they lead to high reproductive success. Some important advances, however, have been achieved since Darwin's work. The genetics of sex has now been clarified, and Fisher (1958) has produced a model to explain sex ratios at conception, a model recently extended to include special mechanisms that operate under inbreeding (Hamilton 1967). Data from the laboratory and the field have confirmed that females are capable of very subtle choices (for example, Petit & Ehrman 1969), and Bateman (1948) has suggested a general basis for female choice and male-male competition, and he has produced precise data on one species to support his argument.

I thank E. Mayr for providing me at an early date with the key reference. I thank J. Cohen, I. DeVore, W. H. Drury, M. Gadgil, W. D. Hamilton, J. Roughgarden, and T. Schoener for comment and discussion. I thank M. Sutherland (Harvard Statistics Department) for statistical work on my *A. garmani* data, H. Hare for help with references, and V. Hogan for expert typing of drafts of the paper. I thank especially E. E. Williams for comment, discussion and unfailing support throughout. The work was completed under a National Science Foundation predoctoral fellowship and partly supported by NSF Grant B019801 to E. E. Williams.

This paper presents a general framework within which to consider sexual selection. In it I attempt to define and interrelate the key variables. No attempt is made to review the large, scattered literature relevant to sexual selection. Instead, arguments are presented on how one might *expect* natural selection to act on the sexes, and some data are presented to support these arguments.

Variance in Reproductive Success

Darwin defined sexual selection as (1) competition within one sex for members of the opposite sex and (2) differential choice by members of one sex for members of the opposite sex, and he pointed out that this usually meant males competing with each other for females and females choosing some males rather than others. To study these phenomena one needs accurate data on differential reproductive success analysed by sex. Accurate data on female reproductive success are available for many species, but similar data on males are very difficult to gather, even in those species that tend toward monogamy. The human species illustrates this point. In any society it is relatively easy to assign accurately the children to their biological mothers, but an element of uncertainty attaches to the assignment of children to their biological fathers. For example, Henry Harpending (personal communication) has gathered biochemical data on the Kalahari Bushmen showing that about two per cent of the children in that society do not belong to the father to whom they are commonly attributed. Data on the human species are, of course, much more detailed than similar data on other species.

To gather precise data on both sexes Bateman (1948) studied a single species, *Drosophila melanogaster,* under laboratory conditions. By using a chromosomally marked individual in competition with individuals bearing different markers, and by searching for the markers in the offspring, he was able to measure the reproductive success of each individual, whether female or male. His method consisted of introducing five adult males to five adult female virgins, so that each female had a choice of five males and each male competed with four other males.

Data from numerous competition experiments with *Drosophila* revealed three important sexual differences: (1) Male reproductive success varied much more widely than female reproductive success. Only four per cent of the females failed to produce any surviving offspring, while 21 per cent of the males so failed. Some males, on the other hand, were phenomenally successful, producing nearly three times as many offspring as the most successful female. (2) Female reproductive success did not appear to be limited by ability to attract males. The four per cent who failed to copulate were apparently courted as vigorously as those who did copulate. On the other hand, male reproductive success was severely limited by ability to attract or arouse females. The 21 per cent who failed to reproduce showed no disinterest in trying to copulate, only an inability to be accepted. (3) A female's reproductive success did not increase much, if any, after the first copulation and not at all after the second; most females were uninterested in copulating more than once or twice. As shown by genetic markers in the offspring, males showed an almost linear increase in reproductive success with increased copulations. (A corollary of this finding is that males tended not to mate with the same female twice.) Although these results were obtained in the laboratory, they may apply with even greater force to the wild, where males are not limited to five females and where females have a wider range of males from which to choose.

Bateman argued that his results could be explained by reference to the energy investment of each sex in their sex cells. Since male *Drosophila* invest very little metabolic energy in the production of a given sex cell, whereas females invest considerable energy, a male's reproductive success is not limited by his ability to produce sex cells but by his ability to fertilize eggs with these cells. A female's reproductive success is not limited by her ability to have her eggs fertilized but by her ability to produce eggs. Since in almost all animal and plant species the male produces sex cells that are tiny by comparison to the female's sex cells, Bateman (1948) argued that his results should apply very widely, that is, to "all but a few very primitive organisms, and those in which monogamy combined with a sex ratio of unity eliminated all intra-sexual selection."

Good field data on reproductive success are difficult to find, but what data exist, in conjunction with the assumption that male reproductive success varies as a function of the number of copulations,[1] support the contention that in all species, except those mentioned below in which male parental care may be a limiting resource for females, male reproductive success varies more than female reproductive success. This is supported, for example, by data from dragonflies (Jacobs 1955), baboons (DeVore 1965), common frogs (Savage 1961), prairie chickens (Robel 1966), sage grouse (Scott 1942), black grouse (Koivisto 1965), elephant seals (LeBoeuf & Peterson, 1969), dung flies (Parker 1970a) and some anoline lizards (Rand 1967 and Trivers, in preparation, discussed below.) Circumstantial evidence exists for other lizards (for example, Blair 1960, Harris 1964) and for many mammals (see Eisenberg 1965). In monogamous species, male reproductive success would be expected to vary as female reproductive success, but there is always the possibility of adultery and differential female mortality (discussed below) and these factors should increase the

1. Selection should favor males producing such an abundance of sperm that they fertilize all a female's available eggs with a single copulation. Futhermore, to decrease competition among offspring, natural selection may favor females who prefer single paternity for each batch of eggs (see Hamilton 1964). The tendency for females to copulate only once or twice per batch of eggs is supported by data for many species (see, for example, Bateman 1948, Savage 1961, Burns 1968 but see also Parker 1970b).

variance of male reproductive success without significantly altering that of the female.

Relative Parental Investment

Bateman's argument can be stated in a more precise and general form such that the breeding system (for example, monogamy) as well as the adult sex ratio become functions of a single variable controlling sexual selection. I first define parental investment as *any investment by the parent in an individual offspring that increases the offspring's chance of surviving (and hence reproductive success) at the cost of the parent's ability to invest in other offspring.* So defined, parental investment includes the metabolic investment in the primary sex cells but refers to any investment (such as feeding or guarding the young) that benefits the young. It does not include effort expended in finding a member of the opposite sex or in subduing members of one's own sex in order to mate with a member of the opposite sex, since such effort (except in special cases) does not affect the survival chances of the resulting offspring and is therefore not *parental* investment.

Each offspring can be viewed as an investment independent of other offspring, increasing investment in one offspring tending to decrease investment in others. I measure the size of a parental investment by reference to its negative effect on the parent's ability to invest in other offspring: a large parental investment is one that strongly decreases the parent's ability to produce other offspring. There is no necessary correlation between the size of parental investment in an offspring and its benefit for the young. Indeed, one can show that during a breeding season the benefit from a given parental investment must decrease at some point or else species would not tend to produce any fixed number of offspring per season. Decrease in reproductive success resulting from the negative effect of parental investment on *nonparental* forms of reproductive effort (such as sexual competition for mates) is excluded from the measurement of parental investment. In effect, then, I am here considering reproductive success as if the only relevant variable were parental investment.

For a given reproductive season one can define the total parental investment of an individual as the sum of its investments in each of its offspring produced during that season, and one assumes that natural selections has favored the total parental investment that leads to maximum net reproductive success. Dividing the total parental investment by the number of individuals produced by the parent gives the typical parental investment by an individual per offspring. Bateman's argument can now be reformulated as follows. Since the total number of offspring produced by one sex of a sexually reproducing species must equal the total number produced by the other (and assuming the sexes differ in no other way than in their

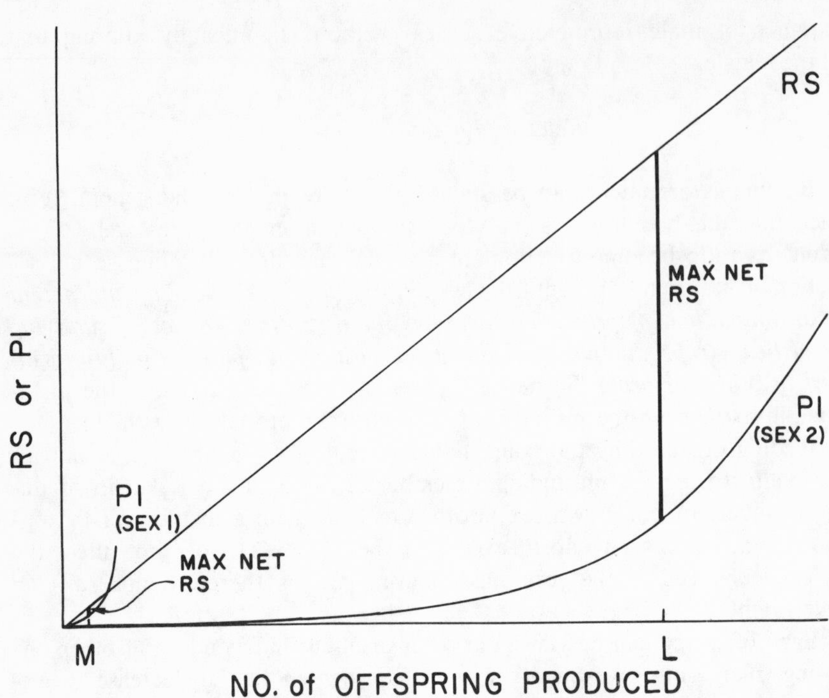

Figure 7.1. Reproductive success (RS) *and decrease in future reproductive success resulting from parental investment* (PI) *are graphed as functions of the number of offspring produced by individuals of the two sexes. At* M *and* L *the net reproductive success reaches a maximum for sex 1 and sex 2 respectively. Sex 2 is limited by sex 1 (see text). The shape of the* PI *curves need not be specified exactly.*

typical parental investment per offspring)[2] then the sex whose typical parental investment is greater than that of the opposite sex will become a limiting resource for that sex. Individuals of the sex investing less will compete among themselves to breed with members of the sex investing more, since an individual of the former can increase its reproductive success by investing successively in the offspring of several members of the limiting sex. By assuming a simple relationship between degree of parental investment and number of offspring produced, the argument can be presented graphically (Figure 7.1). The potential for sexual competition in the sex investing less can be measured by calculating the ratio of the number of offspring that sex optimally produces (as a function of parental invest-

2. In particular, I assume an approximately 50/50 sex ratio at conception (Fisher 1958) and no differential mortality by sex, because I later derive differential mortality as a function of reproductive strategies determined by sexual selection. (Differential maturation, which affects the adult sex ratio, can also be treated as a function of sexual selection.) For most species the disparity in parental investment between the sexes is so great that the assumptions here can be greatly relaxed.

ment alone, assuming the opposite sex's investment fixed at its optimal value) to the number of offspring the limiting sex optimally produces (L/M in Figure 7.1).

What governs the operation of sexual selection is the relative parental investment of the sexes in their offspring. Competition for mates usually characterizes males because males usually invest almost nothing in their offspring. Where male parental investment per offspring is comparable to female investment one would expect male and female reproductive success to vary in similar ways and for female choice to be no more discriminating than male choice (except as noted below). Where male parental investment strongly exceeds that of the female (regardless of which sex invests more in the sex cells) one would expect females to compete among themselves for males and for males to be selective about whom they accept as a mate.

Note that it may not be possible for an individual of one sex to invest in only part of the offspring of an individual of the opposite sex. When a male invests less per typical offspring than does a female but more than one-half what she invests (or vice-versa) then selection may not favor male competition to pair with more than one female, if the offspring of the second female cannot be parcelled out to more than one male. If the net reproductive success for a male investing in the offspring of one female is larger than that gained from investing in the offspring of two females, then the male will be selected to invest in the offspring of only one female. This argument is graphed in Figure 7.2 and may be important to understanding differential mortality in monogamous birds, as discussed below.

Fisher's (1958) sex ratio model compares the parental expenditure (undefined) in male offspring with that in female offspring and suggests energy and time as measures of expenditure. Restatements of Fisher's model (for example, Kolman 1960, Willson & Pianka 1963, T. Emlen 1968, Verner 1965, Leigh 1970) employ either the undefined term, parental expenditure, or the term energy investment. In either case the key concept is imprecise and the relevant one is parental investment, as defined above. Energy investment may often be a good approximation of parental investment, but it is clearly sometimes a poor one. An individual defending its brood from a predator may expend very little energy in the process but suffer a high chance of mortality; such behavior should be measured as a large investment, not a small one as suggested by the energy involved.

Parental Investment Patterns

Species can be classified according to the relative parental investment of the sexes in their young. In the vast majority of species, the male's only contribution to the survival of his offspring is his sex cells. In these species, female contribution clearly exceeds male and by a large ratio.

A male may invest in his offspring in several ways. He may provide his

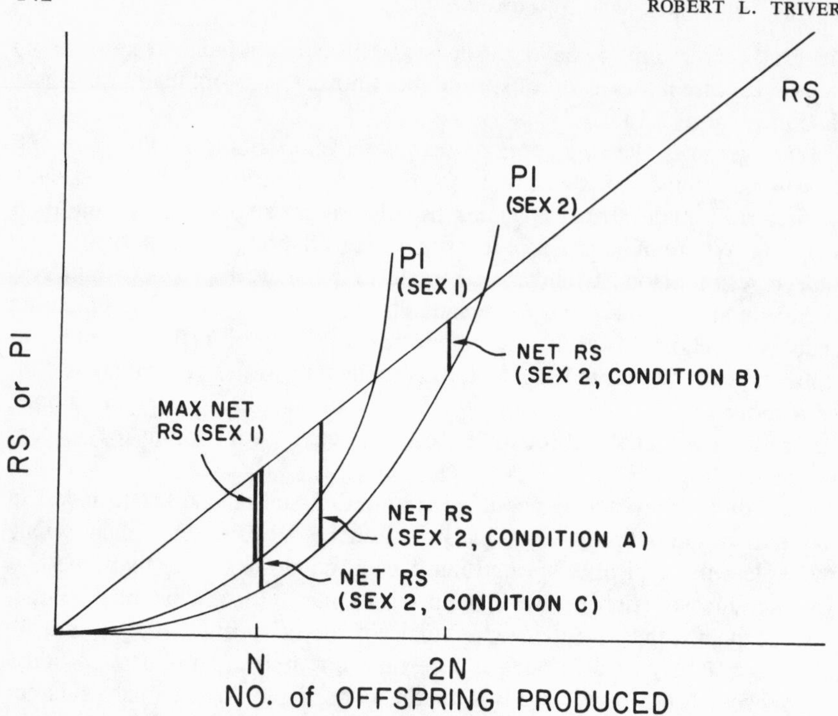

Figure 7.2. RS *and* PI *as functions of the number of offspring produced for two sexes. Sex 2 invests per typical offspring more than half of what sex 1 invests. Condition A: maximum net* RS *for a member of sex 2 assuming he can invest in any number of offspring between* N *and* 2N. *Condition B: net* RS *assuming member of sex 2 invests in* 2N *offspring. Condition C: net* RS *assuming member of sex 2 invests in* N *offspring. If member of sex 2 must invest in an integral multiple of* N *offspring, natural selection favors condition C.*

mate with food as in baloon flies (Kessel 1955) and some other insects (Engelmann 1970), some spiders, and some birds (for example, Calder 1967, Royama 1966, Stokes & Williams, 1971). He may find and defend a good place for the female to feed, lay eggs or raise young, as in many birds. He may build a nest to receive the eggs, as in some fish (for example, Morris 1952). He may help the female lay the eggs, as in some parasitic birds (Lack 1968). The male may also defend the female. He may brood the eggs, as in some birds, fish, frogs, and salamanders. He may help feed the young, protect them, provide opportunities for learning, and so on, as in wolves and many monogamous birds. Finally, he may provide an indirect group benefit to the young (such as protection), as in many primates. All of these forms of male parental investment tend to decrease the disparity in investment between male and female resulting from the initial disparity in size of sex cells.

To test the importance of relative parental investment in controlling sexual selection one should search for species showing greater male than female parental investment (see Williams 1966, pp. 185–186). The best candidates include the Phalaropidae and the polyandrous bird species reviewed by Lack (1968). In these species, a female's parental investment ends when she lays her eggs; the male alone broods the eggs and cares for the young after hatching. No one has attempted to assess relative parental investment in these species, but they are striking in showing very high male parental investment correlating with strong sex role reversal: females tend to be more brightly colored, more aggressive and larger than the males, and tend to court them and fight over them. In the phalaropes there is no evidence that the females lay multiple broods (Höhn 1967, Johns 1969), but in some polyandrous species females apparently go from male to male laying successive broods (for example, Beebe 1925; see also Orians 1969). In these species the female may be limited by her ability to induce males to care for her broods, and female reproductive success may vary more than male. Likewise, high male parental investment in pipefish and seahorses (syngnathidae) correlates with female courtship and bright coloration (Fiedler 1954), and female reproductive success may be limited by male parental investment. Field data for other groups are so scanty that it is not possible to say whether there are any instances of sex role reversal among them, but available data for some dendrobatid frogs suggest at least the possibility. In these species, the male carries one or more young on his back for an unknown length of time (for example, Eaton 1941). Females tend to be more brightly colored than males (rare in frogs) and in at least one species, *Dendrobates aurata,* several females have been seen pursuing, and possibly courting, single males (Dunn 1941). In this species the male carries only one young on his back, until the tadpole is quite large, but females have been found with as many as six large eggs inside, and it is possible that females compete with each other for the backs of males. There are other frog families that show male parental care, but even less is known of their social behavior.

In most monogamous birds male and female parental investment is probably comparable. For some species there is evidence that the male invests somewhat less than the female. Kluijver (1933, cited in Coulson 1960) has shown that the male starling (*Sturnus vulgaris*) incubates the eggs less and feeds the young less often than the female, and similar data are available for other passerines (Verner & Willson, 1969). The fact that in many species males are facultative polygynists (von Haartman 1969) suggests that even when monogamous the males invest less in the young than their females. Because sex role reversal, correlating with evidence of greater male than female parental investment, is so rare in birds and because of certain theoretical considerations discussed below, I tentatively classify most monogamous bird species as showing somewhat greater female than male investment in the young.

A more precise classification of animals, and particularly of similar species, would be useful for the formulation and testing of more subtle hypotheses. Groups of birds would be ideal to classify in this way, because slight differences in relative parental investment may produce large differences in social behavior, sexual dimorphism and mortality rates by sex. It would be interesting to compare human societies that differ in relative parental investment and in the details of the form of the parental investment, but the specification of parental investment is complicated by the fact that humans often invest in kin other than their children. A wealthy man supporting brothers and sisters (and their children) can be viewed functionally as a polygynist if the contributions to his fitness made by kin are devalued appropriately by their degree of relationship to him (see Hamilton 1964). There is good evidence that premarital sexual permissiveness affecting females in human societies relates to the form of parental investment in a way that would, under normal conditions, tend to maximize female reproductive success (Goethals 1971).

The Evolution of Investment Patterns

The parental investment pattern that today governs the operation of sexual selection apparently resulted from an evolutionarily very early differentiation into relatively immobile sex cells (eggs) fertilized by mobile ones (spermatozoa). An undifferentiated system of sex cells seems highly unstable: competition to fertilize other sex cells should rapidly favor mobility in some sex cells, which in turn sets up selection pressures for immobility in the others. In any case, once the differentiation took place, sexual selection acting on spermatozoa favored mobility at the expense of investment (in the form of cytoplasm). This meant that as long as the spermatozoa of different males competed directly to fertilize eggs (as in oysters) natural selection favoring increased parental investment could act only on the female. Once females were able to control which male fertilized their eggs, female choice or mortality selection on the young could act to favor some new form of male investment in addition to spermatozoa. But there exist strong selection pressures against this. Since the female already invests more than the male, breeding failure for lack of an additional investment selects more strongly against her than against the male. In that sense, her initial very great investment commits her to additional investment more than the male's initial slight investment commits him. Furthermore, male-male competition will tend to operate against male parental investment, in that any male investment in one female's young should decrease the male's chances of inseminating other females. Sexual selection, then, is both controlled by the parental investment pattern and a force that tends to mold that pattern.

The conditions under which selection favors male parental investment have not been specified for any group of animals. Except for the case of polygyny in birds, the role of female choice has not been explored; instead, it is commonly assumed that, whenever two individuals can raise more individuals together than one alone could, natural selection will favor male parental investment (Lack 1968, p. 149), an assumption that overlooks the effects of both male-male competition and female choice.

INITIAL PARENTAL INVESTMENT

An important consequence of the early evolutionary differentiation of the sex cells and subsequent sperm competition is that male sex cells remain tiny compared to female sex cells, even when selection has favored a total male parental investment that equals or exceeds the female investment. The male's initial parental investment, that is, his investment at the moment of fertilization, is much smaller than the female's, even if later, through parental care, he invests as much or more. Parental investment in the young can be viewed as a sequence of discrete investments by each sex. The relative investment may change as a function of time and each sex may be more or less free to terminate its investment at any time. In the human species, for example, a copulation costing the male virtually nothing may trigger a nine-month investment by the female that is not trivial, followed, if she wishes, by a fifteen-year investment in the offspring that is considerable. Although the male may often contribute parental care during this period, he need not necessarily do so. After a nine-month pregnancy, a female is more or less free to terminate her investment at any moment but doing so wastes her investment up until then. Given the initial imbalance in investment the male may maximize his chances of leaving surviving offspring by copulating and abandoning many females, some of whom, alone or with the aid of others, will raise his offspring. In species where there has been strong selection for male parental care, it is more likely that a mixed strategy will be the optimal male course—to help a single female raise young, while not passing up opportunities to mate with other females whom he will not aid.

In many birds, males defend a territory which the female also uses for feeding prior to egg laying, but the cost of this investment by the male is difficult to evaluate. In some species, as outlined above, the male may provision the female before she has produced the young, but this provisioning is usually small compared to the cost of the eggs. In any case, the cost of the copulation itself is always trivial to the male, and in theory the male need not invest anything else in order to copulate. If there is any chance the female can raise the young, either alone or with the help of others, it would be to the male's advantage to copulate with her. By this reasoning one would expect males of monogamous species to retain some psychological traits consistent with promiscuous habits. A male would be selected to differentiate between a female he will only impregnate and a female with whom he will also raise young. Toward the former he should be more eager for sex and less discriminating in choice of sex partner than the female toward him, but toward the latter he should be about as discriminating as she toward him.

If males within a relatively monogamous species are, in fact, adapted to pursue a mixed strategy, the optimal is likely to differ for different males. I know of no attempt to document this possibility in humans, but psychology might well benefit from attempting to view human sexual plasticity as an adaptation to permit the individual to choose the mixed strategy best suited to local conditions and his own attributes. Elder (1969) shows that steady dating and sexual activity (coitus and petting) in adolescent human females correlate inversely with a tendency to marry up the socioeconomic scale as adults. Since females physically attractive as adolescents tend to marry up, it is possible that females adjust their reproductive strategies in adolescence to their own assets.

Desertion and Cuckoldry

There are a number of interesting consequences of the fact that the male and female of a monogamous couple invest parental care in their offspring at different rates. These can be studied by graphing and comparing the cumulative investment of each parent in their offspring, and this is done for two individuals of a hypothetical bird species in Figure 7.3. I have graphed no parental investment by the female in her young before copulation, even though she may be producing the eggs before then, because it is not until the act of copulation that she commits the eggs to a given male's genes. In effect, then, I have graphed the parental investment of each individual in the other individual's offspring. After copulation, this is the same as graphing investment in their own offspring, assuming, as I do here, that the male and female copulate with each other and each other only.

To discuss the problems that confront paired individuals ostensibly cooperating in a joint parental effort, I choose the language of strategy and decision, as if each individual contemplated in strategic terms the decisions it ought to make at each instant in order to maximize its reproductive success. This language is chosen purely for convenience to explore the adaptations one might expect natural selection to favor.

At any point in time the individual whose cumulative investment is exceeded by his partner's is theoretically tempted to desert, especially if the disparity is large. This temptation occurs because the deserter loses less than his partner if no offspring are raised and the partner would therefore be more strongly selected to stay with the young. Any success of the partner will, of course, benefit the deserter. In Figure 7.3, for example, desertion by the male right after copulation will cost him very little, if no offspring are raised, while the chances of the female raising some young alone may be great enough to make the desertion worthwhile. Other factors are

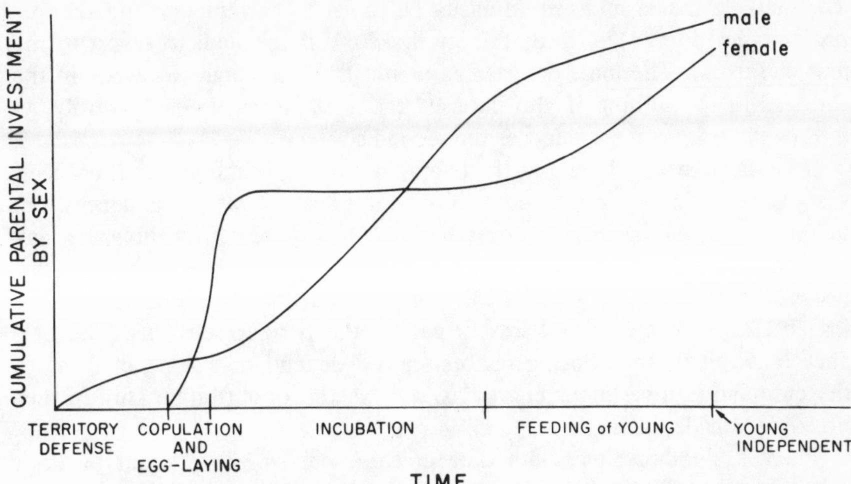

Figure 7.3. Hypothetical cumulative parental investment of a male and a female bird in their offspring as a function of time. Territory defense: *Male defends area for feeding and nest building.* Copulation and egg-laying: *Female commits her eggs to male who commits his defended nest to the female.* Incubation: *Male incubates eggs while female does nothing relevant to offspring.* Feeding of young: *Each parent feeds young but female does so at a more rapid rate.*

important in determining the adaptiveness of abandonment, factors such as the opportunities outside the pair for breeding and the expected shape of the deserter's investment curve if he does not desert. If the male's investment curve does not rise much after copulation, then the female's chances of raising the young alone will be greater and the time wasted by the male investing moderately in his offspring may be better spent starting a new brood.

What are the possible responses of the deserted individual? If the male is deserted before copulation, he has no choice but to attempt to start the process over again with a new female; whatever he has invested in that female is lost. If either partner is deserted after copulation, it has three choices. (1) It can desert the eggs (or eat them) and attempt to breed again with another mate, losing thereby all (or part of) the initial investment. (2) It can attempt to raise the young on its own, at the risk of overexertion and failure. Or, (3) it can attempt to induce another partner to help it raise the young. The third alternative, if successful, is the most adaptive for it, but this requires deceiving another organism into doing something contrary to its own interests, and adaptations should evolve to guard individuals from such tasks. It is difficult to see how a male could be successful in deceiving a new female, but if a female acts quickly, she might fool a male. As time goes on (for example, once the eggs are laid), it is unlikely that a male could easily be fooled. The female could thus be programmed to try the third strategy first, and if it failed, to revert to the first or second. The male deserter gains most if the female succeeds in the third strategy, nothing if she chooses the first strategy, and possibly an intermediate value if she chooses the second strategy.

If neither partner deserts at the beginning, then as time goes on, each invests more and more in the young. This trend has several consequences. On the one hand, the partner of a deserter is more capable of finishing the task alone and natural selection should favor its being more predisposed to try, because it has more to lose. On the other hand, the deserter has more to lose if the partner fails and less to gain if the partner succeeds. The balance between these opposing factors should depend on the exact form of the cumulative investment curves as well as the opportunities for further breeding outside the pair.

There is another effect with time of the increasing investment by both parents in the offspring. As the investments increase, natural selection may favor *either* partner deserting even if one has invested more in the young than the other. This is because the desertion may put the deserted partner in a cruel bind: he has invested so much that he loses considerably if he also deserts the young, even though, which should make no difference to him, the partner would lose even more. The possibility of such binds can be illustrated by an analogous situation described by Rowley (1965). Two neighboring pairs of wrens happened to fledge their young simultaneously and could not tell their young apart, so both pairs fed all six young indiscriminately, until one pair "deserted" to raise another brood, leaving their neighbors to feed all six young, which they did, even though this meant they were, in effect, being taken advantage of.

Birds should show adaptations to avoid being deserted. Females, in particular, should be able to guard against males who will only copulate and not invest subsequent parental effort. An instance of such an adaptation may be found in the red-necked phalarope, *Phalaropus lobatus*. In phalaropes the male incubates the eggs alone and alone cares for the young after hatching (Höhn 1967, Johns 1969), so that a graph of cumulative parental investment would show an intitial large female investment which then remains the same through time, whereas the initial male investment is nil and increases steadily, probably to surpass the female investment. Only the female is vulnerable to being deserted and this right after copulation, since any later desertion by the male costs him his investment in incubation, the young being almost certain to perish. Tinbergen (1935) observed a female vigorously courting a male and then flying away as soon as he responded to the courtship by attempting to copulate. This coy performance was repeated numerous times for several days. Tinbergen attributed it to the "waxing and waning of an instinct," but the behavior may have been a test of the male's willingness to brood the female's eggs. The male under observation was, in fact, already brooding eggs and was courted when he left the eggs to feed on a nearby pond. In order to view a complete egg-laying sequence, Tinbergen destroyed the clutch the male was brooding. Within a half day the female permitted the male sexual access, and he subsequently brooded her eggs. The important point is that the female could apparently tell the difference between a free and an encumbered male, and she withheld sex from the latter. Courtship alternating with flight may be the test that reveals the male's true attachments: the test can show, for example, whether he is free to follow the female.

It is likely that many adaptations exist in monogamous species to guard against desertion, but despite evidence that desertion can be common (Rowley 1965) no one has attempted to analyze courtship with this danger in mind. Von Haartman (1969) has reviewed some evidence for adaptations of females to avoid being mated to a polygynous male, and being so mated is sometimes exactly equivalent to being deserted by the male (von Haartman, 1951).

External fertilization requires a synchrony of behavior such that the male can usually be certain he is not attempting to fertilize previously fertilized eggs. With the evolution of internal fertilization the male cannot be so certain. For many species (for example, most mammals), the distinction is not important because the male loses so little by attempting to fertilize previously fertilized eggs. Where male parental care is involved, however, the male runs the risk of being cuckolded, of raising another male's offspring. For Figure 7.1 it was assumed that the pair copulated with each other and each other only, but the male can usually not be sure that such is the case and what is graphed in such a situation is the male's investment in the *female's* offspring. Adaptations should evolve to help guarantee that the female's offspring are also his own, but these can partly be countered by the evolution of more sophisticated cuckolds.

One way a male can protect himself is to ensure that other males keep their distance. That some territorial aggression of monogamous male birds is devoted to protecting the sanctity of the pair bond seems certain, and human male aggression toward real or suspected adulterers is often extreme. Lee (1969), for example, has shown that, when the cause is known, the major cause of fatal Bushman fights is adultery or suspected adultery. In fact, limited data on other hunter-gathering groups (including Eskimos and Australian aborigines) indicate that, while fighting is relatively rare (in that organized intergroup aggression is infrequent), the "murder rate" may be relatively high. On examination, the murderer and his victim are usually a husband and his wife's real or suspected lover. In pigeons (*Columba livia*) a new male arriving alone at a nocturnal roosting place in the fall is attacked day after day by one or more resident males. As soon as the same male appears with a mate, the two are treated much more casually (Trivers, unpublished data), suggesting that an unpaired male is more threatening than a paired one.

I have argued above that a female deserted immediately after copulation may be adapted to try to induce another male to help raise her young. This factor implies adaptations on the part of the male to avoid such a fate. A simple method is to avoid mating with a female on first encounter, sequester her instead and mate with her only after a passage of time that reasonably excludes her prior impregnation by another male. Certainly males guard their females from other males, and there is a striking difference between the lack of preliminaries in promiscuous birds (Scott 1942, Kruijt & Hogan 1967) and the sometimes long lag between pair bonding and copulation in monogamous birds (Nevo 1956), a lag which usually seems to serve other functions as well.

Biologists have interpreted courtship in a limited way. Courtship is seen as allowing the individual to choose the correct species and sex, to overcome antagonistic urges and to arouse one's partner (Bastock 1967). The above analysis suggests that courtship should also be interpreted in terms of the need to guard oneself from the several possibilities of maltreatment at the hands of one's mate.

Differential Mortality and the Sex Ratio

Of special interest in understanding the effects of sexual selection are accurate data on differential mortality of the sexes, especially of immature individuals. Such data are, however, among the most difficult to gather, and the published data, although important, are scanty (for example, Emlen 1940, Hays 1947, Chapman, Casida, & Cote 1938, Robinette et al. 1957, Coulson 1960, Potts 1969, Darley 1971, Myers & Krebs 1971). As a substitute one can make use of data on sex ratios within given age classes or for all age classes taken together. By assuming that the sex ratio at conception (or, less precisely, at birth) is almost exactly 50/50, significant deviations from this ratio for any age class or for all taken together should imply differential mortality. Where data exist for the sex ratio at birth and where the sex ratio for the entire local population is unbalanced, the sex ratio at birth is usually about 50/50 (see above references, Selander 1965, Lack 1954). Furthermore, Fisher (1958) has shown, and others refined (Leigh 1970), that parents should invest roughly equal energy in each sex. Since parents usually invest roughly equal energy in each individual of each sex, natural selection, in the absence of unusual circumstances (see Hamilton 1967), should favor approximately a 50/50 sex ratio at conception.

It is difficult to determine accurately the sex ratio for any species. The most serious source of bias is that males and females often make themselves differentially available to the observer. For example, in small mammals sexual selection seems to have favored male attributes, such as high mobility, that tend to result in their differential capture (Beer, Frenzel, & MacLeod 1958; Myers & Krebs, 1971). If one views one's capture techniques as randomly sampling the existing population, one will conclude that males are more numerous. If one views one's capture techniques as randomly sampling the effects of mortality on the population, then one will conclude that males are more prone to mortality (they are captured more often) and therefore are less numerous. Neither assumption is likely to be true, but authors routinely choose the former. Furthermore, it is often not appreciated what a large sample is required in order to show significant deviations from a 50/50 ratio. A sample of 400 animals showing a 44/56 sex ratio, for example, does not deviate significantly from a 50/50 ratio. (Nor, although this is almost never pointed out, does it differ significantly from a 38/62 ratio.)

Mayr (1939) has pointed out that there are numerous deviations from a 50/50 sex ratio in birds and I believe it is likely that, if data were sufficiently precise, most species of vertebrates would show a significant deviation from a 50/50 sex ratio. Males and females differ in numerous characteristics relevant to their different reproductive strategies and these characters are unlikely to have equivalent effects on survival. Since it is not advantageous for the adults of each sex to have available the same number of adults of the opposite sex, there will be no automatic selective agent for keeping deviations from a 50/50 ratio small.

A review of the useful literature on sex ratios suggests that (except for birds) when the sex ratio is unbalanced it is usually unbalanced by there being more females than males. Put another way, males apparently have a tendency to suffer higher mortality rates than females. This is true for those dragonflies for which there are data (Corbet, Longfield, & Moore 1960), for the house fly (Rockstein 1959), for most fish (Beverton & Holt 1959), for several lizards (Tinkle 1967, Harris 1964, Hirth 1963, Blair 1960, Trivers, discussed below) and for many mammals (Bouliere & Verschuren 1960, Cowan 1950, Eisenberg 1965, Robinette et al. 1957, Beer, Frenzel, & MacLeod 1958, Stephens 1952, Tyndale-Biscoe & Smith, 1969, Myers & Krebs, 1971, Wood 1970). Hamilton (1948) and Lack (1954) have reviewed studies on other animals suggesting a similar trend. Mayr (1939) points out that where the sex ratio can be shown to be unbalanced in monogamous birds there are usually fewer females, but in polygynous or promiscuous birds there are fewer males. Data since his paper confirm this finding. This result is particularly interesting since in all other groups in which males tend to be less numerous monogamy is rare or nonexistent.

THE CHROMOSOMAL HYPOTHESIS

There is a tendency among biologists studying social behavior to regard the adult sex ratio as an independent variable to which the species reacts with appropriate adaptations. Lack (1968) often interprets social behavior as an adaptation in part to an unbalanced (or balanced) sex ratio, and Verner (1964) has summarized other instances of this tendency. The only mechanism that will generate differential mortality independent of sexual differences clearly related to parental investment and sexual selection is the chromosomal mechanism, applied especially to humans and other mammals: the unguarded X chromosome of the male is presumed to predispose him to higher mortality. This mechanism is inadequate as an explanation of differential mortality for three reasons.

1. The distribution of differential mortality by sex is not predicted by a knowledge of the distribution of sex determining mechanisms. Both sexes of fish are usually homogametic, yet males suffer higher mortality. Female birds are heterogametic but suffer higher mortality only in monogamous species. Homogametic male meal moths are outsurvived by their heterogametic female counterparts under laboratory conditions (Hamilton & Johansson 1965).

2. Theoretical predictions of the degree of differential mortality expected by males due to their unguarded X chromosome are far lower than those observed in such mammals as dogs, cattle and humans (Ludwig & Boost 1951). It is possible to imagine natural selection favoring the heterogametic sex determining mechanism if the associated differential mortality is slight and balanced by some advantage in differentiation or in the homogametic sex, but a large mortality associated with heterogamy should be counteracted by a tendency toward both sexes becoming homogametic.

3. Careful data for humans demonstrate that castrate males (who remain of course heterogametic) strongly outsurvive a control group of males similar in all other respects and the earlier in life the castration, the greater the increase in survival. (Hamilton & Mestler 1969). The same is true of domestic cats (Hamilton, Hamilton & Mestler 1969), but not of a species (meal moths) for which there is no evidence that the gonads are implicated in sexual differentiation (Hamilton & Johansson 1965).

An Adaptive Model of Differential Mortality

To interpret the meaning of balanced or unbalanced sex ratios one needs a comprehensive framework within which to view life historical phenomena. Gadgil & Bossert (1970) have presented a model for the adaptive interpretation of differences between species' life histories; for example, in the age of first breeding and in the growth and survival curves. Although they did not apply this model to sexual differences in these parameters, their model is precisely suited for such differences. One can, in effect, treat the sexes as if they were different species, the opposite sex being a resource relevant to producing maximum surviving offspring. Put this way, female "species" usually differ from male species in that females compete among themselves for such resources as food but not for members of the opposite sex, whereas males ultimately compete only for members of the opposite sex, all other forms of competition being important only insofar as they affect this ultimate competition.

To analyze differential mortality by sex one needs to correlate different reproductive strategies with mortality, that is, one must show how a given reproductive strategy entails a given risk of mortality. One can do this by graphing reproductive success (RS) for the first breeding season as a function of reproductive effort expended during that season, and by graphing the diminution in future reproductive success (D) in units of first breeding season reproductive success. (Gadgil and Bossert show that the reproductive value of a given effort declines with age, hence the need to convert future reproductive success to comparable units.) For simplicity I assume that the diminution, D, results entirely from mortality between the first and second breeding seasons. The diminution could result from mortality in a later year (induced by reproductive effort in the first breeding season) which would not change the form of the analysis, or it could result from decreased ability to breed in the second (or still later) breeding season, which sometimes occurs but which is probably minor compared to the diminution due to mortality, and which does not change the analysis as long as one assumes that males and females do not differ appreciably in the extent to which they suffer this form of diminution.

Natural selection favors an individual expending in the first breeding season the reproductive effort (RE) that results in a maximum net reproductive success (RS—D). The value of D at this RE gives the degree of expected mortality between the first and second breeding seasons (see Figures 7.4 and 7.5). Differences between the sexes in D will give the expected differential mortality. The same analysis can be applied to the nth breeding season to predict mortality between it and the nth + 1 breeding season. Likewise, by a trivial modification, the analysis can be used to generate differences in juvenile mortality: let D represent the diminution in chances of surviving to the first breeding season as a function of RE at first breeding. Seen this way, one is measuring the cost in survival of developing during the juvenile period attributes relevant to adult reproductive success.

SPECIES WITH LITTLE OR NO MALE PARENTAL INVESTMENT

In Figure 7.4, I have graphed RS and D as functions of reproductive effort in the first breeding season for females of a hypothetical species in which males invest very little parental care. The RS function is given a sigmoidal shape for the following reasons. I assume that at low values of RE, RS increases only very gradually because some investment is necessary just to initiate reproduction (for example, enlarging the reproductive organs). RS then increases more rapidly as a function of RE but without achieving a very steep slope. RS finally levels off at high values of RE because of increased inefficiencies there (for example, inefficiencies in foraging; see Schoener 1971). I have graphed the value, f, at which net reproductive success for the female reaches a maximum. Technically, due to competition, the shape of the RS function for any given female will depend partly on the reproductive effort devoted by other females; the graph therefore assumes that other females tend to invest near the optimal value, f, but an important feature of a female's RS is that it is *not* strongly dependent on the RE devoted by other females: the curve would not greatly differ if all other females invested much more or less. I have graphed D as a linear function of RE. So doing amounts to a definition of reproductive effort, that is, a given increment in reproductive effort during the first breeding season can be detected as a proportionately increased chance of dying be-

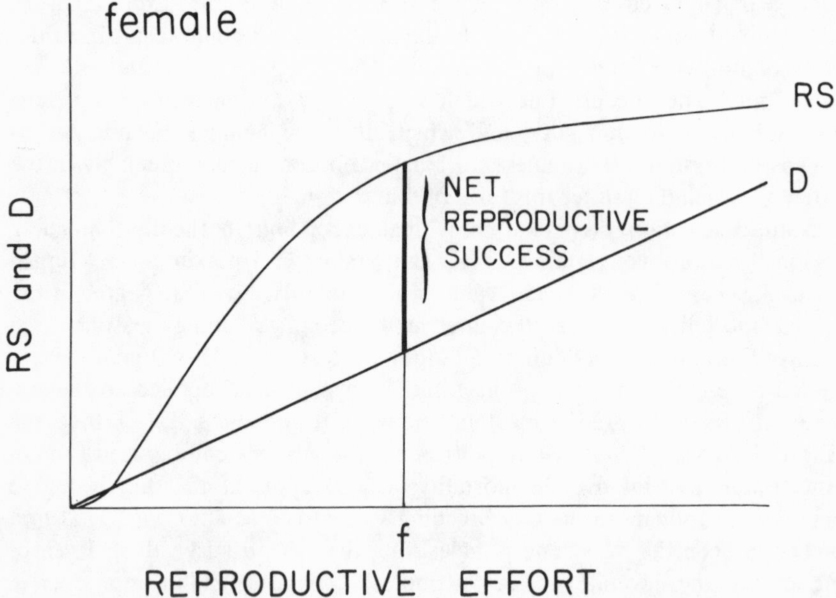

Figure 7.4. Female reproductive success during the first breeding season (RS) *and diminution of future reproductive success* (D) *as functions of reproductive effort during first breeding.* D *is measured in units of first breeding (see text). At* f *the net reproductive success reaches a maximum. Species is one in which there is very little male parental investment.*

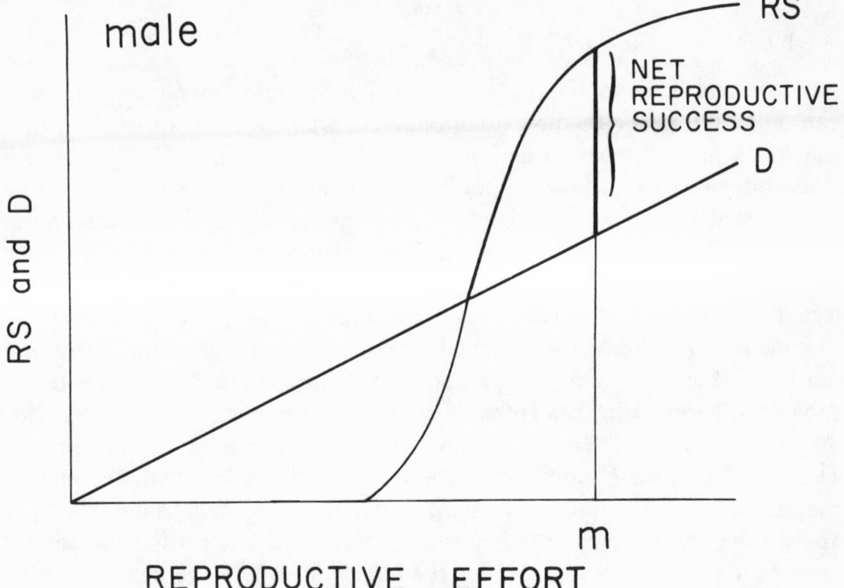

Figure 7.5. Same as Figure 7.4 except that it is drawn for the male instead of the female. At m *the net reproductive success reaches a maximum.*

tween the first and second breeding seasons. Note that reproductive effort for the female is essentially synonymous with parental investment.

Male RS differs from female RS in two important ways, both of which stem from sexual selection. (1) A male's RS is highly dependent on the RE of other males. When other males invest heavily, an individual male will usually not outcompete them unless he invests as much or more. A considerable investment that is slightly below that of other males may result in zero RS. (2) A male's RS is potentially very high, much higher than that of a conspecific female, but only if he outcompetes other males. There should exist some factor or set of factors (such as size, aggressiveness, mobility) that correlates with high male RS. The effect of competition between males for females is selection for increased male RE, and this selection will continue until greater male than female RE is selected as long as the higher associated D is offset by the potentially very high RS. This argument is graphed in Figure 7.5, where the steep slope of RS reflects the high interaction between one male's RS and the RE of the other males. Note that the argument here depends on the existence of a set of factors correlated with high male reproductive success. If these factors exist, natural selection will predispose the male to higher mortality rates than the female. Where a male can achieve very high RS in a breeding season (as in land-breeding seals, Bartholemew 1970), differential mortality will be correspondingly high.

SPECIES WITH APPRECIABLE MALE PARENTAL INVESTMENT

The analysis here applies to species in which males invest less parental care than, but probably more than one-half, what females invest. I assume that most monogamous birds are so characterized, and I have listed reasons and some data above supporting this assumption. The reasons can be summarized by saying that because of their initial large investment, females appear to be caught in a situation in which they are unable to force greater parental investment out of the males and would be strongly selected against if they unilaterally reduced their own parental investment.

Functions relating RS to parental investment are graphed for males and females in Figures 7.6 and 7.7, assuming for each sex that the opposite sex shows the parental investment that results for it in a maximum net reproductive success. The female curve is given a sigmoidal shape for the reasons that apply to Figure 7.4; in birds the female's initial investment in the eggs will go for nothing if more is not invested in brooding the eggs and feeding the young, while beyond a certain high RE further increments do not greatly affect RS. Assuming the female invests the value, f, male RS will vary as a function of male parental investment in a way similar to female RS, except the function will be displaced to the left (Figure 7.7) and some RS will be lost due to the effects of the cuckoldry graphed in Figure 7.8.

Because males invest in parental care more than one-half what females

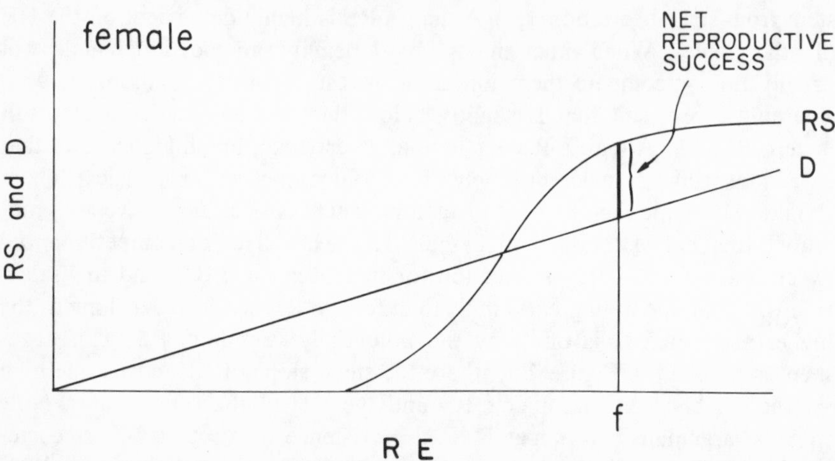

Figure 7.6. Female reproductive success and diminution in future reproductive success as functions of reproductive effort (RE) *assuming male reproductive effort of* m_1. *Species is a hypothetical monogamous bird in which males invest somewhat less than females in parental care (see Figure 7.7 and 7.8).*

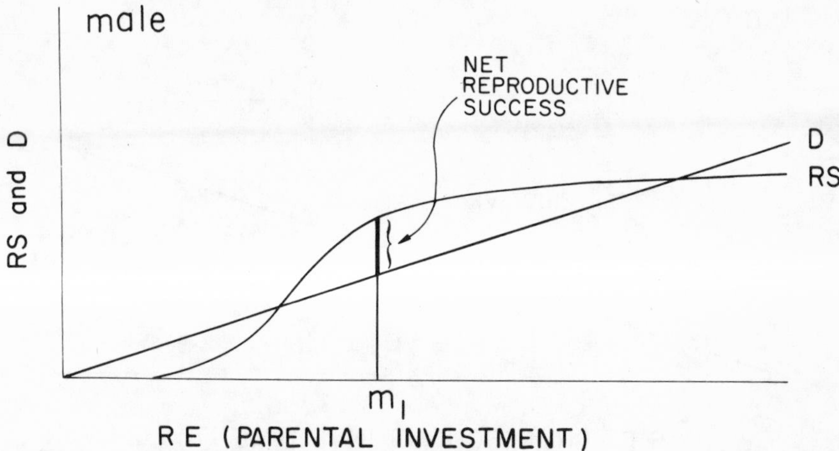

Figure 7.7. Male reproductive success and diminution in future reproductive success as functions of reproductive effort, assuming female reproductive effort of f. *Species is same as in Figure 7.6. Reproductive effort of male is invested as parental care in one female's offspring. Net reproductive success is a maximum at* m_1.

invest and because the offspring of a given female tend to be inseminated by a single male, selection does not favor males competing with each other to invest in the offspring of more than one female. Rather, sexual selection only operates on the male to inseminate females whose offspring he will not raise, especially if another male will raise them instead. Since selection presumably does not strongly favor female adultery and may oppose it (if, for example, detection leads to desertion by the mate), the opportunities for cuckoldry are limited: high investment in promiscuous activity will bring only limited RS. This argument is graphed in Figure 7.8. The predicted differential mortality by sex can be had by comparing D (f) with D ($m_1 + m_2$).

It may seem ironic, but in moving from a promiscuous to a monogamous life, that is, in moving toward *greater* parental investment in his young, the male tends to *increase* his chances of surviving relative to the female. This tendency occurs because the increased parental investment disproportionately decreases the male's RE invested in male-male competition to inseminate females.

Note that in both cases above differential mortality tends to be self-limiting. By altering the ratio of possible sexual partners to sexual competitors differential mortality sets up forces that tend to keep the differential mortality low. In species showing little male parental investment differential male mortality increases the average number of females available for those males who survive. Other things being equal, this increase tends to make it more difficult for the most successful males to maintain their relative ad-

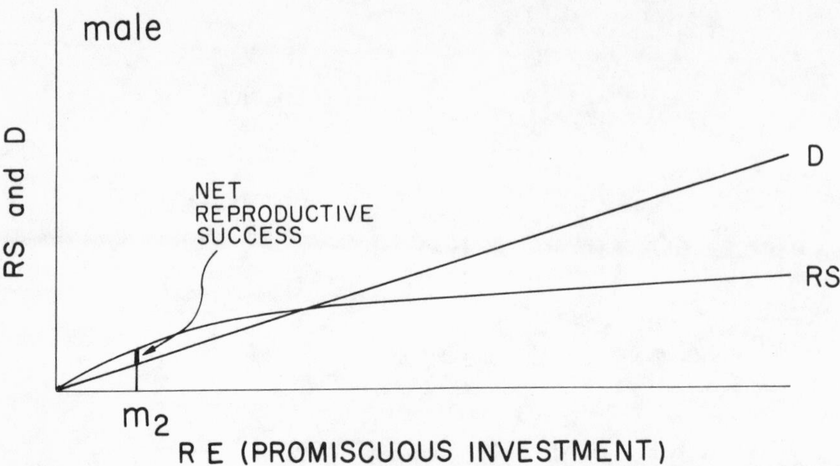

Figure 7.8. Male reproductive success and diminution of future reproductive success as a function of reproductive effort solely devoted to promiscuous behavior. Net reproductive success at m_2 *is a maximum. Same species as in Figures 7.6 and 7.7.*

vantage. In monogamous birds differential female mortality induces competition among males to secure at least one mate, thereby tending to increase male mortality. Such competition presumably also increases the variance in male reproductive success above the sexual differential expected from cuckoldry.

SPECIES WITH GREATER MALE THAN FEMALE PARENTAL INVESTMENT

Since the above arguments were made with reference to relative parental investment and not sex, they apply to species in which males invest more parental effort than females, except that there is never apt to be a female advantage to cuckolding other females, and this advantage is always alive with males. Where females invest more than one-half what males invest, one would predict differential female mortality. Where females invest less than one-half what males invest, one would predict competition, and a resulting differential female mortality.

Male–Male Competition

Competition between males does not necessarily end with the release of sperm. Even in species with internal fertilization, competition between sperm of different males can be an important component of male-male competition (see the excellent review by Parker 1970b). In rare cases, competition between males may continue after eggs are fertilized. For example an adult male langur (*Presbytis entellus*) who ousts the adult male of a group may systematically kill the infants of that group (presumably fathered by the ousted male) thereby bringing most of the adult females quickly into estrus again (Sugiyama 1967). While clearly disadvantageous for the killed infants and their mothers, such behavior, benefiting the new male, may be an extreme product of sexual selection. Female mice spontaneously abort during the first four days of pregnancy when exposed to the smell of a strange male (Bruce 1960, reviewed in Sadleir 1967), a situation subject to several interpretations including one based on male-male competition.

Sperm competition may have important effects on competition between males prior to release of sperm. In those insects in which later-arriving sperm take precedence in fertilizing eggs, selection favors mating with a female just prior to release of eggs, thereby increasing competition at ovulation sites and intensifying selection for a postovulatory guarding phase by the male (see Parker 1970bcd, Jacobs 1955). I here concentrate on male-male competition prior to the release of sperm in species showing very little male parental investment.

The form of male-male competition should be strongly influenced by the distribution in space and time of the ultimate resource affecting male reproductive success, namely, conspecific breeding females. The distribution can be described in terms of three parameters: the extent to which females are clumped or dispersed in space, the extent to which they are clumped or dispersed in time, and the extent to which their exact position in space and time is predictable. I here treat females as if they are a passive resource for which males compete, but female choice may strongly influence the form of male-male competition, as, for example, when it favors males clumping together on display grounds (for example, S. Emlen 1968) which females then search out (see below under "Female Choice").

DISTRIBUTION IN SPACE

Cervids differ in the extent to which females are clumped in space or randomly dispersed (deVos, Broky & Geist 1967) as do antelopes (Eisenberg 1965), and these differences correlate in a predictable way with differences in male attributes. Generally male-male aggression will be the more severe the greater the number of females two males are fighting over at any given moment. Searching behavior should be more important in highly dispersed species especially if the dispersal is combined with unpredictability.

DISTRIBUTION IN TIME

Clumped in time refers to highly seasonal breeders in which many females become sexually available for a short period at the same moment (for example, explosive breeding frogs; Bragg 1965, Rivero & Estevez 1969), while highly dispersed breeders (in time) are species (such as chimpanzees; Van Lawick-Goodall 1968) in which females breed more or less randomly throughout the year. One effect of extreme clumping is that it becomes more difficult for any one male to be extremely successful: while he is copulating with one female, hundreds of other females are simultaneously being inseminated. Dispersal in time, at least when combined with clumping in space, as in many primates, permits each male to compete for each newly available female and the same small number of males tend repeatedly to inseminate the receptive females (DeVore 1965).

PREDICTABILITY

One reason males in some dragonflies (Jacobs 1955) may compete with each other for female oviposition sites is that those are highly predictable places at which to find receptive females. Indeed, males display several behaviors, such as testing the water with the tips of their abdomen, that apparently aid them in predicting especially good oviposition sites, and such sites can permit very high male reproductive success (Jacobs 1955). In the cicada killer wasp (*Sphecius spheciosus*) males establish mating territories around colony emergency holes, presumably because this is the most predictable place at which to find receptive females (Lin 1963).

The three parameters outlined interact strongly, of course, as when very strong clumping in time may strongly reduce the predicted effects of strong clumping in space. A much more detailed classification of species with non-obvious predictions would be welcome. In the absence of such models I present a partial list of factors that should affect male reproductive success and that may correlate with high male mortality.

SIZE

There are very few data showing the relationship between male size and reproductive success but abundant data showing the relationship between male dominance and reproductive success: for example, in elephant seals (LeBoeuf & Peterson 1969), black grouse (Koivisto 1965, Scott 1942), baboons (DeVore 1965) and rainbow lizards (Harris 1964). Since dominance is largely established through aggression and larger size is usually helpful in aggressive encounters, it is likely that these data partly reveal the relationship between size and reproductive success. (It is also likely that they reflect the relationship between experience and reproductive success.)

Circumstantial evidence for the importance of size in aggressive encounters can be found in the distribution of sexual size dimorphism and aggressive tendencies among tetrapods. In birds and mammals males are generally larger than females and much more aggressive. Where females are known to be more aggressive (that is, birds showing reversal in sex roles) they are also larger. In frogs and salamanders females are usually larger than males, and aggressive behavior has only very rarely been recorded. In snakes, females are usually larger than males (Kopstein 1941) and aggression is almost unreported. Aggression has frequently been observed between sexually active crocodiles and males tend to be larger (Allen Greer, personal communication). In lizards males are often larger than females, and aggression is common in some families (Carpenter 1967). Male aggressiveness is also common, however, in some species in which females are larger, for example, *Sceloporus,* (Blair 1960). There is a trivial reason for the lack of evidence of aggressiveness in most amphibians and reptiles: the species are difficult to observe and few behavioral data of any sort have been recorded. It is possible, however, that this correlation between human ignorance and species in which females are larger is not accidental. Humans tend to be more knowledgeable about those species that are also active diurnally and strongly dependent on vision, for example, birds and large mammals. It may be that male aggressiveness is more strongly selected in visually oriented animals because vision provides long-range information on the behavior of competitors. The male can, for example, easily observe another male beginning to copulate and can often quickly attempt to intervene (for example, baboons, DeVore 1965 and sage grouse, Scott 1942).

Mammals and birds also tend towards low, fixed clutch sizes and this may favor relatively smaller females, since large female size may be relatively unimportant in reproductive success. In many fish, lizards and salamanders female reproductive success as measured by clutch size is known to correlate strongly within species with size (Tinkle, Wilbur & Tilley 1970, Tilley 1968).

Measuring reproductive success by frequency of copulation, I have analyzed male and female reproductive success as a function of size in *Anolis garmani* (Figures 7.9 and 7.10). Both sexes show a significant positive correlation between size and reproductive success, but the trend in males is significantly stronger than the trend in females ($p < .01$). Consistent with this tendency, males grow faster at all sizes than females (Figure 7.11) and reach an adult weight two and one-half times that of adult females. The sex ratio of all animals is unbalanced in favor of females, which would seem to indicate differential mortality, but the factors that might produce the difference are not known. Males are highly aggressive and territorial, and large males defend correspondingly large territories with many resident females. No data are available on size and success in aggressive encounters, but in the closely related (and behaviorally very similar) *A. lineatopus,* 85 per cent of 182 disputes observed in the field were won by the larger animal (Rand 1967). Females lay only one egg at a time, but it is likely that larger adult females lay eggs slightly more often

Figure 7.9. Male and female Anolis garmani *copulating face down four feet up the trunk of a cocoanut tree.* Photo by Joseph K. Long.

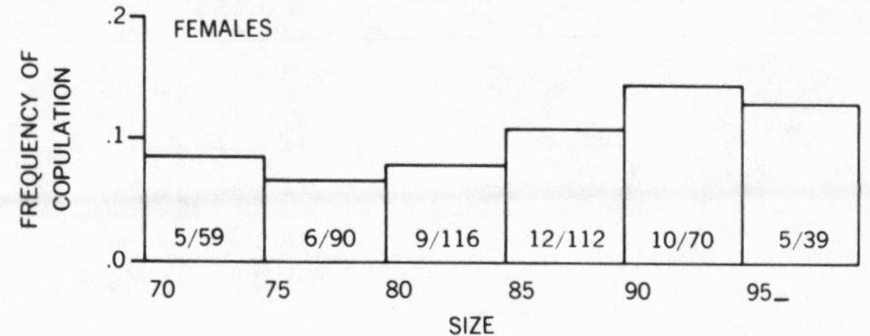

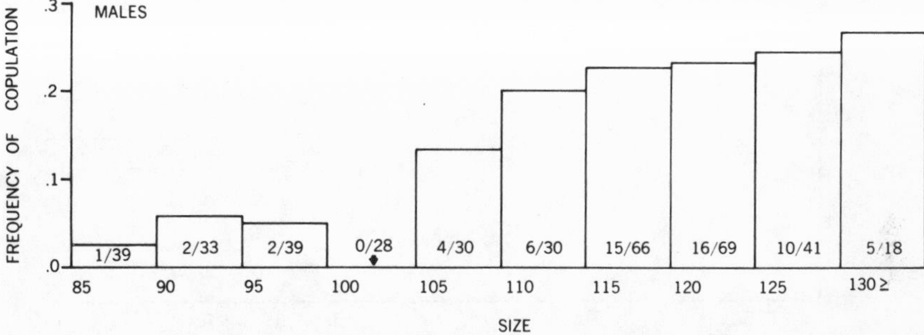

Figure 7.10. Reproductive success in male and female A. garmani *as a function of size. Reproductive success is measured by the number of copulations observed per number of individuals (male or female) in each nonoverlapping 5 mm size category. Data combined from five separate visits to study area between summer 1969 and summer 1971.*

than smaller ones, and this may partly be due to advantages in feeding through size-dependent aggressiveness, since larger females wander significantly more widely than smaller adult ones. An alternate interpretation (based on ecological competition between the sexes) has been proposed for sexual dimorphism in size among animals (Selander 1966), and the interpretation may apply to *Anolis* (Schoener 1967).

METABOLIC RATE

Certainly more is involved in differential male mortality than size, even in species in which males grow to a larger size than females. Although data show convincingly that nutritional factors strongly affect human male survival *in utero,* a sexual difference in size among humans is not detected until the twenty-fourth week after conception whereas differences in mortality appear as soon as the twelfth week. Sellers et al. (1950) have shown that male rats excrete four times the protein females do; the difference is removed by castration. Since males suffer more from protein-deficient diets than females (they gain less weight and survive less well) the sex-linked proteinuria, apparently unrelated to size, may be a factor in causing lower male survival in wild rats (Schein 1950). (The connection between

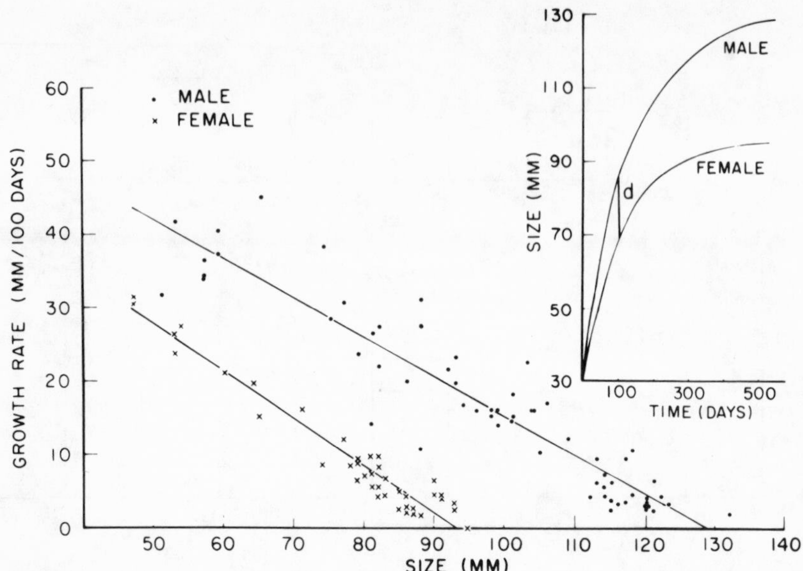

Figure 7.11. Male and female growth rates in A. garmani *as a function of initial size based on summer 1970 recaptures of animals marked 3 to 4 months before. A line has been fitted to each set of data;* d *indicates how much larger a male is when a similar aged female reaches sexual maturity.*

proteinuria and male reproductive success is obscure.) Again, although human male survival is more adversely affected by poor nutritional conditions than female survival, Hamilton (1948) presents evidence that the higher metabolic rate of the male is an important factor increasing his vulnerability to many diseases which strike males more heavily than females. Likewise, Taber & Dasmann (1954) argue that greater male mortality in the deer, *Odocoileus hemionus,* results from a higher metabolic rate. High metabolic rate could relate to both aggressiveness and searching behavior.

EXPERIENCE

If reproductive success increases more rapidly in one sex than the other as a function of age alone (for example, through age-dependent experience), then one would expect a postponement of sexual maturity in that sex and a greater chance of surviving through a unit of time than in the opposite sex. Thus, the adult sex ratio might be biased in favor of the earlier maturing sex but the sex ratio for all ages taken together should be biased in favor of the later maturing sex. Of course, if reproductive success for one sex increases strongly as a function of experience and experience only partly correlates with age, then the sex may be willing to suffer increased mortality if this mortality is sufficiently offset by increases in experience. Selander (1965) has suggested that the tendency of immature male blackbirds to exhibit some mature characteristics may be adaptive in that it increases the male's experience, although it also presumably increases his risk of mortality.

MOBILITY

Data from mammals (reviewed by Eisenberg 1965 and Brown 1966) and from some salamanders (Madison & Shoop 1970) and numerous lizards (Tinkle 1967 and Blair 1960) suggest that males often occupy larger home ranges and wander more widely than females *even when males are smaller* (Blair 1965). Parker (1970a) has quantified the importance of mobility and searching behavior in dung flies. If females are a dispersed resource, then male mobility may be crucial in exposing the male to a large number of available females. Again, males may be willing to incur greater mortality if this is sufficiently offset by increases in reproductive success. This factor should only affect the male during the breeding season (Kikkawa 1964) unless factors relevant to mobility (such as speed, agility or knowledge of the environment) need to be developed prior to the reproductive season. Lindburg (1969) has shown that macaque males, but not females, change troops more frequently during the reproductive season than otherwise and that this mobility increases male reproductive success as measured by frequency of copulation, suggesting that at least in this species, greater mobility can be confined to the reproductive season (see also Miller 1958). On the other hand, Taber & Dasmann (1954) present evidence that as early as six months of age male deer wander more widely from their mothers than females—a difference whose function, of course, is not known. Similar very early differences in mobility have been demonstrated for a lizard (Blair 1960) and for several primates, including man (Jensen, Bobbitt & Gordon 1968).

Female Choice

Although Darwin (1871) thought female choice an important evolutionary force, most writers since him have relegated it to a trivial role (Huxley 1938, Lack 1968; but see Fisher 1958, and Orians 1969). With notable exceptions the study of female choice has limited itself to showing that females are selected to decide whether a potential partner is of the right species, of the right sex and sexually mature. While the adaptive value of such choices is obvious, the adaptive value of subtler discriminations among broadly appropriate males is much more difficult to visualize or document. One needs both theoretical arguments for the adaptive value of such female choice and detailed data on how females choose. Neither of these criteria is met by those who casually ascribe to female (or male) choice the evolution of such traits as the relative hairlessness of both human sexes (Hershkovitz 1966) or the large size of human female breasts (Morris 1967). I review here theoretical considerations of how females might be expected to choose among the available males, along with some data on how females do choose.

SELECTION FOR OTHERWISE NEUTRAL OR DISFUNCTIONAL MALE ATTRIBUTES

The effects of female choice will depend on the way females choose. If some females exercise a preference for one type of male (genotype) while others mate at random, then other things being equal, selection will rapidly favor the preferred male type and the females with the preference (O'Donald 1962). If each female has a specific image of the male with whom she prefers to mate and if there is a decreasing probability of a female mating with a male as a function of his increasing deviation from her preferred image, then it is trivial to show that selection will favor distributions of female preferences and male attributes that coincide. Female choice can generate continuous male change only if females choose by a relative rather than an absolute criterion. That is, if there is a tendency for females to sample the male distribution and to prefer one extreme (for example, the more brightly colored males), then selection will move the male distribution toward the favored extreme. After a one generation lag, the distribution of female preferences will also move toward a greater percentage of females with extreme desires, because the granddaughters of females preferring the favored extreme will be more numerous than the granddaughters of females favoring other male attributes. Until countervailing selection intervenes, this female preference will, as first pointed out by Fisher (1958), move both male attributes and female preferences with increasing rapidity in the same direction. The female preference is capable of overcoming some countervailing selection on the male's ability to survive to reproduce, if the increased reproductive success of the favored males when mature offsets their chances of surviving to reproduce.

There are at least two conditions under which one might expect females to have been selected to prefer the extreme male of a sample. When two species, recently speciated, come together, selection rapidly favors females who can discriminate the two species of males. This selection may favor females who prefer the appropriate extreme of an available sample, since such a mechanism would minimize mating mistakes. The natural selection of females with such a mechanism of choice would then initiate sexual selection in the same direction, which in the absence of countervailing selection would move the two male phenotypes further apart than necessary to avoid mating error.

Natural selection will always favor female ability to discriminate male sexual competence, and the safest way to do this is to take the extreme of a sample, which would lead to runaway selection for male display. This case is discussed in more detail below.

SELECTION FOR OTHERWISE FUNCTIONAL MALE ATTRIBUTES

As in other aspects of sexual selection, the degree of male investment in the offspring is important and should affect the criteria of female choice. Where the male invests little or nothing beyond his sex cells, the female has only to decide which male offers the ideal genetic material for her offspring, assuming that male is willing and capable of offering it. This question can be broken down to that of which genes will promote the survival of her offspring and which will lead to reproductive success, assuming the offspring survive to adulthood. Implicit in these questions may be the relation between her genes and those of her mate: do they complement each other?

Where the male invests parental care, female choice may still involve the above questions of the male's genetic contribution but should also involve, perhaps primarily involve, questions of the male's willingness and ability to be a good parent. Will he invest in the offspring? If willing, does he have the ability to contribute much? Again, natural selection may favor female attentiveness to complementarity: do the male's parental abilities complement her own? Can the two parents work together smoothly? Where males invest considerable parental care, most of the same considerations that apply to female choice also apply to male choice. The alternate criteria for female choice are summarized in Table 7.1.

SEXUAL COMPETENCE

Even in males selected for rapid, repeated copulations the ability to do so is not unlimited. After three or four successive ejaculations, for example, the concentration of spermatozoa is very low in some male chickens (Parker, McKenzie & Kempster 1940), yet males may copulate as often as 30 times in an hour (Guhl 1951). Likewise, sperm is completely depleted in male *Drosophila melanogaster* after the fifth consecutive mating on the same day (Demerec & Kaufmann 1941, Kaufmann & Demerec 1942). Duration of copulation is cut in half by the third copulation of a male dung fly on the same day and duration of copulation probably correlates with sperm transferred (Parker 1970a). In some species females may be able to judge whether additional sperm are needed (for example, house flies; Riemann, Moen & Thorson 1967) or whether a copulation is at least behaviorally successful (for example, sea lions; Peterson & Bartholomew 1967), but in many species females may guarantee reproductive success by mat-

Table 7.1. Theoretical criteria for female choice of males

- I. All species, but especially those showing little or no male parental investment
  - A. Ability to fertilize eggs
    - (1) correct species
    - (2) correct sex
    - (3) mature
    - (4) sexually competent
  - B. Quality of genes
    - (1) ability of genes to survive
    - (2) reproductive ability of genes
    - (3) complementarity of genes
- II. Only those species showing male parental investment
  - C. Quality of parental care
    - (1) willingness of male to invest
    - (2) ability of male to invest
    - (3) complementarity of parental attributes

ing with those males who are most vigorous in courtship, since this vigor may correlate with an adequate supply of sperm and a willingness to transfer it.

When the male is completely depleted, there is no advantage in his copulating but selection against the male doing so should be much weaker than selection against the female who accepts him. At intermediate sperm levels, the male may gain something from copulation, but the female should again be selected to avoid him. Since there is little advantage to the male in concealing low reproductive powers, a correlation between vigor of courtship and sperm level would not be surprising. Females would then be selected to be aroused by vigorous courtship. If secondary structures used in display, such as bright feathers, heighten the appearance of vigorousness, then selection may rapidly accentuate such structures. Ironically, the male who has been sexually most successful may not be ideal to mate with if this success has temporarily depleted his sperm supply. Males should not only be selected to recover rapidly from copulations but to give convincing evidence that they have recovered. It is not absurd to suppose that in some highly promiscuous species the most attractive males may be those who, having already been observed to mate with several females, are still capable of vigorous display toward a female in the process of choosing.

GOOD GENES

Maynard Smith (1956) has presented evidence that, given a choice, female *Drosophila subobscura* discriminate against inbred males of that species and that this behavior is adaptive: females who do not so discriminate leave about ¼ as many viable offspring as those who do. Females may choose on the basis of courtship behavior: inbred males are apparently unable to perform a step of the typical courtship as rapidly as outbred males. The work is particularly interesting in revealing that details of courtship behavior may reveal a genetic trait, such as being inbred, but it suffers from an artificiality. If inbred males produce mostly inviable offspring, then, even in the absence of female discrimination, one would expect very few, if any, inbred males to be available in the adult population. Only because such males were artificially selected were there large numbers to expose to females in choice experiments. Had that selection continued one generation further, females who chose inbred males would have been the successful females.

Maynard Smith's study highlights the problem of analyzing the potential for survival of one's partner's genes: one knows of the adult males one meets that they have survived to adulthood; by what criterion does one decide who has survived better? If the female can judge age, then all other things being equal, she should choose older males, as they have demonstrated their capacity for long survival. All other things may not be equal, however, if old age correlates with lowered reproductive success, as it does in some ungulates (Fraser 1968) through reduced ability to impregnate. If the female can judge the physical condition of males she encounters, then she can discriminate against undernourished or sickly individuals, since they will be unlikely to survive long, but discrimination against such individuals may occur for other reasons, such as the presumed lowered ability of such males to impregnate successfully due to the weakened condition.

In some very restricted ways it may be possible to second-guess the future action of natural selection. For example, stabilizing selection has been demonstrated to be a common form of natural selection (see Mayr 1963) and under this form of selection females may be selected to exercise their own discrimination against extreme types, thereby augmenting the effects of any stabilizing selection that has occurred prior to reproduction. Mason (1969) has demonstrated that females of the California Oak Moth discriminate against males extreme in some traits, but no one has shown independent stabilizing selection for the same traits. Discrimination against extreme types may run counter to selection for diversity; the possible role of female choice in increasing or decreasing diversity is discussed below as a form of complementarity.

Reproductive success, independent of ability to survive is easier for the female to gauge because she can directly observe differences in reproductive success before she chooses. A striking feature of data on lek behavior of birds is the tendency for females to choose males who, through competition with other males, have already increased their likelihood of mating. Female choice then greatly augments the effects of male–male competition. On the lek grounds there is an obvious reason why this may be adaptive.

By mating with the most dominant male a female can usually mate more quickly, and hence more safely, than if she chooses a less dominant individual whose attempts at mating often result in interference from more dominant males. Scott (1942) has shown that many matings with less dominant individuals occur precisely when the more dominant individuals are unable, either because of sexual exhaustion or a long waiting line, to quickly service the female. Likewise, Robel (1970) has shown that a dominant female prevents less dominant individuals from mating until she has mated, presumably to shorten her stay and to copulate while the dominant male still can. A second reason why choosing to mate with more dominant males may be adaptive is that the female allies her genes with those of a male who, by his ability to dominate other males, has demonstrated his reproductive capacity. It is a common observation in cervids that females placidly await the outcome of male strife to go with the victor. DeVore (1965) has quantified the importance of dominance in male baboon sexual success, emphasizing the high frequency of interference by other males in copulation and the tendency for female choice, when it is apparent, to be exercised in favor of dominant males. That previous success may increase the skill with which males court females is suggested by work on the black grouse (Kruijt, Bossema and deVos, *in press*), and females may prefer males skillful at courting in part because their skill correlates with previous success.

In many species the ability of the male to find receptive females quickly may be more important than any ability to dominate other males. If this is so, then female choice may be considerably simplified: the first male to reach her establishes thereby a *prima facie* case for his reproductive abilities. In dung flies, in which females must mate quickly while the dung is fresh, male courtship behavior is virtually nonexistent (Parker 1970a). The male who first leaps on top of a newly arrived female copulates with her. This lack of female choice may also result from the *prima facie* case the first male establishes for his sound reproductive abilities. Such a mechanism of choice may of course conflict with other criteria requiring a sampling of the male population, but in some species this sampling could be carried out prior to becoming sexually receptive.

There are good data supporting the importance of complementarity of genes to female choice. Assortative mating in the wild has been demonstrated for several bird species (Cooch & Beardmore 1959, O'Donald 1959) and disassortative mating for a bird species and a moth species (Lowther 1961, Sheppard 1952). Petit & Ehrman (1969) have demonstrated the tendency in several *Drosophila* species for females to prefer mating with the rare type in choice experiments, a tendency which in the wild leads to a form of complementarity, since the female is presumably usually of the common type. These studies can all be explained plausibly in terms of selection for greater or lesser genetic diversity, the female choosing a male whose genes complement her own, producing an "optimal" diversity in the offspring.

GOOD PARENT

Where male parental care is involved, females certainly sometimes choose males on the basis of their ability to contribute parental care. Orians (1969), for example, has recently reviewed arguments and data suggesting that polygyny evolves in birds when becoming the second mate of an already mated male provides a female with greater male parental contribution than becoming the first mate of an unmated male would. This will be so, for example, if the already mated male defends a territory considerably superior to the unmated male's. Variability in territory quality certainly occurs in most territorial species, even in those in which territories are not used for feeding. Tinbergen (1967), for example, has documented the tendency for central territories in the black-headed gull to be less vulnerable to predation. If females compete among themselves for males with good territories, or if males exercise choice as well, then female choice for parental abilities will again tend to augment intra-male competition for the relevant resources (such as territories). The most obvious form of this selection is the inability of a nonterritory holding male to attract a female.

Female choice may play a role in selecting for increased male parental investment. In the roadrunner, for example, food caught by a male seems to act on him as an aphrodisiac: he runs to a female and courts her with the food, suggesting that the female would not usually mate without such a gift (Calder 1967). Male parental care invested after copulation is presumably not a result of female choice after copulation, since she no longer has anything to bargain with. In most birds, however, males defend territories which initially attract the females (Lack 1940). Since males without suitable territories are unable to attract a mate, female choice may play a role in maintaining male territorial behavior. Once a male has invested in a territory in order to attract a mate his options after copulating with her may be severely limited. Driving the female out of his territory would almost certainly result in the loss of his investment up until then. He could establish another territory, and in some species some males do this (von Haartman 1951), but in many species this may be difficult, leaving him with the option of aiding, more or less, the female he has already mated. Female choice, then, exercised *before* copulation, may indirectly force the male to increase his parental investment *after* copulation.

There is no reason to suppose that males do not compete with each other to pair with those females whose breeding potential appears to be high. Darwin (1871) argued that females within a species breeding early for nongenetic reasons (such as being in excellent physical condition) would produce more offspring than later breeders. Sexual selection, he argued, would favor males competing with each other to pair with such females. Fisher (1958) has nicely summarized this argument, but Lack (1968, p. 157) dismisses it as being "not very cogent," since "the date of breeding in birds has been evolved primarily in relation to two different factors, namely the food supply for the young and the capacity of the female to form eggs." These facts are, of course, fully consistent with Darwin's argument, since Darwin is merely supposing a developmental plasticity that allows females to breed earlier if they are capable of forming the eggs, and data presented elsewhere in Lack (1968) support the argument that females breeding earlier for nongenetic reasons (such as age or duration of pair bond) are more successful than those breeding later (see also, for example, Fisher 1969, and Coulson 1966). Goforth & Baskett (1971) have recently shown that dominant males in a penned Mourning Dove population preferentially pair with dominant females; such pairs breed earlier and produce more surviving young than less dominant pairs. It would be interesting to have detailed data from other species on the extent to which males do compete for females with higher breeding potential. Males are certainly often initially aggressive to females intruding in their territories, and this aggressiveness may act as a sieve, admitting only those females whose high motivation correlates with early egg laying and high reproductive potential. There is good evidence that American women tend to marry up the socioeconomic scale, and physical attractiveness during adolescence facilitiates such movement (Elder 1969). Until recently such a bias in female choice presumably correlated with increased reproductive success, but the value, if any, of female beauty for male reproductive success is obscure.

The importance of choice by both female and male for a mate who will not desert nor participate in sex outside the pair bond has been emphasized in an earlier section ("Desertion and cuckoldry"). The importance of complementarity is documented in a study by Coulson (1966).

CRITERIA OTHER THAN MALE CHARACTERS

In many species male–male competition combined with the importance of some resource in theory unrelated to males, such as oviposition sites may mitigate against female choice for male characters. In the dragonfly *Parthemis tenera* males compete with each other to control territories containing good oviposition sites, probably because such sites are a predictable place at which to find receptive females and because sperm competition in insects usually favors the last male to copulate prior to oviposition (Parker 1970b). It is clear that the females choose the oviposition site and not the male (Jacobs 1955), and male courtship is geared to advertise good oviposition sites. A male maintaining a territory containing a good oviposition site is *not* thereby contributing parental investment unless that maintenance benefits the resulting young.

Female choice for oviposition sites may be an especially important determinant of male competition in those species, such as frogs and salamanders, showing external fertilization. Such female choice almost certainly predisposed these species to the evolution of male parental investment. Female choice for good oviposition sites would tend to favor any male investment in improving the site, and if attached to the site to attract other females the male would have the option of caring more or less for those eggs already laid. A similar argument was advanced above for birds. Internal fertilization and development mitigate against evolution of male parental care in mammals, since female choice can then usually only operate to favor male courtship feeding, which in herbivores would be nearly valueless. Female choice may also favor males who mate away from oviposition sites if so doing reduced the probability of predation.

Where females are clumped in space the effects of male competition may render female choice almost impossible. In a monkey troop a female preference for a less dominant male may never lead to sexual congress if the pair are quickly broken up and attacked by more dominant males. Apparent female acquiescence in the results of male–male competition may reflect this factor as much as the plausible female preference for the male victor outlined above.

Summary

The relative parental investment of the sexes in their young is the key variable controlling the operation of sexual selection. Where one sex invests considerably more than the other, members of the latter will compete among themselves to mate with members of the former. Where investment is equal, sexual selection should operate similarly on the two sexes. The pattern of relative parental investment in species today seems strongly influenced by the early evolutionary differention into mobile sex cells fertilizing immobile ones, and sexual selection acts to mold the pattern of relative parental investment. The time sequence of parental investment analyzed by sex is an important parameter affecting species in which both sexes invest considerable parental care: the individual initially investing more (usually the female) is vulnerable to desertion. On the other hand, in species with internal fertilization and strong male parental investment, the male is always vulnerable to cuckoldry. Each vulnerability has led to the evolution of adaptations to decrease the vulnerability and to counter-adaptations.

Females usually suffer higher mortality rates than males in monogamous birds, but in nonmonogamous birds and all other groups, males usually suffer higher rates. The chromosomal hypothesis is unable to account for the data. Instead, an adaptive interpretation can be advanced based on the relative parental investment of the sexes. In species with little or no male parental investment, selection usually favors male adaptations that lead to high reproductive success in one or more breeding seasons at the cost of increased mortality. Male competition in such species can only be analyzed in detail when the distribution of females in space and time is properly described. Data from field studies suggest that in some species, size, mobility, experience and metabolic rate are important to male reproductive success.

Female choice can augment or oppose mortality selection. Female choice can only lead to runaway change in male morphology when females choose by a relative rather than absolute standard, and it is probably sometimes adaptive for females to so choose. The relative parental investment of the sexes affects the criteria of female choice (and of male choice). Throughout, I emphasize that sexual selection favors different male and female reproductive strategies and that even when ostensibly cooperating in a joint task male and female interests are rarely identical.

References

Bartholomew, G. A. 1970. A model for the evolution of pinniped polygyny. *Evolution* 24: 546–559.

Bastock, M. 1967. *Courtship: An ethological study*. Chicago: Aldine.

Bateman, A. J. 1948. Intrasexual selection in Drosophila. *Heredity* 2: 349–368.

Beebe, W. 1925. The variegated Tinamou *Crypturus variegatus variegatus* (Gmelin). *Zoologica* 6: 195–227.

Beer, J. R., L. D. Frenzel, & C. F. MacLeod. 1958. Sex ratios of some Minnesota rodents. *American Midland Naturalist* 59: 518–524.

Beverton, J. M., & S. J. Holt. 1959. A review of the lifespan and mortality rates of fish in nature and their relation to growth and other physiological characteristics. In *The lifespan of animals,* ed. G. Wolstenhome & M. O'Connor, pp. 142–177. London: J. & A. Churchill.

Blair, W. F. 1960. *The Rusty Lizard*. Austin: University of Texas.

Bouliere, Z. F., & Verschuren, J. 1960. *Introduction a l'ecologie des ongules du Parc National Albert*. Bruxelles: Institut des Parcs Nationaux du Congo Belge.

Bragg, A. N. 1965. *Gnomes of the night*. Philadelphia: University of Pennsylvania Press.

Brown, L. E. 1966. Home range and movement of small mammals. *Symposium of the Zoological Society of London* 18: 111–142.

Bruce, H. 1960. A block to pregnancy in the mouse caused by the proximity of strange males. *Journal of Reproduction and Fertility* 1: 96–103.

Burns, J. M. 1968. Mating frequency in natural populations of skippers and butterflies as determined by spermatophore counts. *Proceedings of the National Academy of Sciences* 61: 852–859.

Calder, W. A. 1967. Breeding behavior of the Roadrunner, *Geococcyx californianus*. *Auk* 84: 597–598.

Carpenter, C. 1967. Aggression and social structure in Iguanid lizards. In *Lizard ecology,* ed. W. Milstead. Columbia, Mo.: University of Missouri.

Chapman, A. B., L. E. Casida, & A. Cote. 1938. Sex ratios of fetal calves. *Proceedings of the American Society of Animal Production* 1938, pp. 303–304.

Cooch, F. G., & M. A. Beardmore. 1959. Assortative mating and reciprocal difference in the Blue-Snow Goose complex. *Nature* 183: 1833–1834.

Corbet, P., C. Longfield, & W. Moore. 1960. *Dragonflies*. London: Collins.

Coulson, J. C. 1960. A study of the mortality of the starling based on ringing recoveries. *Journal of Animal Ecology* 29: 251–271.

———. 1966. The influence of the pair-bond and age on the breeding biology of the kittiwake gull *Rissa tridactyla*. *Journal of Animal Ecology* 35: 269–279.

Cowan, I. M. 1950. Some vital statistics of big game on overstocked mountain range. *Transactions of North American Wildlife Conference* 15: 581–588.

Darley, J. 1971. Sex ratio and mortality in the brown-headed cowbird. *Auk* 88: 560–566.

Darwin, C. 1871. *The descent of man, and selection in relation to sex*. London: John Murray.

Demerec, M., & Kaufmann, B. P. 1941. Time required for *Drosophila* males to exhaust the supply of mature sperm. *American Naturalist* 75: 366–379.

DeVore, I. 1965. Male dominance and mating behavior in baboons. In *Sex and behavior,* ed. Frank Beach. New York: John Wiley and Sons.

deVos, A., P. Broky, & V. Geist. 1967. A review of social behavior of the North American Cervids during the reproductive period. *American Midland Naturalist* 77: 390–417.

Dunn, E. R. 1941. Notes on *Dendrobates auratus*. *Copeia* 1941, pp. 88–93.

Eaton, T. H. 1941. Notes on the life history of *Dendrobates auratus*. *Copeia* 1941, pp. 93–95.

Eisenberg, J. F. 1965. The social organizations of mammals. *Handbuch der Zoologie* 10 (7): 1–92.

Elder, G. 1969. Appearance and education in marriage mobility. *American Sociological Review* 34: 519–533.

Emlen, J. M. 1968. A note on natural selection and the sex-ratio. *American Naturalist* 102: 94–95.

Emlen, J. T. 1940. Sex and age ratios in the survival of the California Quail. *Journal of Wildlife Management* 4: 91–99.

Emlen, S. T. 1968. Territoriality in the bullfrog, *Rana catesbeiana*. *Copeia* 1968, pp. 240–243.

Engelmann, F. 1970. *The physiology of insect reproduction*. Oxford: Pergamon Press.

Fiedler, K. 1954. Vergleichende Verhaltensstudien an Seenadeln, Schlangennadeln und Seepferdchen (Syngnathidae). *Zeitsch. Tierpsych.* 11: 358–416. 358–416.

Fisher, H. 1969. Eggs and egg-laying in the Laysan Albatross, *Diomedea immutabilis*. *Condor* 71: 102–112.

Fisher, R. A. 1958. *The genetical theory of natural selection*. New York: Dover Publications.

Fraser, A. F. 1968. *Reproductive behavior in Ungulates*.London and New York: Academic Press.

Gadgil, M., & W. H. Bossert. 1970. Life historical consequences of natural selection. *American Naturalist* 104: 1–24.

Goethals, G. W. 1971. Factors affecting permissive and nonpermissive rules regarding premarital sex. In *Studies in the sociology of sex: a book of readings,* ed. J. M. Henslin. New York: Appleton-Century-Croft.

Goforth, W., & T. Baskett. 1971. Social organization of penned Mourning Doves. *Auk* 88: 528–542.

Guhl, A. M. 1951. Measurable differences in mating behavior of cocks. *Poultry Science* 30: 687.

Haartman, L. von. 1951. Successive polygamy. *Behavior* 3: 256–274.

———. 1969. Nest-site and evolution of polygamy in European Passerine birds. *Ornis Fennica* 46: 1–12.

Hamilton, J. B. 1948. The role of testicular secretions as indicated by the effects of castration in man and by studies of pathological conditions and the short lifespan associated with maleness. *Recent Progress in Hormone Research* 3: 257–322.

Hamilton, J. B., & M. Johansson. 1965. Influence of sex chromosomes and castration upon lifespan: studies of meal moths, a species in which sex chromosomes are homogenous in males and heterogenous in females. *Anatomical Record* 24: 565–578.

Hamilton, J. B., & G. E. Mestler. 1969. Mortality and survival: comparison of eunuchs with intact men and women in a mentally retarded population. *Journal of Gerontology* 24: 395–411.

Hamilton, J. B., R. S. Hamilton, & G. E. Mestler. 1969. Duration of life and causes of death in domestic cats: influence of sex, gonadectomy and inbreeding. *Journal of Gerontology* 24: 427–437.

Hamilton, W. D. 1964. The genetical evolution of social behavior. *Journal of Theoretical Biology* 7: 1–52.

———. 1967. Extraordinary sex ratios. *Science* 156: 477–488.

Harris, V. A. 1964. *The life of the Rainbow Lizard.* Hutchinson Tropical Monographs. London.

Hays, F. A. 1947. Mortality studies in Rhode Island Reds II. *Massachusetts Agricultural Experiment Station Bulletin* 442: 1–8.

Hershkovitz, P. 1966. Letter to *Science* 153: 362.

Hirth, H. F. 1963. The ecology of two lizards on a tropical beach. *Ecological Monographs* 33: 83–112.

Höhn, E. O. 1967. Observations on the breeding biology of Wilson's Phalarope (*Steganopus tricolor*) in Central Alberta. *Auk* 84: 220–244.

Huxley, J. S. 1938. The present standing of the theory of sexual selection. In *Evolution,* ed. G. DeBeer. New York: Oxford Univ. Press.

Jacobs, M. 1955. Studies in territorialism and sexual selection in dragonflies. *Ecology* 36: 566–586.

Jensen, G. D., Bobbitt, R. A. & Gordon, B. N. 1968. Sex differences in the development of independence of infant monkeys. *Behavior* 30: 1–14.

Johns, J. E. 1969. Field studies of Wilson's Phalarope. *Auk* 86: 660–670.

Kaufmann, B. P., & Demerec, M. 1942. Utilization of sperm by the female *Drosophila melanogaster*. *American Naturalist* 76: 445–469.

Kessel, E. L. 1955. The mating activities of baloon flies. *Systematic Zoology* 4: 97–104.

Kikkawa, J. 1964. Movement, activity and distribution of small rodents *Clethrionomys glareolus* and *Apodemus sylvaticus* in woodland. *Journal of Animal Ecology* 33: 259–299.

Kluijver, H. N. 1933. Bijrage tot de biologie en de ecologie van den spreeuw (*Sturnus vulgaris* L.) gedurende zijn voortplantingstijd. *Versl. Plantenziektenkundigen dienst, Wageningen* 69: 1–145.

Koivisto, I. 1965. Behaviour of the black grouse during the spring display. *Finnish Game Research* 26: 1–60.

Kolman, W. 1960. The mechanism of natural selection for the sex ratio. *American Naturalist* 94: 373–377.

Kopstein, F. 1941. Über Sexualdimorphismus bei Malaiischen Schlangen. *Temminckia,* 6: 109–185.

Kruijt, J. P, I. Bossema, & G. J. deVos. *In Press.* Factors underlying choice of mate in Black Grouse. *15th Congr. Intern. Ornith.,* The Hague, 1970.

Kruijt, J. P., & J. A. Hogan. 1967. Social behavior on the lek in Black Grouse, *Lyrurus tetrix tetrix* (L.) *Ardea* 55: 203–239.

Lack, D. 1940. Pair-formation in birds. *Condor* 42: 269–286.

————. 1954. *The natural regulation of animal numbers.* New York: Oxford University Press.

————. 1968. *Ecological adaptations for breeding in birds.* London: Methuen.

LeBoeuf, B. J., & R. S. Peterson. 1969. Social status and mating activity in elephant seals. *Science* 163: 91–93.

Lee, R., 1969, King Bushman violence. Paper presented at meeting of American Anthropological Association, November, 1969.

Leigh, E. G. 1970. Sex ratio and differential mortality between the sexes. *American Naturalist* 104: 205–210.

Lin, N. 1963. Territorial behavior in the Cicada killer wasp *Sphecius speciosus* (Drury) (Hymenoptera: Sphecidae.) I. *Behaviour* 20: 115–133.

Lindburg, D. G. 1969. Rhesus monkeys: mating season mobility of adult males. *Science* 166: 1176–1178.

Lowther, J. K. 1961. Polymorphism in the white-throated sparrow, *Zonotrichia albicollis* (Gmelin). *Canadian Journal of Zoology* 39: 281–292.

Ludwig, W., & C. Boost. 1951. Über Beziehungen zwischen Elternalter, Wurfgrösse und Geschlechtsverhältnis bei Hunden. *Zeitschrift fur indukt. Abstammungs und Vererbungslehre* 83: 383–391.

Madison, D. M., & Shoop, C. R. 1970. Homing behavior, orientation, and home range of salamanders tagged with tantalum–182. *Science* 168: 1484–1487.

Mason, L. G. 1969. Mating selection in the California Oak Moth (Lepidoptera, Droptidae). *Evolution* 23: 55–58.

Maynard Smith, J. 1956. Fertility, mating behaviour and sexual selection in *Drosophila subobscura. Journal of Genetics* 54: 261–279.

Mayr, E. 1939. The sex ratio in wild birds. *American Naturalist* 73: 156–179.

————. 1963. *Animal species and evolution.* Cambridge: Harvard University Press.

Miller, R. S. 1958. A study of a wood mouse population in Wytham Woods, Berkshire. *Journal of Mammalogy* 39: 477–493.

Morris, D. 1952. Homosexuality in the Ten-spined Stickleback (*Pygosteus pungitius*). *Behaviour* 4: 233–261.

————. 1967. *The naked ape.* New York: McGraw Hill.

Myers, J., & C. Krebs. 1971. Sex ratios in open and closed vole populations: demographic implications. *American Naturalist* 105: 325–344.

Nevo, R. W. 1956. A behavior study of the red-winged blackbird. 1. Mating and nesting activities. *Wilson Bulletin* 68: 5–37.

O'Donald, P. 1959. Possibility of assortative mating in the Arctic Skua. *Nature* 183: 1210.

————. 1962. The theory of sexual selection. *Heredity* 17: 541–552.

Orians, G. H. 1969. On the evolution of mating systems in birds and mammals. *American Naturalist* 103: 589–604.

Parker, G. A. 1970a. The reproductive behavior and the nature of sexual selection in *Scatophaga stercoraria* L. (Diptera: Scatophagidae) 2. The fertilization rate and the spatial and temporal relationships of each sex around the site of mating and oviposition. *Journal of Animal Ecology* 39: 205–228.

———. 1970b. Sperm competition and its evolutionary consequences in the insects. *Biological Reviews* 45: 525–568.

———.1970c. The reproductive behaviour and the nature of sexual selection in *Scatophaga stercoraria* L. (Diptera: Scatophagidae) VI. The adaptive significance of emigration from the oviposition site during the phase of genital contact. *Journal of Animal Ecology* 40: 215–233.

———. 1970d. The reproductive behaviour and the nature of sexual selection in *Scatophaga stercoraria* L. (Diptera: Scatophagidae). VI. The adaptive sig-evolution of the passive phase. *Evolution* 24: 774–788.

Parker, J. E., F. F. McKenzie, & H. L. Kempster. 1940. Observations on the sexual behavior of New Hampshire males. *Poultry Science* 19: 191–197.

Peterson, R. S., & G. A. Bartholomew. 1967. *The natural history and behavior of the California Sea Lion*. Special Publications #1, American Society of Mammalogists.

Petit, C., & L. Ehrman. 1969. Sexual selection in *Drosophila*. In *Evolutionary biology,* vol. 5, ed. T. Dobzhansky, M. K. Hecht, W. C. Steere. New York: Appleton-Century-Crofts.

Potts, G. R. 1969. The influence of eruptive movements, age, population size and other factors on the survival of the Shag (*Phalacrocorax aristotelis* L.). *Journal of Animal Ecology* 38: 53–102.

Rand, A. S. 1967. Ecology and social organization in the Iguanid lizard *Anolis lineatopus*. *Proc. U.S. Nat. Mus.* 122: 1–79.

Riemann, J. G., D. J. Moen, & B. J. Thorson. 1967. Female monogamy and its control in house flies. *Insect Physiology* 13: 407–418.

Rivero, J. A., & A. E. Estevez. 1969. Observations on the agonistic and breeding behavior of *Leptodactylus pentadactylus* and other amphibian species in Venezuela. *Breviora No.* 321: 1–14.

Robel, R. J. 1966. Booming territory size and mating success of the Greater Prairie Chicken (*Tympanuchus cupido pinnatus*). *Animal Behaviour* 14: 328–331.

Robel, R. J. 1970. Possible role of behavior in regulating greater prairie chicken populations. *Journal of Wildlife Management* 34: 306–312.

Robinette, W. L., J. S. Gashwiler, J. B. Low, & D. A. Jones. 1957. Differential mortality by sex and age among mule deer. *Journal of Wildlife Management* 21: 1–16.

Rockstein, M. 1959. The biology of ageing insects. In *The lifespan of animals,* ed. G. Wolstenhome & M. O'Connor, pp. 247–264. London: J. A. Churchill.

Rowley, I. 1965. The life history of the Superb Blue Wren *Malarus cyaneus*. *Emu* 64: 251–297.

Royama, T. 1966. A re-interpretation of courtship feeding. *Bird Study* 13: 116–129.

Sadleir, R. 1967. *The ecology of reproduction in wild and domestic mammals.* London: Methuen.

Savage, R. M. 1961. *The ecology and life history of the common frog.* London: Sir Isaac Pitman and Sons.

Schein, M. W. 1950. The relation of sex ratio to physiological age in the wild brown rat. *American Naturalist* 84: 489–496.

Schoener, T. W. 1967. The ecological significance of sexual dimorphism in size in the lizard *Anolis conspersus*. *Science* 155: 474–477.

———. 1971. Theory of feeding strategies. *Annual Review of Ecology and Systematics,* 2: 369–404.

Scott, J. W. 1942. Mating behavior of the Sage Grouse. *Auk* 59: 477–498.

Selander, R. K. 1965. On mating systems and sexual selection. *American Naturalist* 99: 129–141.

———. 1966. Sexual dimorphism and differential niche utilization in birds. *Condor* 68: 113–151.

Sellers, A., H. Goodman, J. Marmorston, & M. Smith. 1950. Sex differences in proteinuria in the rat. *American Journal of Physiology* 163: 662–667.

Sheppard, P. M. 1952. A note on non-random mating in the moth *Panaxia dominula.* (L.) *Heredity* 6: 239–241.

Stephens, M. N. 1952. Seasonal observations on the Wild Rabbit (*Oryctolagus cuniculus cuniculus* L.) in West Wales. *Proceedings of the Zoological Society of London* 122: 417–434.

Stokes, A., & H. Williams. 1971. Courtship feeding in gallinaceous birds. *Auk* 88: 543–559.

Sugiyama, U. 1967. Social organization of Hanuman langurs. In *Social communication among primates,* ed. S. Altmann. Chicago: University of Chicago Press.

Taber, R. D., & R. F. Dasmann. 1954. A sex difference in mortality in young Columbian Black-tailed Deer. *Journal of Wildlife Management* 18: 309–315.

Tilley, S. 1968. Size-fecundity relationships and their evolutionary implications in five Desmognathine salamanders. *Evolution* 22: 806–816.

Tinbergen, N. 1935. Field observations of East Greenland birds. 1. The behavior of the Red-necked Phalarope (*Phalaropus lobatus* L.) in Spring. *Ardea* 24: 1–42.

———. 1967. Adaptive features of the Black-headed Gull *Larus ridibundus* L. *Proceedings of the International Ornithological Congress* 14: 43–59.

Tinkle, D. W. 1967. The life and demography of the Side-blotched Lizard, *Uta stansburiana. Miscellaneous Publications of the Museum of Zoology, University of Michigan* 132: 1–182.

Tinkle, D., H. Wilbur, & S. Tilley. 1970. Evolutionary strategies in lizard reproduction. *Evolution* 24: 55–74.

Tyndale-Biscoe, C. H. and R. F. C. Smith. 1969. Studies on the marsupial glider, *Schoinobates volans* (Kerr). 2. Population structure and regulatory mechanisms. *Journal of Animal Ecology* 38: 637–650.

Van Lawick-Goodall, J. 1968. The behavior of free-living chimpanzees in the Gombe Stream Reserve. *Animal Behaviour Monographs* 1: 161–311.

Verner, J. 1964. Evolution of polygamy in the long-billed marsh wren. *Evolution* 18: 252–261.

———. 1965. Selection for sex ratio. *American Naturalist* 99: 419–421.

Verner, J., & M. Willson. 1969. Mating systems, sexual dimorphism, and the role of male North American passerine birds in the nesting cycle. *Ornithological Monographs* 9: 1–76.

Williams, G. C. 1966. *Adaptation and natural selection.* Princeton: Princeton University Press.

Willson, M., & E. Pianka. 1963. Sexual selection, sex ratio, and mating system. *American Naturalist* 97: 405–406.

Wood, D. H. 1970. An ecological study of *Antechinus stuartii* (Marsupialia) in a Southeast Queensland rain forest. *Australian Journal of Zoology* 18: 185–207.

8

ROBERT K. SELANDER
UNIVERSITY OF TEXAS

Sexual Selection and Dimorphism in Birds

Introduction

The signal importance of birds in the development and history of the theory of sexual selection is well known. Darwin (1871) cited many avian examples in his general statement of the theory in Chapter 8, and devoted four chapters to an account of sexual selection and dimorphism in birds, in which secondary sexual characters are more conspicuous and diversified than in any other class of vertebrates. As Ghiselin (1969, p. 225) notes: "The remarkable complexity of Darwin's thought is particularly well revealed in his discussion of sexual dimorphism in birds . . . [in which] he interrelates the major themes in *The Descent of Man*—namely, behavior, the laws of variation, and natural selection—to construct one of the most sophisticated arguments in his system." Birds also have figured prominently in the formulations of Wallace (1889) and other critics and proponents of rival theories, in the writings of the early students of animal coloration and behavior (Poulton 1890, Mottram 1915, Hingston 1933), and in the analyses of Fisher (1930), Huxley (1938abc, 1943), Maynard Smith (1958), Mayr (1942, 1963), and others who have translated Darwin's contributions into the language and conceptual framework of the synthetic theory of evolution. And much of the ecological and ethological research that provides a basis for modern interpretations of sexual dimorphism and other phenomena that Darwin sought to explain deals with birds.

I am indebted to R. S. Ralin for her expert assistance in the preparation of this review, and to the editor, B. G. Campbell, for his understanding and patience. I thank M. T. Ghiselin, G. H. Orians, and R. H. Wiley for comments on the manuscript.

My research is supported by grants from the National Institutes of Health (GM-15769) and the National Science Foundation (GB-15664).

My purpose in this review is to discuss selected examples of sexual dimorphism in birds arising from sexual selection and other causes. I shall evaluate, where pertinent, Darwin's contribution to an understanding of the phenomenon, and emphasize the ways in which modern research in population biology has advanced our understanding of the evolutionary processes involved. I have been particularly concerned with problems relating to the evolution of mating systems (and thus indirectly or directly to sexual dimorphism in morphology, physiology, and behavior), all of which are ultimately ecological in nature. My viewpoint will seem biased or enlightened, depending on the reader's philosophy, in the following respect. Accepting the position that Darwinian selection at the level of the individual is sufficient to explain the origin of adaptations, including those involved in complex social systems, I have not been concerned with "group selection" hypotheses and other approaches implying that "biotic adaptations" ("population" or "species adaptations") can exist at the expense of individual fitness (see review in Williams 1966).

The Theory of Sexual Selection

GENERAL BACKGROUND

Darwin introduced the thoery of sexual selection to account for certain characters and patterns of variation that did not appear to be explicable in terms of natural selection for adaptations promoting success in the "struggle for existence." In brief, his thoery was proposed to explain the existence of characters, "the acquisition of which is strictly due to reproductive advantage [over individuals of the same sex]." As Huxley (1963) has shown, Darwin was actually concerned with the possibility of distinguishing two modes of selection: *survival* (=natural) *selection* and *reproductive* (=sexual) *selection.* Strictly speaking, all characters directly affecting reproduction should be attributed to sexual selection, including those that facilitate copulation and fertilization and those involved in parental care. But Darwin and later writers restricted application of the term *sexual selection* to display characters or weapons that function shortly before and at the time of mating, that is, characters rather directly involved in obtaining mates and copulations.

Sexual dimorphism is of interest in that it shows that there is a class of characters (morphological, behavioral, and other) differentially expressed in the sexes because of sexual variation in ways of maximizing fitness (Fisher 1930). With regard to both survival and reproduction, adaptations may or may not be similar in the sexes. Thus, males and females may identically exploit a food niche and as a consequence be monomorphic in trophic features; or they may be differentially adapted for niche exploitation or other activities affecting survival. Similarly, displays and other adaptations for reproduction (including displays functioning in the maintenance of breeding territories and in courtship) may or may not be similar in the sexes. The central problem is to analyze the environmental and other conditions responsible for the variable combinations of survival- and reproduction-enhancing adaptations occurring in different species. Although particular attention has been given to sexual variation in these combinations, this aspect is, in a sense, secondary to the larger problem.

Although Darwin was concerned almost exclusively with sexual dimorphism, he was aware that with regard to a given character sexual selection may act uniformly on males and females, thus producing sexually selected monomorphism.[1] Of special interest to Darwin were display characters that by their extreme expression or development would seem to decrease the probability of survival. Because these characters could not be interpreted as adaptations maximizing "vigor" and hence survival, their existence seemed to refute the theory of natural selection and therefore required explanation. Although modern definitions of natural selection in terms of differential perpetuation of alleles and gene complexes (Dobzhansky 1970) remove the conceptual difficulty Darwin faced, there remains the intriguing problem of the causal bases of sexual variation in adaptive strategy. The phenomena that the theory of sexual selection attempted to explain form only a part, albeit a major one, of the larger picture of differential adaptation in individuals of populations.

In reviewing the Darwinian theory of sexual selection, both Fisher (1930) and Huxley (1938a) stressed the fact that two principles are involved: in Huxley's terminology, *epigamic selection* (involving behavioral interactions between male and female) and *intrasexual selection* (involving interactions among males or, less frequently, among females). The distinction is useful theoretically, although in practice it is often extremely difficult to differentiate between the effects of these two types of selection. Many authors, unjustifiably ignoring the intrasexual part of Darwin's theory, have restricted the concept of sexual selection to the epigamic aspect, as did Sibley (1957, p. 173) in defining sexual selection as "the reproductive advantage accruing to those genotypes which provide the stronger heterosexual stimuli." Wynne-Edwards (1962) and others have argued that Darwin himself considered the epigamic aspect more important than the intrasexual, but a careful reading of Darwin shows that this notion is erroneous. In Chapter 8 Darwin clearly expresses his position: "We shall further see, and it could never have been anticipated, that the power to charm the female has *sometimes been more important* than the power to conquer other males in battle" (italics mine). Perhaps because the epi-

1. Obviously the application of sexual selection theory cannot logically be limited to the so-called secondary sexual characters. The conventional system of classifying characters in relation to their sexual distribution and function is in many respects unsuitable for discussions of evolutionary processes.

gamic aspect of his theory was the more novel, and hence the more likely to be rejected by his critics, Darwin examined it in greater detail. But in general discussions of his theory he was usually careful to mention both epigamic and intrasexual aspects.

No purpose would be served by an extensive analysis of the diverse reasons that various authors have rejected or misinterpreted in whole or in part the theory of sexual selection, beginning with A. R. Wallace and continuing to the present. Wallace's rejection of the epigamic aspect of Darwin's theory clearly can be attributed to his dualistic philosophy, which would not allow even the rudimentary "aesthetic sense" in lower animals that seemed to be implied in the concept of mate selection on the basis of color or pattern. (Choice on the basis of animalistic "vigor" was acceptable, however.) Although Wallace's (1889) own theory of the origin of sexual dimorphism has certain elements of ingenuity, it is on the whole poorly reasoned and demonstrates severe deficiencies in his concept of causality. Yet Wallace's views remain influential. For example, Grant (1963, p. 243) believes that Wallace's "brilliant analysis" discredited the epigamic aspect of Darwin's theory, which Grant thinks does not provide a satisfactory explanation of "the development of ornamentation and song in the male sex." My own view is that Darwin's theoretical and descriptive contributions have for the most part been validated by modern work in population biology.

SOME DIFFICULTIES ENCOUNTERED BY DARWIN

Darwin's theory of sexual selection is, on the whole, less tightly reasoned than his theory of natural selection. But the evolution of differential adaptation of the sexes is an exceedingly complex subject, and its analysis demands integration of information and theory from several biological disciplines, such as genetics and behavior, that were in a primitive state in Darwin's time. Considering the limited resources of information (much of it anecdotal and erroneous) and relevant theory available to Darwin, the synthesis he achieved seems all the more remarkable. Before discussing the more significant aspects of Darwin's contribution, I should like to mention some areas in which Darwin encountered problems he was unable to resolve.

Darwin did not understand the fundamental reason why it is generally the male which is more strongly modified by sexual selection. Therefore he was forced to conclude that it is "the great eagerness" of the males that has "indirectly led to their much more frequently developing secondary sexual characters." To support this "explanation" he suggested that males are more variable than females, thus providing more material for sexual selection. But the argument becomes nearly circular when he notes that secondary sexual characters are extraordinarily variable and are usually confined to the males. At one point he comes close to grasping the solution to the problem of sexual variation in "eagerness" when he notes that "on the whole the expenditure of matter and force by the two sexes is probably nearly equal, though effected in very different ways and at different rates." This statement has a startlingly modern ring, and, indeed, an explanation of the problem can be developed along this general line (Williams 1966).

The relative variability of characters influenced by sexual selection has never been properly investigated. Darwin did not always make a clear distinction between intrapopulation and interpopulation variation, as, for example, in discussing ocelli in the Lepidoptera (Chapter 4). I suspect that age and seasonal factors contribute heavily to the variability of certain male secondary sexual characters, since from a genetic standpoint there is no reason to believe that they should be any more or any less variable than other characters. Unusual variability might be expected in characters subserving the function of individual recognition (Marler 1960, Marler & Hamilton 1966, and various chapters in Hinde 1969), or if there were a premium on novelty for its own sake, but these possibilities have yet to be evaluated.

Because of a paucity of information on sex ratios and breeding ecology of birds, Darwin had considerable difficulty in accounting for the existence of certain types of sexual dimorphism in monogamous species, and was therefore led to construct a complex and subtle argument that many authors have found less than fully convincing. Although we still do not fully understand the ways in which sexual selection affects monogamous forms, there is no justification for altogether ruling out sexual selection in monogamous species as some authors have done. Darwin's suggestion that a selective advantage (in terms of larger brood size) accrues to males chosen by reason of superior display characters by early breeding females was verified and extended by Fisher (1930). Of course, provided the appearance, behavior (including "vigor"), or circumstances (for example, possession of a breeding territory of superior quality) of a male reflects his Darwinian fitness, selection for female discrimination is expected to occur, even in monogamous forms with balanced sex ratios. As Williams (1966, p. 184) explains, "A male whose general health and nutrition enables him to indulge in full development of secondary sexual characters, especially courtship behavior, is likely to be reasonably fit genetically. Other important signs of fitness would be the ability to occupy a choice nesting site and a large territory, and the power to defeat or intimidate other males." Since it would be advantageous for a male "to pretend to be highly fit whether he is or not," Williams (1966, p. 184) envisions an "evolutionary battle of the sexes," involving "skilled salesmanship among the males and an equally well-developed sales resistance and discrimination among the females."

In considering sexual selection that involves female choice in monogamous species, it should be remembered that a monogamous mating system does not imply a balanced quaternary sex ratio as Darwin and certain other authors believed. There is considerable evidence that males outnumber females in many groups of monogamous birds, including ducks and various passerines (Lack 1954, French 1959, Bellrose et al. 1961), presumably because of higher mortality rates in females, resulting from their more extensive and demanding role in reproduction (egg production; incubation and other forms of parental care).

As Fisher (1930) and others have noted, intrasexual selection may contribute to the development of sexual dimorphism in monogamous species, even if epigamic selection is relatively unimportant. For example, competition among males for breeding sites in short supply (or for superior sites) will promote the development of secondary sexual characters that function in agonistic interactions.

Greatly puzzled by what we now know as sex-limited and sex-influenced variation, Darwin analyzed in detail the relationship in birds "between the period of development of . . . characters and the manner of their transmission," and finally arrived at an interpretation expressed in two "laws" of inheritance: (1) Variations first appearing in either sex at a late period in life tend to be developed in the same sex alone. (2) Variations first appearing early in life in either sex tend to be developed in both sexes. Most of the material in Chapters 15 and 16 reflects Darwin's attempt to understand the distribution of secondary sexual characters in birds and to demonstrate that these laws provide a causal explanation for characters limited by sex, season, or age. But, lacking a valid genetic theory, he often went astray, as when he doubted that a character first developed in both sexes could through selection be limited in its expression to one sex alone (see Fisher 1930). His lengthy and involved discussions of "Inheritance at Corresponding Periods of Life," "Inheritance Limited by Sex," and so forth are largely unsatisfactory and will not be reviewed here. Most of the problems Darwin was concerned with were long ago resolved by geneticists and endocrinologists.

Darwin apparently failed to grasp the notion that it is advantageous for secondary sexual characters to be expressed sexually and temporally only when they are required. Because he relied too heavily on his laws of inheritance, he also had difficulty accepting Wallace's suggestion that the plumage of females can be modified (apart from that of males) for protection against predators. It is particularly surprising that Darwin doubted that the dull colors of marsh birds have evolved for the sake of rendering the birds inconspicuous to predators. Since he believed that secondary sexual characters occurring in both sexes were developed first in males and subsequently transmitted to females, he failed to appreciate the significance of mutual display in promoting monomorphic bright plumages (Huxley 1923). Finally, as Huxley (1938ab) and others have noted, Darwin erred in attributing to sexual selection too much of avian plumage color and pattern (such as the black color of crows and many marine birds and the white color of herons).

Sexual Differences in Adaptation for Feeding

In Chapter 13 Darwin (1871) alluded to "certain differences between the sexes which apparently depend on differences in their habits of life," and could therefore be accounted for by natural selection. The striking sexual dimorphism in bill structure in the huia (*Neomorpha acutirostris*) was cited as a prime example of differential adaptation for feeding (Figure 8.1). But Darwin also realized that even small sexual differences in trophic structures may have ecological significance, for he noted that the slightly (9 per cent) larger bill of the male goldfinch (*Carduelis carduelis*) enables it to feed on seeds of the teasel, which cannot be exploited efficiently by the smaller-billed female (see Newton 1967).

In many birds the sexes differ in size and proportions of the bill and other body parts (Amadon 1959). Recent work has shown that this dimorphism sometimes has ecological significance in adapting males and females to different subniches and thereby reducing intersexual competition for food (Hutchinson 1965, see review in Selander 1966). However, it is often difficult to determine the ultimate causes of ecological sexual dimorphism since sexual selection for dimorphism in body size also produces in trophic structures associated differences that secondarily result in differential niche utilization (Selander 1965, 1966, Holyoak 1970). Darwin appreciated this problem in discussing the goldfinch, in which it is likely that, as Newton (1967) showed, the bills of males are larger simply because males are on the average bigger birds than females. However, in some species natural selection for optimal size of trophic structures opposes sexual selection favoring increased dimorphism in body size. Thus, for example, the house sparrow (*Passer domesticus*) is sexually monomorphic in bill and skull dimensions, presumably because in both sexes selection maintains bill size at the optimum for utilization of food resources, but the species is dimorphic in size of other body parts and in body weight (Selander & Johnston 1967, Johnston & Selander 1971). In general, small degrees of sexual difference in bill size occur in omnivorous species, which like the house sparrow exploit food supplies that are sufficiently abundant to permit extensive sexual overlap in utilization. Conversely, marked sexual dimorphism in bill size, with associated differences in niche utilization is characteristic of food specialists, especially those that take large items of food (Selander 1966). Schoener (1965) has demonstrated a parallel rela-

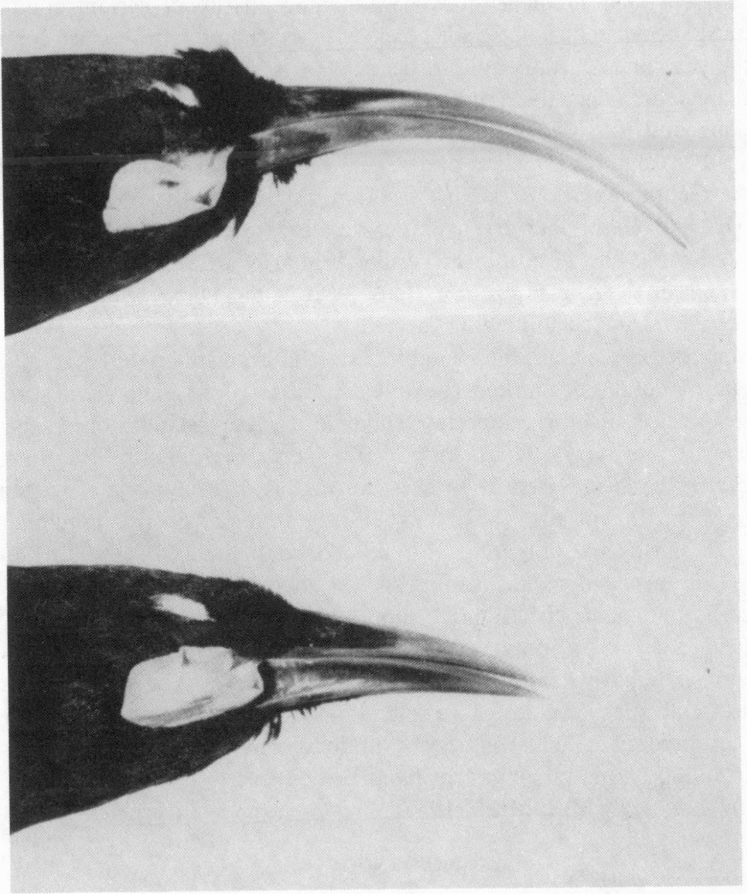

Figure 8.1. Sexual dimorphism in bill size and structure in the huia (Neomorpha acutirostris). *Female above, male below* (*after Selander 1966*).

tionship between food size and abundance and interspecific difference in bill size among sympatric congeneric species.

Strong sexual selection associated with polygynous and other nonmonogamous mating systems often produces a marked increase in male body size because of the advantage of large size in epigamic display and in intermale dominance relations at communal display grounds or colonial breeding sites, and invariably the bill also becomes strongly dimorphic. In some species the advantage of large size in behavioral interactions may be so great that this consequence of sexual selection in a sense forces males to exploit suboptimal food subniches, with the result that mortality rates are higher in males than in females. However, male and female exploitation of different food subniches may be advantageous under certain conditions. In most species males need not be closely associated with females for much of the year and are thus able to occupy areas where they can specialize in their own subniche; this adaptation may be facilitated by unisexual winter flocking and the use of different feeding areas (Selander 1966). In any event, both natural selection and sexual selection can promote dimorphism in the feeding apparatus, and it is often difficult to distinguish their separate effects. Only when the trophic structures alone are modified can we conclude that the dimorphism results primarily or wholly from selection for differential niche utilization. This is so in the huia and also in certain woodpeckers and other feeding specialists.

Among the melanerpine woodpeckers dimorphism in bill size may be absent, moderate, or marked (Selander & Giller 1963). The greatest dimorphism occurs in three species endemic to the islands of Hispaniola (*Centurus striatus*), Guadeloupe (*C. herminieri*), and Puerto Rico (*Melanerpes portoricensis*). In these forms, as in woodpeckers in general, dimorphism in bill size (also tongue size) is much greater than in other body dimensions. Compared with related continental species, the greater sexual dimorphism of the insular species increases by approximately one-third the total span of bill length represented in a population (Figure 8.2).

Field studies of foraging in the insular species *C. striatus* and *M. portoricensis* have demonstrated that males specialize in probing and females in gleaning (Table 8.1) (Selander 1966, Wallace & Selander 1972). In these species sexual differences in foraging behavior equal or exceed those found in many sympatric pairs of congeneric species in continental North America (MacArthur 1958, Brewer 1963). In the less dimorphic

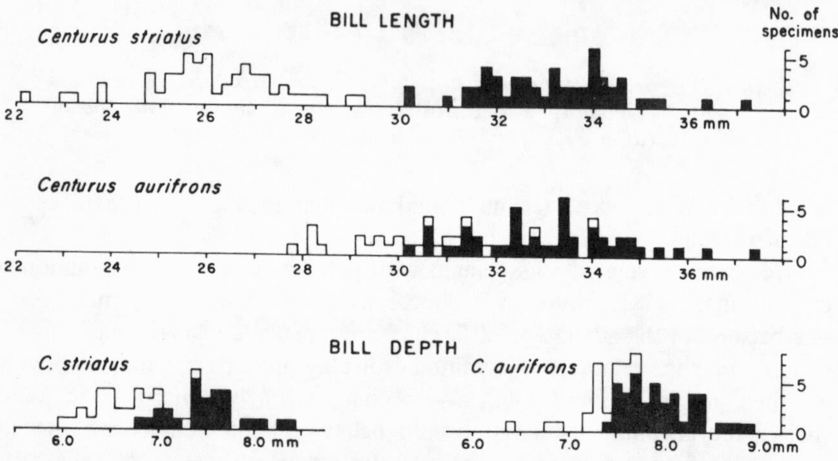

Figure 8.2. Individual and sexual variation in bill length and bill depth in the Hispaniolan woodpecker (Centurus striatus) *and the golden-fronted woodpecker* (C. aurifrons) (*after Selander 1966*).

Table 8.1. Sexual variation in foraging behavior in insular woodpeckers (after Selander 1966, and Wallace 1970)

Species and Sex	Number of Foraging Records	Per cent of Foraging Records Involving: probing	pecking and excavating	gleaning	$\chi^2_{(2)}$
Centurus striatus (Hispaniola)					
Male	671	37	23	40	71.5
Female	975	23	16	61	$(P < 0.001)$
Melanerpes portoricensis (Puerto Rico)					
Male	295	28	45	27	30.5
Female	261	18	32	50	$(P < 0.001)$
Centurus carolinensis (Texas)					
Male	119	40	20	40	3.1
Female	85	36	13	51	$(P > 0.10)$

continental melanerpines sexual differences in foraging are, as expected, less marked.

The conspicuous intraspecific adaptive radiation that certain insular species of woodpeckers achieve through ecological sexual dimorphism apparently depends on a reduction in intensity of interspecific competition resulting from the absence or rarity on the islands of other woodpeckers and birds of similar adaptive type (Selander 1966; see also Snow 1966, and Schoener 1968, for a related discussion of dimorphism in insular lizards). Where opportunity for speciation through geographical isolation exists (Lack 1947, Mayr 1963), as in archipelagos, new species can arise to exploit the unoccupied insular niches and habitats. But even where there is no opportunity for speciation, a single species population may achieve some degree of adaptive radiation through expansion of its ecological range, which under certain conditions involves sexual variation in niche utilization.

Recent work (Ligon 1968, Jackson 1970, Kilham 1970, Kock, Courchesne & Collins 1970) on woodpeckers of the genus *Dendrocopos* indicates that ecological sexual dimorphism is often primarily behavioral, without obvious morphological correlates, and that in some species agonistic interactions involving male dominance over the female function to maintain spatial separation of the sexes while foraging. Apparently certain habitats

Table 8.2. Sexual dimorphism in size in some North American falconiform birds (calculated from data in Friedmann 1950) (after Selander 1966)

Form	*Wing Length of females* (mm)*	*Percentage Difference between Sexes†*		
		wing	*bill*	*tarsus*
Accipiter striatus striatus	182	18.3	20.8	10.9
Accipiter s. velox	200	14.6	18.9	9.1
Accipiter cooperii	260	11.1	14.7	9.8
Accipiter gentilis atricapillus	334	2.5	7.2	7.0
Falco sparverius sparverius	195	6.1	4.0	0.5
Falco columbarius columbarius	208	9.1	12.0	5.2
Falco albigularis albigularis	220	14.0	12.9	7.9
Falco tinnunculus tinnunculus	252	3.4	13.7	5.3
Falco femoralis femoralis	271	11.0	14.0	6.8
Falco mexicanus	343	12.7	15.3	7.9
Falco peregrinus anatum	356	11.8	16.2	6.8
Falco rusticolus obsoletus	403	9.5	10.2	4.0

*Provides an indication of body size.
†Female larger than male in all species.

are best exploited for food when males and females of similar bill size forage over different areas (for example, different strata, dead versus live limbs), while others are best utilized when strongly dimorphic males and females work over the same areas but use different foraging techniques.

As Amadon (1959) has noted, "reversed" sexual size dimorphism has developed independently in several groups of predatory birds—the frigate-birds (Fregatidae), jaegers and skuas (Stercorariidae), owls (Strigiformes), and hawks and their allies (Falconiformes). Although males and females of strongly dimorphic falconiforms such as various accipiters and falcons (Table 8.2) take different types and sizes of prey (Cade 1960, Höglund 1964, Storer 1966, Mueller & Berger 1970), workers do not agree on the causal basis for the dimorphism underlying differential niche utilization. Amadon (1959) believed that the larger size of the female evolved as a protection for the young against male predation ("anti-cannibalism" theory), but Storer (1966) questioned this interpretation on good grounds. Cade (1960) and Willoughby and Cade (1964) and, recently, Brown and Amadon (1970) suggested that there is an advantage in having the female dominant over the male to facilitate pairing.[2] However, like Storer (1966), Frochot (1967), and others, I believe the basic adaptive function of the dimorphism lies in differential niche utilization (Selander 1966); that the

2. Attempts to experimentally demonstrate disruptions in pairing where there is little size difference between pair members (Willoughby & Cade, 1964) are not likely to produce evidence bearing on the problem at hand, since size dimorphism imposed ultimately by the distribution and abundance of prey items would secondarily influence the dominance relationships of pair members.

dimorphism is "reversed" is perhaps explicable in terms of an advantage of a large female in producing large eggs. The pair-bond hypothesis of Cade and Amadon is unsatisfactory for *Accipiter,* in which the largest species, the goshawk (*A. gentilis*), is only moderatley dimorphic in size (Table 8.2), apparently because it specializes on a narrower range of food types than do other accipiters (Höglund 1964, Storer 1966). The Cade-Amadon hypothesis also does not explain the fact that there is less size dimorphism in the sparrow hawk (*Falco sparverius*) than in larger species of falcons. Perhaps the explanation is that *F. sparverius* feeds on relatively abundant, small food items (mostly insects). A similar explanation has been advanced to account for lesser degrees of sexual dimorphism among the smaller species of owls (Earhart & Johnson 1970).

The adaptive significance of size dimorphism in monogamous shorebirds is not entirely clear. But whatever the reasons, sexual variation in size in shorebirds, whether "normal" or "reversed," is associated with differential feeding behavior. For example, Holmes and Pitelka (1968) showed that the diets of males and females of the pectoral sandpiper (*Calidris melanotos*) and the red-backed sandpiper (*C. alpina*) at Barrow, Alaska, differ about as much as do those of the two species (Figure 8.3). At the

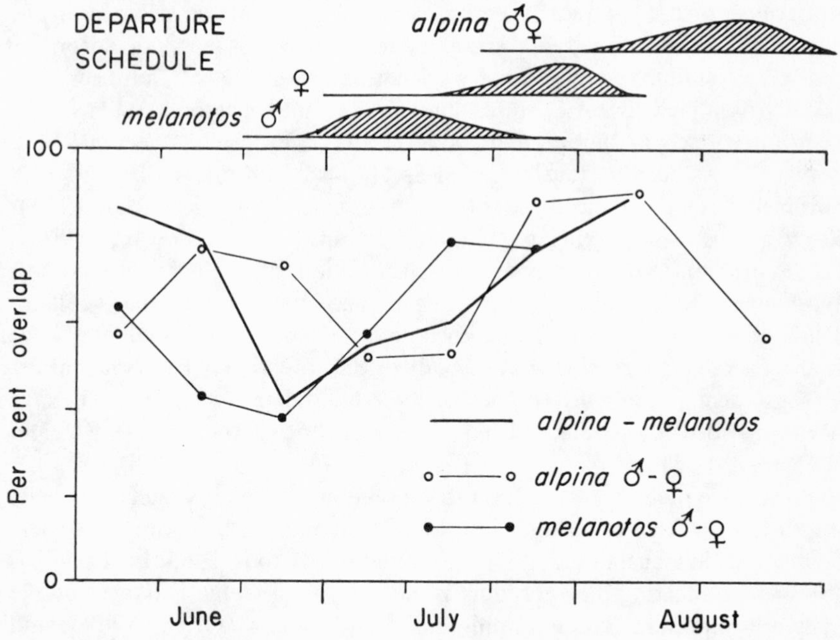

Figure 8.3. Sexual and interspecific variation in indexes of diet similarity (per cent overlap) in two species of Calidris *sandpipers. Schedule of departure from nesting area shown at top (after Holmes & Pitelka 1968).*

end of the nesting season, when the adults of *C. melanotos* and of two other *Calidris* species have already left the nesting area, the diets of males and females of *C. alpina* diverge. At that time, especially good separation of feeding by the sexes may be advantageous because individuals are molting and depositing premigratory fat, or perhaps a contraction of areas that provide food is involved.

Mating Systems and Sexual Selection

Darwin (1871) identified and later authors (Fisher 1930, Huxley 1938ab, Selander 1965) have emphasized a relationship between type of mating system and strength of sexual selection. It has been long recognized that large degrees of sexual dimorphism in morphology are almost invariably associated with nonmonogamous mating systems, and recent work has shown that evolutionary shifts from monogamy to polygamy and polybrachygamy (promiscuity) also involve a complex of interrelated changes in population structure, physiology, and behavior, only some of which were known to Darwin (Selander 1965). However, not until recently have serious attempts been made to understand the ultimate causes of variation in mating system.

Because of the complexity and coadapted nature of the behavioral and ecological factors underlying social systems, it is perhaps not surprising that the evolutionary consequences of mating systems have often been mistakenly identified as their causes and that nonmonogamous systems have been interpreted as biotic adaptations produced by group selection. Thus polygamy has been variously viewed as: (1) an adjustment or solution to "problems" of unbalanced sex ratios (Armstrong 1947, Kendeigh 1952); (2) a means of regulating population fecundity (Wynne-Edwards 1962); (3) a mechanism for optimal size distribution of biomass (DeVore & Washburn 1963); and (4) a means of accelerating evolution (Gilliard 1962, 1969, Sick 1967). But neither data nor additional hypotheses have been generated by these theories, and no purpose would be served in reviewing them. Thorough critiques of the biotic adaptation hypothesis have been provided by Crook (1965), Lack (1966), Wiens (1966), and Williams (1966).

Productive modern research on the evolution of mating systems has been influenced by the realization that: (1) mating systems are ecological adaptations influencing the fitness of individuals (Crook 1965, Lack 1968); (2) factors affecting the reproductive success of the female as well as the male are important in determining the mating system (Orians 1969); and (3) unbalanced sex ratios, delayed maturation of males, increased sexual dimorphism, and the like are consequences rather than causes of mating systems (Selander 1965).

THE CLASSIFICATION OF MATING SYSTEMS

The gamut of mating relationships in birds extends from permanent monogamy, in which male and female establish a life-long and exclusive "pair-bond,"[3] to a situation in which the sexes meet only momentarily for copulation (Table 8.3). The terms *monogamy* and *polygamy* carry the implication of a ritualized pair-bond (Armstrong 1964). The term *promiscuity* (or promiscuous polygamy) is conventionally employed to designate the situation in which mating occurs without establishment of a pair-bond or with formation of a bond of very short duration, and invariably promiscuity implies multiple matings involving two or more partners (Selander 1965, Verner & Willson, 1966, 1969). Unfortunately, however, the term *promiscuous* connotes a lack of discrimination in choice of partners and is therefore inappropriate as far as the mating systems of birds and other higher vertebrates are concerned. While males of some species, especially those having non-monogamous mating systems, are relatively undiscriminating (Selander 1965), females are highly selective in their choice of mates; the adaptive bases for this sexual difference have been discussed by Fisher (1930), Bateman (1949), Manning (1965), Williams (1966), Orians (1969), and others. For this reason, Armstrong (1964) proposed to substi-

Table 8.3. Classification of mating systems in birds

A. Pair-bond of considerable duration (a few days at least, and usually the major part of a breeding season or longer).
   1. Monogamy. Exclusive relationship involving one male and one female. Temporal classification: seasonal or permanent.
   2. Polygamy. An individual mating with two or more individuals in a single breeding season. Temporal classification: simultaneous (harem polygamy) or successive (restricted polygamy). Spatial classification: nonterritorial, monoterritorial, or polyterritorial.
      a. Polygyny. Male mating with several females.
      b. Polyandry. Female mating with several males.

B. Pair-bond very brief (an hour or so at most) or absent.
   1. Monobrachygamy. An individual mating with one individual in a breeding season; perhaps not represented in birds.
   2. Polybrachygamy ("promiscuity"). An individual mating with two or more individuals in a breeding season.
      a. Polybrachygyny. Male mating with several females.
      b. Polybrachyandry. Female mating with several males.

3. This widely used term is difficult to define. Hinde (1964, p. 581) notes that "pair formation implies that a number of social responses, potentially elicitable by any member of the species, become more or less limited to one individual; at the same time other responses (e.g., aggressive ones) become inhibited towards the partner. When paired, the mates often tend to keep together for much of the time, and may show a special type of searching behaviour if they lose contact."

tute "transient multiple pairing" for "promiscuity," and as a technical term I suggest *polybrachygamy* (many brief matings) (Table 8.3).

MATING SYSTEMS AS ECOLOGICAL ADAPTATIONS

The social systems of birds have been reviewed and analyzed in relation to ecological factors by Crook (1965) and Lack (1968). With regard to mating systems the major problems are to explain why over 90 per cent of bird species are monogamous and to determine the particular combinations of ecological factors that have led independently in various groups to the evolution of polygamy and polybrachygamy.

Monogamy. It is probable, as Lack (1954) maintains, that the number of offspring a female or a pair raises has evolved under the influence of natural selection to correspond to what on the average is the largest number for which sufficient energy can be mobilized. Lack (1968) interprets the prevalence of monogamy among birds as indicating that in most situations two parents can feed the young and hence raise more offspring than can the female feeding alone. The argument can, of course, be extended to all cases in which cooperation of any type by two parents results in the raising of more young than could be raised by a single adult. It follows that polygamy can evolve only under ecological conditions that permit one parent's role in nest building and parental care to be severely reduced, and that polybrachygamy can develop only when one parent can be fully emancipated from these duties (Snow 1963, Crook 1965).

That monogamy is more frequent in nidicolous birds (95 per cent of subfamilies; 93 per cent of species) than in nidifugous birds (77 per cent of subfamilies; 83 per cent of species) (Table 8.4) is not surprising. However, the persistence of monogamy in groups of birds that show little or no male participation in parental care is puzzling. For example, most sandpipers (Scolopacidae) are monogamous, although generally only one parent incubates and cares for the brood, and the nidifugous young forage for themselves from hatching. For migratory species breeding at high northern latitudes, Lack (1968) suggests that the explanation may lie in the advantage of arriving on the breeding grounds already paired, the monogamous habit assisting in retention of a mate and thus facilitating rapid breeding in a short season. A similar explanation has been proposed by Lack (1968) for the persistence of monogamy in most ducks (Anatinae), in which the male has essentially no role in parental care. In a few ducks of the genera *Cairina, Sarkidiornis,* and *Biziura* that are resident at southern latitudes, the mating system is polybrachygamous, but the ecological factors predisposing these forms to this mating system are poorly understood.

Table 8.4. Relation of diet to mating system in birds (after Lack, 1968)

A. Nidicolous Species

Main Diet	Percentage of Species with Indicated Mating System		
	monogamous	*polygynous*	*polybrachygynous*
Land animals	42	0	0
Land animals and plants	27	x*	4
Aquatic animals	5	0	0
Seeds	11	1	0
Fruit	8	0	2
Total (nidicolous)	93	1	6

B. Nidifugous Species

Main Diet	Percentage of Species with Indicated Mating System				
	monogamous	*polygynous*	*polybrachygynous*	*polyandrous*	*polygynous and polyandrous*
Land animals	12	0	0	0	0
Land animals and plants	4	0	x	2	0
Aquatic animals	36	0	x	x	0
Aquatic plants	14	0	x	0	0
Land plants	17	8	2	0	4
Total (nidifugous)	83	8	2	2	4
All birds	92	2	6	0.4	—

*x indicates less than 0.5 per cent.

Among birds that are brood parasites, polybrachygamy might have been expected to be the universal mating system. However, while the Viduinae and the Indicatoridae are polybrachygynous, the parasitic cuckoos (Cuculidae) and cowbirds (Icteridae) apparently are monogamous. This variation remains to be explained.

Polygyny. Since polygyny is invariably advantageous to males, Orians (1969), drawing on information from his own work with blackbirds (Orians 1961) and the work of Verner (1963, 1964) on marsh wrens, reasons that its presence or absence depends primarily on its advantage or disadvantage to females, and that the mating system will be determined by female choice of mates among the available males. When the male parental role in a species is extensive and involves possession of a territory that will supply all or a major part of the food for the young, the female should base her choice on an assessment of the quality of the territory and the probability that the male is capable of and disposed toward assuming parental duties. (Since males probably also recognize and compete for good territories, a female's choice of a good territory may guarantee a mate of high fitness. If factors other than the amount of food that can be supplied to young limit brood size, male parental care may be of little consequence, and, as Orians (1969) points out, female choice should be based strictly on the phenotype of the male and the quality of the territory.[4] For example, limitations of food for egg production or possibly the adaptiveness of a small, cryptic nest (Snow 1970), may set the clutch size so low that male feeding of young is unnecessary.

If the mean reproductive success of males and females is positively correlated with the quality of the territory, variation between territories held by unmated and already mated males may be sufficiently large that the expected reproductive success of a female is higher if she mates with a male who already has one mate but occupies a territory in superior habitat rather than with an unmated male on poor habitat (Figure 8.4). The "polygyny threshold" (Verner & Wilson 1966) is the difference in quality of habitats occupied by mated and unmated males required to make a polygynous mating advantageous for a female. Where the difference in mean reproductive success of females in monogamous and polygynous matings is small and variation in quality of the habitat is great, conditions are particularly favorable for an increase in the frequency of polygyny. An important point developed by Orians (1961, 1969) is that polygyny is likely to develop among species in which feeding areas are widespread but nesting sites are restricted.

A number of predictions made from the Orians-Verner model have been confirmed by studies of mating systems in birds. If the model is correct, females of polygynous species should mate with already mated males, even when unmated males are readily available. This has been demonstrated in the long-billed marsh wren (*Cistothorus palustris*) (Verner 1964, Verner & Engelsen 1970), red-winged blackbird (*Agelaius phoeniceus*) (Orians 1961, Haigh 1968), and great-tailed grackle (*Quiscalus mexicanus*) (Selander & Giller 1961, Kok 1970). Additionally, the average reproductive success per female and the number of females mated with a given male should not be negatively correlated, a prediction Haigh (1968) confirmed for the red-winged blackbird. For this species, the advantages of the polygynous mating system to both males and females are clearly demonstrated by Haigh's two-year study of breeding success in monogamous and polygynous matings in a marsh-nesting population in Washington (Table 8.5). The most significant finding is that the number of young fledged per

4. When pair formation in a species takes place in winter flocks before nesting territories are established or when females nest apart from the males, females must select mates on the basis of male characters alone (Verner 1964). Then increased emphasis on display behavior centered on the attributes of the male rather than on those of a territory is expected (see discussion in Orians & Christman 1968). This expectation is realized in birds of paradise, grouse, and other polybrachygamous species.

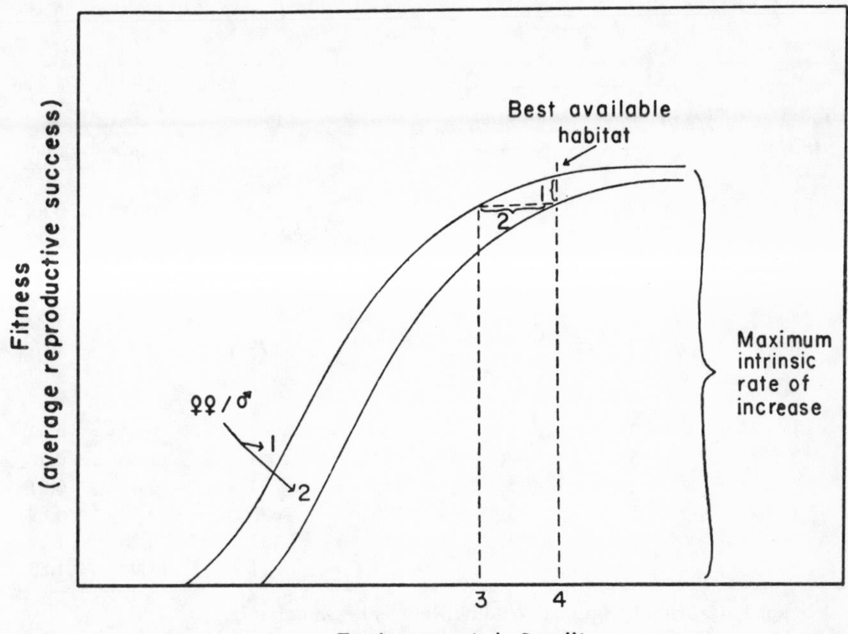

Figure 8.4. Orians-Verner model of conditions necessary for the evolution of polygyny. Average reproductive success is assumed to be correlated with environmental quality, and females are assumed to choose their mates from available males. Distance 1 is the difference in fitness between females mated monogamously and those mated bigamously in the same environment. Distance 2 is the polygyny threshold, *which is the minimum difference in quality of habitat held by males sufficient to make bigamous matings by females favored by natural selection (after Orians 1969).*

female averaged higher for polygynous males than for monogamous males in both years of study.

According to an analysis by Verner and Wilson (1966), only 14 (5 per cent) of the 291 species of North American passerines are regularly polygynous or polybrachygamous; of these, 11 (9 icterids) breed in marshes, prairies, or savannah-like habitats. These authors have proposed that the spatial range of productivity of these habitats is unusually great compared to other habitats, and that marshes in particular provide a rapidly renewed insect source that can be exploited by several females without depletion. However, Lack (1968, p. 30) considers "the postulated correlation with open habitats to be very doubtful, as it rests mainly on the species in one family, the Icteridae . . . and so might be coincidental." Haartman (1969) found no obvious prevalence of marsh and grassland inhabitants among

Table 8.5. Reproductive success of monogamous and polygynous matings in the red-winged blackbird (after Haigh 1968)*

Number of Females per Male	*Number of Males Studied*	*Total Active Nests*	*Total Eggs Laid*	*Total Young Fledged*	*Young Fledged per*	
					male	*female*
			1966			
1	8	9	33	7	0.88	0.88
2	14	37	110	22	1.57	0.78
3	11	38	119	49	4.45	1.48
4	7	39	105	29	4.14	1.03
5	9	52	172	57	6.33	1.27
6	3	22	70	29	9.66	1.61
			1967			
1	7	8	30	3	0.43	0.43
2	15	40	112	21	1.40	0.70
3	14	52	157	34	2.43	0.81
4	7	36	120	25	3.57	0.89
5	5	35	120	31	6.20	1.24
6	1	6	23	11	11.00	1.83

*Studied at Turnbull National Wildlife Refuge, Washington.

the 5 per cent of European passerines that are regularly polygynous. Nor did he find evidence of a correlation between feeding habits or food milieu and polygyny. Rather, the main correlation with mating system seems to be nest site, as noted earlier by Kluijver et al. (1940).

Many polygynous species have domed nests or nest in holes. Haartman (1969) suggests that polygyny is facilitated in closed-nesting species because: (1) the male is less important in driving off predators and in covering the eggs; (2) safety of the nests makes possible the evolution of slower growth rates in nestlings; and (3) good insulation reduces the maintenance costs of nestlings. A reduction in food required per unit time by nestlings reduces the "need" for the male to assist in parental care, thus setting the scene for polygamy. Haartman notes that while restricted availability of nest sites may to some degree facilitate polygyny among hole-nesters it cannot be invoked for species with (self-built) domed nests.

The Ploceidae (weaver birds) have been extensively analyzed by Crook (1962, 1964, 1965) and more recently by Lack (1968) in an attempt to understand factors that affect mating systems and dispersion (Table 8.6). In the subfamily Ploceinae, forest species nest solitarily in monogamous pairs, are primarily insectivorous, and are morphologically monomorphic, both sexes wearing bright plumages throughout the year. But species that inhabit grasslands and savannas nest colonially or in "grouped territories," are polygynous with few exceptions, are graminivorous and exploit food in areas near the nesting colonies, and are markedly dimorphic sex-

Table 8.6. Relation of food and habitat to breeding dispersion and mating system in Ploceidae (after Lack 1968)

	Number of Species in Indicated Category						
	dispersion type				*mating system*		
Main Food and Habitat	*solitary (or 2–4 pairs together)*	*grouped territories*	*colonial*	*solitary or colonial*	*monogamous*	*polygynous*	*either monogamous or polygynous*
			Ploceinae				
Insects							
Forest	17	0	1	0	17	0	0
Savannah	4	0	2	0	5	0	1
Insects and seeds							
Forest	2	0	0	1	3	0	0
Savannah	1	0	4	3	1	4	3
Grassland	1	0	0	1	1	(1?)	0
Seeds							
Savannah	0	1	16	0	2	10	1
Grassland	0	13	3	0	0	14*	0
			Bubalornithinae and Passerinae				
Insects and seeds							
Savannah	3	0	17	4	14	1	0
Alpine	1	0	0	0	1	0	0
Seeds							
Savannah	0	0	2	0	1	0	0

*In addition, one species is polybrachygamous.

ually; the female is cryptically colored, as is the male in the nonbreeding season. Intermediate conditions with respect to nesting dispersion and mating system are found in those ploceine species in intermediate ecological categories.

Crook, following Armstrong (1955), believed that monogamy in the Ploceinae is favored when food for the young is scarce, while polygyny evolves where food is plentiful and assistance of the male is not essential in rearing broods. Hence, the graminivorous species feed on temporarily abundant food, but as noted by Lack (1968, p. 47), "the difficulty in this explanation is that nearly all other tropical graminivorous birds are monogamous." Also, that male assistance in rearing the young is unnecessary does not alone provide a sufficient explanation for the evolution of polygyny. I agree with Lack that the Orians-Verner argument can be extended to explain variation in mating systems in the Ploceinae. For the polygynous species there is evidence that nesting sites are very limited, whereas food resources are abundant. Presumably the male must spend a relatively large part of his effort in holding a territory (which reduces his contribution to parental care), while the female must pair with an already mated male if she is to obtain a good nesting site. Probably the degree of restriction in amount of nesting substrate in relation to abundance of food and population size is the important factor in the origin of polygyny among the weaver birds.

Crook believes that in the Ploceinae monogamy has evolved from polygyny several times. One case involving the black-faced dioch (*Quelea quelea*) is particularly interesting, since this is one of the few colonial grassland species that is monogamous. Two factors apparently are involved. Because *Quelea* nests in gigantic colonies (an average colony may consist of 500,000 pairs!) it is able to overexploit food resources in adjacent foraging areas, so that journeys for food may be very long; consequently it is advantageous for both male and female to care for the brood. Additionally, greater mortality of females due to starvation (and dependent in part on the adverse effects of competition with males) during the dry season and in the critical period when seeds germinate at the beginning of the rainy season leads to a quaternary sex ratio strongly unbalanced in favor of males (see discussion and references in Crook & Ward 1968, and Crook & Butterfield 1970).

The Icteridae provide some striking parallels with the Ploceidae in regard to appearance, dispersion, and mating systems (Figure 8.5), but fail to show a similar relationship between mating system and diet (Lack 1968). The icterid equivalent of *Quelea* is the tricolored blackbird (*Agelaius tricolor*), in which "with the development of extreme coloniality and the utilization of distant feeding grounds, strong selective pressure in favor of male particpation in feeding the young has apparently caused an evolution back toward a more monogamous situation and more equal divi-

Figure 8.5. Convergent evolution in New World Icteridae and African Ploceinae (and a pipit): (a) monogamous insectivorous Icterus galbula *and* Malimbus scutanus *(b) polygynous marshland* Agelaius phoeniceus *and* Euplectes orix, *both in grouped nesting territories (c) extremely colonial* Agelaius tricolor *and* Quelea quelea *(d) colonial* Zarhynchus wagleri *and* Ploceus cucullatus *(e) grassland* Sturnella neglecta *and a pipit* Macronyx croceus *(f) brood parasitic* Molothrus ater *and* Anomalospiza imberbis *(after Lack, 1968).*

sion of labor between the sexes" (Orians 1961, p. 308). The species is less polygynous (usually no more than two females per male) than the closely related red-winged blackbird (three or four females per male), and the extent of the male's participation in parental care is greater.

In many species of birds the frequency of polygyny among males varies spatially and temporally (Williams 1952, Sauer & Sauer 1966). In populations of the long-billed marsh wren (*Cistothorus palustris*) that Verner (1964) studied in Washington, 30 to 50 per cent of males were polygynous (mostly bigamous), but only 5 per cent were polygynous in a population at Sapelo Island, Georgia (Kale 1965), possibly because the population density in relation to the total amount of optimal habitat was not so great that wrens were forced to occupy marginal habitat. A similar explanation many account for variation in polygyny–monogamy proportions in populations of the wren (*Troglodytes troglodytes*) (contra Armstrong 1955, who attempted to link it to availability of food).

Polygyny is uncommon in nonpasserine birds. Harem polygyny occurs in the turkeys (Meleagridae) and in many of the larger species of Phasianidae, in which harem members disperse to nest solitarily. But the peacock and some other pheasants are polybrachygynous (Morris 1957), and the smaller forms of the family, including the quails and partridges, are monogamous. Studies of the jungle fowl (Kruijt 1964, Collias et al. 1966, Collias & Collias 1967a) and of feral populations of the domestic fowl (McBride, Parer & Foenander 1969) reveal the existence of a complex social organization involving both dominance hierarchies and territoriality in males, but as yet we have no analysis of the ecological and evolutionary aspects of the polygynous mating system (Lack 1968). Several of the ratites apparently are polygynous, but only for the ostrich (*Stuthio camelus*) is the mating system well understood (Sauer & Sauer 1966). In this species one to three females lay their eggs in a common nest, and incubation and parental care are performed by the male and the dominant hen.

Surprisingly there is no clear relationship between clutch size and mating system in birds (Skutch 1949, Haartman 1954, 1955, Klomp 1970). It might have been expected that a reduction would accompany the evolution of polygyny, but apparently this is not so, and we may conclude that polygyny evolves where the female can feed the young and is not forced to reduce clutch size. Not unexpectedly, however, the evolution of polygyny usually involves a reduction in amount of male parental care per brood (Verner & Willson 1969). In many species, a staggering of reproductive cycles of females mated to a polygynous male permits the male to participate in feeding the nestlings (Verner 1964), and also to "guard" the female against the approaches of other males until she is incubating.

In sum, Lack (1968) and Haartman (1969) have demonstrated that an understanding of the evolution of polygyny cannot be derived from a purely statistical analysis of species in terms of diet or other isolated aspects of their ecology. Diet per se seems to be at most a subsidiary cause of monogamous habits in birds. Some correlations can be made, but they are probably fortuitous, being, as Lack notes, related to associated differences in habitat distribution. The Orians-Verner model represents the most significant recent advance in our understanding of the evolution of mating systems.

Polybrachygyny. This mating system, which has evolved in numerous unrelated groups of birds, is characterized by an absence of pair-bonds, a persistent seeking of matings by males, and a failure of males normally to participate in any phase of parental care. While it is difficult to identify common predisposing ecological factors among groups, the central problem is to determine why the male stops assisting in care of the young. Once this has occurred, the male is free to devote his whole time and energy to the business of obtaining matings.

Some insight into the problem of the evolution of polybrachygyny may be provided by an examination of the Icteridae, in which this mating system has developed independently in two colonially nesting groups, the larger grackles of the genus *Quiscalus,* and the oropendolas (*Gymnostinops* and related genera). In both, polybrachygyny probably developed from the successive polygyny of colonially nesting species, as represented by the Brewer's blackbird (*Euphagus cyanocephalus*) (Williams 1952, Horn 1968), in which feeding occurs off the territory.[5]

Polygyny in the Brewer's blackbird is of the successive type: a male pairs with a female, guards her continuously against the advances of other males until her clutch is completed, and then repeats the sequence with another female. The male assists the females in feeding the nestlings or fledglings. This behavior is adaptive for the male, since by guarding the female he has maximized the probability that the young are his own.

In the polybrachygynous great-tailed grackle (*Quiscalus mexicanus*) adult males establish territories in trees or marsh vegetation; nesting is colonial, with over 100 nests being found in large trees (Selander & Giller 1961, Selander & Hauser 1965, Kok 1970). Females, attracted to the colony site by the displays and vocalizations of the males, build nests within the territory of a male and defend a small area around the nest site against the intrusions of other females (minimal distance between nests is about two feet). Males, which take no part in nest-site selection, nest building, incubation, or care of the young, spend 75 to 80 per cent of their time on their

5. Current theory (reviewed in Horn 1968) holds that colonial nesting is adaptive primarily in aiding the exploitation of spatially and temporally variable food supplies. The evolution of colonial nesting and of nonmonogamous mating systems are largely separate problems although influenced by some common factors (see Collias & Collias, 1969).

territories, alternating almost continuously between agonistic interactions with other territorial or intruding males and solicitation displays directed to females. Although a male may briefly leave his territory to solicit females gathering nesting material or to feed, most of his time is spent on the territory. Males recognize individual females, for they do not solicit females that are incubating or feeding young.

An important difference between the polygynous Brewer's blackbird and the polybrachygynous great-tailed grackle is that the male of the first species focuses attention on the defense of his female, while that of the second species is primarily concerned with maintenance of a nesting territory and makes no serious attempt to follow and guard the females nesting in his territory. To understand the evolution of polybrachygyny in *Quiscalus,* it may be instructive to imagine a situation in which competition for nesting territories is severe and the breeding of females relatively synchronous. Under these conditions it might be advantageous for a territorial male to forego guarding (which involves frequent absences from the colony) and to remain more or less constantly on his territory, devoting his full effort to its defense and to attracting females and stimulating them to copulate. There is an increased chance that a female nesting in the territory of one male will be fertilized by another, but statistically the territorial male has the advantage, since he displays to her at the nest as she builds. Thus the female's behavioral tendencies can be adjusted over a period of several days through habituation and other forms of conditioning. Most copulations occur on the nesting territory.

Once established, the polybrachygynous system apparently is not easily lost, even when the ecological picture changes. Thus the great-tailed grackle remains polybrachygynous even though it now occupies for the most part agricultural and other man-influenced habitats and is presently not limited as far as nesting sites are concerned. However, the behavior patterns associated with parental care remain latent in the male (Selander 1970), so that polygyny or even monogamy could re-evolve under the appropriate selection pressures.

The polybrachygynous icterids are unusual in that the males are closely associated with the nesting females. In other groups in which this mating system has evolved, females nest singly apart from the display grounds of the males and generally visit the males only for copulation. Among birds, polybrachygyny is about as frequent in nidicolous as in nidifugous species; polybrachygynous passerines tend to be frugivorous (Snow 1963), but this relationship is perhaps fortuitous (Lack 1968). Among the larger families of birds, polybrachygyny is the common mating system only in the hummingbirds (Trochilidae). Some other families in which this mating system has evolved are the Indicatoridae, Pipridae, Cotingidae, Paradisaeidae, Icteridae, Ploceidae, Menuridae, Tetraonidae, Phasianidae, Anatidae, Otididae, Meleagridae, and Scolopacidae (see review in Lack 1968).

No serious effort has been made to identify factors influencing the evolution of the polybrachygynous mating system in nonpasserine birds. The polybrachygyny of certain grouse and other birds may have developed from harem polygyny as represented in the jungle fowl. Here we can imagine a situation in which any advantages that a female might derive from association with a male are outweighed by other factors, such as increased danger of detection by predators (Braestrup 1963, Crook 1965). Once pair-bond behavior is lost, parental behavior will soon be lost in males, since they will be unable to identify their own young, and it is only advantageous for males to care for their own progeny.

Possibly body size is a factor in the development of polybrachygyny, as a tendency for this mating system (or polygyny) to occur in species of relatively large size has been noted in grouse, bustards, pheasants, and icterids (Amadon 1959). Perhaps in certain groups, such as the grouse, disassociation of the sexes, leading to nonmonogamous mating systems, is more likely to occur in large species because individuals are relatively more conspicuous to predators. But even for small birds, such as the hummingbirds and manakins, the primary predisposing factor may be intense predation pressure at or near the nest site, such that disassociation of the sexes is, on balance, adaptive (Snow 1970). It is probably significant that almost without exception females of polybrachygynous species nest singly (for concealment) and are cryptic in behavior and plumage.

As Hjorth (1970) points out, disassociation of the male from the female (and the loss of parental care by the male) may or may not lead to the aggregation of males in arenas or communal display sites. Among the grouse (Tetraonidae), various types of organization of display activites occur (Table 8.7). Some species display collectively, but solitary display occurs in several genera as well as in perhaps the majority of polybrachygynous birds, including most hummingbirds, birds of paradise and bower birds, and manakins. Where it occurs, the value of male aggregation must be considerable, since groups presumably would often be especially vulnerable to predation. Among grouse collective display is rare in forest species; all the lek forms are birds of open country.

Considerable insight into factors promoting social aggregation of males is provided by Snow's (1963) analysis of the polybrachygynous manakins (Pipridae) and Hjorth's (1970) studies of the grouse.

In the manakins, all displays in which two or more males are associated together (generally at traditional display grounds) are called *collective* or *group* displays. Two types are distinguished: *lek displays,* where the males clearly are rivals, each occupying his own perch or court; and *true communal displays,* in which the males take equal parts in a joint performance. Lek displays are characteristic of the genera *Manacus* and *Pipra,* while true communal displays occur in *Chiroxiphia.* To account for the development of group displays, Snow (1963) suggests that with loss of the pair-

Table 8.7 Mating systems and display organization in Tetraonidae (after Hjorth 1970)

Mating System	*Organization of Display Activities*	*Genus or Species*	*Comments*
Monogamy	Solitarily displaying	*Tetrastes*	Pair may spend a great part of year together but male does not take part in rearing progeny
		Lagopus	Tendency to polygyny in red grouse and rock grouse; in latter, male does not care for young
Polybrachygyny	Solitarily displaying	*Bonasa*	Tendency to territory clustering
		Canachites	
		Falcipennis	
		Dendragapus	Unorganized collective display (rare)
	Collectively displaying		
	1. Less well-organized gatherings; territory boundaries vaguely defined	*Tetrao urogallus*	*T. parvirostris* apparently less territorial than
	2. Well-organized gatherings on traditional places (arenas); = true lek species	*Lyrurus mlokosiewiczy*	
	(*a*) Single-cluster type; territory boundaries normally well defined in mating time	*Lyrurus tetrix* *Pedioecetes* *Tympanuchus cupido* and *pallidicinctus*	*T. urogallus* In high-number years, tendency to split large leks into portions, or to establish satellite leks close to arena
	(*b*) Multicluster type; territory boundaries vaguely defined	*Centrocercus*	Each cluster normally centered around special "mating spots"

bond the coordination between the sexes necessary for successful mating comes to depend increasingly on the female's response to the stimulus provided by the courting male. Because there is no opportunity for the gradual overcoming of aggression and fear, as in the process of pair formation, all balancing of behavioral tendencies (Morris 1956, Tinbergen 1965) must be achieved in a few seconds of highly coordinated mutual activity in which the male plays the leading role. Accordingly, a group of *n* males displaying together may have an attractive and stimulating power more than *n* times as great as that of a male displaying solitarily. If so, the evolution of group displays will follow, unless accompanied by increased danger from predators or by other disadvantages. The group can advertise itself much more continuously and effectively than can a lone bird, and, perhaps more importantly, the mutual stimulation among males results in bursts of display that are far more impressive than anything an individual can achieve. Similarly, for the collective displays of grouse Hjorth (1970) reports that the display intensity of each participant is far greater on big leks than on small leks; also, the carrying power of the advertising song and, hence, its influence on distant females vary with the number of singing males (Figure 8.6).

The upper limit of size of groups of displaying males will be set by the distances that the females must travel to visit the display grounds. If all the males in a large area are concentrated in one display ground, a few males establishing a much smaller display ground nearer the outlying nesting

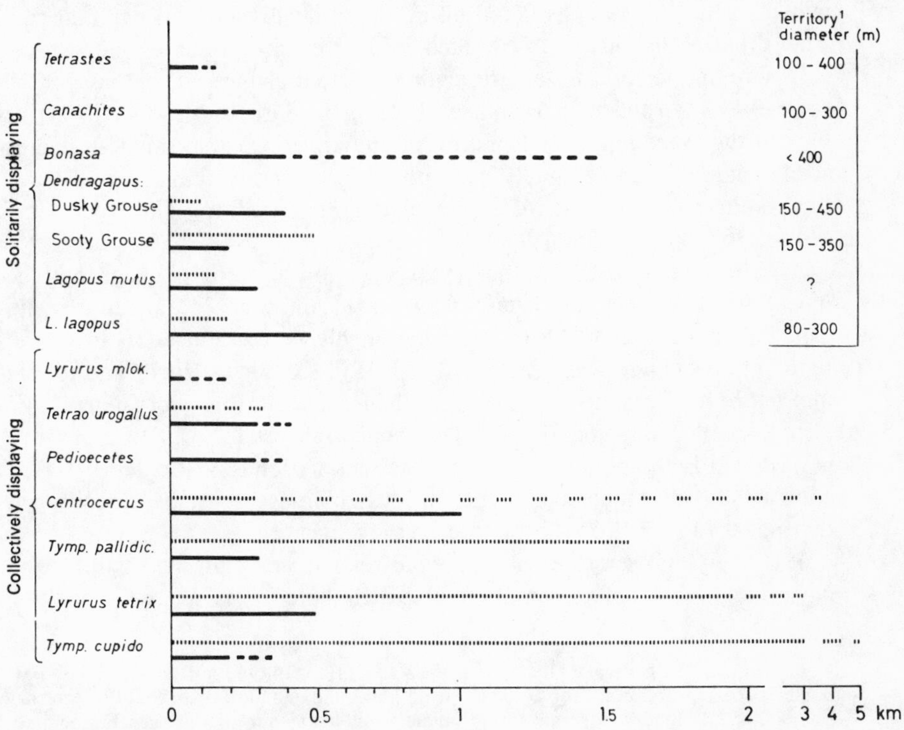

Figure 8.6. Carrying distances of advertising signals in grouse. Continuous line: *nonvocal acoustic signals or visual signals.* Vertically dashed line: *vocalizations.* Broken line: *a carrying power considered uncommon. For solitarily displaying species, territorial ranges are indicated at upper right* (*after Hjorth 1970*).

areas may have an advantage. Hence there is a balance of advantages, producing a roughly even dispersion of display grounds throughout the areas of suitable breeding habitat.

True communal display is exemplified by the manakin genus *Chiroxiphia* (Snow 1963). In *C. pareola* each display perch is dominated by a single male, who attracts neighboring males to "dance" with him. But when a responsive female is present, he is able to keep his neighbors away. Thus the synchronized "cartwheel" dance (Gilliard 1959a) and other joint male displays serve to attract females. Whether the visitors are other adult males with their own perches nearby or are younger, subordinate males getting the benefit of practice remains to be determined. Copulation is preceded by a different display by a single male, presumably the perch "owner." The lek is maintained by a balance between the aggressive and social tendencies of males, but true communal display depends on the temporary breaking down of the aggressive component.

Reversed sexual roles and polyandry. Rarely in the course of avian evolution has the male assumed all duties of incubation and parental care. This situation has generally resulted in a reversal of roles of the sexes in courtship and territorial defense, with correlated changes in the "direction" of sexual dimorphism in plumage. Thus in phalaropes the female arrives first on the breeding grounds, takes the initiative in pair formation, aggressively guards the male against the approaches of other females, and leaves the nesting area while the male is incubating or brooding (Tinbergen 1935, Höhn 1965, 1967, Johns 1969).[6]

The hormonal basis for the reversed dimorphism in plumage and behavior in phalaropes has been studied in recent years.[7] The most significant findings are that androgens occur in higher concentration in ovaries than in testes (Dyrenfurth & Höhn 1963, Höhn & Cheng 1967) and that females produce much less prolactin than males (Höhn & Cheng 1965, Nicoll, Pfeiffer & Fevold 1967). The incubation patch, formation of which is mediated by both testosterone and prolactin (Johns & Pfeiffer 1963), is confined to the male, and the nuptial plumage, which is androgen-dependent (Johns 1964), is brighter in the female.

It is likely that sex reversal of normal roles in courtship and parental behavior evolved from a condition in which both sexes shared equally in

6. Contrary to general belief, phalaropes are monogamous, not polyandrous. Pair-bond formation and constant association of male and female are probably necessary, since it would be advantageous for the male to incubate only if the eggs he incubates were produced by a female he had fertilized. It is noteworthy that male phalaropes have retained the (adaptive) behavior of copulating with females other than their mates when the opportunity arises (Tinbergen 1935, Johns 1969).

7. That a reversal in body size dimorphism has not occurred in the phalaropes (the female is larger than the male—26 per cent in the Wilson phalarope—as in most shorebirds) is consistent with the idea that large size in female shorebirds is adaptive in permitting the production of large eggs.

parental care.[8] Perhaps increasing need for territorial defense or for reduction in biomass on the breeding grounds made it advantageous for one pair member to reduce the extent of participation in incubation and brooding. There is an element of chance involved,[9] and in some proportion of cases it is the female that has taken on other duties.

Once a reversal in roles has been achieved and the female contribution to parental care is relatively small, the way is open to polyandry, especially when the amount of good nesting habitat is in short supply (as in the case of polygyny). Polyandry has evolved at least five times in birds—in button-quail (Turnicidae), painted snipes (Rostratulidae), lillytrotters (Jacanidae), rails (Rallidae), and tinamous (Tinamidae). Among the last-named group, the mating system is particularly variable; some species have successive polyandry, others harem polygamy, and still others monogamy (see review in Lack 1968). Our understanding of polyandry in tinamous and other birds is too fragmentary to warrant further discussion.

The Consequences of Sexual Selection

The evolutionary shift from monogamy to polygamy or polybrachygamy has profound effects on morphology, behavior, physiology, and ecology, the full extent of which we have only recently begun to explore (Selander 1965). Because the number of matings a male of a monogamous species may obtain is severely limited, characters promoting survival have greater adaptive value relative to those subject to sexual selection than do such characters in polygamous and polybrachygamous species, since a male of a monogamous species that survives to a given age has a greater probability of mating than does a male of a nonmonogamous species, in which intermale competition for females is intensified. Consequently, the degree of development of secondary sexual characters is generally held within moderate limits. Characters such as large size, conspicuous plumage signals, and strong copulatory and aggressive tendencies in males are highly adaptive in facilitating the holding of superior nesting or display territories or in otherwise establishing high social rank and in attracting and stimulating females, but they render the individual more vulnerable to predators or otherwise reduce the probability of survival. Thus such characters develop only to the point where increasing mortality leads to a lessening of competition among males. Eventually an equilibrium is established where the fitness of individual males is maximal.

8. Höhn's (1967) theory that "a hereditary deficiency of prolactin appeared in females" is not sufficient, since it fails to explain how genes that produce a deficiency come to predominate *in populations.*

9. Lewontin (1969) emphasizes that the determination of which alternative stable state a given dynamic system evolves to is a function of variation and the starting point.

In polygynous or polybrachygynous species, the number of matings a male may obtain is potentially very large, and there is an increased selective premium on characters that function in intrasexual and epigamic interactions directly related to mating. Characters promoting survival of the male have a relatively smaller influence on total fitness, and, as Darwin's theory predicts (Fisher 1930, Huxley 1938b), sexually selected characters may develop to a point where mortality rates are much higher in males than in females.

The following discussion is concerned with some of the major consequences of sexual selection in birds, especially as they are manifested in nonmonogamous species.

SEXUAL DIMORPHISM IN MORPHOLOGY

In many groups the correlation between mating system and degree of sexual dimorphism in body size and in color, form, and pattern of the plumage and soft parts is so strong that the mating type can be inferred with reasonable certainty from the degree of dimorphism. However, where selection for cryptic coloration is intense, it may override sexual selection. Thus, polygyny in the grassland-inhabiting meadowlarks (*Sturnella*) has not produced the degree of sexual dimorphism in color seen in other polygynous icterids, and polygynous wrens do not show increased sexual dimorphism. The polybrachygynous great snipe (*Capella media*), which displays at night and depends largely on vocal rather than visual communication, has cryptic plumage. For the polybrachygynous bearded bellbird (*Procnias averano*), Snow (1970) suggests that the method of feeding (flying out to pluck fruit) is incompatible with the evolution of ornate plumes, which would be obstructive and easily damaged.

While increased size dimorphism is characteristic of nonmonogamous species of the Icteridae (Selander & Giller 1960), grouse (Tetraonidae), bustards (Otididae), and certain other families (Amadon 1959), no conspicuous relationship exists between mating system and body size dimorphism in the manakins (Pipridae), birds of paradise and bower birds (Paradisaeidae), and hummingbirds (Trochilidae). It is notable that when the male is much larger than the female, such as in grouse, agonistic and courtship displays generally involve erection of the feathers or other behavior that increases the apparent size of the male, whereas size is a lesser feature of display in the more monomorphic types of birds. Another notable feature is that in grouse, turkeys, icterids, bustards, shorebirds, pheasants, and anatids the extreme of sexual dimorphism in body size is reached when the male is roughly twice the mass of the female.

Large size of males may be adaptive primarily in intrasexual contexts, but it may also be significant in courtship. For example, in the turkey the contrast between the female and male sizes is an important factor contributing to her receptive "crouching" for copulation (Schein & Hale 1965).

In most monogamous birds, males are on the average slightly larger than females, and there is evidence that small sexual differences in mean body weight or in bill size are related to the problem of maintaining proper dominance relationships among pair members. In the herring gull (*Larus argentatus*) the male member of a pair invariably has the larger bill (Tinbergen 1960, Harris & Jones 1969), and the same is true for several other shorebirds (Soikkeli 1966, Jehl 1970). For the monogamous stilt sandpiper (*Micropalama himantopus*) and least sandpiper (*Calidris minutilla*) Jehl (1970) found that pairs with the greatest size difference in bill length are earliest to hatch young. Perhaps the size difference promotes rapid pair formation in arctic habitats, where it may be advantageous to breed as early as possible in the spring so that the young will hatch when food is plentiful. But whether the primary selective advantage of bill dimorphism pertains to mate selection (as Jehl [1970] believes) or to differential niche utilization is problematical.

Following a similar line of reasoning, Hamilton (1961) suggested that plumage dimorphism in migratory temperate zone orioles and warblers facilitates rapid pair formation (by promoting rapid sex recognition and reducing intersexual hostility) once the birds arrive on the breeding grounds. However, it remains to be determined whether the tendency for resident tropical zone species to be monomorphic (with bright plumage) and temperate zone species to be dimorphic is related to differences in the extent of participation in defense of territory.

Among African parrots of the genus *Agapornis,* solitary nesters are strongly sexually dimorphic in color of the face, breast, and bill, whereas the colonially nesting species are monomorphic, with bright coloration. Perhaps, as Dilger (1960) suggests, signaling of the same information facilitates the coordination of group activity in the more highly social, colonial forms, but differences in nest-hole defense behavior may also be involved. Both males and females of the monomorphic forms defend the entrance hole against intruders of either sex. In certain hummingbirds sexual monomorphism is a result of selection for similar aggressive signals when both males and females hold feeding territories (Wolf 1969).

Not all dimorphism in body size can be attributed to sexual selection. Among monogamous hole-nesting ducks the protection against predators afforded by nesting in cavities with small entrance holes has favored retention of or reduction in body size in the female, with the consequence that sexual size dimorphism is marked, especially in the larger species (Bergman 1965).

Where ecological conditions permit, it is adaptive for males to lose the conspicuous signals of breeding plumage in the nonbreeding season. But two molts a year may not be energetically feasible; then we would expect sexual dimorphism to be less marked than in the other case. Understandably, many birds have signal characters, such as colored wattles and pouches or patches of feathers, that can be concealed when the male is not displaying. This arrangement may be beneficial both in reducing risks of detection by predators and in facilitating flocking or other social behavior (Hamilton & Barth 1962). For example, the shoulder-patch display of certain grouse is intimately associated with subordinace, avoidance, and female soliciting. Male black grouse "may sit peacefully together in trees when feeding, with the white [shoulder-patch] spots fully exposed, only to start behaving aggressively as soon as other display features are demonstrated" (Hjorth 1970).

One way for males of nonmonogamous species to employ conspicuous display features and yet avoid increased mortality is to substitute objects for secondary sexual characters. By removing the central tuft of grass from the display ring of a male Jackson's whydah (*Euplectes Jacksoni*), Van Someren (1945) demonstrated that the tuft may possess more significance to the hen than does the displaying male. From studies of the whydahs and bishop birds, Emlen (1957) formally developed the hypothesis that females' choices may be for aspects of the territory and its nesting habitat rather than for the male territory holder alone. When the male is only one component of a "total situation" the female selects, the increasing importance of objects in courtship may permit a reduction of secondary sexual characters in the male. Sexual selection is in a sense transferred from plumage to object, and adjustments in relative emphasis of the male per se or of nests, bowers, or other inanimate objects become possible. This notion is original with Gilliard (1956, 1969), for although Darwin (1871) was aware of the function of the bowers of bower birds in courtship, he did not express the "transferral" idea.

Recent work on multiple nest-building behavior in weaverbirds (Crook 1963, Hall 1970) and wrens emphasizes the importance of nests in courtship. In the wren (*Troglodytes aedon*) (Kendeigh 1941), the house wren (*T. troglodytes*) (Kluijver et al. 1940, Armstrong 1955), and the long-billed marsh wren (*Cistothorus palustris*) (Verner 1965), males lead prospective mates to nests and display nearby. There has been a shift in releasers associated with courtship from the males themselves to their courting structures. Verner (1965) makes the interesting point that these wrens are the only North American passerines that are regularly polygamous but are not sexually dimorphic in plumage. When a nest of the African village weaverbird is repeatedly rejected by females—and especially when it starts to fade—the male tears it down and builds a fresh one in its place (Collias & Collias 1970).

Gillard's transferral hypothesis was suggested by negative correlations in the paradise and bower birds between the development of "showy" male plumage and the development and use of bowers. Two levels of correlation have been identified. First, the birds of paradise, which do not build bowers, have by and large greater development of elaborate and conspicuous plumes and coloration than do the bower builders. Second, within the bower birds, the same relationship appears to hold—fancy "houses and jewelry" seem to have been substituted for colorful plumage. For example, in *Amblyornis macgregoriae* the male, which wears a long, brilliant golden-orange crest, builds a simple, undecorated bower. In *A. subalaris* the male crest is shorter and the bower somewhat more elaborate. Finally, in *A. inornatus* the male, which builds an extremely elaborate bower decorated with berries, shells, and piles of flower, lacks a crest and is in plumage almost indistinguishable from the female.

Evidence of transferral is also available for the avenue builders (*Chlamydera*) (Gillard 1959b). In Lauterbach's bower bird (*C. lauterbachi*), in which the male builds an unusually large, complex bower of sticks and pebbles and displays with a red berry in his bill, male and female have similar dull plumages. In *C. cerviniventris,* which is also monomorphic, dull and lacks a crest, head-turning behavior is interpreted by Gilliard (1959b, 1969) as a "relict movement dating from the time when the species had such a crest," but other interpretations are possible: it could be a "cut-off" appeasement pattern. Hence it is hardly a "strong line" of evidence for the transferral effect. It is obvious that much more field work will have to be done before we have a satisfactory picture of the evolution of the bower birds.

Courtship feeding in birds may involve elements of transferral, but the subject has yet to be fully analyzed in this regard (Lack 1940, 1941, Johnston 1962). Hinde (1956) suggests that it leads to habituation to the male's proximity, and notes that it is common in "aggressive" species.

BEHAVIOR

In much of the early behavioral literature a sharp distinction was made between "display" (communication in intermale interactions) and "courtship" behavior, but the dichotomy is artificial and misleading, as shown originally by Hingston (1933; see also Huxley 1938c). Ethologists have now clearly demonstrated that many of the signaling movements, sounds, and structures (releasers) that birds use in sexual behavior (pair formation and solicitation for copulation) are similar to those employed in agonistic interactions (Morris 1956, Tinbergen 1954, 1965, Bastock 1967). Indeed, in many birds, notably in certain grouse (Hjorth 1970) and other polybrachygynous forms, little if any distinction can be made between the agonistic and sexual displays of the male.

Some of the ways in which behavioral interactions between pair members are affected by dimorphism in plumage color are shown by Dilger's

(1960) study of the monogamous *Agapornis* parrots. Male courtship in the dichromatic species involves relatively little conflict between attack/ escape and copulation tendencies (males are relatively "unafraid" of females). However, the monomorphic species have evolved a compensatory "diethism": during copulation the female ruffles the feathers of the head, throat, and wrist in an appeasing display that functions to "remind" the male of her sex.

In the weakly dimorphic common grackle (*Quiscalus quiscula*) mutual ruff-out display with song (having a strong aggressive tendency) is a conspicuous part of early pair-bond formation behavior: gradually the male dominates as the female appeases with solicitation display (Ficken 1963, Yang & Selander 1968). But in the polybrachygynous boat-tailed grackle (*Q. major*) the female never threatens the male; ruff-out display and song are employed only in interactions with other females. Finally, in some populations of the great-tailed grackle (*Q. mexicanus*) the song has been lost in the female (Selander & Giller 1961).

Characteristically in nonmonogamous species the period of maximum testicular development and of reproductive display of males is lengthened to include all or most of the breeding season, and the amount of time and energy devoted to display and associated activities is greatly increased. For example, in the polygamous African weaverbird (*Ploceus cucullatus*) most of the male's energy over a maintenance level goes into building and displaying nests; some nine to ten nests are woven for every one from which a brood eventually is fledged (Collias & Collias 1967b). Additionally, the displays of nonmonogamous birds are "exaggerated" in form and the repertoire of signals is greater in males than in females. In icterids, males of strongly polygynous species have a greater variety of vocal signals than do females (Orians & Christman 1968), whereas in monogamous or weakly polygynous species the number is about the same.

Sexual selection associated with polygyny and polybrachygyny produces in males markedly increased levels of "sex drive," together with lowered thresholds of response to stimulation by feminine characters, since strong persistence in courtship is an especially important factor in mating success (Selander & Dickerman 1963, Selander 1965, Hjorth 1970). Moreover, intermale competition for territories or high positions in dominance hierarchies selects for unusually strong aggressive tendencies, and these may in turn place a high premium on those morphological and behavioral characters of the female that reduce the probability that she will elicit overly aggressive male responses, especially at the time of courtship and copulation. It is also probable that the disadvantage of performing overly hostile responses to females at the time of mating limits the degree to which aggressiveness evolves in males (Selander 1965). In any event, the sexual displays of polygynous and, especially, polybrachygynous species are generally characterized by unusually strong aggressive and copulatory elements in the male and marked submissiveness in the female.

Since the whole of sexual selection theory rests on the idea of competitively determined unequal reproductive success among members of one sex (usually the male), evidence that in polybrachygynous birds the majority of matings are in fact performed by a minority of the adult males is critical. Also, because the epigamic aspect has so often been denied, evidence for the existence of female choice is of interest. Before proceeding, I may note that for a variety of species we now have indisputable evidence both of strongly disproportionate reproductive contributions among males and of deliberate selection of mating partners by females. The important question, as yet not fully answered, is: Why are females selective and what are the criteria of choice?

Studies of behavior in the domestic chicken (Guhl 1962) and domestic and wild turkeys (Hall & Schein 1962, Watts 1968) demonstrate that strong aggressive and copulatory tendencies are critical components of the behavior of successful males. Although the dominant male (top-ranking in peck order) in a flock of chickens does not court or attempt to tread so often as his immediate inferior, he copulates most frequently, fertilizes the most eggs, and sires the most chicks (Guhl & Warren 1946). Among the determinants of peck-order rank are body weight and strength, innate level of aggressiveness, hormonal titers, experience, and general level of health. (Since the female is normally passive in courtship, it is not surprising that while aggressiveness in hens is positively correlated with social status it is negatively correlated with frequency of being courted, frequency of giving the sexual crouch, and, hence, frequency of mating [Schjelderup-Ebbe 1935].) Similarly, in the turkey most or all matings are completed by males that have established high social rank by agonistic display and fighting, partly (but only partly) because dominant males interfere with mating attempts of males of low social status. In general most females in a flock prefer the same males. Ehrman (Chapter 7) reviews here the experimental work of Lill and Wood-Gush (1965) demonstrating that female chickens assortatively mate with males on the basis of physical characters (plumage color, other aspects of morphology) and vocalizations rather than quantitative differences in male courtship displays.

Hjorth's (1970) monographic study of grouse emphasizes the importance of the male's behavior in adjusting the behavioral tendencies of the female. A successful male must threaten and appease in proper balance, so the female will not flee but will, nonetheless, be completely subordinate and remain in a fixed position for copulation. Surprisingly, even in strongly dimorphic lek species the sex of an individual is "recognized" largely by behavior rather than by plumage or other morphological features: sexually mature females behave differently to male threat than do males. According to Hjorth (1970, p. 501), "toward females . . . the function of threat is to display superiority to such a degree that a complete subordinance from the female's side eventually appears." Probably much learning by the male is involved in developing the best technique for inducing females to remain on his territory and later to squat before him (Kruijt & Hogan 1967). In some species, females apparently return to a site where they have been treated with "balanced threat"; thus abiotic recognition marks of the arena may replace a poor recognition of males with whom they have had earlier experience.

Factors influencing female choice have been examined by Kruijt and Hogan (1967) in the black grouse (*Lyrurus tetrix*), a species in which females prefer to mate with males that hold territories in the center of the lek. In this study, more than 85 per cent of the matings were performed by four central males, and some males failed to copulate. Kruijt and Hogan showed that the probability that a male will copulate with a receptive female is proportional to the amount of time the female spends on his territory, and they suggested that because central territories are smaller than peripheral ones the density of males is a factor influencing the female's preference for central territories. Also, females are known to approach fighting males, and central males do more fighting than peripheral males. The timing of the male's squatting (appeasing) and circling at various distances apparently influences the amount of time a female spends in a male's territory. Some males are more efficient than others; in other words, successful males have a better "balance" of tendencies. But why are these the central males? It would seem that the central males are the more highly aggressive individuals and also the more experienced ones capable of properly presenting "balanced threat" to the females.

The social system in the ruff (*Philomachus pugnax*) is exceedingly complex, involving lek behavior and a unique behavioral-morphological polymorphism of males (Hogan-Warburg 1966). *Resident males* occupy residences (territories) spaced 1 to 2 meters apart at the lek. *Satellite males* do not hold territories but instead seek to remain on the territories of the resident males. Since overt aggressive behavior is never shown by satellite males and their escape tendency is low, the net effect of their behavior is to strongly appease the resident male (Table 8.8). The degree to which residents tolerate satellites varies from lek to lek, depending on size. On large leks satellites are fiercely attacked, and only a few succeed in settling down on a residence. But on small leks residents do not normally attack satellites, and all are accepted as "guests" on residences.

Females visiting a lek wander singly or in groups through the territories of a number of resident males. Copulation occurs only after a female expresses a choice by crouching. When a female crouches on a singly occupied residence, she in effect chooses the resident male, but on multiply occupied residences the female sometimes makes an actual choice of the

Table 8.8. Behavior patterns of males of the ruff on the lek (after Hogan-Warburg 1966)

Shown by:	Resident Male				Marginal Male			Satellite Male		
With Respect to:	*R*	*M*	*S*	♀	*R*	*M*	♀	*R*	*S*	♀
Attacking acts										
Wing beating	+	–	±	–	–	(+)	–	–	–	–
Feather pulling	+	–	±	–	–	(+)	–	–	–	–
Grappling	+	–	±	–	–	(+)	–	–	–	–
Kicking	+	+	–	–	–	(+)	–	–	–	–
Jumping	+	–	±	–	–	(+)	–	–	–	–
Pecking	+	+	+	–	–	(+)	–	–	–	–
Forward postures										
Hidden-tail forward	+	–	–	–	–	–	–	–	–	–
Spread-tail forward	+	+	+	–	–	–	–	–	–	–
+ Bill thrusting	+	+	+	–	(+)	(+)	–	–	–	–
Up-tail forward	–	–	–	+	–	–	–	–	–	–
Low forward	+	–	–	–	–	–	–	–	–	–
Oblique postures										
Normal oblique posture	+	+	∓	–	(+)	–	–	∓	–	–
+ Bill thrusting	+	+	∓	–	(+)	–	–	–	–	–
+ Head jerk	+	–	–	–	(+)	–	–	∓	–	–
Oblique posture with perpendicular bill	–	–	∓	–	–	–	–	∓	–	–
Head-back posture	–	–	–	–	(+)	–	–	–	–	–
+ Head jerk	–	–	–	–	(+)	–	–	–	–	–
Low-wing posture	–	–	–	+	–	–	–	–	–	–
+ Wing lifting	–	–	–	+	–	–	–	–	–	–
Strutting	–	–	–	–	–	–	–	–	–	+
Upright postures										
Wing fluttering and flutter jumping	–	–	–	+	–	–	+	–	–	+
Puffed upright	–	–	–	+	–	–	–	–	–	–
Tiptoe	–	–	–	–	–	–	–	+	–	+
Cone upright	–	–	–	–	+	–	–	–	–	–
Sleek upright	–	–	–	–	+	–	–	+	–	–
Horizontal postures										
Squat	–	–	+	+	–	–	(+)	+	–	+
Half-squat	–	–	∓	–	–	–	–	–	–	–
Low horizontal	–	–	+	+	–	–	(+)	∓	–	+

R = resident males
M = marginal males
S = satellite males

\+ = occurs normally
(+) = occurs infrequently
– = does not occur normally

In cells where two signs are given, the upper sign refers to behavior shown on large leks, the lower sign to behavior shown on small leks. Signs in all columns except with respect to females refer to the occurrence of behavior on the lek when no females are present.

resident or a satellite by twisting until she is parallel to him. At larger leks most matings are performed by a few males on singly occupied residences; females crowd around one or two of these males, who frequently copulate with several females in succession.[10] (A crouching or copulating female attracts other females and stimulates them to crouch also at a particular residence.) On small leks, though, females prefer either residents or satellites on multiply occupied territories. Why this difference exists is not clear. Hogan-Warburg feels that female choice is based on features of individual males, for females may select a certain satellite male regardless of the residence where he is located; indeed they follow him from residence to redidence. Because residents are likely to tolerate a "preferred" satellite and because satellites select those residences that females prefer, the "most attractive" resident and satellite males usually end up together. Although the degree of development and brilliance of the male nuptial plumage directly influences a female's choice, the preferred resident or satellite males are not characterized by a specific color or pattern of plumage.

Preferred residences on small or large leks have one important feature in common: the occupants (resident and satellite, if present) periodically interrupt squatting to perform other behavior. Female crouching usually takes place only after a male rises from the squat (shows a relatively strong aggressive tendency?). "By visiting different residences the female may finally, by trial-and-error, find a residence with a riser(s) which provides her with the proper stimulation to crouch" (Hogan-Warburg 1966, p. 197). Inexperienced females are probably influenced more by specific behavioral features of the male, morphological features of the male's plumage, and the behavior of other females on the lek, but choice by experienced females is more likely to depend on conditioning to a particular male or residence. Thus an experienced female may have learned that on small leks males on a doubly occupied residence are more likely to interrupt squatting than is a single male. Why this is so has yet to be explained.

Two major themes emerge from an analysis of mating behavior in grouse, the ruff, and other polybrachygynous birds. First, a female prefers to mate with a male that presents a properly "balanced threat"—that is, with a male that displays in such a way that the female's own behavioral tendencies are adjusted to permit contact and copulation. Since experience plays an important part in the development of the male's "courting technique," in general it is the older males that are chosen. Second, females choose to mate with the dominant males in a hierarchy or, in the case of lek species, with the more aggressive males. The net result is that females strongly tend to mate with aggressive older males. And the adaptiveness of this tendency seems clear, at least in regard to the fitness of the female's

10. On a large lek studied by Hogan-Warburg (1966), 59 per cent of the 53 copulations recorded were preformed by 3 of the 19 resident males; 8 of the residents never copulated; and only 2 of the 23 satellites copulated.

male progeny, since as Fisher (1930, p. 143) noted, "the success of an organism in leaving a numerous posterity is not measured only by the number of its surviving offspring, but also by the quality or probable success of these offspring." Moreover, a female's choice of a highly aggressive male, whether based on direct assessment or on his position in a dominance hierarchy or on a lek (central versus peripheral territory) also maximizes the probability that her progeny will be generally well endowed with respect to elements of fitness dependent on survival (Braestrup 1966). For a male in a superior position must be in good physiological condition and, importantly, must have survived for several years. In a sense, then, females mate preferentially with males all aspects of whose fitness have been "demonstrated." I believe that Darwin intuitively understood these relationships when he postulated that the most efficient male display would be correlated with greater general "vigor."

Mathematical models for Darwin's concept of sexual selection, in which a constant sexual preference is assumed in all females, and Fisher's (1930) concept, in which the sexual preference will itself be subject to selection, were developed by O'Donald (1962), who showed that combinations of close-linked factors (super-genes) controlling female preference and advantageous male characters should evolve with extreme rapidity.

SEX RATIOS

A satisfactory analysis of the relationships between sex ratios and mating systems is precluded by the paucity of reliable information on sex ratios in avian populations. The formerly popular notion that polygamy and polybrachygamy evolve as adaptive solutions to "problems" created by strongly unbalanced quaternary sex ratios has been replaced by the concept that unbalanced sex ratios are consequences of differential mortality in males and females resulting ultimately from intense sexual selection in nonmonogamous mating systems (Willson & Pianka 1963, Selander 1965). For at least one species, the polybrachygynous great-tailed grackle, the cause-and-effect relationship is clear (Table 8.9). At the nestling stage the sex ratio is balanced, but in October, two months after the breeding season, the sex

Table 8.9. Sex ratios in Quiscalus *grackles (after Selander 1965)*

Age Group	*Period*	*Method of Determination*	*Number of Individuals*	*Per Cent Males*
Nestling*	April–June	Dissection	244	50.8
Adult and first-year†	October	Count at roost	939	42.8
	March	Count at roost	1349	29.2

**Q. mexicanus* and *Q. major*
†*Q. mexicanus* only

ratio among first-year and adult birds is 1 male to 1.34 females. During the winter, differential mortality (males die at twice the rate of females) further unbalances the sex ratio, until in March, a month before the breeding season begins, the ratio is 1 male to 2.42 females. The higher mortality rate of males is believed to be in part a consequence of their being more vulnerable to predators because of their conspicuous coloration and behavior and because of their disproportionately large tails, which impede rapid flight. It is also probable that the large size of males (mean body weight 183 grams versus 122 grams in females), while highly adaptive in intrasexual competiton for territories at the breeding colonies, is above optimum for efficient foraging, and that males are therefore more likely to starve when food is in short supply in midwinter.

Working with the dimorphic, polygynous red-winged blackbird, Haigh (1968) attempted to test Fisher's theory that the primary sex ratio is adjusted so that the total parental energy expenditure incurred in raising young of each sex is equal and is not influenced by differential mortality beyond the period of parental care. Individually, male red-winged blackbirds are 1.4 times as expensive to raise as females, both absolute and relative growth rates being higher in males. Although Haigh's study suggests that on a population basis total energy expenditure is greater for males than females, the results are equivocal because of uncertainties concerning the accuracy of estimates of the primary sex ratio and the degree of differential mortality in the two-week fledgling period of dependency. Recently Emlen (1968) has questioned Fisher's conclusion that the primary sex ratio is independent of postparental care mortality, but support for the hypothesis has been provided by Leigh (1970).

MATURATION RATES

In many polygynous and polybrachygynous species females breed in their first year, while males do not breed until their second year or later. The breeding plumage in males is not assumed until the second year (weaver finches, icterids, manakins) or later (bellbirds, bower birds, and birds of paradise), and the subadult plumage is cryptic or intermediate between the juvenile-female plumage and that of the adult male (Selander 1958). In the lyrebird (*Menura superba*) the elaborate plumage of the male does not mature until the birds are seven or eight years old (and the transition takes three to four years), although displays and singing commence at one year of age (Smith 1965).

In nonmonogamous icterids, the testes in first-year males recrudesce later in the breeding season than do those of adult males (Selander & Hauser 1965, Payne 1969), and at maximum size they are smaller, although active spermatogenesis occurs (Figure 8.7). Presumably androgen titers also are lower, a factor perhaps correlated with the lesser intensity of dis-

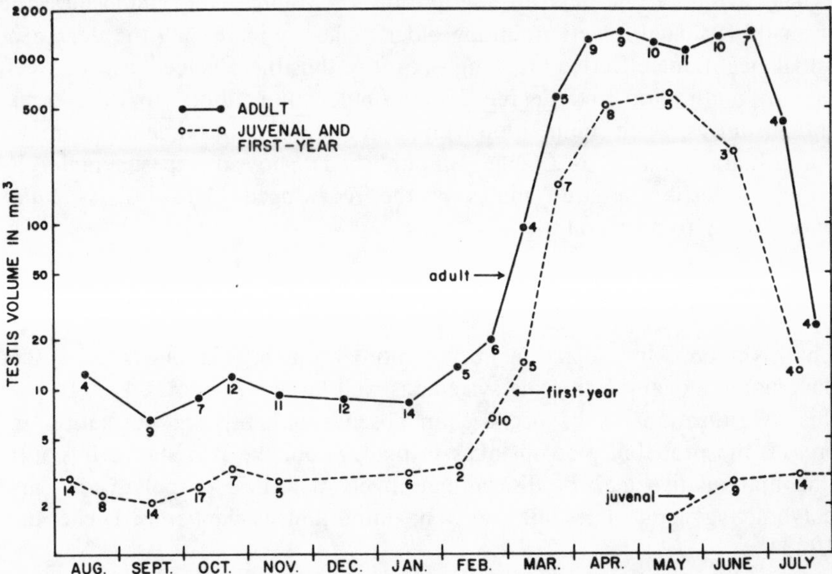

Figure 8.7. Seasonal testis volume cycle of the great-tailed grackle (Quiscalus mexicanus) *in the Austin region, Texas. Numbers below points indicate sample sizes (after Selander & Nicholson 1962).*

play characteristic of young birds. It should be noted that in *Quiscalus* and other icterids the dull first-year plumage does not result from lesser androgen titers during molt, since in species of this family, as in the majority of birds, plumage color is independent of hormonal control.

To explain delayed maturation, I have suggested that there is a low probability that young males will obtain matings in competiton with older, experienced males. This has two aspects: failure to obtain a territory and failure to properly adjust the behavioral tendencies of females, in part because of lack of experience in presenting "balanced threat" or in nest building (Verner & Engelsen 1970), bower building, or other activities related to courtship. This probability must be weighed against the increased risks to survival that a male takes in assuming full breeding plumage and competing for territory and matings in its first year (see Gadgil & Bossert 1970). If the risks are great, selection will reduce the rate of maturation (Selander 1965), producing a "floating population" of nonbreeding males. In general, a lesser tendency for delay in maturation rates occurs in species in which display mainly involves movement and sounds, with relatively weak emphasis on morphological features as signals. Yearling male sharp-tailed grouse (*Pedioecetes phasianellus*) perform the elaborate dancing display as intensely as do adult males, but in this species the breeding plumage of males is much more cryptic than in other polybrachygynous grouse (Hjorth 1970).

The evolution of delayed maturation of young males intensifies the strength of sexual selection among older males by increasing the degree of imbalance in the effective breeding sex ratio; thus there is feedback between rate of maturation and degree of intermale competition. In exceptional circumstances, when competition with adult males is reduced, first-year males may obtain matings, as Orians (unpublished) showed experimentally by removing territorial adult males of the red-winged blackbird (*Agelaius phoeniceus*) from colonies.

INTERSPECIFIC INTERACTIONS

That sympatric hybridization occurs more frequently among species that have nonmonogamous mating systems is well known (Mayr 1942). In part this hybridization results because an absence of pair-bond formation increases the probability of mistakes in mating, but the persistence in courtship and relative lack of discrimination characteristic of polygynous and polybrachygynous males may also be important (Selander & Dickerman 1963).

Possibly selection for rapid and correct species recognition, especially on the part of the female, is in part responsible for the species-specificity of male social signals used in courtship in ducks and certain other groups of birds (Sibley 1957), but the effects of sexual selection and selection for species-specificity are similar and therefore difficult to distinguish. A tendency for reduction in degree of sexual plumage dimorphism in insular species of birds is often attributed to relaxed selection for species-specificity of male signals (Sibley 1957, Grant 1965), but no quantitative analysis is available. Moreover, interpretation of such a tendency is difficult, since alternative explanations are possible in terms of variation in duration of pair-bond, social structure of populations, intensity of competition for nesting sites, predation pressure, and other aspects of life history (see Gaymer et al. 1969, Thielcke 1969, Kear 1970).

Concluding Comment

Allen (1969) has shown how ignorance of and confusion about Darwinian theory and lack of imagination among naturalists created a climate favorable to de Vries' mutation theory at the turn of the century, leading to an "eclipse" of Darwinism (Huxley 1943). Lacking an appreciation for adaptation and the populational aspects of evolution, the mutationists assigned to natural selection a minor role in the evolutionary process and essentially dismissed the theory of sexual selection. As a consequence, no real progress in the understanding of sexual selection could be made until the mutationists' hold on evolutionary biology was broken in the late 1930's with the emergence of new schools of genetics, systematics, and ecology that led to neo-Darwinism and the current synthetic theory of evolution. Still, another 20 years elapsed before more than a handful of ecologists and behaviorists were to seriously concern themselves with the evolution of adaptations and the distinction between proximate and ultimate causes (Orians 1962, Cain 1964, Tinbergen 1967).

In recent years the study of social systems has demonstrated the immense power of natural selection (including sexual selection) and the complexity and subtlety of adaptations it can generate (Lack 1968). The present review shows, I believe, that the theory of sexual selection is essentially correct as stated by Darwin—a conclusion reached earlier by Huxley (1938ab) and Maynard Smith (1958). That *The Descent of Man* has remained for a century the prime reference on the evolutionary aspects of sexual variation testifies both to Darwin's remarkable breadth of thinking and almost total grasp of the complex problem of sexual variation and to the degree to which this area has been neglected. Major modern contributions have been to show that problems of the evolution of social systems, mating systems, and sexual dimorphism are ultimately ecological in nature and to integrate Darwin's ideas with genetics and ethology. Significantly, all recent advances in our understanding of such phenomena as dispersion, reproductive rates, mating systems, sexual dimorphism, and other complex adaptations have come from the rigorous application of the principles of Darwinian selection.

References

Allen, G. E. 1969. Hugo de Vries and the reception of the "mutation theory." *J. Hist. Biol.* 2: 55–87.

Amadon, D. 1959. The significance of sexual difference in size among birds. *Proc. Amer. Phil. Soc.* 103: 531–536.

Armstrong, E. A. 1947. *Bird display and behavior.* New York: Oxford Univ. Press.

————. 1955. *The wren.* London: Collins.

————. 1964. Polyandry. In *A new dictionary of birds,* ed. A. L. Thomson, pp. 655–656. New York: McGraw-Hill.

Bastock, M. 1967. *Courtship: an ethological study.* Chicago: Aldine.

Bateman, A. J. 1949. Analysis of data on sexual isolation. *Evolution* 3: 174–177.

Bellrose, F. C., T. G. Scott, A. S. Hawkins, & J. B. Low. 1961. Sex ratios and age ratios in North American ducks. *Bull. Illinois Nat. Hist. Surv.* 27: 391–474.

Bergman, G. 1965. Der sexuelle Grössendimorphismus der Anatiden als Anpassung an des Höhlenbrüten. *Commentationes Biologicae, Soc. Sci. Fenn.* 28: 1–10.

Braestrup, F. W. 1963. The function of communal displays. *Dansk Ornithol. Forenings Tidsskrift* 57: 133–142.

————. 1966. Social and communal display. *Phil. Trans. Royal Soc. London,* Ser. B, 251: 375–386.

Brewer, R. 1963. Ecological and reproductive relationships of the blackcapped and Carolina chickadees. *Auk* 80: 9–47.

Brown, L., & D. Amadon. 1970. *Eagles, hawks and falcons of the world.* New York: McGraw-Hill.

Cade, T. J. 1960. Ecology of the peregrine and gyrfalcon populations in Alaska. *Univ. Calif. Publ. Zool.* 63: 151–290.

Cain, A. J. 1964. The perfection of animals. In *Viewpoints in biology,* Vol. 3, ed. J. D. Carthy & C. L. Duddington, pp. 36–63. London: Butterworth.

Collias, N. E., & E. C. Collias. 1967a. A field study of the red jungle fowl in north-central India. *Condor* 69: 360–386.

————. 1967b. A quantitative analysis of breeding behavior in the African village weaverbird. *Auk* 84: 396–411.

————.1969. Size of breeding colony related to attraction of mates in a tropical passerine bird. *Ecology* 50: 481–488.

————. 1970. The behavior of the west African village weaverbird. *Ibis* 112: 457–480.

Collias, N. E., E. C. Collias, D. Hunsaker, & L. Minning. 1966. Locality fixation, mobility and social organization within an unconfined population of red jungle fowl. *Anim. Behav.* 14: 550–559.

Crook, J. H. 1962. The adaptive significance of pair formation types in weaver birds. *Symp. Zool. Soc. London* 8: 57–70.

————. 1963. Comparative studies on the reproductive behavior of two closely related weaver bird species (*Ploceus cucullatus* and *P. nigerrimus*) and their races. *Behaviour* 21: 177–232.

————. 1964. The evolution of social organization and visual communication in the weaver birds (Ploceinae). *Behaviour* (Suppl. 10), pp. 1–178.

————. 1965. The adaptive significance of avian social organization. In *Social organization of animal communities,* ed. P. E. Ellis, pp. 181–218. *Symp. Zool. Soc. London* 14.

Crook, J. H., & P. A. Butterfield. 1970. Gender role in the social system of *Quelea.* In *Social behaviour in birds and mammals,* ed. J. H. Crook, pp. 211–248. London and New York: Academic Press.

Crook, J. H., & P. Ward. 1968. The *Quelea* problem in Africa. In *The problems of birds as pests,* ed. R. K. Murton & E. N. Wright, pp. 211–229. *Symp. Inst. Biol.* 17. London and New York : Academic Press.

Darwin, C. 1871. *The descent of man, and selection in relation to sex.* London: John Murray.

DeVore, I., & S. L. Washburn. 1963. Baboon ecology and human evolution. In *African ecology and human evolution,* ed. F. C. Howell and F. Bourlière, pp. 335–367. Chicago: Aldine.

Dilger, W. C. 1960. The comparative ethology of the African parrot genus *Agapornis. Zeit. f. Tierpsychol.* 17: 649–685.

Dobzhansky, T. 1970. *Genetics of the evolutionary process.* New York: Columbia Univ. Press.

Dyrenfurth, I., & E. O. Höhn. 1963. Steroid hormone content of the gonads of phalaropes and certain other birds in relation to sexual behavior in phalaropes. *J. Physiol.* 169: 42–43.

Earhart, C. M., & N. K. Johnson. 1970. Size dimorphism and food habits of North American owls. *Condor* 72: 251–264.

Emlen, J. M. 1968. A note on natural selection and the sex ratio. *Amer. Nat.* 102: 94–95.

Emlen, J. T., Jr. 1957. Display and mate selection in the whydahs and bishop birds. *Ostrich* 1957: 202–213.

Ficken, R. W. 1963. Courtship and agonistic behavior of the common grackle, *Quiscalus quiscula*. *Auk* 80: 52–72.

Fisher, R. A. 1930. *The genetical theory of natural selection*. Oxford: Clarendon Press.

French, N. R. 1959. Life history of the black rosy finch. *Auk* 76: 159–180.

Friedmann, H. 1950. The birds of North and Middle America. Part 11. *Bull. U.S. Natl. Mus.* 50: 1–793.

Frochot, B. 1967. Reflexions sur les rapports entre predateurs et proies sur les rapaces. II. L'influence des proies sur les rapaces. *Terre Vie* 1: 33–62.

Gadgil, M., & W. H. Bossert. 1970. Life historical consequences of natural selection. *Amer. Nat.* 104: 1–24.

Gaymer, R., R. A. A. Blackman, P. G. Dawson, M. Penny, & C. M. Penny. 1969. The endemic birds of Seychelles. *Ibis* 111: 157–176.

Ghiselin, M. T. 1969. *The triumph of the Darwinian method*. Berkeley: Univ. California Press.

Gilliard, E. T. 1956. Bower ornamentation versus plumage characters in bower-birds. *Auk* 73: 450–451.

————. 1959a. Notes on the courtship behavior of the blue-backed manakin (*Chiroxiphia pareola*). *Amer. Mus. Novitates* 1942: 1–19.

————. 1959b. A comparative analysis of courtship movements in closely allied bower-birds of the genus *Chlamydera*. *Amer. Mus. Novitates* 1936: 1–8.

————. 1962. On the breeding behavior of the cock-of-the-rock (Aves, *Rupicola rupicola*). *Bull. Amer. Mus. Nat. Hist.* 124: 31–68.

————. 1969. *Birds of paradise and bower birds*. Garden City, New York: National History Press.

Grant, P. R. 1965. Plumage and the evolution of birds on islands. *Syst. Zool.* 14: 47–52.

Grant, V. 1963. *The origin of adaptations*. New York: Columbia Univ. Press.

Guhl, A. M. 1962. The behaviour of chickens. In *The behaviour of domestic animals,* ed. E. S. E. Hafez, pp. 491–530. Baltimore: Williams and Wilkins.

Guhl, A. M., & D. C. Warren. 1946. Number of offspring sired by cockerals related to social dominance of chickens. *Poultry Sci.* 25: 460–472.

Haartman, L. von. 1954. Der Trauerfliegenschnäpper. III. *Acta Zool. Fenn.* 83: 1–96.

————. 1955. Clutch size in polygynous species. *Proc. 11th Intern. Ornithol. Congr.*, Basel, pp. 450–453.

————. 1969. Nest-site and evolution of polygamy in European passerine birds. *Ornis Fenn.* 46: 1–12.

Haigh, C. R. 1968. *Sexual dimorphism, sex ratios and polygyny in the red-winged blackbird*. Ph.D. thesis, Univ. Washington, Seattle.

Hale, E. B., & M. W. Schein. 1962. The behaviour of turkeys. In *The behaviour of domestic animals,* ed. E. S. E. Hafez, pp. 531–564. Baltimore: Williams and Wilkins.

Hall, J. R. 1970. Synchrony and social stimulation in colonies of the black-headed weaver *Ploceus cucullatus* and Vieillot's black weaver *Melanopteryx nigerrimus*. *Ibis* 112: 93–104.

Hamilton, T. H. 1961. On the functions and causes of sexual dimorphism in breeding plumage of North American species of warblers and orioles. *Amer. Nat.* 45: 121–123.

Hamilton, T. H., & R. H. Barth, Jr. 1962. The biological significance of season change in male plumage appearance in some New World migratory bird species. *Amer. Nat.* 96: 129–144.

Harris, M. P., & P. H. Jones. 1969. Sexual differences in measurements of herring and lesser black-backed gulls. *Brit. Birds* 62: 129–133.

Hinde, R. A. 1956. A comparative study of courtship of certain finches (Fringillidae). *Ibis* 98: 1–23.

————. 1964. Pair formation. In *A new dictionary of birds,* ed. A. L. Thomson, pp. 581–582. New York: McGraw-Hill.

————. (ed.). 1969. *Bird vocalizations.* Cambridge: Cambridge Univ. Press.

Hingston, R. W. G. 1933. *The meaning of animal colour and adornment.* London: E. Arnold.

Hjorth, I. 1970. Reproductive behaviour in Tetraonidae, with special reference to males. *Viltrevy* 7: 183–596.

Hogan-Warburg, A. J. 1966. Social behavior of the ruff, *Philomachus pugnax* (L.). *Ardea* 54: 109–229.

Höglund, N. H. 1964. Über die Ernährung des Habichts (*Accipiter gentilis* Lin.) in Schweden. *Viltrevy* 2: 271–328.

Höhn, E. O. 1965. *Die Wassertreter* (*Phalaropidae*). Wittenberg: Siemsen Verlag.

————. 1967. Observations on the breeding biology of Wilson's phalarope (*Steganopus tricolor*) in central Alberta. *Auk* 84: 220–244.

Höhn, E. O., & S. C. Cheng. 1965. Prolactin and the incidence of brood patch formation and incubation behaviour in the two sexes of certain birds with special reference to phalaropes. *Nature* 208: 197–198.

————. 1967. Gonadal hormones in Wilson's phalarope (*Steganopus tricolor*) and certain other birds in relation to plumage and sex behaviour. *Gen. Comp. Endocrinol.* 8: 1–11.

Holmes, R. T., & F. A. Pitelka. 1968. Food overlap among coexisting sandpipers on northern Alaskan tundra. *Syst. Zool.* 17: 305–318.

Holyoak, D. T. 1970. Sex-differences in feeding behaviour and size in the carrion crow. *Ibis* 112: 397–400.

Horn, H. S. 1968. The adaptive significance of colonial nesting in the Brewer's blackbird (*Euphagus cyanocephalus*). *Ecology* 49: 682–694.

Hutchinson, G. E. 1965. *The ecological theater and the evolutionary play.* New Haven: Yale Univ. Press.

Huxley, J. S. 1923. Courtship activities in the red-throated diver (*Colymbus stellatus* Pontopp.); together with a discussion of the evolution of courtship in birds. *J. Linn. Soc.* 35: 253–292.

————. 1938a. The present standing of the theory of sexual selection. In *Evolution,* ed. G. R. deBeer, pp. 11–42. Oxford: Clarendon Press.

————. 1938b. Darwin's theory of sexual selection and the data subsumed by it, in the light of recent research. *Amer. Nat.* 72: 416–433.

————. 1938c. Threat and warning coloration in birds, with a general discussion of the biological functions of colour. *Proc. 8th Intern. Ornithol. Congr.,* Oxford, pp. 430–455.

————. 1943. *Evolution: the modern synthesis.* First ed. New York: Harper & Row.

————. 1963. *Evolution: the modern synthesis.* Rev. ed. New York: Harper & Row.

Jackson, J. A. 1970. A quantitative study of the foraging ecology of downy woodpeckers. *Ecology* 51: 318–323.

Jehl, J. R. 1970. Sexual selection for size differences in two species of sandpipers. *Evolution* 24: 311–319.

Johns, J. E. 1964. Testosterone-induced nuptial feathers in phalaropes. *Condor* 66: 449–455.

————. 1969. Field studies of Wilson's phalarope. *Auk* 86: 660–670.

Johns, J. E., & E. W. Pfeiffer. 1963. Testosterone-induced incubation patches of phalarope birds. *Science* 140: 1225–1226.

Johnston, R. F. 1962. A review of courtship feeding in birds. *Bull. Kansas Ornithol. Soc.* 13: 25–32.

Johnston, R. F., & R. K. Selander. 1971. Evolution in the house sparrow. II. Adaptive differentiation in North American populations. *Evolution* 25: 1–28.

Kale, W. H., II. 1965. Ecology and bioenergetics of the long-billed marsh wren in Georgia salt marshes. *Bull. Nuttall Ornithol. Club* 5: 1–142.

Kear, J. 1970. The adaptive radiation of parental care in waterfowl. In *Social behaviour in birds and mammals,* ed. J. H. Crook, pp. 357–392. London & New York: Academic Press.

Kendeigh, S. C. 1941. Territorial and mating behavior of the house wren. *Illinois Biol. Monogr.* 18: 1–120.

————. 1952. Parental care and its evolution in birds. *Illinois Biol. Monogr.* 22: 1–356.

Kilham, L. 1970. Feeding behavior of downy woodpeckers. I. Preference for paper birches and sexual differences. *Auk* 87: 544–556.

Klomp, H. 1970. The determination of clutch-size in birds: a review. *Ardea* 58: 1–124.

Kluijver, H. N., J. Ligtvoet, C. Van Den Ouwelant, & F. Zegwaard. 1940. De levenswijze van den winterkoning *Troglodytes tr. troglodytes* (L.). *Limosa* 13: 1–51.

Koch, R. F., A. E. Courchesne, & C. T. Collins. 1970. Sexual differences in foraging behavior of white-headed woodpeckers. *Bull. So. Calif. Acad. Sci.* 69: 60–64.

Kok, O. B. 1970. *Behaviour of the great-tailed grackle* (Quiscalus mexicanus). Ph.D. thesis, Univ. Texas, Austin.

Kruijt, J. P. 1964. Ontogeny of social behaviour in Burmese red junglefowl (*Gallus gallus spadiceus*). *Behaviour* (Suppl. 12). pp. 1–201.

Kruijt, J. P., & J. A. Hogan. 1967. Social behavior on the lek in black grouse, *Lyrurus tetrix tetrix* (L.) *Ardea* 55: 203–240.

Lack, D. 1940. Courtship feeding in birds. *Auk* 57: 169–178.

————. 1941. Courtship feeding—a correction and further records. *Auk* 58: 56.

————. 1947. *Darwin's finches.* Cambridge: Cambridge Univ. Press.

————. 1954. *The natural regulation of animal numbers.* Oxford: Clarendon Press.

————. 1966. *Population studies of birds.* Oxford: Clarendon Press.

————. 1968. *Ecological adaptations for breeding in birds.* London: Methuen.

Leigh, E. G., Jr. 1970. Sex ratio and differential mortality between the sexes. *Amer. Nat.* 104: 205–210.

Lewontin, R. C. 1969. The bases of conflict in biological explanation. *J. Hist. Biol.* 2: 34–45.

Ligon, J. D. 1968. Sexual differences in foraging behavior in two species of *Dendrocopos* woodpeckers. *Auk* 85: 203–215.

Lill, A., & D. G. M. Wood-Gush. 1965. Potential ethological isolating mechanisms and assortative mating in the domestic fowl. *Behaviour* 25: 16–44.

MacArthur, R. H. 1958. Population ecology of some warblers of northeastern coniferous forests. *Ecology* 39: 599–619.

Manning, A. 1965. Drosophila and the evolution of behaviour. In *Viewpoints in biology,* Vol. 4, ed. J. D. Carthy & C. L. Duddington, pp. 125–169. London: Butterworths.

Marler, P. 1960. Bird songs and mate selection. In *Animal sounds and communication,* ed. W. E. Lanyon & W. N. Tavolga, pp. 348–367. Washington, D. C: Amer. Inst. Biol. Sci.

Marler, P., & W. J. Hamilton, III. 1966. *Mechanisms of animal behavior.* New York: Wiley.

Maynard Smith, J. 1958. Sexual selection. In *A century of Darwin,* ed. S. A. Barnett, pp. 231–244. Cambridge: Harvard Univ. Press.

Mayr, E. 1942. *Systematics and the origin of species.* New York: Columbia Univ. Press.

———. 1963. *Animal species and evolution.* Cambridge: Harvard Univ. Press.

McBride, G., I. P. Parer, & F. Foenander. 1969. The social organization and behaviour of the feral domestic fowl. *Anim. Behav. Monogr.* 2: 126–181.

Morris, D. 1956. The function and causation of courtship ceremonies. In *L'instinct dans le comportement des animaux et de l'homme,* ed. P.-P. Grassé, pp. 261–286. Fondation Singer-Polignac. Paris: Masson et Cie.

———. 1957. The courtship of pheasants. *Zoo Life* 12: 8–13.

Mottram, J. C. 1915. The distribution of secondary sexual characters amongst birds, with relation to their liability to the attacks of predators. *Proc. Zool. Soc. London,* pp. 663–678.

Mueller; H. C., & D. D. Berger. 1970. Prey preferences in the sharp-shinned hawk: the roles of sex, experience, and motivation. *Auk* 87: 452–457.

Newton, F. 1967. The adaptive radiation and feeding ecology of some British finches. *Ibis.* 109: 33–98.

Nicoll, C. S., E. W. Pfeiffer, & H. R. Fevold. 1967. Prolactin and nesting behavior in phalaropes. *Gen. Comp. Endocrinol.* 8: 61–65.

O'Donald, P. 1962. The theory of sexual selection. *Heredity* 17: 541–552.

Orians, G. H. 1961. The ecology of blackbird (*Agelaius*) social systems. *Ecol. Monogr.* 31: 285–312.

———. 1962. Natural selection and ecological theory. *Amer. Nat.* 96: 257–263.

———. 1969. On the evolution of mating systems in birds and mammals. *Amer. Nat.* 103: 589–603.

Orians, G. H., & G. M. Christman. 1968. A comparative study of the behavior of red-winged, tricolored, and yellow-headed blackbirds. *Univ. Calif. Publ. Zool.* 84: 1–81.

Payne, R. B. 1969. Breeding seasons and reproductive physiology of tricolored blackbirds and redwinged blackbirds. *Univ. Calif. Publ. Zool.* 90: 1–137.

Poulton, E. B. 1890. *The colours of animals, their meanings and use, especially considered in the case of insects.* London: Kegan Paul, Trench, Trübner.

Sauer, E. G. F., & E. M. Sauer. 1966. The behavior and ecology of the South African ostrich. *Living Bird* 5: 45–75.

Schein, M. W., & E. B. Hale. 1965. Stimuli eliciting sexual behavior. In *Sex and behavior,* ed. F. A. Beach, pp. 440–482. New York: Wiley.

Schjelderup-Ebbe, T. 1935. Social behavior in birds. In *Handbook of social psychology,* ed. C. Murchison, pp. 947–972. Worcester, Mass.: Clark Univ. Press.

Schoener, T. W. 1965. The evolution of bill size differences among sympatric congeneric species of birds. *Evolution* 19: 189–213.

———. 1968. The *Anolis* lizards of Bimini: resource partitioning in a complex fauna. *Ecology* 49: 704–726.

Selander, R. K. 1958. Age determination and molt in the boat-tailed grackle. *Condor* 60: 353–376.

———. 1965. On mating systems and sexual selection. *Amer. Nat.* 99: 129–141.

———. 1966. Sexual dimorphism and differential niche utilization in birds. *Condor* 68: 113–151.

———. 1970. Parental feeding in a male great-tailed grackle. *Condor* 72: 238.

Selander, R. K., & R. W. Dickerman. 1963. The "nondescript" blackbird from Arizona: an intergeneric hybrid. *Evolution* 17: 440–448.

Selander, R. K., & D. R. Giller. 1960. First-year plumages of the brown-headed cowbird and red-winged blackbird. *Condor* 62: 202–214.

———. 1961. Analysis of sympatry of great-tailed and boat-tailed grackles. *Condor* 63: 29–86.

———. 1963. Species limits in the woodpecker genus *Centurus* (Aves). *Bull. Amer. Mus. Nat. Hist.* 124: 213–274.

Selander, R. K., & R. J. Hauser. 1965. Gonadal and behavioral cycles in the great-tailed grackle. *Condor* 67: 157–182.

Selander, R. K., & R. F. Johnston. 1967. Evolution in the house sparrow. I. Intrapopulation variation in North America. *Condor* 69: 217–258.

Selander, R. K., & D. J. Nicholson. 1962. Autumnal breeding of boat-tailed grackles in Florida. *Condor* 64: 81–91.

Sibley, C. G. 1957. The evolutionary and taxonomic significance of sexual dimorphism and hybridization in birds. *Condor* 59: 166–191.

Sick, H. 1967. Courtship behavior in the manakins (Pipridae): a review. *Living Bird* 6: 5–22.

Skutch, A. F. 1949. Do tropical birds rear as many young as they can nourish? *Ibis* 91: 430–455.

Smith, L. H. 1965. Changes in the tail feathers of the adolescent lyrebird. *Science* 147: 510–513.

Snow, B. K. 1966. Observations on the behaviour and ecology of the flightless cormorant *Nannopterum harrisi*. *Ibis* 108: 265–280.

———. 1970. A field study of the bearded bellbird in Trinidad. *Ibis* 112: 299–329.

Snow, D. W. 1963. The evolution of manakin displays. *Proc. 13th Intern. Ornithol. Congr.*, Ithaca, pp. 553–561.

Soikkeli, M. 1966. On the variation in bill and wing length of the dunlin (*Calidris alpina*) in Europe. *Bird Study* 13: 256–269.

Storer, R. W. 1966. Sexual dimorphism and food habits in three North American accipiters. *Auk* 83: 423–436.

Thielcke, G. 1969. Geographic variation in bird vocalizations. In *Bird vocalizations,* ed. R. A. Hinde, pp. 311–339. Cambridge: Cambridge Univ. Press.

Tinbergen, N. 1935. Field observation of east Greenland birds. 1. The behaviour of the red-necked phalarope (*Phalaropus lobatus* L.) in spring. *Ardea* 24: 1–42.

———. 1954. The origin and evolution of courtship and threat display. In *Evolution as a process,* ed. J. Huxley, A. C. Hardy, & E. B. Ford, pp. 233–250. London: Allen & Unwin.

————. 1960. *The herring gull's world.* Rev. ed. New York: Basic Books.
————. 1965. Some recent studies of the evolution of sexual behavior. In *Sex and behavior,* ed. F. A. Beach, pp. 1–33. New York, Wiley.
————. 1967. Adaptive features of the black-headed gull *Larus ridibundus* L. *Proc. 14th Intern.Ornithol. Congr.,* Oxford, pp. 43–59.
Van Someren, V. D. 1945. The dancing display and courtship of Jackson's whydah (*Coliuspasser jacksoni* Sharpe). *J. East African Nat. Hist. Soc.* 18: 131–141.
Verner, J. 1963. Song rates and polygamy in the long-billed marsh wren. *Proc. 13th Intern. Ornithol. Congr.,* Ithaca, pp. 299–307.
————. 1964. Evolution of polygamy in the long-billed marsh wren. *Evolution* 18: 252–261.
————. 1965. Breeding biology of the long-billed marsh wren. *Condor* 67: 6–30.
Verner, J., & G. H. Engelsen. 1970. Territories, multiple nest building, and polygyny in the long-billed marsh wren. *Auk* 87: 557–567.
Verner, J., & M. F. Willson. 1966. The influence of habitats on mating systems of North American birds. *Ecology* 47: 143–147.
————. 1969. Mating systems, sexual dimorphism, and the role of male North American passerine birds in the nesting cycle. *Ornithol. Monogr.* 9: 1–76.
Wallace, A. R. 1889. *Darwinism: an exposition of the theory of natural selection with some of its applications.* London: Macmillan.
Wallace, R. A. 1970. *Sexual dimorphism, niche utilization, and social behavior in insular species of woodpeckers.* Ph.D. thesis, Univ. Texas, Austin.
Wallace, R. A., & R. K. Selander. 1972, in preparation. Ecological aspects of sexual dimorphism in woodpeckers.
Watts, C. R. 1968. Rio Grande turkeys in the mating season. *Trans. 33, N. Amer. Wildl. and Nat. Resources Conf.,* pp. 205–210.
Wiens, J. A. 1966. On group selection and Wynne-Edwards' hypothesis. *Amer. Sci.* 54: 273–287.
Williams, G. C. 1966. *Adaptation and natural selection: a critique of some current evolutionary thought.* Princeton: Princeton Univ. Press.
Williams, L. 1952. Breeding behavior of the Brewer blackbird. *Condor* 54: 3–47.
Willoughby, E. J., & T. J. Cade. 1964. Breeding behavior of the American kestrel (sparrow hawk). *Living Bird* 3: 75–96.
Willson, M. F., & E. R. Pianka. 1963. Sexual selection, sex ratio, and mating system. *Amer. Nat.* 97: 405–407.
Wolf, L. L. 1969. Female territoriality in a tropical hummingbird. *Auk* 86: 490–504.
Wynne-Edwards, V. C. 1962. *Animal dispersion in relation to social behaviour.* Edinburgh: Oliver & Boyd.
Yang, S. Y., & R. K. Selander. 1968. Hybridization in the grackle *Quiscalus quiscula* in Louisiana. *Syst. Zool.* 17: 107–143.

9

JOHN HURRELL CROOK
BRISTOL UNIVERSITY

Sexual Selection, Dimorphism, and Social Organization in the Primates

Introduction

Darwin's references to primates in *The Descent of Man* (1871) were both frequent and well-scattered throughout a text devoted to evolutionary principles of significance in most animal phyla. It was however clear that of all the taxa that interested him the primates were of unique and most direct importance for human descent. Furthermore, the evolutionary origin of the differences between man and woman seemed to Darwin, as to contemporary ethologists, to be more comprehensively explicable when considered in the light of primate evolution as a whole.

In most animal groups the sexes differ not only in the character of their generative organs, their primary sexual attributes, but also in their secondary sexual characteristics, features not directly concerned with the mating act but which are highly diagnostic of the sex to which an individual belongs. These diverse secondary features vary from those barely concerned with reproduction at all to those characteristics which, although not functional in mating itself, are of major reproductive support in bringing the

I am indebted to Dr. John Goss-Custard and my ethological colleagues (1972) at Bristol for extensive discussions on the theme of this paper in the summer of 1970. Working separately, John and I thought out the likely relations between the social and environmental factors involved (254–267) and compared our independently derived conclusions. The close similarity between our final positions gives us some confidence in their reliability and heuristic value. I am also grateful to Dr. Adam Kendon for a long conversation on human courtship and to Mr. David Crawford for useful criticisms of earlier graphical representations of Figures 9.1 and 9.2. Dr. Pelham Aldrich-Blake kindly read and commented on the final manuscript. My personal research on the Gelada baboon in Ethiopia was financed by the Wenner Gren Foundation for Anthropological Research, The Royal Society, and by Bristol University.

two sexes together or into a situation in which mutual courtship and mating sequences may commence. Many differences between the sexes are related particularly to the competition that characteristically occurs between males, either for territory, or for possession of a female or several females. Secondary sexual characteristics, those important in competition for a mating partner and those functional in support of mating itself, typically appear when an individual reaches reproductive maturity. Both are generally considered to be products of sexual selection. Darwin describes at length the difference between natural selection and sexual selection and summarizes his findings as follows.

> Sexual selection depends on the success of certain individuals over others of the same sex in relation to the propagation of the species; whilst natural selection depends on the success of both sexes, at all ages, in relation to the general conditions of life. The sexual struggle is of two kinds; in the one it is between the individuals of the same sex, generally the male sex, in order to drive away or kill their rivals, the females remain passive; whilst in the other, the struggle is likewise between the individuals of the same sex, in order to excite or charm those of the opposite sex, generally the females, which no longer remain passive, but select the more agreeable partners. . . Variability is the necessary basis for the action of selection and is wholly independent of it. It follows from this, that variations of the same general nature have often been taken advantage of and accumulated through sexual selection in relation to the propagation of the species, and through natural selection in relation to the general purposes of life. Hence secondary sexual characters, when equally transmitted to both sexes can be distinguished from ordinary specific characters only by the light of analogy. The modifications acquired through sexual selection are often so strongly pronounced that the two sexes have frequently been ranked as distinct species or even as distinct genera. Such strongly marked differences must be in some manner highly important; and we know that they have been acquired in some instances at the cost not only of inconvenience, but of exposure to actual danger (1871, p. 398).

Darwin used several criteria for distinguishing secondary sexual characteristics.

1. The features acquired by sexual selection are confined to one sex.
2. The features develop fully only at sexual maturity.
3. The features often appear only during the reproductive season.
4. Males are in most species the most active in courtship and in the context of reproduction make use of their offensive weapons in competitive encounters with male rivals and of their courtship display characteristics in the presence of females to attract them.

He further inferred the operation of sexual selection from the observation that individuals of the one sex are capable of feeling a strong antipathy or preference for certain individuals of the opposite sex. These feelings are the basis on which sexual selection operates. Persistent selection for mating of animals possessing certain qualities would lead to the perpetuation of these features in succeeding generations and the emergence of marked morphological and behavioral differentiation of the sexes. The two main principles involved are on the one hand *epigamic* or *intersexual selection* and, on the other, *intrasexual selection* (Huxley 1938ab,) the former resulting from a reproductive advantage accruing to individuals with the stronger heterosexual stimili (Sibley 1957) and the latter from advantages accruing from the possession of morphological and behavioral features that increase reproductive potential through the successes they secure in competitive rivalry between members of the same sex, usually male.

Huxley (1923, 1938ab), Fisher (1929), Selander (1965) and Orians (1969) have all emphasized the important link between sexual selection and the nature of a species mating system. The development of especially exaggerated male morphological and display characteristics is characteristically related to the occurrence of polygyny. Huxley (1923) was the first to show that the occurrence of mating systems involving intense sexual selection was dependent upon the ecology of the species; aspects of the environment including food resources and predation pressure affecting the extent to which polygyny (and the emergence of features linked with this mating system) was advantageous or disadvantageous to the individuals concerned. This important approach was not developed by ethologists until relatively recently for a variety of historical reasons (see Crook 1970a), and was first applied broadly in comparative studies of avian societies in individual taxonomic families (Immelmann 1962, Crook 1964) and then in studies of the class as a whole (Brown 1964, Crook 1965, Lack 1968). In 1966 Crook and Gartlan applied the method in a first attempt at an explanation of the diversity of social systems in primates, particularly those of the terrestrial Old World species that were the best known at that time. It was apparent to these authors that sexual selection as well as direct ecological adaptation was involved in the social evolution of these systems. Field studies of primates are currently developing rapidly and improving greatly in quality. Crook (1970b) recently undertook a broad based review of much of the work available up to 1969 but without further emphasis on the significance of sexual selection. In this article I treat first the occurrence of sexual dimorphism throughout the primates, second, the importance of sexual selection as an aspect of social selection in the evolution of social organizations and lastly the current state of inference from these studies to the condition of man.

Sexual Dimorphism in the Primates

The main morphological characteristics in which the sexes of the primates differ are as follows:

1. Weight and muscular development.
2. Body dimensions such as head and body length and tail length.
3. Pelage color and markings, often in the region of the face.
4. Possession of particular anatomical features such as long canines, a bulbous nose (in *Nasalis*) or gular pouches (for example, *Pongo*), shoulder capes or manes, skull characteristics, especially the development of nuchal and sagittal crests in males, baldness, permanent skin ridges and skin coloration, especially on face and sometimes on chest and/or ischial areas.
5. Occurrence of maturational, seasonal or periodic morphological changes directly associated with reproduction; skin color (for example, scrotum) in males, sexual swellings in ischial region of females associated with skin color changes of the same and other areas during the ovulation phase of the estrous cycle.

From this list it is apparent that a wide range of features may differentiate the sexes, some permanently but others only during a mating period or, as in the female, only during the ovulation phase of the estrous cycle. Generally speaking the features that are pronounced in males often seem to have to do with competition with other males while female features relate particularly to the timing of mating and the advertisement of sexual readiness at the height of estrus. Throughout the primates the larger size of the male sex is a recurrent theme. DeVore and Washburn (1963) and Altmann and Altmann (1970, p. 209) are inclined to attribute this to the significance of size and strength to the defensive role of adult males of value to the troop as a protection from predators. Other authors (Crook & Gartlan 1966, Struhsaker 1969) stress the likely importance of size in intrasexual competition in the rivalry between males for females. In this case the size increase is preadaptive to the male's defensive role. In either case if, as DeVore and Washburn (1963) pointed out, such increase occurred without a proportionate decrease in male representation in local populations the maintenance of the larger male biomass would cut into the food resources available for females, particularly under conditions of food poverty. In addition, since recruitment of young per capita is the key to biological success, female body size is within limits likely to decrease allowing a larger number of individuals for the same biomass. As we shall see, the disproportion in the sizes of the sexes varies in species of differing ecological adaptation and a higher representation of adult females is common. Furthermore, females commence breeding at an earlier age than do males. Jolly (1963) has suggested that the growth of capes, in the hamadryas baboon for example, achieves an apparent extra increase in male size but with little cost in metabolic requirements.

In compiling a brief survey of sex differences in primates I have made extensive use of Napier and Napier's handbook (1967) which comprises an authoritive distillation of primate facts available at that date. It is clear from the material available to these authors that the sample sizes of measured cadavers vary enormously from species to species and that in making numerical comparisons the most that can be established are sets of differential trends. The findings are nevertheless of considerable interest.

TREE SHREWS, LEMURS, LORISES

Although the tree shrews may no longer be considered primates (Martin 1968) they undoubtedly show characteristics close to those of the insectivore ancestors of the order. These small mammals reveal a range of forms from the completely arboreal to the terrestrial. Most of them feed on fruit, insect and vertebrate resources. Little is known of their life in the wild, available reports showing only that they occur most usually either solitarily or in pairs with perhaps a temporary formation of small familial groups consisting of a male, female and offspring for a period following reproduction. Captivity observation suggests pair living to be usual, the animals possessing both a sleeping nest and a nest in which the young are reared. Territorial or pathway marking with urine and secretion from other glands is most usually performed by males.

Napier and Napier (1967) provide a number of measures of weight that allow estimation of the percentage of the males weight shown by females. Where possible these authors compare the mid-points of the ranges of measurements. In weight females are 85 per cent of the males weight in *Ptilocercus,* 90 per cent in *Tupaia,* 99 per cent in *Urogale* and 106 per cent in *Anathana.* With respect to head and body length (excluding tails) the figures for the same genera are 96 per cent, 100 per cent and 108 per cent (two species), 99 per cent and 106 per cent. In other words dimorphism is slight. This finding, together with the fact that extreme dimorphism is relatively infrequent in primates and largely confined to the Old World Anthropoidea, indicates that marked morphological and behavioral dimorphism is not a primitive characteristic of primates but has evolved in certain genera in relation to particular patterns of living. The further implication is that sexual selection has exerted a profound influence only in these same forms and not in others. It certainly does not appear to have been a major factor in the evolution of tree shrews.

Among the lemurs differences between the sexes are likewise slight. Most lemurs live solitarily or in small mother-litter families perhaps sometimes associated with a male in a loose community structure. In the larger species individuals live in small groups including one or more males. Groups larger than ten and including several males are found only in the genus *Lemur* itself which is also a partly terrestrial form (Petter 1962, Jolly 1966). Only in *Lemur* is there a development of sexual dichromatism (*L. macaco, L. mongoz*). In this genus we find changes in the genitalia of the female in association with estrus, changes in size associated with reddening. The social organization of *Lemur* is not only more elaborate, the social units containing more individuals than other lemurs, but it also differs interestingly from comparable groups in the Anthropoid monkeys where sex dimorphism is equally or more pronounced. Compared with *Macaca* for example, in which there are commonly more adult females than males in a social unit, *Lemur catta* (and also *Propithecus verreauxi*) has either a more or less equal adult sex ratio or a preponderance of males. The breeding seasons of these lemurs are extremely short and aggression likewise very limited in time. Apart from the mating season males are either not particularly dominant or, although ranked with respect to one another, subordinate to females (*L. catta*) (Jolly 1966). Therefore, in these lemurs a relative absence of dimorphism is linked to an absence of the male dominance so commonly characteristic of Anthropoidea and there is a markedly seasonal limitation on aggression between males. In addition, moreover, the complex social hierarchies, cooperative alliances and social subterfuge typical of the more dimorphic and hierarchically organised Anthropoidea are noticeably absent. Perhaps by strictly confining mating and births to limited seasons the lemurs have avoided the emergence of the sexually dimorphic and socially competitive demographic structures of Anthropoidea, but they have also failed to develop the complex social skills upon which the more elaborate aspects of primate social life appear to depend.

Little sexual dimorphism occurs in lorises. In *Loris* the females weigh about 82 per cent as much as the males but are of about the same head and body length. In *Nycticebus* the figures are 92 per cent and 94 per cent; in *Perodicticus* 91 per cent and 105 per cent. In *Galago* however, measures show females roughly 76 per cent and 83 per cent of males (two species). The greater dimorphism of this species may perhaps be associated with Dominique's (pers comm) observations that large males contact several females in a community and evidently exclude lighter weight males from access to them. The acquisition of females by previously peripheral males is linked with increases in weight of the latter. It is not yet known however how far this type of social organization may not also occur in Lorisid species with less marked dimorphism.

NEW WORLD MONKEYS

From the figures available dimorphism in weight is very slight in the Ceboidea: indeed in some cases females exceed the males in weight. Some representative measurements are shown on the opposite page.

In *Alouatta* the male is bearded and possesses a specialized larynx used in the production of loud calls that maintain spacing between groups (see Chivers 1969). In *Brachyteles* there are slight color contrasts between the sexes. Such dichromatism is more marked in *Cebus* and *Pithecia.* In *Ateles* the female is the heavier animal and male dominance behavior is not ap-

Genus	*Weight (% Female in Male)*	*Head/Body length (%)*
Alouatta	about 80	81
Aotus	85	100
Ateles	103	105
Brachyteles	—	95
Cacajao	—	90
Callithrix	93	101
Cebus	78	91
Lagothrix	85	99
Pithecia	89	87
Saguinus	102–112	91

parent. Likewise in *Saguinus* the female is the heavier and, although not longer in head-body length, the tail length is 108 per cent of males. The female is also the more aggressive animal and performs marking behavior. As also in *Callithrix* the male commonly takes care of the baby for long periods. In many south American monkeys facial markings are pronounced in both sexes but commonly these do not differ between the sexes. The evolution of facial markings thus may have more to do with the prevention of interspecific hybridization than with sex-related behavior. The evolution of diversity in these patterns appears to have followed complex rules (Hershkovitz 1968).

These figures reveal a general tendency for males to outweigh females but by only a small amount. Figures of this type occur mainly in species living in party sizes of about 20 or 30 animals and which are primarily vegetarian. The *Ateles* tends to form monosexual parties and disperse broadly from a large communal tree roost. The Tamarin, *Saguinus*, probably lives in monogamous pairs and like some other South American monkeys is quite largely carnivorous. Whether this fact is connected with the unusual size of the female and her aggressive behavior remains unknown. Clearly much more information is required on the Ceboidea before generalizations relating to dimorphism, ecology and behavior can be made.

OLD WORLD MONKEYS

Table 9.1 summarizes the main features of morphological sex dimorphism in the Old World Monkeys. In general the difference in weight between the sexes is more pronounced than in almost all other primates. No less than nine genera have females characteristically weighing 70 per cent or less than the males (*Cercopithecus, Cynopithecus, Erythrocebus, Papio, Presbytis,* (*P. entellus* only), *Theropithecus, Macaca, Mandrillus, Nasalis*). Of these the most extreme weight dimorphism is found in *Mandrillus, Papio, Erythrocebus* and *Nasalis* where the female is close to half the weight of the male. The least dimorphism is found in *Colobus* and

Table 9.1. Sexual dimorphism in Old World Monkeys

Genus	*Weight*	*Dimensions* *head-body length (HB), tail length (T)*	*Other features*
	(Female as % of male)		
Cercocebus	No figure	87 (HB) 86–91 (T)	Sexual swelling in estrous female of moderate extent. No color change in perineum.
Cercopithecus	about 70	About 80 (HB) and 94 (T)	Sex skin changes in color in females of subgenera *Athenopithecus* and *Miopithecus* and some pelage contrast in latter. Vivid blue scrotum in *Cercopithecus.*
Colobus	93–97	93–98 (HB) in *Procolobus* 101 (HB)	Large canines in males. Sex swelling in females of *Piliocolobus.*
Cynopithecus	63	85 (HB)	Long canines in male.
Erythrocebus	54	No figures.	Scrotum of adult male is bright blue. Male shows aloof behavior fitting role of watch dog for group.
Papio	50 (*P. anubis*)	81 (HB) 83 (T) Both figures for *P. anubis.*	Marked development of mane in *P. hamadryas.* Small male mane also in *P. papio.* Sex swellings in estrous females. Canines developed in males.
Presbytis	68 in *P. entellus* but 92–99 in other sp. groups.	94 (HB)	Canines longer in males.

Pygathrix	No figure	95 (HB) 91 (T)	
Rhinopithecus	No figure	85 (HB) 95 (T)	Some clear dimorphism in some spp.
Theropithecus	70	71 (HB)	Marked development of mane and canines in males and different shape of chest patch. Major sex-skin changes in females in estrus.
Macaca	64 in *M. fascicularis* 69 in other species	Female about 95 per cent of male in HB. Range, male 442–700 mm (n = 115 and 81) and female 432–680 mm, see Napier & Napier 1967, p. 406.	Prominent canines in males, which also have continuous brow-ridge over nose. Seasonal enlargement and reddening of testis in *M. mulatta*. Sex-skin changes occur in most species in females: swellings pronounced in *sylvana, mulatta, assamensis* and *cyclopis,* not marked in *speciosa, fuscata, radiata, nemestrina*. Color: reddens or goes purple in all spps. except *sylvana* and *fascicularis* where color is grey-blue. In *sinica* females have redder faces. In *mulatta* face reddens in estrus in 10 per cent females.
Mandrillus	Female about half male weight.	No precise figures but female about half size male.	Sex-skin swelling and bright color in female. Extreme dimorphism in facial skin paterns and coloration.
Nasalis	57	90 (HB) Females have shorter tails at 84 per cent of males.	Long, bulbous drooping nose in male.

Female feature expressed as per cent of male usually derived from comparisons of midpoints of ranges of the two sexes given in Napier & Napier 1967.

Presbytis (other than *P. entellus*) suggesting that Colobine monkeys may not be as dimorphic as Cercopithecids. The canines are commonly more developed in males than females (especially in *Theropithecus, Papio, Cynopithecus* and *Macaca*). Shoulder capes or manes are pronounced in *Papio hamadryas* and *Theropithecus* and to a lesser extent in the northern populations of *Papio papio* and *P. anubis*. The long bulbous and drooping nasal organ of *Nasalis* may well be associated with loud calling which is thought to function in the spacing of groups.

The most extreme combinations of dimorphic characteristics are found in the genera *Mandrillus* (size, color, extreme contrasts in facial patterning and coloration), *Theropithecus* (size, mane, canines, chest patch contrasts), *Papio hamadryas* (size, mane and canines) and *Erythrocebus* (size and build). It is certainly not an accident that all these animals are both terrestrial and live in one-male reproductive groups[1] in which the males play the predominant behavior roles that structure group behavior (dominant leadership in *Theropithecus, P. hamadryas* and probably also in *Mandrillus;* watch dog and defender in *Erythrocebus*).

The occurrence of manes is most characteristic of harem forming species of arid African environments and may be a consequence of intrasexual selection enhancing signals used in competitive rivalry. If this were so an apparent increase in size is accomplished without an increase in the individual's biomass proportional to its appearance. In arid areas this would be helpful since the male needs little metabolic energy to maintain merely a long coat of hair. Jolly (1963) suggests that manes attract females to a harem owner: the hair acting as a strong stimulus for grooming and band formation and maintenance. The mane is thus interpreted by him as a consequence of intersexual selection favoring a feature that enhances the attractiveness of the male for the female.

While dimorphism in weight is marked in *Macaca* it is not associated with other major contrasts. This genus lives in multimale rather than one-male groups but the males are organised in complex relationships reflecting dominance and other status characteristics. In *Cercopithecus,* most species of which are arboreal, one-male groups occur in many species but without extreme dimorphism. The association between terrestrial life and one-male groups seems particularly diagnostic for the extreme development of dimorphism in these animals. It is argued that this enhancement is due to strong intrasexual selection operating most markedly in such groups (see further pp. 257–267).

Perhaps the most interesting differences between the sexes concern the complex diversity of changes in the "sexual skin" of females. These changes, occurring in the perineal area and sometimes also in other areas

1. Within the genus *Mandrillus,* the Drill is suspected, on available field evidence, to live in one-male groups (Gartlan pers. comm.). The Mandrill has yet to be studied in the field.

of the body, may include gross and complicated swellings (*Cercocebus, Pilicolobus, Papio, Mandrillus,* certain *Macaca* species). These changes develop in estrus and are usually at a maximum at approximately the time of ovulation. W. Wickler (1967), in an extensive review, argues that the presentation by a female of the posterior to a male constitutes the main precopulatory mating invitation in the majority of Cercopithecid primates. In certain species the effectiveness of presentation has evidently been increased by the provision of timely color changes and swellings that can hardly fail to attract the male's attention. In the rhesus monkey the surface of these swellings aids in the dissemination of odor which functions as a pheromone in activating male behavior (Michael & Keverne 1968, 1970). As Darwin emphasized (1876) the extensive development of these elaborate anatomical and behavioral secondary sexual epigamic characters may be considered a consequence of the action of intersexual selection although Keverne (1970) thinks their primary adaptation might have lain in temperature regulation. As yet, it remains totally unclear as to why only certain Cercopithecoid species have developed these fantastic sexual attractants and not others. There is little doubt from the information reviewed by Wickler that there have been several cases of parallel evolution since the morphological features involved in one species are not always the same in others. Why some species have not developed such characteristics at all remains a puzzle. There is no close association with patterns of ecology or social grouping since swelling and color changes occur almost haphazardly in arboreal and terrestrial animals living in either one-male or multimale reproductive units. However, there is perhaps a tendency for these developments to be associated with ground living.

Wickler (1967) also discusses some remarkable resemblances in color and design between the hind quarters of males (particularly the ischial, circum-anal and scrotal regions) and those of the females of the same species. Many Cercopithecoid primates live either in one-male groups, from which adolescent males are commonly ejected by the adult male owner, or in multimale groups in which complex status hierarchies develop among the males based upon age and size, kinship and affiliative behavior (see review, Crook 1970b). The protection assured by remaining in a group is probably considerable, especially in terrestrial species living in areas also inhabited by numerous mammalian predators. Wickler argues plausibly that in these Cercopithecoid societies the males utilize the female presentation gesture as a means to reduce the likelihood of aggression from a more dominant older male. The adoption of female type submissive behavior by younger and weaker males not only reduces the likelihood of a damaging fight but also reduces the pressure by superiors to leave the group. Such behavior thus increases group cohesion. Wickler argues that the effectiveness of the appeasement signal is enhanced by the inclusion of elements that mimic (intraspecifically and intersexually) the females' signal characteristics. In a number of male cercopithecoids the features of the posterior that resemble those of the female are striking, and different anatomical derivations are found in different species.

Wickler (1967) reports, for example, that in estrus the perineal area of the female *Cercopithecus aethiops centralis* reddens and the vulvar margins, between which peeps the conspicuously red clitoris, become blue. The anogenital region of the male has a scarlet perineum and a bright blue scrotum below which the scarlet penis is visible. Viewed from behind, the juxtaposition of these organs resembles the design of the females posterior markedly. Males of other *Cercopithecus* species also show color patterns posteriorly, the resemblance of which to female patterns remains to be established because the necessary observations are lacking. Wickler gives details of numerous other such resemblances between the sexes including the massive red buttocks of the male hamadryas, color similarities in *Macaca mulatta* and the remarkable ischial swellings of male and female Red and Olive Colobus monkeys. Here the swellings are permanent features of both sexes from puberty and, although derived from different anatomical features in each species, show remarkable similarities in form.

The gelada baboon is of especial interest (Wickler 1963). The elaborate changes in the female perineal area include a waxing and waning of the red coloration, the tumescence of bare skin areas and the appearance of pearly white vesicles around the edges. As menstruation approaches the color fades and the vesicles enlarge in correlation with the luteal phase of the ovarian cycle (Matthews 1956, on captive animals). The female also possesses a patch of bare skin on the chest quite strikingly similar in design to the posterior and which also changes in color and vesiculation.

During 1965 the writer worked in the Ethiopian highlands studying the social behavior of the wild gelada. He obtained data important to Wickler's theory but which can only give partial support to it. Females in estrus, when their chest color is most red, consort particularly closely with their males and mating occurs. In a small number of the copulations observed the males examined the female chests closely pushing the nose and lips near to the skin. The bare skin areas on the belly and between the legs were likewise examined before the male moved around behind the female to examine the vulva. Copulatory mounting followed. In many more sequences this preliminary examination was omitted and mounting proceeded directly after presentation. Possibly examinations only occur during the first few matings when a female has come into estrus and is approaching the male. It is thus demonstrated that the chest patches are indeed involved in copulatory sequences in wild geladas. However, the resemblances between the color changes on chest and ischial areas are not as close as Wickler supposed. Correlations between the states of these structures (Table 9.2) shows that in many animals in estrus when the chest is most red and the vesicles well developed and pink the perineal skin is a dark purplish grey color. In late estrus the vesicles become white and the perineal areas a paler pink. Lactating mothers and females out of estrus mostly have pink perineal areas when the chest is flesh colored or very pale pink with no vesicles at all. Vesicle development and color changes do however vary in phase anteriorly and posteriorly throughout the cycle. While these field data are far from conclusive it seems strange that if the red chest color should be most attractive to males the perineal areas should be most red at precisely the time when mating would appear to be inappropriate. Possibly an odor acting as a pheromone may be present on these surfaces and be of more importance than color alone.

Table 9.2. Relations between coloration of chest skin patches and ischial areas during the estrous cycle of female Theropithecus gelada

Chest development in females	*Ischial skin color: bright pink*	*Ischial skin color: pale pink*	*Ischial skin color: purplish grey*	*Totals*
a. No vesicles. Pale pink skin. Not in estrus.	46	5	6	57
b. Large pink vesicles. Pink skin. Full estrus.	7	2	27*	36
c. Small white vesicles. Paler skin. Late estrus.	10	4	9	23
d. Maternal females suckling young. Flesh colored or pale pink chests. No vesicles.	26	14	3	43
Totals	89	25	45	159

Field observations: Binoculars (×10), Telescope (×60). Distances between 12–200 metres. Numbers represent summed totals per category from counts in three areas in Semyen, Ethiopia, in February and in March, 1965.

*R. Dunbar (*in litt.*), currently working in Ethiopia, suggests that the high representation of females with grey ischial areas in this sample is due to a large representation of young preparous animals.

Wickler also suggested that the nipples of the female, which in the adult female gelada lie closely together in the mid-line of the chest and which are often long and pendulous, are signal imitations of the lips of the vulva. However, in sexually mature preparous females the nipples are small and lie well apart; nevertheless, the animals are manifestly popular with their males. Long nipples are particularly characteristic of maternal females and appear to arise in the course of suckling. The babies take both into the mouth at once. The signal function of these structures in copulatory behavior is thus by no means demonstrated.

Field comparisons between the time spent sitting by geladas and baboons (*Papio anubis*) were made by the writer and Aldrich-Blake (1968). The gelada was not only found to spend a vastly greater time feeding than the baboon but also to do almost all of it in a sitting position. Assuming a need for a morphological signal informing males of the female's sexual condition it seems the rear end of the gelada would indeed be inappropriate as it is seen relatively little. It is thus reasonable to suppose the action of a selection pressure enhancing cyclic changes on the chest, which were possibly originally important in temperature control, to produce a sexual "releaser." Those females with the most effective chests would attract most matings over many generations and supposedly leave most offspring. It does not appear essential, however, for the signal to be an exact copy of the ischial design, and indeed we find it is not. In view of the baby and juvenile geladas' prolonged interest in the nipples with which they may play as well as obtain nourishment, an interest in this area is likely to continue into adulthood so that any color development is likely to have significance. While it is not possible to refute Wickler's plausible suggestion on this evidence the extent to which the chest patches really copy the perineal area remains to a degree subjective.

The chest patch of the male gelada is flesh colored in subadults and red in mature males. Prolonged field observation revealed no incident in which intermale posturing involving a dynamic chest display occurred. Certainly there is no parallel with the presenting of large buttocks by males to dominants in other species. Juvenile male geladas in fact sometimes present in the normal way to the adult male of their group during infrequent agonistic encounters. The area presented has no resemblance to the female posterior being dull grey in color. Gelada males are however fond of sitting on a prominent rock with the chest well exposed. It seems not improbable that the chest may then function as a distance signal to other animals of both sexes announcing the presence and position of a harem "overlord." The signal may deter other males from interference with females near the male and thus, rather than being a protective mechanism for a weak male, the chest may contribute to the reproductive success of powerful individuals. Intrasexual selection may thus maintain in the male secondary sexual characteristics originally developed in the female.

Although Wickler's arguments are generally compelling there remain numerous further inconsistencies in the data. In the female rhesus macaque for example a sexual skin swelling occurs only during maturation and disappears in the adult although the red color remains. In the male talapoin there is no correspondence between the pattern of the male genitalia and that of the female swelling. And again why some species and not others have followed this course of signal evolution remains unknown. In spite of these doubts one may perhaps conclude that Cercopithecoid primates have repeatedly but independently evolved signals in the male sex that appear to mimic those used by the female in sexual presentation. The functions of such male signals are not however necessarily homologous in different species.

It seems probable that in these complex status oriented societies the high level of aggression among males and their greater size may be related to relatively longer periods of sexual (mating) potency in males than in females. Breeding seasons appear primarily to be a function of female reproductive seasonality rather than of male periodism. If this suggestion were found to be true there are numerous implications. As Wickler (1967) points out, although Zuckerman's (1932) argument favoring a sexual basis for higher primate society has not been substantiated (Lankaster & Lee 1965) in the form in which he presented it, sexual motivation of males, even though not overtly expressed, may account in some measure for their continual concern with either intersexual bonding in one-male units or dominance ranking in multimale reproductive units respectively even when females are nonreceptive. The competitive nature of Cercopithecoid, as compared with lemur societies (see p. 236), also gives rise to numerous behavioral elaborations including social subterfuge and agonistic buffering (Kummer 1967, Crook 1970c, Deag & Crook 1971). Indeed, although in *Rhesus,* testis size is large during the mating period and small during the birth season (changes which may perhaps be connected with a rise and fall in spermatogenesis), it remains unclear how far male sexual inactivity may be a function of female inactivity nor to what extent residual sexual motivation may affect behavior when females are not receptive. Nor, of course, is it known in what way these factors vary between species with long or short breeding seasons. Experimental testing is clearly needed to examine these points.

Male Cercopithecoid primates utilize the sexual mounting behavior sequence not only in the context of mating but also as an expression of dominance over another individual, commonly an animal that has recently shown submission through "presenting". Mounting as a nonsexual behavior pattern differs in detail from the sexual performance and seems rarely to include more than a token thrusting. In a number of primates (hamadryas, the chimpanzee, squirrel monkey, rhesus) the mounting is accompanied by penile erection and in some forms penile erection itself is emancipated from its simple sexual function to emerge as a social display normally connoting an assertion of status. Alpha male squirrel monkeys show thigh spreading and penile erection in a display directed towards the face of a subordinate animal (Ploog, Blitz, & Ploog 1963).

The direct utilization of the male genitals and their anatomical modification as display characters is, as Wickler (1967) shows, a feature of Ceboid rather than Cercopithecoid behavior. Of particular interest is the finding that just as males mimic female genital characteristics in the Cercopithecoidea so in certain Ceboids do the females mimic the male characteristics. The female squirrel monkey (*Saimiri*) uses the male type genital display as an expression of dominance and shows mimicry of male genitalia through possession of a large clitoris and a pseudoscrotal enlargement dorsal to it. Other species show similar modifications. In *Ateles* (in which females are larger than males) and *Alouatta* (where this is not so) the long pendulous clitoris and pseudoscrota must perform some social function that as yet remains to be elucidated. Possibly the female mimicry of male characteristics in Ceboids is linked to quite fundamental contrasts in the relationship between the sexes when compared to those characteristic of the Cercopithecoidea that more usually show male mimicry of female features. Much here remains to be explored and the ever present question as to why some species and not others, commonly close relatives, show intraspecific and intersexual mimicry is unresolved.

In many nonprimate mammals and in some species of lower primates the penis is utilized in a second connection, namely urine marking of territory. Wickler argues, rather questionably, that the conspicuous exhibition of the colorful penis by sitting baboons and *Cercopithecus aethiops* forms part of a visual position-marking display indicating the location of the troop by dominant male animals acting as markers around the edge of the troop. He also points out that the colors and the patterning of the face in the male mandrill have a close resemblance to features of its genital region although this is in fact less vivid than the face itself. The mandrill (so far as is known) does not display its genitalia directly,[2] indeed, as Wickler rather coyly remarks, all it has to do to achieve the same effect is to look at someone. The possibility that mandrills live in one-male groups resembling those suspected by Gartlan for the drill adds point to this suggestion and indicates a possible function in the defence of a "harem" in the poorly lit conditions of the Congo rain forest. These suggestions can only be substantiated by more detailed field observations than are at present available.

THE APES AND MAN

Sexual dimorphism in terms of the percentage of the males' weight shown by females is most striking in the orang utan (bornean orang 43 per cent, sumatran 54 per cent) and in the gorilla (50 percent approx). In both these animals contrasts in size and weight are supported by other characteristics, nuchal and sagittal crests on the skull and the grey back of mature gorilla males and, in orang males, the development of cheek flanges and the gular pouch. Some 70 per cent of orang males also develop sagittal and nuchal crests. Dimorphism is slight in weight in *Hylobates* (93 per cent), *Symphalangus* (92 per cent, head-body length 102 per cent) and *Pan* (90 per cent, head-body length 94 per cent). In *Hylobates* there are color contrasts in pelage in *H. concolor* and *H. hoolock* but not in *H. lar* or *H. agilis*. *Symphalangus* males have large preputal tufts of hair and sometimes develop sagittal crests. Female chimpanzees show sex swellings in estrus and tend to be more bald than males at maturity. These characteristics correlate in gibbons and siamangs with monogamous territorial life and in the chimpanzee with the open-group (Reynolds 1966) promiscuous

2. Darwin (1876), quoting a German correspondent J. von Fischer, records the presentation of a captive young male Mandrill to humans, other monkeys, and a mirror.

type of life in which dominance ranking is not especially pronounced. The extreme dimorphism of the gorilla is associated with the formation of small social units led by a particular adult male. These enormous creatures exhibit fearsome displays as a form of threat when disturbed. Doubtless the size development here is in part a direct consequence of selection favoring defence from predators. Gorillas are otherwise slow moving non-arboreal and unprotected apes. Intrasexual selection may however have played some initial role in the evolution of size contrasts of the sexes in this species since a form of spacing involving a reduction in the frequency of large males may be advantageous. The related chimpanzee operates its open-group life largely in relation to fruit finding (Reynolds 1965), and since it can seek security in trees it is not exposed to such risks from predation as is the gorilla. The absence of marked dimorphism may be related to this relatively noncompetitive manner of life. Sexual swellings are shown by female chimpanzees and presentation plays a diverse role in many social contexts. Mimicry is however not developed in this species.

Homo sapiens shows many attributes peculiar to each sex. We may list some of these as follows (see Dengrove 1961).

Character	*Man*	*Woman*
Conception and infant mortality	120 conceived against 100 women but only 105 on average survive to birth	In first year of life death rate less than man by 25%
Size	Larger	Smaller (80% of male weight 94% of height)
Strength	More muscular Higher metabolic rate More powerful heart and more red corpuscles per cc	Less muscular. Lower metabolic rate
Energy utilization	Generally more wasteful	Generally more efficient
Longevity	Shorter (mean life expectancy N. Americans 67 years)	Longer (73 years)
Sex maturity	Later	Earlier
Sexual 'drive'	Tends to decrease between ages 30-45+	Tends to increase between age 30-45+ (See Packard 1968, Chap. 24)
Skin	Loses 'complexion' after puberty	Retains 'complexion' well into maturity
Hair	Bearded, more body hair after puberty Baldness common	No beard, less body hair Baldness rare
Chest area	Small nipples	Rounded breasts especially when adolescent, areolar area around nipples
Voice	"Breaks" at puberty to lower tone.	Retains paedomorphic tone, higher pitch than adult male

Darwin (1871), noting the main anatomical contrasts in this list, saw that they were similar to those found in other primates and he ascribed them generally to the same cause: sexual selection. He attributed the size and strength of man primarily to intrasexual selection but argued for epigamic selection with respect to the beauty of women. He also thought that many racial differences could be attributed to contrasts in sexual selection operating together with natural selection in isolated populations. Thus differences in preferred types of beauty could impose a selection favoring certain types of build and facial feature rather than others. Darwin argued that the superior strength of men meant that the male sex played a predominant role in the choice of mate, and that this is culturally reinforced in many societies. He did not deny however that in some cultures women had a greater say, even choice, in their marriage partner. In particular he thought that beards (in bearded races) could be due to female selection operating over generations. Both Darwin and, more recently, Dobzhansky (1962) point out that, while in principle sexual selection could occur in this way, in man as in other species there are numerous barriers to its operation. Marriage rules and other social mechanisms for the control of love are an exceedingly complex aspect of kinship systems (Fox 1967a, Goode 1959) and leave little room for a biologically based choice of mate through simple interpersonal encounter. Furthermore, since in tribal societies virtually all women marry, the case for differential selection is poor because the less beautiful are not known to be less fecund than the more beautiful. Mating out of wedlock, elopement, and choice of second partners may, however, still allow some effect of selection. In any case the crystallisation of sex differences and race features must have belonged to a particularly remote phase of human history so that current customs, even those of primitive peoples, may not be particularly relevant. One must also remember that evidence for the natural selection of racial characters in relation to such things as climate, food resources, and incidence of sunlight is as good, if not considerably better, than the evidence for sexual selection (Dobzhansky, Chapter 4).

It seems highly likely that early in human history a number of closely correlated changes in socio-sexual behavior emerged as a co-adaptation forming a new grade of social organization in nonforest conditions. These associated trends included:

1. Development of a more carnivorous diet, use of tools in hunting, and the emergence of language as a control system governing intentions to act within hunting groups.
2. Development of upright posture freeing the hands and permitting better vision and faster running but incurring difficulties for women in labor. Baby very immature at birth and requiring long-term care.
3. All-male groups tend to specialize as hunting parties operating from a home base of the larger troop.

4. Tendency to form long-term bonds between the sexes to reduce intermale rivalry and social antagonism but more particularly to provide secure social environment for rearing of young. Woman's psychosocial attributes become more suited to homemaking and support, man's to outward exploration, hunting and control over events.
5. To aid in bond maintenance sexual activity is enhanced through sexual selection. Improved bonds provide security for children and hence a greater contribution to later generations from the effective bond formers. Women cease to show estrus and are sexually responsive more or less continuously. Coition becomes very frequent and highly rewarding. Bond formation is also associated with powerful changes in affect: the emergence of love and tenderness in their characteristic human form.

In 1871 Darwin argued that the reduction of hair on the human body was the result of sexual selection. He pointed out that hair loss is common in the development of secondary sexual characters in other primates and that women are generally less hairy than men. It seems therefore that the bareness of the female skin was selected because of its attractiveness to males and, as Darwin remarks, the character later became typical of both sexes. Almost a century later in his popular book *The Naked Ape* Desmond Morris related these changes to numerous other aspects of human sexual morphology particularly those described by Masters & Johnson (1966). Morris' provocative synthesis makes sense of several features of human anatomy inadequately explained before. The trendy manner in which his material is presented should not blind academics to the heuristic quality of his work. Although much of it is hunch and unsupported hypothesis, *The Naked Ape* not only suggests wide areas for more rigorous thought and research but also foreshadows a major shift in the popular "image" of man. After considering alternative viewpoints Morris argues that hair reduction in the human species is adaptive in facilitating touch contact of special importance in the production of sexual affect in courtship and mating. Morris's subsidiary argument that loss of body insulation was also adaptive in ensuring heat loss after sprinting on the hunt is far fetched. Other hunting animals have not lost their fur. In the tropics where man arose, the need for an insulating layer of hair is not marked even at night and would not necessarily prevent hair reduction where strong selection in its favor was operating. Furthermore the naked ape presumably undressed at a stage in history at which caves and other shelters could have been used at night. As man moved into colder areas the use of clothes as insulators became significant.

Associated with nakedness are the following features: the rounded breasts of the young woman, the formation of highly sensitive lips, the large size of the erect human penis compared to that of other primates, the development of female orgasm, the reddening of flushing of areas of skin during coition, and the vaso-dilation of lips, soft parts of the nose, ear lobes, nipples, areolar area of pigmented skin around the nipples, and genitals. All these changes appear associated with the production of high sexual affect through skin stimulation and excitation of erogenous zones, particularly the genitals. Through making sex sexier, as Morris puts it, the reward value of partnership in mating is increased and the pair bond maintained. Promiscuity is reduced through sexual love for one's mate and by the rivalry and aggression of other males already in possession of the other females.

Many of the surface areas of the female function as sexual attractants or visual releasers for male appetitive sexual behavior. Developing Wickler's discussion of the intrasexual mimicry involved in the evolution of the female gelada's chest patch, Morris argues that as human beings moved from the posterior to the anterior mating position consequent upon the evolution of upright body posture so the relevant sexual releasers moved to a frontal location. Whereas, with the old primate mating posture the buttocks and tumescent genital area were probably the prime sexual releasers, in the frontal approach these signals are mimicked by the rounded breasts and lips. Oral inspection of the vulva is changed to lip-to-lip oral activity—the kiss. However as Goodhart (1964) and Crook & Gartlan (1966) have pointed out it is perhaps not so much breast shape as the visual stimulus provided by the areolar zone around the nipple that may be the more critical "releaser." This feature may be due however to a subsequent signal development enhancing further the effect of the original mimicry. Wickler himself (see Eibl-Eibesfeldt 1970, p. 437) evidently disagrees with Morris and argues for a derivation of breast shape as a signal from an emphasis on the offering of the breast as a female contact gesture to the male. He therefore sees the significance of the breast as part of the maternal complex undoubtedly involved in the human courtship pattern. The areolar area furthermore may be of significance in guiding the baby to the nipple. Although the breasts of multiparous women are perhaps only effectively provocative when sexual arousal is high it is exactly these features of young women which comprise a more or less continuous visual signal. Young women in search of mates will naturally be those most likely to show effective sexual signaling. Anthropological evidence does not however necessarily confirm this viewpoint. In many primitive socieities women are habitually topless without occasioning rampant and pervasive sexuality. Indeed the more usual female sexual enticement is exposure of the genitals (Ford & Beach 1952). The role of the breasts in sexual enticement in modern western society is thus probably culturally induced as a consequence of their being clothed provocatively. One must remember that showing an ankle was once considered almost as interesting as unzipping a blouse.

One should perhaps distinguish between signals that function at a distance (body form, gait—high heels enhancing the provocative body movements of the walking female, breast deportment—the "sweater girl"), middle distance signals (voice quality and tone, complexion), close visual signals (areolar tumescence, body flush, eye glitter, pupillary distension) and contact signals (epidermal touch quality, breast tumescence, lip-feel, genital sensation and body scent). For men visual signals play a major part in initial sexual arousal and this doubtless accounts for the greater emphasis on distance and middle distance signals in women. While a number of visual signals emanating from the male are important for a woman (athletic deportment and movement, buttocks, eye glitter and pupillary distention) the contact signals and the feedback generated by male stimulation of her own body generally appear to be of greater importance, perhaps reflecting the more inward receptive psychological character of the woman compared with the outgoing penetrative aspect of male behavior.

The middle distance signals of women are particularly contrasted with those of men in that they retain characteristics apparent in both sexes in childhood but lost in man after puberty. The retention of paedomorphic features (e.g. unbroken voice, retention of childlike complexion and more rounded body form), suggests that a greater degree of neoteny has been positively sexually selected in women than in men. This is also apparent in certain aspects of female courtship behavior (p. 273).

Turning now to certain morphological characteristics of the human male it is strange that no effective explanations have been proposed until very recently for such features as the large (among primates) phallus, beards, and certain postural features. In his 1966 paper Wickler discusses the significance of the brightly colored penis in higher primates and presents his findings in relation to man. The display of the penis by dominant male baboons supposed by Wickler to be marking an area utilized by their troop may, he suggests, in man, take the form of exaggerated phallocrypts, ritual artifacts, fetishes and ithyphallic sculptures apparently used in certain ancient and modern cultures as protective boundary markers. In Papua, males of certain tribes enhance the penis with a sheath commonly made of gourd which is kept in an erect position by means of a waist string. The penis sheath may in some cases extend as high as the middle of the chest (see also Eibl-Eibesfeldt 1970). Dani men (Harrer 1964) tap excitedly upon these sheaths with their fingernails when aroused by any novelty. Hewes' (1957) work suggests that male sitting postures characteristically tend to reveal the penis while those of women tend to cover the genital area.

Unfortunately anthropological evidence does not clearly support Wickler's (1966) viewpoint. In a discussion of the Dani attire Heider (1969) points out that the penis sheath is associated neither with erotic practises nor with a social system stressing hierarchical ranking of males. He considers that "individual differences in attire . . . are more sartorial than status linked" and, while the Dani male may select a sheath for the day much in the way a western male may select a necktie to express his personality or mood, there is as little differentiation in attire as there is minimal status differentiation in the group. Indeed the Dani men consider sexual modesty to be the only reason for wearing a sheath. On fitting a new one a polite gentleman turns his back on company to do so. Nevertheless the sheath is part of the male identity kit since women never wear them except in victory celebration dances when they parade in other decorative items of male attire as well. Heider comments on the use of phallocrypts in other New Guinean, South American and African tribal cultures and discusses the codpiece of medieval Europe. While Westermarck and Benedict interpreted these forms of dress as a form of sexual exhibitionism, Heider was unable to confirm the use of such attire as sexual symbolism in the people he studied.

Morris (1967) states that in addition to the lips the fleshy part of the human nose becomes dilated in sexual arousal. Given that the large projecting nose of man is an almost unique feature among higher primates (see p. 240 for discussion of *Nasalis*) he suspects a hidden signal function for this structure not unconnected with sex. A Wickleresque approach would suggest a comparison here with the mandrill in which the design of the genital area is repeated in mimicry on the face (p. 246). It is tempting to suggest that the nose mimics the phallus and the beard the pubic hair. The word nose is symbolic for penis in some cultures and a reference to cutting off noses in India caused wild hilarity among young men, which was explained to the author in this sense. The fact that noses occur in both sexes does not of course help this particular argument.

Beards are more certainly related to adult male status and authority and are perceived as having this effect even in modern western society, especially when associated with the greying of the hair and the assumption of culturally attributed roles requiring a degree of veneration (for example, Orthodox Priests). In some beardless peoples (for example, Maori) facial tatooing or scarring has replaced the beard. The practice of shaving the face seems related to a cultural de-emphasis of male hierarchical organization and an emphasis on more equality between the sexes than is catered for biologically. A further effect of shaving is perhaps the reduction of intense status rivalry between males and an increase in democratic attitudes (see Freedman 1968, Hallpike 1969). The use of a beard in modern society is various. It may disguise the chinless wonder but, on the other hand, among hippies it seems to re-emphasize the old biological sex difference although, in this case, in a subculture not given to hierarchical male ranking, but oriented instead toward a sexual equality often combined with a degree of promiscuity. Here the beard and hair generally seems to play an epigamic role in which selection is as much (if not more) allocated to the females as to the males and in which intrasexual male competition is culturally reduced. Indeed the hippy use of hair may recall an ancient function of face and head hair in primitive man. Jolly (1970), pointing out the many evolutionary parallels between gelada baboons and men, notes that both have extensive devleopments of hair on the anterior parts of the male body. He suggests that such hair may be important in attracting females sexually and in the formation and maintenance of sexual bonds. Hippy society also reveals the increased license for sexual choice allocated to modern women compared to medieval and ancient cultures. Clearly, the development of diverse cultures and subcultures radically effects the significance attributed to phylogenetically ancient sex characteristics.

The difficulty with Morris' arguments is that they are essentially panglossian. Any anatomical character that fits a largely preconceived pattern is seen as being all for the best in the best of all sexual worlds. Changes in appearance that may be mere concomitants of autonomic arousal are given adaptive significance for which there is little evidence other than presupposition. For example, while it is plausible that the reddening of the enlarged *labia minora* in women can be visually perceived by their mates the frequency of such observation must be very low indeed. Even in the hypothetical state of affairs presumed to exist when protohominid ancestors mated in the posterior position it seems unlikely that this reddening would necessarily have been a visual signal since it occurs in the plateau phase of sexual excitement when the male would probably have been mounting. We should note also that this color change associated with mating must be functionally different from sex-skin changes in other primates which are associated with the phases of estrus. The *glans penis* also changes color late in the plateau phase but no one has yet suggested a signal function for this, presumably because, except in masturbation, the penis is then well inserted in the vagina.

In any case it is possible to think up alternative evolutionary explanations for many of the sex characteristics without adopting Morris' scheme. Projecting noses may prevent rain falling in the nasal aperture in an upright ape, nasal vasocongestion and the flaring of the nostrils may be linked to the hyperventilation that occurs in coition and to the facial expression associated with the inhalation of scent (flemen) in other mammals. Likewise the development of the lips may perhaps be associated as much with suckling and oral exploration as with visual stimulation. These hypotheses are unfortunately largely untestable and one opinion is not worth much more than another. The fact that Morris' story hangs together particularly well may tell us more about his skill as a writer than about the validity of his views. As Jolly (1970) remarks, speculations of this kind have about as much scientific value as the "Just So" stories. Jolly's own work illustrates how evolutionary hypotheses can be validated only through exhaustive comparative behavioral and anatomical investigations at levels additional to that from which the originally suggestive data were derived.

In my opinoin the main point made by Morris is most likely to be correct while the minor points are probably faulty. In all probability the evolutionary development of hair reduction, increased skin sensitivity and tactile changes involving skin tension were all associated with increasing the tactile sensations of coital body contact especially in the frontal presentation. Likewise the breasts of young women taken together with other features (limb contour, complexion, and the like) seem to represent the main visual sexual releasers for the male. While the latter features may have been due to straightforward intersexual selection by ancient males the former features have probably been selected in both sexes for their effect in improving sexual rewards, in inducing sexual love and in maintaining pair bonds. The same is also likely to be true for the presence of orgasm in women and the absence of the more typical mammalian estrus. The functional significance of all these correlated changes is most plausibly seen within the context of the adaptations of seed-eating and of later partially carnivorous protohominids to open country life with associated shifts in social organization.

Sexual Selection and Social Organization

Many writers since Darwin have discussed the association between enhanced sexual dimorphism and various types of polygynous social structure (Birds: Sibley 1957, Orians 1961, 1969, Crook 1964, 1965, Verner 1964, Selander 1965, Lack 1968; Seals: Nutting 1891; Ungulates: Jarman 1968, Estes 1966, Leuthold 1966). In most of these cases however the polygynous association is limited in time to a mating season, bond formation is commonly weak and in some cases membership of a "harem" is quite inconstant so that the male-female interaction resembles closely the form of promiscuity occurring on a lek. Longer term more bonded associations between the sexes are found only in a few ungulates and rodents, certain carnivora and in higher primates. Higher primate demes are characteristically divided spatially and socially into cohesive long-term reproductive units of a relatively constant membership and in which distinctive patterns of socio-sexual association occur. A number of classifications of higher primate social organizations have been attempted; the differences between them are attributable to the steady inflow of new information. Here we focus for convenience particularly on the better known Cercopithecoidea and classify the species under two sociotypes (after Crook, in prep., see also 1970a).

SOCIOTYPE A. THE ONE-MALE/ALL-MALE GROUP SYSTEM

This sociotype comprises primate populations divided socially into "one-male" reproductive groups (that is, groups of sexually mature females with their young, each group containing only one mature male or sometimes one together with one other younger animal) and "all-male" groups. The spatial dispersion of these groups varies considerably from (1) situations in forests where one-male groups occupy territories from which solitary males are more or less excluded (*Cercopithecus mitis,* Aldrich-Blake 1970b) through (2) cases in which one-male groups and all-male groups each move in a large home range, showing some degree of range overlap with their neighbors (Patas monkey, Hall 1966) to (3) cases in which the two types of groups associate in herds under good feeding conditions but tend otherwise to forage separately (Gelada, Crook 1966), and (4) those in which one-male units associate in bands together with peripheral non-reproductive males (Hamadryas, Kummer 1968).

SOCIOTYPE B. THE MULTIMALE GROUP SYSTEM

This sociotype comprises populations socially divided into cohesive groups containing several adult males together with a rather larger number of females and their offspring. The males characteristically sort themselves into a complex social hierarchy the organization of which is determined by affiliative relations and kinship. Within this sociotype varieties occur depending on (1) the extent and duration of consort relations between the sexes at mating, (2) the division of the group into central and peripheral sections (the behavior of members of the latter constrained to a degree by the assertive competitive presence of central animals) and (3) the extent to which males show competitive behavior, social subterfuge and the utilization of babies or infants in "agonistic buffering" (see Crook 1970b, Deag & Crook 1971). Some multimale groups inhabit topographically defended territories (namely, *Cercopithecus aethiops*); others occupy large overlapping home ranges. Solitary males occur outside the troops in several of the societies studied but this condition is unlikely to be a permanent one for any given individual.

Most species may be allocated without difficulty to either Sociotype A or B, but some may show either or both types of grouping pattern at contrasting locations in the species range. Some of these populations have groups which are territorial, while others occupy apparently undefended home ranges. Species with this complex variability in social organization occur in the leaf-eating monkeys (Colobinae).

In general one-male groups of forest Cercopithecids that live at relatively high population densities occur in territories. One-male groups are also found on undefended and overlapping home ranges or in systems of congregation and dispersal depending on local and seasonal food item dispersion. These last are found particularly in relatively arid regions of Africa that experience long dry seasons. Multimale groups occur in a variety of forest arboreal species and in savanna baboons and macaques inhabiting country relatively rich in food. The leaf eaters occur in a variety of forests and show marked intraspecific variation including both A and B grouping patterns in their social organizations.

Attempts at explaining the diversity of social structures in Cercopithecid primates have arisen from studies on correlations between social organizations and aspects of the species' ecology. For example Crook & Gartlan (1966) argued that one-male group systems were well adapted to terrestrial open-country habitats with seasonal food poverty in long dry seasons because with patchy food distribution dispersion in small parties would be advantageous. Were the parties larger, competition between the members would not enable all animals to gain enough nourishment. The reduction in the number of adult males to a single animal per reproductive group was seen as adaptive in that it allowed a greater proportion of the available food to be apportioned to females responsible for rearing young. A study of the gelada baboon (Crook 1966) suggested that all-male groups tended not to exploit quite the same areas as the reproductive units thus reducing indirect competition for food between the sexes even more. Similar findings are reported in greater detail for certain Rhodesian ungulates by Jarman (1968). Crook and Gartlan argued that in richer savanna areas the greater food availability and its apparently less patchy distribution allows a tighter congregation of animals into larger groups. This feature itself was considered to be an adaptation to the higher predation pressures of these areas. The multimale type of organization evidently results from the relaxation of food poverty so that the broad dispersion of "surplus" males and their separate ranging from the reproductive unit is of no particular survival value to either sex. Indeed their incorporation in a single large reproductive group may be interpreted as advantageous, again primarily in the context of protection from predation.

In forests the occurrence of one-male groups has been attributed to a different pattern of year round fluctuation and shortage in the food resources affecting very dense populations. A degree of food poverty is considered to be an omnipresent threat that at times makes the rearing of young difficult. In these circumstances one-male groups would once more be adaptive (see more detailed discussions in Aldrich-Blake 1970a, Crook 1970a and below).

Competition between males for females that are sexually receptive is likely to occur in all these social systems although it will be regulated differently in each according to the dispersion of individual animals and the composition of the groups in which they live. It follows that sexual selection of at least the intrasexual kind is likely to be occurring in all types of group.

In the evolutionary history of social structures it seems unlikely that adaptation to ecology and sexual selection have operated independently, the structures forming first as it were and then acting as receptacles for sexual selection or, conversely, sexually selected attributes leading to certain types of social structure which were then related to ecology. Both processes must have operated together throughout primate history. However, to gain some impression of the relative importance of the two processes it is necessary to consider group size and manner of dispersion separately from group composition. Here we must, for reasons of space, concern ourselves primarily with group composition although it is essential to outline briefly current views on group size and dispersion (for a full discussion together with a review of primate field studies see the primate chapter in Crook, in prep., from which much of the following argument is drawn).

The key factors determining group size and manner of dispersion appear to be (1) predation pressures, (2) food item abundance and dispersion and (3) the spatial frequency of other key resources such as water holes and sleeping sites. The extent and pattern of predation will vary with the size and character of the monkey concerned. In general where predation is a constant threat, as in the case of arboreal monkeys subject to eagle predation (especially on young) or terrestrial rich savanna primates living in an area full of large and small felid and canid predators, the larger the group the greater the probability of detecting danger and the less likely that any given individual will be taken due to the cover the presence of others provides (see theoretical examination of these postulates in Vine 1971). Conversely the formation of large groups is less likely in areas containing only sparse predator populations feeding primarily on other species or where some members at least of the primate population are very large and frightening (mandrill, hamadryas, gorilla).

The nature and abundance of the food resource is inferred to be a key limiting factor in population dynamics and dispersion. Food may be (1) either evenly dispersed in space or patchy, (2) seasonally variable in abundance or relatively nonseasonal and (3) of relatively high or low density (in terms of biomass per unit area). In forests (compared to savanna) food is generally at high density, relatively nonseasonal (although certain important items of diet fluctuate seasonally in availability) and more or less evenly dispersed (although again certain items of diet are rarer than others in terms of spatial frequency). Under these conditions large numbers of monkeys at high population densities are supported and it is suspected that, except during periods when food is superabundant, the numbers present may reach an asymptote in balance with food availability. The risk of predation especially on young animals makes group life of advantage. Since most forest species so far studied live in territorial groups or space themselves by intergroup avoidance without topographical defense the question arises as to how the relationship between the area of more or less exclusive use and the number of animals in a group is determined.

Theoretically, as the numbers in a group rise so must the demand on the food content of the territory and hence eventually also on the space needed for a range sufficient to support the group. The amount of ranging (travelling and food foraging) a group must do per day depends on numerous factors, particularly on the density of the various food items. The territory size will be related to the ranging pattern that occurs in it. Indeed it is an expression of this pattern. Since it is literally a fruitless activity to explore areas just foraged by others the optimum population distribution is expressed in separate exclusive areas of a size adequate to meet the needs of a group under the worst conditions regularly likely to occur. This means that at other times food will be superabundant. Indeed, under such conditions, large polyspecific associations may then occur with a much reduced emphasis on niche division and territory maintenance (Gautier & Gautier-Hion 1969).

The area defensible[3] by a group is however unlikely to be a simple function of the numbers of the group. As Aldrich-Blake (1970b) points out, if the group's requirement for foraging in terms of area is large it cannot detect intrusions into this space either because the intruders are out of sight or because they cannot be heard. On the other hand a group with small foraging requirements (area) can hear it neighbors, patrol borders or rush to borders when intruders are heard and so maintain an exclusive area with little cost in terms of energy expended. In such a situation there will clearly be an optimum numerical density suited to the most efficiently defensible space. Since either (1) attempts to defend essentially indefensible areas and (2) foraging in areas exploited by others are both nonadaptive procedures in terms of time and energy expenditure, it is argued that the optimum group size will be that at which the defensible area provides an adequate provision of food under the normally existing range of conditions. For many African Cercopithecoid primates living in forests this number appears to be about a dozen (Struhsaker 1969). The dispersion pattern is maintained by methods of defense involving a ritualized display often occurring after dawn in which nearest neighboring groups announce their location and indulge in visual and/or vocal encounters. Such behavior maintains spacing with little expenditure of energy. In addition, as the group grows through reproduction, certain individuals, commonly young males with or without females, are excluded from the group so that the numbers present remain roughly constant. Presumably certain young, perhaps the more assertive, will remain to replace the adults that are aging or which die. It seems then that the numbers in a territory of forest-dwelling monkeys are probably as much determined by limits of space in terms of defensibility as they are by the feeding area requirements of the group. This relationship is illustrated in the form of a model depicted in Figures

3. See J. L. Brown (1964) for discussion of "defendability" in relation to the diversity of avian territorial systems.

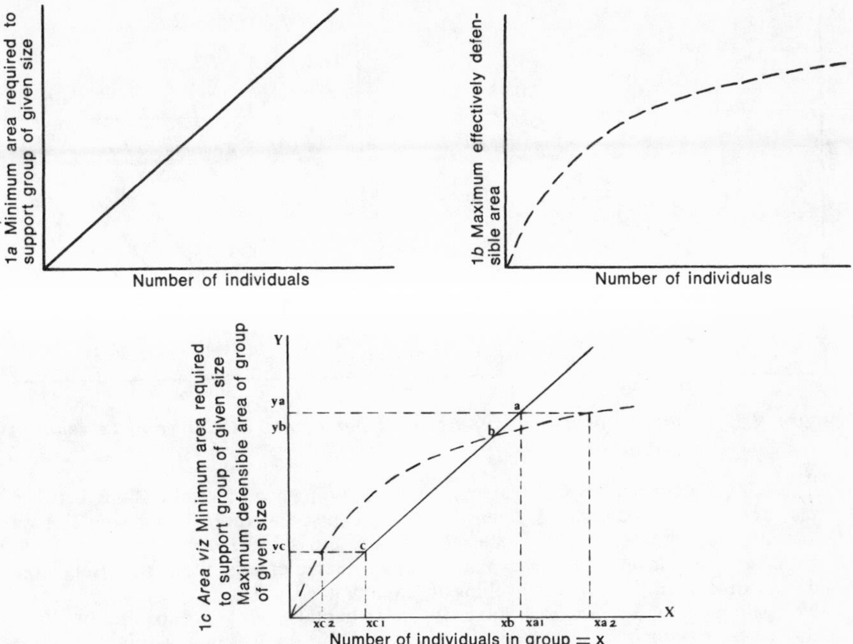

Figure 9.1. Relations between food availability, defensible area, and number of individuals in groups.

1. Given that group formation is adaptive in relation to predation pressures the size of groups in a given habitat depends upon a relation between food density and exploitation on the one hand and on the other hand, the defensible area containing adequate resources for the group.
2. The area which contains the minimum food requirements of a group increases with the number of individuals in the group (1*a*) given that, in this model, food items are treated as being evenly distributed.
3. The area defensible by a group increases decrementally with group size (1*b*)—with small groups an increase in numbers improves defensibility of a given territory (or allows expansion), but with large groups requiring big foraging areas the addition of an animal or two has little or no effect on the defensibility of such an area. The maximum defensible area is that at which exclusion of others can be enforced effectively without energy and time expenditure curtailing other activities to a prohibitive degree.
4. In 1*c* the plot of the relations between number of individuals in a group against the minimum area required to support the group (the linear relationship) and the defensible area (decremental relationship) are shown superimposed. With large numbers (*xa*2) the theoretically defensible area does not contain sufficient food to support the group. Indeed the area (*ya*) can only support *xa*1 individuals. Some members would therefore have to leave the group. With small numbers (*xc*2) the animals can defend an area *yc* but this area has enough food to support a population *cx*1. This group can therefore increase in size.

   Point b represents the number of individuals at which (for this habitat) the occupied area is both effectively defensible and which contains sufficient food to maintain the group. Groups will tend to approximate in size to a value given by this point. The value will vary with the food resources of the habitat (in richer areas the gradient will be less steep) and with the amount of food required by individuals of the species concerned.

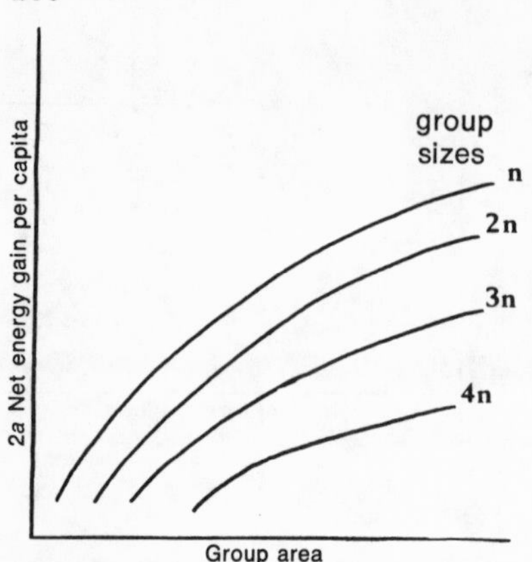

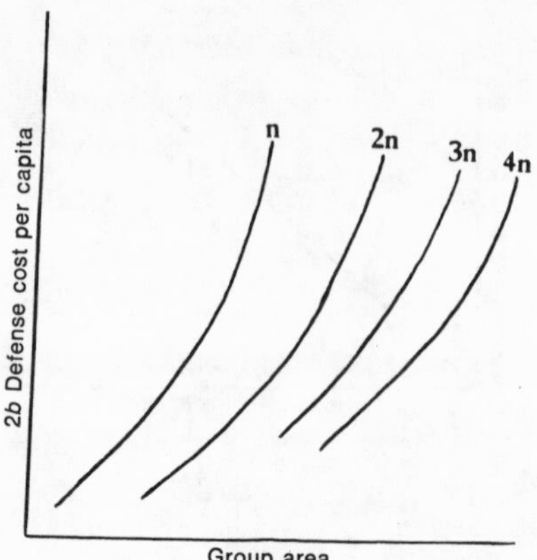

Figure 9.2. Resource gain and defense cost per capita in time and in relation to group area.

1. The relations considered in Figure 9.1 are a consequence of relationships between resource gain per capita and defense cost per capita in groups of varying size on variably sized home ranges. These relations are envisaged here.
2. In 2a net gain in energy per capita increases decrementally with increasing area due to time-energy costs in travelling to exploit it (See 3).
3. Net gain per capita per area increases decrementally with group size (n — 4n) due to factors such as increased direct and indirect competition within the group and hence further time-energy costs in travel. There comes a point at which increased home range size is of little value due to the high costs of exploiting it.
4. In 2b, assuming an equal work load per capita, the cost in defense per capita would rise with the area to be defended. The same cost will secure a larger area for larger groups but this increase is treated as decremental. With large areas the addition of an animal will make no appreciable difference to defense. In fact, of course, most of the defense load falls to a male or males (see text) usually with a degree of female collaboration.

9.1 and 9.2. Whether such groups are one-male or multimale may perhaps depend on the diet of the species and the food availability within the defended area. One-male groups in forests may be most usual where the population density is often near a food controlled asymptote yet with periods of food superabundance of frequently long duration. This could be due to a regulation of numbers more by intrinsic social processes than by direct food shortage (see Watson & Moss 1970). The evidence remains slight (see Aldrich-Blake 1970ab, Crook 1970b, and below).

In rich savanna country, food resources are less abundant and more widely spread (that is density is less per given area) than in forest and in addition show more seasonal variation in both these parameters. The foraging area is normally far too big to be defended in any other than a highly intermittent manner. Macaques, baboons and other primates of such areas commonly move in large overlapping home ranges, and the spatial separation of the groups are usually maintained by mutual avoidance. Group cohesion seems to vary considerably from one population to another and may be related to the predation experience of the population. Thus animals moving in open country with good all round observation may fan out when foraging in a condition resembling that of terrestrial primates living in less food rich areas (Altmann & Altmann 1970, Aldrich-Blake et al. 1971).

Where food resources are seasonally sparse and distributed in patches, as seems to be the case in the more arid areas of Africa, not all members of a large group travelling as a coherent body would encounter sufficient food items unless they scattered. Separate ranging in small parties is a fact characteristic of patas monkeys at almost all seasons except when water is so short that congregation around the wells is essential (Struhsaker & Gartlan 1970). This behavior is typical too of geladas except when food is abundant in the rains (Crook 1966). Hamadryas bands also tend to scatter when foraging (Kummer 1968) as do certain anubis baboon troops in a comparable habitat (Aldrich-Blake et al. 1971). The variance in troop size in both rich and poor savanna habitats is large and may possibly eventually be related to local ranging conditions. Figures 9.3 and 9.4 depict models relating party size and dispersion, time-energy expenditure in food exploitation per capita, resource patchiness and seasonality in food abundance.

The process of group splitting has been studied only in multimale groups of the Japanese macaque and in the rhesus populations on Cayo Santiago Island. It is perhaps related here more to social instability in large groups than to direct effects of food shortage. Nevertheless it seems likely that as numbers in a given deme expand, the smaller groups of younger animals (also isolates) may be forced to live in suboptimal habitats or to live partly on ranges already foraged by existing and more dominant groups.

Little can be said at present about the control of dispersion in animals such as the Colobines which show marked intraspecific variation in social organization. Here again, however, associations with ecology are apparent and future research may prove them to be similar in kind to those discussed (see Crook 1970b and in prep. for a review of the relevant field studies of these sociotypes).

We may now turn to a consideration of the factors controlling the composition of the groups in these various sociotypes. Essentially this demands an explanation as to why males are excluded more from reproductive units of Sociotype A than from those of Sociotype B. We will argue that the greater degree of exclusion in Sociotype A is a function of social processes in the group which are a consequence of behavior traits (especially but not exclusively of males) that have been subject to certain forms of social selection operating in particular environments over many generations. In particular they are due to an aspect of sexual selection little considered by either Darwin or subsequent writers: the competition between males not merely for access to sexually receptive females but less

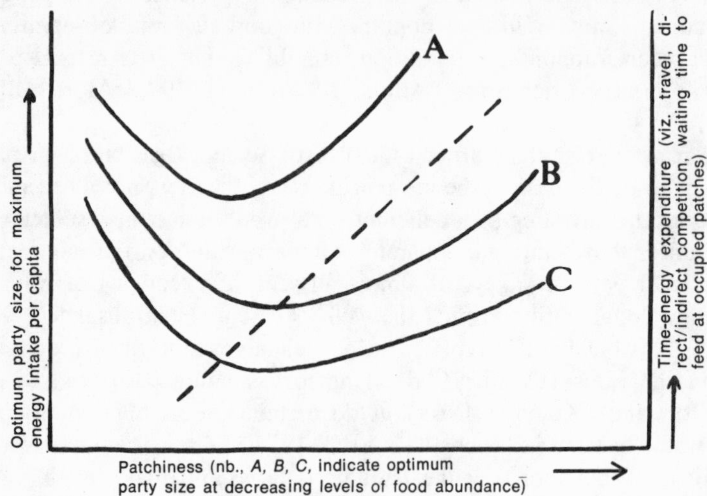

Figure 9.3. Relations between party size, time-energy expenditure per capita, resource patchiness and resource abundance in hypothetical open country habitats with originally evenly dispersed resource items.

1. By patchiness is meant that the originally evenly dispersed food items are concentrated into limited portions of a given area—the patches themselves being evenly distributed and the total biomass of food in the area unchanged. With increasing patchiness the number of patches decreases with an increase in biomass of food per patch till all food is dumped in a single patch.
2. With increasing patchiness group members are a) forced into greater indirect/direct competition at patches and b) some (the more subordinate) will have to travel to another patch before getting a feed.
3. Groups will increase per capita net gain in food intake by splitting into small parties. With nonpatchy evenly dispersed food the dispersion of members in a coherent group will be related to the dispersion of food items (that is, the inter-item distance). With high frequency of patches party size at first may remain large but as patches get fewer the party sizes will decrease as competition and travelling between patches rises. As patches become fewer still party size will once more rise as individuals opt to attempt competition at a large rich patch rather than to travel in search of an unseen one.
4. The time-energy expenditure in nonforaging activities per capita increases with patchiness.
5. Figure 9.3 depicts three levels of abundance *A*, *B*, *C* in decreasing order of plenty. Resource availability per patch under the terms of this model depends on both patchiness and the overall food abundance. The more food available in a patch the larger a party it can accommodate. With a high food abundance (*A*) party size will decrease less with medium patch frequencies than under poorer conditions (*B*).
6. Under very poor feeding conditions (*C*) optimum party size falls very low and recovery at the few but richer patches at high patchiness values is slow. This is because while time-energy expenditure in travel, competition and perhaps waiting is high the rewards per patch are now low (that is, noncompensatory). Under such conditions individuals may be forced to search for food elsewhere before having fed (sufficiently) at a given patch. Small groups are likely to persist under these conditions and to show a high level of nomadism combined with great skills at patch finding.

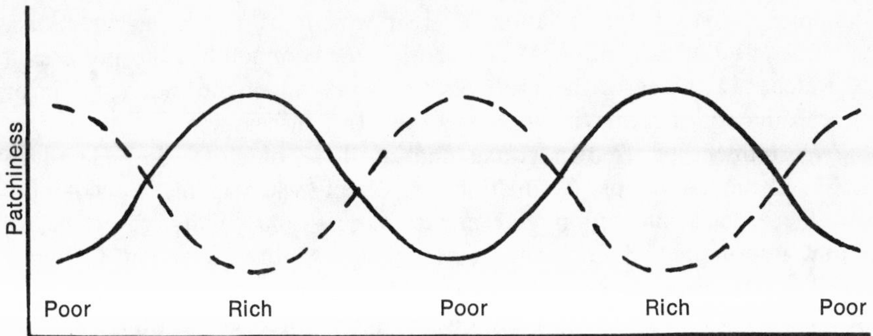

Figure 9.4. Relations between patchiness of food resources, optimum party size for maximum intake per capita, and seasonality in food abundance.

—— = Optimum party size, varies with the richness of the environment and inversely with patchiness

. . . . = Patchiness, varies with the poverty of the food environment

1. Where food abundance fluctuates seasonally patchiness is likely to increase as food resources fall.
2. Under these circumstances party sizes are likely to fall in the food-poor seasons and the frequency of parties rise.
3. Exactly this state of affairs is apparent in certain populations of Gelada baboons studied in Ethiopia (Crook 1966).

directly, for the resources whereby they can maintain a group of females with whom young are reared almost to maturity.

Darwin (1871) argued that competition over females would lead to the enhancement of male characteristics that ensure success in reproduction. "Sexual selection depends on the success of certain individuals over others of the same sex in relation to the propagation of the species." Darwin's word "propagation" is usually understood to mean fertilization leading to recruitment to the population. This usage is an inevitable consequence of most papers on sexual selection in vertebrates taking their examples from birds, in which sexually selected characteristics are most pronounced among polygynous species where males often do little other than compete for females and then fertilize them. A fresh categorization of the processes involved in sexual selection is desirable in order to emphasise the additional meaning of "propagate"; namely, to rear to maturity. Differential success in this process between males has not before been adequately discussed probably because it involves competition for environmental commodities in addition to that for receptive females, thereby comprising a selective complex not easy to disentangle.

Natural selection is the consequence of the tendency for animals to increase in numbers to an asymptote at which a complex socio-demographic regulation of numbers develops in relation to the prevailing limiting factors in the ecological economy of the species. These latter factors legislate

(Solomon 1964) the population level at which the regulation functions. Natural selection is a result of competition for commodities the possession of which (1) increases the probability of survival of the individual prior to reproduction, (2) maximizes its reproductive success and (3) maximizes the recruitment of its own young and/or those of close kin (Hamilton 1963) to the population. Competition is "direct" when agonistic encounters or other social interaction determines success and "indirect" when no actual interindividual encounter is involved. Natural selection is therefore "environmental" when it is primarily in relation to indirect competition, or "social" when it is primarily in relation to direct competition.

Social selection then is that process leading to the evolutionary enhancement of morphological allesthetic and behavioral characteristics that function within a social system to provide biological advantages to the individual in relation to survival prior to reproduction, the formation of zygotes and the birth and rearing to maturity of young or the progeny of close kin. Direct competition, often by means of ritualized display, is usually involved. Social selection results from (*a*) effects of competition between the subject and others of either sex with respect of commodities essential to survival in a situation that will allow an attempt at reproduction, (*b*) competition for access to preferred members of the opposite sex for mating and (*c*) effects of competition between subjects for access to commodities in the environment essential for the rearing of their young to reproductive age. Of these *b* is the process most commonly referred to as sexual selection. Social selection is undoubtedly one of the main evolutionary processes responsible for the emergence of both individual and group behavioral characteristics.

Crook & Gartlan (1966) argued that within multimale troops sexual selection (social selection *b* above) would lead to the enhancement of behavioral and morphological characteristics that increase the frequency with which males obtain mating with ovulating females. It is reported particularly from multimale troops of baboons that competition between males leads to the formation of a dominance hierarchy in which the high ranking animals are those that most frequently secure matings with females at ovulation. Other males mate at other stages of the female cycle, mostly during the early onset of receptivity when the female's behavior is more promiscuous. In *Papio* multimale groups the approach of ovulation is signalled by the ischial swelling which act as both a visual and an olfactory (R. Michael, personal communication) stimulus telling the dominant males when to associate. Consorting between the dominant male and an estrous female may last from a few hours to a day or so. In such a system it seems that characteristics determining male dominance are likely to be propagated, hence the formation of marked status hierarchies and the evolution of sexual dimorphism particularly as a consequence of increased male size. Young males in such a system are not able to obtain matings likely to yield offspring until they are mature and large enough to challenge established animals.

While ranking of this kind is common in multimale troops the relation between high rank and exclusive access to ovulating females is not perhaps certainly established. Carpenter (1942) reported a close correlation between the dominance rank of a male and his access to receptive females in rhesus monkeys. Altmann (1962) reported that female rhesus in estrus associated closely with one male at a time but that these males could change in a succession of estrus periods. Making certain assumptions he derived a model that suggested that in a multimale group where the ranks of the males equal one-third of the number of sexually mature nonpregnant females then the males are demarcated sharply into those that obtain access and those that do not. Struhsaker (1967) suggested that in his savanna vervet monkeys there was a relation between high dominance and copulatory success. Papers by DeVore (1965) and Saayman (1970) also suggest this to be true for baboons. However some evidence (R. Michael, personal communication) suggests that in macaques females tend to be more promiscuous and to form less enduring consortships than do baboons. It may well be that the correlation between rank and the frequency of successful impregnation is weaker in some species than in others. In multimale groups generally the extent to which social selection type *b* (sexual selection) is operative depends on the extent to which the males present maintain a differential access to females at the critical phase of the estrus cycle. Since rank in terms of mating and rank in terms of access to other commodities do not always correlate and since dominance has social functions additional to simple mating procedures (Rowell 1966) the significance of such behavior in relation to social selection is probably more complex than appears evident at the present time. The whole very important question demands detailed investigation.

We now turn to the densely populated arboreal forest monkeys of Sociotype A. We have argued that here the most adaptive dispersion pattern consists in small groups defending territories of optimum size in relation to defensibility and food value. Young animals must disperse lest at times of food shortage the defended area become insufficient to supply the needs of the individuals living in it. The defended areas and group sizes, it was argued, are on average adjusted to the least productive periods of the annual cycle so that food superabundance may well occur at other times. Given that populations tend to grow to an asymptote representing the level at which the resources available in the environment balance the demands made upon them, we may argue that behavioral adjustments maintaining the recruitment efficiency of the group members will be related to social changes increasing the efficacy of environmental exploitation.

Since the sex ratio at birth appears to be at parity, one would expect an equal distribution of sexes throughout the territories providing that no factor operated to unbalance the dispersion. Small groups containing several reproductive males and females would then be expected. Given that group members compete for commodities in short supply and that some males are commonly excluded from reproductive groups, one may infer that some form of competition between males has arisen as a major factor shifting the sex-ratio in reproductive groups in favour of females. An evolutionary consequence of such competition would be the more aggressive domineering behavior of the males in most species.

Competition within groups cannot be directly for food alone because if this occurred between equally matched sexes it would tend to lead to the departure or starvation of females and males in about equal proportion and a heavier loss of young. Indeed when emigration occurred there should then be no reason why it should lower male representation. The shift in sex representation may therefore be in part a consequence of social selection type *b:* traditional male intrasexual selection. Indeed, as Orians (1969) has pointed out, sexual selection of this type is likely to operate more in mammalian than avian populations, since males are usually but little involved in the direct rearing, feeding and care of young. Evidence perhaps in favor of this viewpoint in Primates is that in multimale systems there is a tendency for a proportion of males to move from one reproductive group to another although, this is not necessarily always related to ranking (for example, *Papio* baboons, Altmann & Altmann (1970); Lolui vervets, Gartlan 1966). Males also occur as solitaries. In addition, the lower representation of the adult male in multimale systems seems due to a process of male exclusion probably associated with a higher mortality per age group than for females.

A male that succeeds in excluding all rivals from a territorial group has acquired all the females for mating and all the available food resources for them and their offspring. Females are not likely to wander, providing the male accompanying them functions efficiently sexually and in territorial maintenance. The male's behavior may however not be as straightforward as it appears. For example, we have no information on the duration of the association between a male and the females on his territory nor do we know whether or not males of one-male groups in the forest switch territories (as does the vervet in a multimale territorial situation). It is of interest here that a male *Presbytis entellus* on taking over a group of females destroyed the former male's young and mated with the females himself (Sugiyama 1967) suggesting a "deliberate" effort to place his own genes on the production line.

Until we know more about male-female bonding in forest monkeys we cannot tell whether social selection type *b* or *c* is more important in the origination of forest one-male groups. Groups in which bonds did not exist, in which males were mobile between groups and yet in which only one male could remain in the group, would still provide major feeding advantages to females at times of short supply and would allow a male to fertilize numerous females. Although the ecological value of other-male exclusion is only operative when food shortage is actually present, exclusion may have predictive value for survival when shortage occurs. So mobile a male would however not necessarily be assuring a food resource for *his own young* through his territorial activities.

In fact, since males usually remain defending their territories beyond the mating season their control of resources must effect the ability with which the females feeding on the preserves can rear young. This effect will moreover be just as important when mating is more or less aseasonal. Furthermore, since females commonly join with males in defensive displays, a degree of cooperation and bonding that lasts for at least a reproductive cycle seems highly likely. The survival value of male behavior thus lies perhaps as much in the securing of female cooperative behavior in the defense of territory as a resource on which progeny can be reared as in the prevention of mating by other males. Social selection type *c* thus appears to be of more importance than sexual selection of the classical type.

We may further argue that were sexual selection (social selection *b*) the only operative factor there would be no necessity for the territory owner to exclude other males at all times from it. In multimale groups the subordinate males mate regularly with females in the early state of estrus. With respect to mating it is only of advantage to the dominant to control access to females when they are about to ovulate. Furthermore, the freedom allowed to other males to mate with females within the dominant male's group probably tends to reduce the tension between the males in the area. Actual geographical exclusion of males from a dominant animal's range must therefore have more to do with assuring the growth and survival of his offspring than merely the control of access to his estrous females.

We turn now to the one-male groups of open country primates: geladas, patas and hamadryas. The patas one-male group living in its big, largely exclusive home range in a severely seasonal grassland environment represents precisely the situation in which the above arguments would apply most strongly. The exclusion of nonreproductive males is marked and they apparently occupy ranges other than those occupied by the bisexual groups, ranges that on ecological examination may well prove to be suboptimal for the species. We have already accounted for the dispersal systems of geladas and hamadryas in terms of their patchy seasonally varying food resources in what are for primates extreme habitats. As Crook & Gartlan (1966) suggested, it will be of advantage to the females of highly mobile and nonterritorial one-male groups if, on the discovery of a food patch, there is only one bulky male present to compete with them indirectly for the often limited supply. Furthermore the single male by locating good food reserves and leading his group to them is assuring the greatest availability of food to the females bearing his own young. These groups seem well bonded and appear to endure as intact structures prehaps over several years, even when associating with other groups on areas of food superabundance. The selection pressure most likely to have been operative here is thus again social selection of type *c*. Indeed it is the long-term incorporation of the male into the female-young reproductive group that distinguishes the sex relations of advanced primates from those of most other mammals. Whereas the various types of polygynous association are usually of short-term duration (for example, in the Pinnipedia and Bovid Artiodactyla) and mostly explicable in terms of the operation of social selection type *b,* it is clear that in primates, as in certain Carnivores, additional evolutionary processes are at work.

The majority of Cercopithecid species probably live in one-male reproductive groups with attendant surplus males. For the exclusion process to prove effective it is essential that surplus males exploit rather different ground (or different resources on the same ground) than the bisexual units (see Figure 9.5). This appears to be the case in the patas monkey (Hall 1966), and the foraging dispersion of geladas (Crook 1966) appears to limit competition between the two types of group. The hamadryas dispersion does not on present knowledge appear to conform to expectations but no details of the foraging behavior of nonreproductive males have yet been published to show whether the proposition holds in this case or not. For that matter we do not yet know to what degree forest arboreal males in the solitary state utilize resources also used by the reproductive groups; under conditions of abundance they probably indeed do do so. In theory one would expect surplus males to occupy suboptimal areas and possibly to suffer a higher mortality rate as individuals than those in the reproductive units, as has been demonstrated for certain Ungulates (Jarman 1968).

If multimale primate groups are exceptional, under what conditions can they arise? One can see that in a rich environment the relatively long duration of periods of superabundance might increase the population of supernumerary males to a degree that the effort spent by harem owners in excluding them was not worthwhile. Further, the presence of additional males would not only increase the protective value of the group to the individual by a simple increase in numbers but also, because males are generally the stronger, more assertive animals, they are most likely to play the protective roles already reported in field studies of baboons. We know too that in multimale groups of macaques and baboons complex affiliative relations develop between the males. Here their cooperative behavior in controlling quarrels within the group, in protecting mothers and infants, and in watchfulness and sometimes active defence against predators becomes a vital aspect of group life. Vandenbergh (1967) showed that when parties of *Rhesus* were placed on small islands a basic group of females emerged

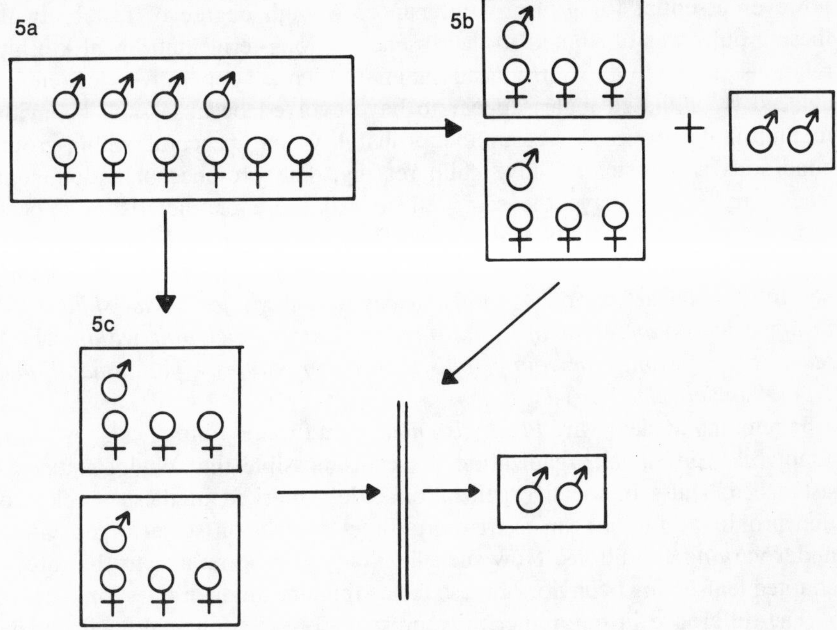

Figure 9.5. The effect of one-male group formation on the apportioning of available food.

1. A group of ten animals comprising four males and six females (that is a typical multimale group) (see 5a) may devide into (5b) two harems with an all-male group in the vicinity or (5c) into two harems with the all-male group foraging elsewhere.
2. In 5a, given that the males are heavier than the females, let us consider food as allocated 50–50 between the sexes rather than the 40–50 ratio that would obtain were individual weights equal throughout the group. Each male thus gets 12.5 per cent and each female 8.3 per cent of the available food.
3. In 5b 12.5 per cent of available food still goes to each harem male and each female gets 8.3 per cent. 25 per cent goes to the females of each harem collectively and 25 per cent to the excluded males. Each harem gets 37.5 per cent of the available food and the two sexes still get 50 per cent each.
4. In 5c the excluded all-male group has departed elsewhere so that the available food is re-apportioned among the remaining 6 females and two males. Assuming that the competitive male does not require more than an equal part of the reallocated 25 per cent, since, even before departure, males were unlikely not to get all they wanted at the expense of females, the reallocation may be made at 3.1 per cent approx per head. Harem males thus get 15.6 per cent of total and females 11.4 per cent each. Total male consumption is now 31.2 per cent and female consumption 58.8 approx. Under actual food deprivation the proportion going to males may increase slightly.
5. The argument assumes no male altruism with respect to the females. If in 5c food shortage increased so that 15.6 per cent of available food was insufficient to maintain the harem males they might tend to increase their intake through direct competition and so decrease the food available to females. Indirect competition would presumably remain in the ratio of the sexes present taking into account the difference in the biomass and food requirements of each sex.

as the most stable element. The presence of a dominant adult male was however essential for group maintenance. A high degree of instability in these groups was attributed to the absence of long-term matrilineal kinship relations among the introduced animals. The cooperative tendencies evinced by affiliated males appear to have evolved because such behavior in multimale groups increases the probability that peaceful within-group conditions will foster effective child rearing. The presence of a dominant leader appears to have the same effect. All these characteristics appear to increase the probability that young within the group will be reared successfully. What is really being selected is a combination of assertive mating control (social selection *b*) with a behavioral *basis for social skills used in affiliative cooperation in establishing a secure social unit within which females forage and rear young. This appears to comprise yet an additional type of social selection* (*d*).

It remains unclear why *Presbytis entellus* and other Colobines show such adaptability in social organization. It seems possible that phylogenetic resistance to shifts in social organization is less marked in these species so that proximate factors can exert more direct control on social organization under varying conditions. How such flexibility can be related to the forest-adapted leaf-eating behavior of these forms remains an open question.

The difference in the numerical representation of adult male and female monkeys in both multimale and one-male group systems is partly due to the fact that males mature later than females. This too would appear to be a consequence of social selection types *b* and *c*. Young sexually mature males are unlikely to be large enough, experienced enough or socially skilled enough to compete effectively with older animals, particularly in the context of sexual and sex-bonding behavior. Indeed attempts at too early an age could be not only futile but damaging both physically and psychologically. Deferment of maturity allows the animal additional time for behavioral and physical development before making individual claims for ranking precedence and access to females.

In that the Cercopithecoidea presumably arose from more lemur-like forebears, insectivorous and nocturnal, we must imagine that their social structures have originated from relatively dispersed organizations like those of *Microcebus* or *Galago* and passed through a more integrated stage resembling lemur in the course of adaptation to a diurnal forest existence. It remains unknown whether adaptation to terrestrial open-country life involved an emergence of a multimale system from a more frequent one-male group system in forests, but in that forest fringe must have been inhabited before more arid environments, it seems plausible. Likewise the evolution of arid country one-male groups from multimale units appears, as Kummer (1968) suggests, plausible. This implies that shifts between socio-types A and B occurred in either direction several times in Cercopithecid evolution. Table 9.3 shows that some five stages appear to be needed for such

Table 9.3. Evolutionary steps between multimale and one-male groups

	Sequence from multimale to one-male reproductive unit	*Sequence from one-male to multimale unit*
START	1. Splitting of multimale group into smaller parties for foraging.	1. Tendency for congregation of one-male and all-male groups.
↓	2. Tendency for adult males to avoid one another and to keep to separate parties.	2. Tendency for females to disperse about herd and associate briefly with nongroup males.
DIRECTION OF CHANGE	3. Tendency for adult males to associate with affiliated females as a result of extended consort links or kinship.	3. Tendency for males to accept presence of nongroup males near females and pay less attention to group maintenance.
↓	4. Tendency for affiliated females to cohere as a party and not to mate with other males.	4. Males compete for estrous females irrespective of group affiliation.
FINISH	5. Tendency for males to drive off nongroup males that approach. This leads to a) increased intergroup spacing perhaps with territorial displays and to b) evolution of displays that regulate ownership of females and bonding to them.	5. Emergence of male hierarchy and various degrees of female promiscuity and mating consortships. No exclusive subgroup affiliation. Operation of Social Selection type (d).

evolutionary sequences. Each of these must involve rather complex adjustments at both the level of social tradition and the level of genetically determined behavioral traits. The sequence also demonstrates a number of mechanisms of importance in ensuring the existence or nonexistence of intersexual bonding and its adaptive significance. Bonding is due, firstly, to male techniques involving persistent retention and reinforcement of affiliation and, secondly, to female willingness to accompany the male and to cooperate or to submit to his training procedures.

There is little evidence to suggest that a female's bonding with a particular male necessarily precludes her tendency to promiscuous mating. Nevertheless bonding systems tend to act as constraints on female infidelity which of course may also occur outside the immediate period of ovulation so significant to the mate. Males in a polygamous system have a more open bond than females in that they may add females to their group if they can. Kummer's work shows that hamadryas males commonly endeavour to do so. Restraint on males arises not from the sex partner but from the competitors of his own sex. Bonding limits to a degree the number of females available to an actively copulating male since attentions to females outside the group would occasion marked resentment. In multimale groups, by contrast, widespread promiscuity is possible, although this does not necessarily mean widespread access to ovulating females. Clearly, female sexual behavior here is not limited to a single male.

Male bonding techniques are expensive in time and energy that could be spend in other activities. The selection pressures maintaining such behavior must be strong. As we have suggested the prime function of bonding is not so much to ensure mating with a particular female as to create a social structure within which resources can be made available most effectively to growing young. The one-male group has evolved as the optimal rearing unit in the ecological circumstances concerned. The degree to which female geladas or hamadryas are satisfied by such an arrangement seems related to the leadership qualities of the "overlord." If he is successful in preventing social disturbance and finding ample food then her offspring are likely to thrive.

The leadership and food-finding skills of the old experienced harem owners of these open country species are likely to be of a high order. Indeed their presence in congragations of geladas and hamadryas may contribute to the effective nourishment of more than their own reproductive group. The emergence of old male leaders in hamadryas bands, the great degree of attention paid to them, their role as decision makers in determining the direction of foraging, all indicate the high information value of an experienced animal in a social unit larger than his own group. The continued incorporation of these wise old beasts in the social structure long after some of them have ceased an active reproductive life involves the establishment of important systems of tolerance and cooperation, of notification and obedience that mark the hamadryas as one of the most socially evolved primates.

Both the multimale and the one-male *Papio* social organizations function as rearing units of great complexity based fundamentally on differential effects of ecological factors upon a common base of social selection ensuring reproductive efficiency from one generation to another. In these systems one becomes aware of the emergence of complex cultural attributes which have broad significance for animals that are of less close kinship than direct progeny. In this these baboons foreshadow the further developments of culture in man.

Some Ethological Approaches to Sex roles in Modern Man

Whether or not we accept Morris' explanation of the origin of the prime human sex differences, there can be little doubt that many of these contrasts, so similar to those in other primates, must be due to social processes common to many primates. Recent examinations of the probable course of early human social history suggest that, as with other open-country terrestrial primates, man developed a polygamous and later a mainly monogamous mating system with long term but not necessarily life-long bonding.

The system was probably derived originally from a more open society akin to that of chimpanzees living in forests (see Fox 1967b, Reynolds 1966, Crook 1970b, Jolly 1970). Unfortunately no protohominid society remains extant upon which to test these ideas by a comparative method although Reynolds has noted certain similarities between chimpanzees and hunter-gatherer societies of man. Recent Japanese work (for example, Itani & Suzuki 1967) shows that forest fringe chimpanzees appear to have a rather more tightly organized baboon type of society than do those living in forests. For the present only speculation can lead us beyond these suggestions. Gorilla, orang-utan and gibbon societies all appear to be specializations to particular ecologies and their ways of living need not concern us further here.

In view of the rigor with which complex human cultures and kinship systems regulate the choice of spouse uncontaminated evidence for the behavioral basis of sexual selection (social selection *b*) at the distant epoch when the socio-morphological contrasts were particularly influenced by genetic change is hard if not impossible to come by. Indeed, the modern "permissive society" with its tolerance of free partner choice by both sexes on a largely reciprocal basis only mildly influenced by social tradition and taboo may possibly approximate in some ways to the primordial selective situation. Although there are primitive societies in which the gender roles as we know them in the West are almost completely reversed, the majority of societies and major world civilizations apportion sex roles in ways that westerners would have little difficulty in recognizing (see Henriques 1960). Cultural factors indubitably play a major role in the details of intersexual relations in every society but on the whole there does appear to be some kind of species-specific ground plan from which major deviations are rare.

Although the scientist as voyeur is still a rare phenomenon and our knowledge of the courtship process remains extraordinarily slight a number of suggestions may perhaps be made.[4]

Young women appear to be attractive to young men owing to the combination of paedomorphic and secondary sexual signal characteristics which they present to them initially at a distance. Hairlessness, voice tone, complexion and girlish behavior all have a childlike character that in ethological terms appear to lower the probability of a male aggressive response or to appease if one is present. These same characteristics are likely to reduce male fear and anxiety on closer approach and to permit sexual expression. The male begins to display in various "show-off" performances including physical prowess (such as, dancing), exhibitions of virtuosity in the social graces, in demonstrations of charm and sensitive virility. These

4. I am greatly indebted to Adam Kendon for a constructive discussion of this theme. A number of his ideas are incorporated into the argument presented.

displays attract the female's attention and provide the basis upon which she may choose to respond to or to reject the male's approach: or more usually, simply fail to observe them. The closer approach of this physically stronger and potent individual is however likely to be alarming so that, at this point, the male commonly switches his behavior. He begins to exhibit childishness mainly in the form of play, teasing, self-mockery, smiles and laughter, above all, contact tenderness. Such childlike behavior seems highly likely to stimulate not only a reciprocal sexual tenderness but also maternal aspects of the female care-giving behavior. In a successful courtship the male acquires the admiration and maternal support of a potential spouse (and child-bearer) while the female gains the virile protectiveness of a male (who in this resembles not only her own father but also foreshadows the protectiveness to be provided to her children) and his sexual admiration of her. Both gain the profound satisfaction of sex-play and the performance of the sexual consummatory act. The significance of a successful courtship is underlined by considering the likely results of misalignments. A sexual approach by a male without adequate play when matched, for example, with a sexually attractive female showing inadequate subordination is likely to lead not to bond formation but rather to unproductive rape. The delicate balance between these behaviors and their reciprocal effects in terms of subjectively experienced affect underlie furthermore the extent to which the fantasy life of the partners is likely to be fulfilled through projection.

From the purely ethological viewpoint this sequence has much in common with courtship in birds and often mammals (for example see Butterfield 1970). The long duration of the bond so formed is in part a consequence of the peculiarities of the human sexual system and it leads to the emergence of the family as the reproductive unit in which young can be safely reared. If our argument is roughly correct it follows that genetic factors influencing not only the emergence of morphological and behavioral signals but also the maturation of "deep structures" underlying culture contingent patterns of emotional behavior and fantasy life are likely to have been positively selected at every successful long-term bond formation. Furthermore it is highly likely that selection may have also influenced the ability of the sexes to learn the social skills basic to the playing of the appropriate gender role. This is suggested by the early emergence of psychological contrasts between the sexes important in the development of appropriate sexual identity (Erikson 1968). The biological roots of human sexual behavior are different in the two sexes and likely to be fundamental determinants in the differentiation of mature personality.

These points of view are relevant to the problem of the relations between the adult sexes in modern western society. The biologist cannot but look with a profound scepticism on social policies based on simplistic psychological theories derived not from ethology but from one or other of the behaviorist schools of learning theory. The naive idea of a psychological "equality" of the two sexes and of their total interchangeability in the performance of social roles has gained support from certain studies purporting to demonstrate that gender role is determined simply through developmental conditioning. This view ignores totally the significance of genetic and physiological differences between the sexes that in current research are shown to exert profound effects during the behavioral maturation of the growing organism. The important social and cultural effects program an already differentiating organism.

Clearly the role of women must undergo major changes in modern society, particularly with the provision of family aids, day nurseries for young children and perhaps through the emergence of forms of communal living in which the restrictive nuclear family unit is no longer the context for most if not all forms of intimate personal behavior (see Hedgepeth & Stock 1970). Equally the repressive treatment of women in the economic sphere needs immediate and generous redress. Nevertheless the remodeling of society according to unwise policies could impose excessive strain on many individuals of both sexes. There may well be a limit beyond which the trends affecting women in our currently male oriented educational systems could produce highly disruptive results. Those concerned with Women's Liberation would be wise to ponder the biological and psychological complementarity of the two sexes and their deep emotional needs for partnership as a counter to the notion of a poorly defined "equality." Health may well lie in an emphasis on contrast and complementarity rather than upon similarity.[5]

This article has of necessity dealt mainly with theory and speculation—some of which is highly controversial. This aspect appears unavoidable in the context of an extraordinary lack of adequate knowledge or research in the problem areas discussed. The ethological approach to primates including man is likely to provide us with major new insights and orientations in the near future. In the meantime the message is clear, a great deal of research and the accummulation of carefully established fact is a vital prerequisite for the formulation of sensible policies regarding human sex roles in modern society. Caution is essential if an improved mental health of both sexes rather than even further social and emotional disruption is to emerge.

Summary

1. Darwin showed that the characteristics of a species acquired by sexual selection are usually confined to one sex, develop fully at sexual matur-

5. For a further discussion of the biological and social bases of sex based behavior differentiation in man see my article *Darwinism and the sexual politics of primates* written subsequently to this paper and to be published in the proceedings of the conference entitled *L'Origine dell' Uomo* (Rome, October 1971) by the Academia Nazionale dei Lincei, Rome, 1972. The conference, like this book, was prepared in celebration of the centenary of the publication of Darwin's *The Descent of Man.*

ity, often appear only in the mating season and are a consequence of either intra- or inter-sexual selective processes. He discussed the evolution of human secondary sexual characteristics within the general context of primate and mammalian evolution as a whole.

2. Sexual selection in higher vertebrates including primates is often most apparent in the features of species showing polygynous mating systems. Primate sexes differ in weight and muscle development, pelage color, skull and skin characteristics and in the occurrence of maturational, seasonal or periodic morphological changes especially in association with the estrous cycle of the female.
3. Sexual dimorphism is little marked in tree shrews, lorises or lemurs. In the Ceboidea, females of some species equal or exceed males in size. In addition female genitalia in some species may mimic those of the male. Insufficient information is yet available to interpret these Ceboid features socio-ecologically or to compare them effectively with the range of variation apparent in the Old World primates. The most marked physical dimorphism is found in the Cercopithecoidea. Discussion is centred particularly upon W. Wickler's studies of cercopithecoid sexual morphology and upon the reliability of his theoretical conclusions. Many of the secondary sexual characters of these animals are evidently associated with the highly competitive nature of their societies, necessitating the frequent use of submissive gesturing by both sexes and male displays indicative of dominance.
4. Contrasts in morphology between the human sexes relate closely to those found in other primates. The original interpretation of the "naked ape" by Darwin is discussed in the context of D. Morris' recent opinions. Although these viewpoints are poorly supported by anthropological evidence, are notably panglossian and largely unverifiable, hair loss in *Homo* probably developed together with an increased skin sensitivity, a behavioral emphasis on contact-comfort, loss of estrus and the development of female orgasm. These characters were part of an adaptive complex related to a new and specifically human grade of social organization, some primordial aspects of which appear to have been paralleled by the gelada baboon.
5. An explanation of the diversity of social structures in the Cercopithecoidea stresses the interaction between adaptations due to environmental selection and those due to social selective processes. Both are viewed as operating together throughout the history of higher primates. Contrasts between species in the spatial dispersion and size of groups are analyzed and simple socio-ecological models presented in graphical form. The sex roles in the composition of these grouping patterns are then discussed in relation to social selection of four kinds arising from (*a*) interindividual competition for commodities essential for permitting an attempt at reproduction, (*b*) competition for access to preferred

mates (inter- and intra-sexual selection), (*c*) competition for access to resources essential for rearing one's own young to reproductive age and (*d*) (p. 270) the effects of affiliative cooperation in establishing a social unit effective in foraging for and protecting the young of the collaborators and their close kin. Among higher primates social selection types *c* and *d* are of major importance and their effects apparent to a degree not seen in other mammalian orders.

6. The rigor with which most human societies regulate choice of spouse means that evidence for natural (not over-culturally controlled) sexual selection in man and evidence for its importance in the evolution of protohominid society is almost impossible to obtain. Possibly the extreme freedom of spouse choice in some areas of contemporary western society reveal the biological basis of this process. Human courtship is related to the contrasting morphological and physiological attributes of the two sexes. The resulting complex appears to be adapted to the effective rearing of young in social units of small size with a tendency to long-term bonding between the sexes. This system is seen as the product of thousands of years of socio-ecological evolution almost all of which occurred prior to the emergence of complex civilizations. Much research on the personal needs of the sexes in modern society is required before sociologists can safely prescribe what social roles may be appropriate to what class of player.

References

Aldrich-Blake, F. P. G. 1970a. Problems of social structure in forest monkeys. In *Social behaviour in birds and mammals,* ed. J. Crook. London and New York: Academic Press.

————. 1970b. *The ecology and behaviour of the Blue Monkey* Cercopithecus mitis stuhlmani. Doctoral Thesis. Bristol University Library.

Aldrich-Blake, F. P. G., T. K. Bunn, R. I. M. Dunbar, & P. M. Headley. 1971. Observations on baboons (*Papio anubis*) in an arid region in Ethiopia. *Folia Primat.* 15: 1–35.

Altmann, S. A. 1962. A field study of the sociobiology of rhesus monkeys. *Macaca mulatta. Ann. N.Y. Acad. Sci.* 102: 338–435.

Altmann, S. A. & J. Altmann. 1970. Baboon Ecology. African Field Research. *Bibliotheca Primatologica,* vol. 12.

Brown, J. L. 1964. The evolution of diversity in avian territorial systems. *Wilson Bulletin* 76: 160–169.

Butterfield, P. A. 1970. The pair bond in the Zebra Finch. In *Social behaviour in birds and mammals,* ed. J. Crook. London and New York: Academic Press.

Carpenter, C. R. 1942. Sexual behaviour of free-ranging rhesus monkeys (*Macaca mulatta*). *J. Comp. Psychol.* 33: 113–142, 143–162.

Chivers, D. 1969. On the daily behaviour and spacing of free-ranging howling monkey groups. *Folia Primat.* 10: 48–102.

Crook, J. H. 1964. The evolution of social organisation and visual communication in the weaver birds (Ploceinae). *Behaviour* Supplement 10. Brill, Leiden.

————. 1965. The adaptive significance of avian social organisations. *Symp. zool. Soc. Lond.* 14: 181–218.
————. 1966. Gelada baboon herd structure and movement: a comparative report. *Symp. zool. Soc. Lond.* 18: 237–258.
————. 1970a. Social behaviour and ethology. In *Social behaviour in birds and mammals,* ed. J. H. Crook. London and New York: Academic Press.
————. 1970b. The Socio-ecology of Primates. In *Social behaviour in birds and mammals,* ed. J. H. Crook. London and New York: Academic Press.
————. 1970c. Sources of cooperation in animals and man. *Soc. Sci. inform.* 9: 27–48.
————. In preparation. *Social systems and evolutionary ecology.*
Crook, J. H. & P. Aldrich-Blake 1968. Ecological and behavioural contrasts between sympatric ground-dwelling primates in Ethiopia. *Folia Primat.* 8: 192–227.
Crook, J. H. & J. S. Gartlan 1966. Evolution of primate societies. *Nature* 210: 1200–1203.
Darwin, C. 1871. *The descent of man and selection in relation to sex.* London: John Murray.
————. 1876. Sexual selection in relation to monkeys. *Nature* 15: 18–19.
Deag, J. & J. H. Crook 1971. Social behaviour and "agonistic buffering" in the wild Barbary Macaque, *Macaca sylvana,* L. *Folia Primat.* 15: 183–200.
Dengrove, E. 1961. Sex differences. In *The encyclopaedia of sexual behaviour.* Vol. 2, ed. A. Ellis & A. Abarbanel, pp. 931–38. London: The Corsano Co.
DeVore, I. 1965. Male dominance and mating behaviour in baboons. In *Sex and behaviour,* ed. F. A. Beach. New York: Wiley.
DeVore, I. & S. L. Washburn. 1963. Baboon ecology and human evolution. In *African ecology and human evolution,* ed. F. Clark Howell & F. Bourliere. Chicago: Aldine.
Dobzhansky, T. 1962. *Mankind evolving.* New Haven: Yale University Press.
Eibl-Eibesfeldt, I. 1970. *Ethology. The biology of behaviour.* New York: Holt, Rinehart and Winston.
Erikson, E. H. 1968. *Identity, youth and crisis.* London: Faber.
Estes, R. D. 1966. Behaviour and life history of the wildebeeste (*Connochaetes taurinus* Burchell) *Nature,* 212: 999–1000.
Fisher, R. A. 1929. *The genetical theory of natural selection.* Oxford: Clarendon Press.
Ford, C. S. & F. A. Beach 1952. *Patterns of sexual behaviour.* London: Methuen.
Fox, R. 1967a. *Kinship and marriage.* London: Penguin Books.
————. 1967b. In the beginning: aspects of hominid behavioural evolution. *Man* 2: 415–433.
Freedman, D. G. 1968. A biological view of man's social behaviour. In *Social behaviour from fish to man,* ed. W. Etkin. Chicago: University of Chicago Press.
Gartlan, J. S. 1966. *Ecology and behaviour of the Vervet Monkey. Lolui Island. Lake Victoria, Uganda,* PhD. Thesis. Bristol University.
Gautier, J. P. & A. Gautier-Hion 1969. Les associations polyspecifiques chez les Cercopithecidae du Gabon. *La Terre et la Vie* 2: 164–201.
Goode, W. J. 1959. The theoretical importance of love. *Amer. Social. Rev.* 24: 38–47.
Goodhart, C. B. 1964. A biological view of toplessness. *New Scientist* 23: 588–560.
Hall, K. R. L. 1966. Behaviour and ecology of the wild Patas monkey *Erythrocebus patas* in Uganda. *J. Zool.* 148: 15–87.

Hallpike, C. R. 1969. Social hair. *Man* 4: 256–264.

Hamilton, W. D. 1963. The evolution of altruistic behaviour. *Amer. Nat.* 97: 354–356.

Harrer, H. 1964. *I come from the Stone Age.* London: Rupert Hart-Davis.

Hedgepeth, W. & D. Stock. 1970. *The alternative. Communal life in New America.* London: Collier-MacMillan.

Heider, K. G. 1969. Attributes and categories in the study of material culture: New Guinea Dani attire. *Man* 4: 379–391.

Henriques, F. 1960. *Love in action, the sociology of sex.* London: MacGibbon and Kee.

Hershkovitz, P. 1968. Metachromism or the principle of evolutionary change in mammalian tegumentary colours. *Evolution* 22: 556–575.

Hewes, G. W. 1957. The anthropology of posture. *Sci. Amer.* 196: 123–132.

Huxley, J. S. 1923. Courtship activities in the Red Throated Diver (*Colymbus stellatus* Pontopp) together with a discussion of the evolution of courtship in birds. *J. Linn. Soc.* 35: 253–292.

————. 1938a. The present standing of the theory of sexual selection. In *Evolution: essays on aspects of evolutionary biology,* ed. G. R. DeBeer. New York and Oxford: Oxford University Press.

————. 1938b. Darwin's theory of sexual selection and the data subsumed by it in the light of recent research. *Amer. Nat.* 72: 416–433.

Immelmann, K. 1962. Beiträge zu einer vergleichenden Biologie australischer Prachtfinken (Spermestidae). *Zool. Jahrb. Syst.* 90: 1–196.

Itani, J. & A. Suzuki 1967. The social unit of chimpanzees. *Primates* 8: 355–381.

Jarman, P. 1968. *The effect of the creation of Lake Kariba upon the terrestrial ecology of the middle Zambezi, with particular reference to the large mammals.* Ph.D. Thesis. Manchester University Library.

Jolly, A. 1966. *Lemur behaviour; a Madagascan field study.* Chicago: University of Chicago Press.

Jolly, C. J. 1963. A suggested case of evolution by sexual selection in Primates. *Man* 63: 177–178.

————. 1970. The seed-eaters: a new model of hominid differentiation based on a baboon analogy. *Man* 5: 5–26.

Keverne, E. B. 1970. *Investigation of the sexual behaviour of rhesus monkeys by operant techniques combined with free cage studies.* Ph.D. Thesis. London University Library.

Kummer, H. 1967. Tripartite relations in Hamadryas baboons. In *Social communication among Primates,* ed. S. A. Altmann. Chicago: University of Chicago Press.

————. 1968. Social organization of Hamadryas baboons. *Bibliotheca Primatologica,* vol. 6.

Lack, D. 1968. *Ecological adaptations for breeding in birds.* London: Methuen.

Lancaster, J. B. & R. B. Lee 1965. The annual reproductive cycle in monkeys and apes. In *Primate behaviour. Field studies of monkeys and apes,* ed. I. DeVore. New York: Holt, Rinehart and Winston.

Leach, E. R. 1958. Magical hair. *J. R. Anthrop. Inst.* 88: 147–164.

Leuthold, U. 1966. Variations in territorial behaviour of Uganda Kob (*Adenota kob thomasi* (Neumann, 1896). *Behaviour* 27: 215–258.

Martin, R. D. 1968. Reproduction and ontogeny in the Tree Shrews (*Tupaia belangeri*) with reference to their general behaviour and taxonomic relationships. *Z. fur Tierpsychol.* 25: 409–495, 505–532.

Masters, W. H. & V. E. Johnson. 1966. *Human sexual response.* London: J. and E. Churchill.

Matthews, L. Harrison. 1956. The sexual skin of the Gelada baboon *Theropithecus gelada*. *Trans. zool. Soc. Lond.* 28: 543–552.

Michael, R. P. & E. B. Keverne 1968. Pheromones in the communication of sexual status in Primates. *Nature* 218: 746–749.

———. 1970. Primate sex pheromones of vaginal origin. *Nature* 225: 84–85.

Morris, D. 1967. *The naked ape*. London: Jonathan Cape.

Napier, J. R. & P. H. Napier. 1967. *A handbook of living primates*. London and New York: Academic Press.

Nutting, C. C. 1891. Some of the causes and results of polygamy among the Pinnipedia. *Amer. Nat.* 25: 103–112.

Orians G. H. 1961. The ecology of Blackbird (*Agelaius*) social systems. *Ecol. Monogr.* 31: 285–312.

———. 1969. On the evolution of mating systems in birds and mammals. *Amer. Nat.* 103: 589–603.

Packard, V. 1968. *The sexual wilderness*. London: Longmans Green.

Petter, J. J. 1962. Recherches sur l'ecologie et l'ethologie des Lemuriens malgaches. *Mem. du Mus. Nat. de l'hist. Naturelle* Ser. A. 27: 1–146.

Ploog, D. W., J. Blitz, & F. Ploog 1963. Studies on social and sexual behaviour of the squirrel monkey (*Saimiri sciureus*). *Folia Primat.* 1: 29–66.

Rowell, T. E. 1966. Hierarchy in the organisation of a captive baboon group. *Anim. Behav.* 14: 420–443.

Reynolds, V. 1965. Some behavioural comparisons between the chimpanzee and the mountain gorilla in the wild. *Am. Anthrop.* 67: 691–706.

———. 1966. Open groups in Hominid evolution. *Man* 1: 441–452.

Saayman, G. S. 1970. The menstrual cycle and sexual behaviour in a troop of free ranging Chacma baboons (*Papio ursinus*). *Folia Primat.* 12: 81–100.

Selander, R. K. 1965. On mating systems and sexual selection. *Amer. Nat.* 99: 129–141.

Sibley, C. G. 1957. The evolutionary and taxonomic significance of sexual dimorphism and hybridisation in birds. *Condor* 59: 166–191.

Solomon, M. E. 1964. Analysis of processes involved in the natural control of insects. In *Advances in ecological research*, ed. J. B. Crag, Vol. 2. London & New York: Academic Press.

Struhsaker, T. T. 1967. Behaviour of vervet monkeys (*Cercopithecus aethiops*). *University of California Publications in Zoology* 82: 1–64.

———. 1969. Correlates of ecology and social organisation among African Cercopithecines. *Folia Primat.* 11: 80–118.

Struhsaker, T. T. & J. S. Gartlan 1970. Observations on the behaviour and ecology of the Patas monkey (*Erythrocebus patas*) in the Waza Reserve, Cameroon. *J. Zool.* 161: 49–63.

Sugiyama, Y. 1967. Social organisation of Hanuman Langurs. In *Social communication among Primates*, ed. S. A. Altman. Chicago: University of Chicago Press.

Vandenbergh, J. G. 1967. The development of social structure in free ranging rhesus monkeys. *Behaviour* 29: 179–194.

Verner, J. 1964. Evolution of polygamy in the long billed marsh wren. *Evolution* 18: 252–261.

Vine, I. 1971. The risk of visual detection and pursuit by a predator and the selective advantage of flocking behaviour. *J. theor. Biol.* 30: 405–422.

Watson, A. & R. Moss. 1970. Dominance, spacing behaviour and aggression in relation to population limitation in vertebrates. *British Ecological Society Symposium* 10: 167–220.

Wickler, W. 1963. Die biologischer Bedeutung auffallend farbiger, nackter Hautstellen und innerartliche Mimikry der Primaten. *Naturw.* 50: 481–482.

————. 1966. Ursprung und biologische Deutung des Genital prasentierens mannlicher Primaten. *Z. Tierpsychol.* 23: 422–437.

————. 1967. Socio-sexual signals and their intra-specific imitation among Primates. In *Primate ethology,* ed. D. Morris. London: Weiderfeld and Nicolson.

Zuckerman, S. 1932. *The social life of monkeys and apes.* London: Kegan Paul.

10

ROBIN FOX
RUTGERS UNIVERSITY

Alliance and Constraint: Sexual Selection in the Evolution of Human Kinship Systems

Introduction

I want here to explore the possibilities of using a sexual selection theory to explain the origins of cultural restraints on mate selection in man. The most universal and important of such restraints is acknowledged to be the taboo on sexual intercourse and marriage between members of the immediate family. While many exceptions to this rule are known, it is nevertheless one of the more universal of all rules and its significance has to be interpreted. It lies at the back of all systems of kinship and marriage, and represents a basic ground rule of such systems. When it is abrogated it is usually done so for a special effect which is recognized, in the same way a poet can abrogate the normal rules of grammar in language in order to gain an effect. We must quickly distinguish between sexual intercourse and marriage here and say that we will be primarily concerned with the latter. A rule against sexual intercourse with members of the immediate family clearly precludes marriage with them (in practice if not in theory), but it is possible to have a rule against marriage which waives the regulation on sexual intercourse. This becomes important when we come to discuss the phenomenon of *exogamy* which pertains more precisely to rules against marriage (first defined by McLennan 1864). Usually the two rules are isomorphic in that rights over women in marriage include rights over their

This chapter was prepared while the author was in receipt of a Special Fellowship from the National Institute of Mental Health under the sponsorship of Dr. David A. Hamburg and the Department of Psychiatry, Stanford University School of Medicine. The preparation of the manuscript was facilitated by a grant from the Rutgers University Research Council. The basic argument of this chapter has been further elaborated by Lionel Tiger and Robin Fox in *The Imperial Animal* (New York: Holt, Rinehart, & Winston, 1971).

sexual services, but again it need not be so and the distinction should be made. Rules about marriage, in short, have to do with the allocation of rights over women, and while one may be forbidden to marry a particular class of women one need not be forbidden to have sexual intercourse with them. This is an important point in which human marriage and animal mating differ, and represents perhaps the crucial breakthrough in the "hominization" process: man became the exogamous animal. At some point in the evolution of his behavior he began to define social units and to apply rules about the recruitment of people to these units and the allocation of women amongst them. Typically he forbade men to mate with their mothers, sisters and daughters, and then with the women of more widely defined social units such as clans or moieties. This kind of exogamic rule, that one should find mates outside one's own social unit, is at the root of all human social organization. Its relation to sexual selection is immediately apparent in that it is an assortative mating procedure of a rather elaborate kind. The modern theory of kinship in fact sees all kinship systems as sets of rules regarding the allocation of women as mates, or the "circulation" of women among the kinship units in the society. Whether or not the cultural allocation of women corresponds to the actual breeding systems depends of course on who actually gets to impregnate the women. But since the rules of allocation include rights to sexual services and offspring, most societies make some effort to make the rules and the facts coincident, with severe penalties for those (particularly the women) who deviate.

In studying the actual processes of sexual selection in man one needs to know a great deal more than just the rules of mate selection. These merely set the parameters within which the players operate. The rules of chess tell us how to play the game, they do not tell us how any particular player will operate. The rules of kinship and marriage likewise divide up the world for any person into "marriageable" and "unmarriageable" parties, but the breeding success of any individual is not governed solely by these rules. Their importance for human social life lies rather in the fact that although they are basically procedures of assortative mating they operate to govern areas of social interaction other than mating in a way that is specific to our species. Before we try to study the "strategies" of sexual selection, therefore, we should try to understand what lies behind the "rules" of the game, since these map out the broad areas within which selection has to operate.

I will adopt an evolutionary approach here on the grounds that if human behavior is the end product of an evolutionary process then we must try to understand the selection pressures that have operated to produce it. This is not to say that any particular item of human culture can be located in the genome, but that certain general features of human behavior on which the existence and operation of human culture depends are in a real sense a part of the biological nature of man (Fox 1970). Lévi-Strauss (1949) has noted three features which have this generality and which he thinks are directly linked to the basic taboo on incest: the exigency of the rule as rule, the notion of reciprocity, and the synthetic nature of the gift. Roughly interpreted this means that man is a rule-obeying creature, that he engages in exchange behavior, and that between two persons who have exchanged a special relationship exists. Kinship systems then are systems of rules about the exchange of women and the relationships set up by this exchange. By the same token economic systems are about the exchange of goods and services, and communication systems about the exchange of information, and the like. Even more fundamental than these processes is the other "faculty" that Lévi-Strauss examines at length, (1962a, 1962b) that is, the ability to name and classify, depending as it does on the existence of a capacity for language, itself rooted in the biology of the species (Lenneberg 1967, Lancaster 1968). The picture of the human being that emerges is of a creature that will spontaneously classify the elements of its social and nonsocial universe, make rules about the items so classified, exchange these items, and set up relationships between the exchanging parties. Kinship systems, then, involve the classification of the universe of kin, the making of rules about which categories are marriageable and unmarriageable, the exchange of the women so classified and ruled upon, and the setting up of relationships among the exchangers. The essence of the incest taboo is that consanguine or "own" women become defined as *objects of exchange* rather than *objects of use* as far as mating is concerned. The prohibition of incest therefore is the most truly primitive of rules since it is the rule needed to start off the whole process.

I would like to go one step further back in the evolutionary process than Lévi-Strauss in an attempt to show how all the factors he deals with are indeed linked together in the evolution of human behavior, to show in other words how they got into the beast. Kinship systems link us more directly to the beasts than any other subsystems of human culture in that they are in effect breeding systems. The social system of a group of nonhuman primates *is* the breeding system; this is what it is about, and this was the case with our prehuman primate ancestors. It was then the evolution from prehuman breeding systems to human kinship systems that was the crucial turning point in our hominization. It follows that many general features of our species-characteristic behavior, which we now apply in numerous cultural subsystems, had their origin in the processes that led to this transition.

The processes involved were largely to do with the inhibition of sexuality and aggression and the development of cortical as opposed to hormonal control over these areas of behavior (Beach 1965, Ford & Beach 1952, Spuhler 1959). The thesis I want to propose here is that the growth of the human neo-cortex, on which rests all the developments that Lévi-Strauss outlines, was very much a function of sexual selection pressures favoring animals with greater cortical control. The following will be a critical elaboration of an argument begun some years ago (Fox 1962) and developed later into an ambitious theory of hominid behavioral evolution (Fox 1967b). I will present a résumé of the theory, consider some objections to it, attempt to resolve these, and then try to link it up with the view of the nature of kinship systems as seen by Lévi-Strauss.

Theory of the Evolution of Cortical Control

In presenting the theory I will be deliberately personal and autobiographical since it may be of some interest to trace its development and vicissitudes.

The theory originated in an attempt to find a biological basis for the relative universality of the incest taboo on the grounds that anything that was general for the species must have some location in the biology of the species. It became obvious that what was involved here was a general tendency to *avoid* sexual relationships of certain kinds, and that this tendency had to be considered apart from the culturally imposed *taboos* on sexual relationships. Even, for example, where there are no overt taboos, specific interdictions or severe punishments, certain types of sexual encounter tend to be avoided. Two processes seemed to be at work: on the one hand people avoided sexual relationships seemingly because they found them painful, distasteful or uninteresting, and on the other hand they placed interdictions on certain relationships regardless of the feelings involved. The relative uniformity of avoidance of sexuality between members of the immediate family, irrespective of the varying content of the taboos, suggested that, to borrow a modern analogy, there was something in the wiring. The only thing previously suggested as being in the wiring of the human organism was an anti-incest instinct, and for obvious reasons this is not a good explanation of anything. I therefore tried out the idea that various learning patterns might be involved and that these might lead to the development of unconscious inhibitions. The only thing I assumed to be in the wiring at this point was a high-intensity sex drive of a high degree of malleability, hence, subject to easy conditioning. I was particularly intrigued by the idea that drives of high intensity were liable to "go into reverse" if they reached a peak. High-intensity drives, to put it crudely, frightened the organism which automatically inhibited the drive (Fox 1962).

I saw the learning of sexual behavior taking either of two major paths. Either it was on an "easy schedule" with little repression of affect or expression, or it was on a "tough schedule." In the first case immature opposite sex organisms (for example, siblings) would develop avoidance behavior naturally; in the second case they would not, but they would develop fears. Whether or not they would develop guilt seemed to depend on other factors than those involved in the sex learning. The foregoing is too simple a summary, but the outcome was a notion that intense fear of incest, where this occurred, stemmed from a repressive separation of "siblings" such that they could not learn a natural avoidance, whereas more muted and less fearful reactions to incest were produced if the siblings could interact when immature. In the latter case they would tend not to want each other as sexual partners anyway. There were other combinations and permutations but this is the drift of the argument.

Clearly several things are left out. This discussion deals only with "siblings" and does not adequately cover parent-child incest. I concluded that some "more comprehensive" theory of the nature of hetero-sexual interaction was necessary to include all forms of incest.

The "more comprehensive" theory obviously would have to do with the inhibitory processes we have mentioned. These operate at two levels as we have seen: on the one hand the organism is capable of developing through learning certain unconscious inhibitions; on the other hand it is also capable of instituting certain highly conscious cultural inhibitions. The first are "avoidances," the second 'taboos', in my private language. I became rapidly convinced, after reading, for example, Count's excellent article (1958), that the answer lay in understanding the evolution of the central nervous system and the brain and the relations between these and behavior. In other words, evolution produced a creature capable of, on the one hand, the development of complex learned unconscious inhibitions and, on the other, of complex learned conscious inhibitions. By what mechanisms had this come about, and what did these mechanisms tell us about the nature of the inhibitory process?

What is involved here is the evolution of certain potentials, certain capacities to learn certain things. I was not looking for instinctive mechanisms. There is no nature/nurture issue here. What is innate (in the wiring) is the capacity to be programmed in certain ways (Fox 1970). But it was also clear that we were moving far beyond the restricted issue of the incest taboo. These capacities involved the whole range of human abilities. One did not only inhibit, consciously or unconsciously, the sexual drive vis-à-vis immediate family members. The capacity to inhibit spread across all drives, and conscious taboos have been placed on a wide range of behaviors.

All this had to do with the growth of cortical control over behavior at the expense of hormonal control, the final outcome of which was the neocortical function we call consciousness. The more that the species dispensed with hormonal control over sexual behavior, for example, the more it depended on learned controls, first of a physiological nature (my "avoidances") and later of both these and conscious controls (my "taboos"). These latter, however, had to have some of the same nature as both hormonal and learned physiological responses, that is, immediacy and effectiveness. In a sense, having replaced instincts by customs, the latter had to function in much the same way as instincts. Their advantage in adaptational terms lay in their range and flexibility. They could be extended, changed and manipulated very rapidly. But to the evolving hominids, those customs (taboos and more positive injunctions) which natural selection had fixed, had to be obeyed like the instinct they had deposed. External controls were not enough, and this is where the mechanism of guilt comes in. Guilt seems to be a highly evolved system of internal control directed towards learned customs. It has been argued that much learned behavior exhibits the same rigidity and predictability as instinct and indeed Russell & Russell (1961) argue that the term should be extended to cover it. A great deal of what the anthropologist calls "unconscious culture" (Kluckhohn 1941, 1943) and what Whiting (1959) has referred to as "learning other than by direct tuition" comes under this head. Hence a combination of rigid habit, unconscious assumptions, and conscious sanctions serves to replace instinct, and guilt can operate on all these mechanisms to keep the members of the group in line. The incest syndrome is an almost universal example of all these evolutionary products at work, hence its particular interest.

I concluded that the idea of a specific "anti-incest instinct" being in the wiring was erroneous but that "what has been produced is a syndrome of biological characteristics surrounding the sex drive, and that most important of evolutionary mechanisms—conscience" (Fox 1967a, p. 69). If, I argued, the natural selection theory of incest taboos was correct, that is, that they were necessary to prevent disorder and genetic stagnation, (Aberle et al. 1963), then the evolving animal had to develop "the capacity to inhibit personal desires in favour of group rules (Fox 1967a, p. 69)." This capacity obviously has more general application than just to intra-familiar sex, but what was intriguing was the idea that the control of sexuality and aggression in the family situation may well have been the origin of this tendency which is the root of truly human behavior generally. If this were so, then all the concern over incest in anthropological theory would indeed be warranted and the contention that the incest taboo was the basis of society would be proved—but not quite for the reasons previously advanced.

The human animal then evolved "a syndrome of genetically-determined behaviours which made the pubescent human in particular susceptible to guilt and other forms of conditioning surrounding the sexual-aggressive drives" (Fox 1967a, p. 70). "I have not," I admitted, "any direct evidence here, except to say that it seems easier to induce guilt over sex than over any other drive (hunger isn't in the picture), with aggression not far behind. And it is a physiological fact that cortical control of sexual activity distinguishes the higher apes and man from other animals."

The theories I was leaning on, those advanced by Slater (1959) and Aberle and his co-authors (1963), assumed much about the proto-hominids that did not tally with the growing knowledge we had about the nonhuman primates. Insofar as primates had any kind of group organization, I argued, it was based on a hierarchy and not on family groups. "The units involved were hierarchical males versus non-hierarchical males rather than 'fathers' versus 'sons' within a nuclear family" (Fox 1967a). Thus, while I was prepared to look with a friendly eye on the Freudian theory of the primal horde—as at least asking the right questions—I was disinclined to see the processes involved as pertaining to the family, which I saw as a later compromise arrangement. Thus the tendencies to inhibit sexual and aggressive drives were probably developed in this wider total group context, and later focused on the family when it developed and became the center of all these mechanisms, and in particular the process of internalization of the group norms; the process by which, to use the poetic language of Talcott Parsons, the objective norms of the group become the subjective need dispositions of the actor. Durkheim (1915), of course, saw this as basic to human social action, and saw collective rituals as necessary to the "reinforcement" of the internalization process whereby the collective conscience became a part of the individual conscience. But he did not ask what Lorenz has dubbed the basic evolutionary question, "How come?" Freud did, and we should pay more serious attention to his answer than we have (Freud 1952).

But to recapitulate: We have reached the point where the next line of attack is to link the growth of cortical control over sexual and aggressive behavior with the development of the neo-cortex generally and to link both to the conditions of social life that we assume to have characterized the evolving hominids. If our suppositions are correct, we should find that the expansion of the cortex is intimately linked with the process of sexual and aggressive inhibition.

To this end we should turn to the evolution of the brain. The hominid brain, it is often asserted, evolved very rapidly. The exact meaning and implication of this has been subjected to considerable scrutiny which we will examine later, but for the moment let us take this as a basic fact. The brain of *Australopithecus africanus* averaged 600 ccs some 1.75 million years ago—not much larger than the chimpanzee's. The brain of *Homo erectus,* by about 600,000 years ago, stood somewhere between 750 and 1200 ccs coming into the lower limits of the *sapiens* range. *Homo sapiens neanderthalensis* reaches the peak with an average somewhere between 1400 and 1700 ccs, and *Homo sapiens sapiens* manages to average about 1350 ccs, with a range of 900–2000 ccs. These are very rough estimates but the trend is clear enough: bigger and faster.

This rate of increase, which Caspari (1963) suggests is in the A or very rapid range, has been attributed to a number of factors. Thus Washburn has cited the use of tools and the advent of systematic hunting (1959, 1960, 1965). Lancaster (1968) stresses speech and development of true language, and so on. All these are *cultural* factors which stress what Montagu (1968) has called the "reciprocal feedback interaction" between cultural and somatic evolution. All of these factors, and Etkin (1954) would include the "nuclear family" as one, it is argued, put pressure on the evolving hominid groups such that the more able (cortically controlled) animals survived and reproduced. However, we are still a long way from anything very specific regarding the growing control of sex and aggression. We could say that in general the needs of a hunting, speaking, cooperating, tool-using animal would lead to this control. But is there not something else that puts into the wiring of the creature these features we have discussed?

It is at this point that sexual selection enters the picture, since with the argument poised at this stage I encountered the work of Michael Chance, first through a stray remark of his at the end of one of his articles (Chance 1962a). Commenting on the rapid evolution of the hominid brain he remarked that such rapidity probably required "some special form of breeding system." Turning to his other work (Chance & Mead 1953, Chance 1962b) I discovered what this form of breeding system was: one based on a hierarchy, or as he would prefer to say, "rank ordered social relations" (Chance 1967). This led me to elaborate, probably prematurely, the theory which brings us to the heart of our topic (Fox 1967b). Chance had put forward a theory to account for the fact that the higher primates had bigger and better brains than other mammals, and had suggested that the same theory might well apply to the protohominids. This theory was essentially to do with the development of inhibitions over sexual and aggressive behavior, and it linked these directly to the growth of the neocortex and increasing cortical control over these areas of behavior. Grafted onto the "tools, talk and hunting" syndrome it could tie up all the loose ends with breathtaking simplicity.

Let me briefly summarize Chance's argument. It is undoubtedly, he says, a sexual selection argument: "This is clearly a case of sexual selection as proposed by Darwin, involving the intra-sexual selection component as proposed by Huxley" (see Huxley 1914). His major premise is derived from Zuckerman (1932) and concerns the state of "constant mating provocation" that exists among primates in that the females are receptive for a longer period of the year and for a larger fraction of the estrous cycle than in any other mammal. The premise had to be questioned in the light of present knowledge (see Lancaster & Lee 1965), but for the moment we will grant it and quibble later. This constant provocation leads to constant competition among the males and the establishment of a breeding hierarchy. Chance was largely concerned with baboons and macaques in that these were, like our own ancestors, terrestrial savanna-dwelling primates and the ones about which most was known. The "classic" picture of the sociospatial system of a baboon-macaque troop is that of a concentric circle (for details see articles in DeVore 1965b, and Altmann 1965). In the center of the group are the large males and around them the females and immature infants. Ranged around this central core are the "subdominant" males who are candidates for places at the center. At the edges of the group are the "peripheral males": young animals who have left their mothers after about a year and older animals who have not made it to a more central position. These latter are the most vulnerable to predation, disease, and other factors that ensure a high death rate.

Among the central males a hierarchy is established with the alpha male taking precedence in the use of space, the obtaining of choice foods, and above all in the impregnation of females. As females come into estrus they may be mounted by subdominant males, as they may be when they approach menstruation, but at the peak of estrus they are taken over by the dominant male and copulate exclusively with him. The pair form a "consort relationship" which may last for a few days or a week. The period of consortship corresponds to the period of ovulation, and hence only the alpha male will pass on genes to the next generation.

His position will be constantly threatened, but once established the dominance hierarchy tends to be fairly stable, and is maintained by ritualized agonistic and deferential postures. In large troops more than one male will of course be involved in breeding, but again position in the hierarchy is the determining factor. The young males must try to work their way into the hierarchy and will gain a place either by displacing an incumbent, or by taking his place when he dies, or by leaving the group and trying elsewhere.

The survival of the individual male and his chances of success in breeding depend on his capacity to *equilibrate,* roughly speaking, his capacity to control his sexual and aggressive drives. "Equilibration demands of the animal an intensification of the control over its emotional responses, both facilitatory and inhibitory" (Chance 1962b, p. 125). Because of the number of contrasting stimuli presented and the number of rather close decisions that have to be made, *the successful animal has to control its emotional responses rather than simply act them out.* Chance then postulates that the enlargement of the neo-cortex was "an anatomical adaptation to the circumstances requiring an equilibrational response" (loc. cit.). (This is essentially my summary in Fox 1967b.)

The amagdaloid nucleus and its connections in particular control rage and other emotions, and this organ is more developed in primates than in any other mammals because, Chance is saying, to survive in the breeding arena of terrestrial primate society one controlled one's emotions or lost out. The "socionomic index" (following Carpenter 1942) is usually heavily in favor of males (on average 1 male to 4 females) and this points to the fact that uncontrolled males never make the hierarchy and either go to the peripheries of the group or leave it altogether. Chance's conclusion sums up the link between his concerns and mine. "We therefore conclude that the ascent of man has been due in part to a competition for social position, giving access to the trigonal sphere of social activity in which *success was rewarded by a breeding premium,* and that at some time in the past, a group of primates, by virtue of their pre-eminent adaptation to this element and consequent cortical enlargement, became pre-adapted for the full exploitation of the properties of the mammalian cortex" (p. 128, my italics). This exploitation included the development of tool making, hunting, language and other aspects stressed previously. If we then marry this to Chance's remark about the "special breeding structure" necessary for rapid cortical evolution, the picture we have of protohominid life is competitive and polygynous with the more dominant males having the "breeding premium" and so hurrying on the process of neo-cortical development. I have tried to summarize the qualities of the dominant male in the protohuman group as follows: controlled, cunning, cooperative, attractive to the ladies, good with the children, relaxed, tough, eloquent, skillful, knowledgeable and proficient and in self-defense and hunting. It also helps to have a high-ranking mother, it seems (Kawamura 1965, Kaufmann 1966, 1967, Koford 1963, Sade 1965, 1967).

I have been deliberately brief in this summary since an adequate and detailed account of the Chance thesis and its implications would take a book. As I have said, what is exciting about it is the possibility of somehow using it to tie up all the loose ends. Thus we were looking for something that would link the general human capacity for inhibition at various levels with the growth of the neo-cortex and the emotions of sex and aggression. The "syndrome of genetically-determined behaviours which made the pubescent animal in particular susceptible to guilt and other forms of conditioning surrounding the sexual-aggressive drives" could be summed up as Chance's "equilibration" process which developed in response to pressures to control sex and aggression and hence to selection in favor of those animals with greater capacity to inhibit drives. I concluded: "The whole process of enlarging the neo-cortex to take-off point was based on a competition between the dominant and sub-dominant males in which those which survived were those best able to control and inhibit, and hence time, their responses. Here then are the beginnings of deferred gratification, conscience and guilt, spontaneous inhibition of drives, and many other features of a truly human state" (Fox 1967b). Included among the "truly human features," of course, would be the extreme sensitivity to matters of sex and aggression in the maturing animal when faced with dominant males and their females; that is, the elements of my incest "avoidance." And with the growth of language and conscious rules, the capacity for guilt over these sensitive areas. (But note that while avoidance can be learned, guilt has to be taught.)

All this reasoning fits in with the doubts I had expressed about incest theories based on the "nuclear family hypothesis." The basic fact of the hierarchy was allowed for and indeed became central, and much about human incestuous behavior made more sense when viewed in this evolutionary framework than when it was linked to the "preservation" of the nuclear family. I do not want to go into the detailed logic of the working out of this argument here, and it should suffice to say that arguments which lump all incest together probably fog the issue. They attempt to answer the question "why incest taboos?" as though incest were a homogeneous phenomenon, which it is not. (A point made strongly by Count in 1958 and reiterated by myself in 1962.) The three possibilities involve different considerations. As far as we can tell from the monkey evidence, there is, for example, little or no incest between mother and son (Imanishi 1965, Sade 1965). The mother is to her son a dominant animal, and mating requires that the female partner be subdominant. The possibilities of mating between siblings are problematical, and it seems that when a young male manages to get into the hierarchy he may or may not mate with his sisters. This depends largely on demographic factors. (See Slater 1959 for similar considerations regarding proto-human groups.) On the other hand the possibility of the father's mating with his daughters is quite high. The father is a dominant animal in control of all the females; the son/father is subdominant and will only get to the females (*any* females) eventually if he learns to control his sexual approaches to his father's females and his aggression toward the father himself. The father's control of his daughters, while at first for mating purposes, at some point passed over into his control of them for political purposes. In either case the son had to be careful.

I am here using the Freudian primal-family-horde language simply to be graphic. As we have seen, the issue is not fathers vs. sons but dominant males of the group vs. sub-dominant males of the group. Fathers and sons as social role players do not exist in our primate groups (although *mothers* and sons do) and we must constantly remember that it is the structure of the total group that we must consider.

Loosely then, we can say that the picture that emerges here is one of the evolution of human sexual behavior in a dominance context and in the context of the total breeding group. The young male had to be sexy and aggressive, but he had to be able to control his sexuality and aggression until such time as he was mature and could take his full place in the hierarchy. (Initiation, I suggested, was really all to do with this problem.) He had to be susceptible to conditioning in the areas of sex and aggression to a high degree in order to survive, and once a permanent assignment of mates became the rule he met the most intensive "trial" of his equilibrational facilities within the immediate family circle. The upshot of this selection process was to produce a creature who was capable of becoming extremely guilty about his sexuality and aggression toward those who were immediately dominant and nurturant toward him. What is more, this process, essentially concentrated on the breeding system, was itself responsible for the growth of the neo-cortex and hence of control and inhibition and eventually consciousness itself.

There evolved then what I described as a 'package deal' in which the following all developed as functions of each other: control over sex and aggression, intelligence and consciousness, feelings about status and personal well being, group loyalty, conscience and guilt, sensitivity to incestuous impulses, identification with and rebellion against the older generation, possessiveness over females and sexual jealousy, the desire for variety in sex life, and many others. All these are part and parcel of the evolution of the brain; part of the "feedback reciprocal interaction." If we include the selective effects of tools, hunting and language, by linking them to the breeding process as further criteria of dominance and hence conferring a "breeding privilege," then our sexual selection theory is complete, perhaps too complete.

Difficulties with the Theory

In this section I will outline some of the difficulties with, and objections to, the theory.

1. The first difficulty is one I have explored before but about which a little more can now be said. It involves the distinction between two different kinds of baboon social systems which I labeled Baboon 1 (common baboons and macaques) and Baboon 2 (hamadryas and gelada baboons). Chance concentrated on the former which has the kind of system we have already described (the "concentric circle"). Baboon 2, on the other hand, lives in large troops of up to four hundred animals the subunits of which are one-male groups or harems. These groups consist of one mature adult male with several females and sometimes a "junior partner," a kind of apprentice younger male who is tolerated by the dominant male. The dominant male herds his females, threatening any males that approach them and chasing them if they stray too far. He delivers a characteristic punishment, the neck bite, to inattentive females. The whole troop only comes together closely at night for sleeping; during the day the effective unit is the one-male group.

What is the significance of this behavior? On the Fox extension of the Chance theory we have to assume that the breeding system of the hominids before and during the transition to humanity fulfilled the criteria laid down by Chance for the rapid evolution of the neo-cortex. That is, it had to be based on sexual competition and a breeding hierarchy, this being the only kind of system that would select out the more cortical males and totally exclude the others. So the question becomes: To what extent can we say that the mating patterns of the pre-, proto-, and true hominids during the Pliocene and early Pleistocene measured up to these criteria? We know next to nothing about the Pliocene of course with regard to hominid fossils, but we do know that it was a long period of drought. I noted in the 1967 paper that Napier (1964), Campbell (1966) and Crook & Gartlan (1966) had independently come to the conclusion that primate social systems were adaptations to ecological niches and that presumably over time these adaptations become fixed. They agreed that the hominids had moved from the forest to the forest edge, through the woodland savannah to the dry savannah. This latter move, during the Pliocene, was crucial, since in terms of the ecological adaptation theory it involved a move from the Baboon 1 to the Baboon 2 type of social system. If we assume that the evolving hominids had to make a similar adaptation, then the question becomes: Does a social system of Baboon type 2 meet the criteria Chance put forward for a system conducive to rapid brain growth?

Some factors are against this. For a start there is not constant mating provocation since breeding is markedly seasonal, another ecological adaptation like the one-male group itself. There is no hierarchy in the Baboon 1 sense either. On the other hand there is considerable sexual antagonism. But since all mating takes place within the one-male group, during the breeding season males are not competing with each other as they might be in a Baboon 1 situation. Another major difference lies in the way harems are formed. In 1967 I noted that we were very much in the dark over this, but Kummer's work now presents us with the startling picture of the subadult males kidnapping and adopting year-old females and behaving maternally to them. These females eventually become the harem of their foster father. He later takes on an apprentice who might also adopt young females and so on (Kummer 1968).

Is there really a problem however? For one thing it is doubtful that the hominids would have made this particular adaptation since in their anatomical and cortical development they were taking a very different path from the baboons. But even if they had adopted the one-male group system, some of the same features would have been at work. The differences are not as startling as they appear at first. The major emphasis in pointing out the differences has been on the permanence of the mating relationship in the one-male group as opposed to the transience of the consort relationship in Baboon 1. But this is more apparent than real. In small groups at least of Baboon 1 type, the alpha male continues to be very much in command of the females even when he is not mating with them. They are all, in a sense, his females, and he tolerates juniors mounting them only when the females are not in peak estrus. In a large group this may be slightly different in that several consort relationships will be taking place at once with the high ranking males possessing the females. At the limits of their ranges in areas of scarce food, however, Baboon 1 troops usually approximate the one-male group situation.

In either case, the basic truth remains that the young males have to sit on the outskirts of the group and work their way back in. In Baboon 1 they have to find a place in the hierarchy by becoming tolerated as "cadets" and then moving into the breeding system. In Baboon 2 they have to work their way back in as apprentices. In either case equilibration is needed, and if the protohominids adopted either system this would have been just as true for them.

We have always to remember, that insofar as the hominids ended up in the early pleistocene as potential men while the baboons were stuck with being baboons and have stayed that way, that it must have been a very different creature that came out of the forests in the first place. Too much emphasis on the specialized adaptations of baboons like the gelada and hamadryas is perhaps misplaced. The protohominids were surely adapting to the same conditions, but they were adapting with a different anatomy and with the growing use of predation and tools. In reconstructing the evolution of their social behavior, therefore, we had best stick to more general features; and of these, hierarchical competition for a breeding privilege remains the most general. Each primate species, including our ancestors, makes its own kind of adaptation within the general framework of this competitive system.

2. We now come to the problem of the chimpanzee. Reynolds (1966ab) argues that we cannot simply dismiss the chimpanzee while espousing with admiration the baboon. The chimpanzee is a higher ape and is closely related to us while the baboon is a monkey and is not; chimpanzees and man share a close common ancestor and we are very alike. If we are to choose a model for our ancestor then why not the chimpanzee? The answer usually given is that the chimpanzee stayed in the forest while our ancestor moved out onto the savannas. A problem arises since, if our hypothesis is correct, how does the chimpanzee with its promiscuous breeding system come to have such a relatively large brain? Clearly its abilities are in excess of its achievements.

Perhaps we should take seriously the Kortlandt & Kooij (1963) notion that the ancestral chimpanzee, like the ancestral man, took to the woodland savanna, but that the chimpanzee went back to the forest lacking tools and permanent bipedalism, while the protohominids soldiered on. This idea might have been thought fanciful, but recent Japanese work suggests that the chimpanzee formerly had a much wider distribution and did indeed live in open territory. It is also clear from this work that when faced with open country the chimpanzee groups organize themselves very tightly in obvious expectation of attacks from predators (Itani 1968). The rather free and easy existence they live in the forest is an existence of refuge groups that have escaped predation and may not be a good clue to their evolution. Groups in savanna country, for example, exclude young, subadult males.

Reynolds thinks that the hominid ancestor must have been like the chimpanzee, but that he became adapted permanently to life on the plains.

He sees various chimpanzee-like patterns as pre-adaptations to a plains life. But here we must be wary. If the chimpanzee got his large brain on the savanna, then the chimpanzee we see today is not the one who lived in the miocene forests nor could he be like our putative ancestor. We cannot project the contemporary chimpanzee back into our ancestry any more than we can the gelada baboon. But it may well be that our ancestor was in many ways more chimp-like than baboon-like; for example, a semi-brachiator and knuckle walker rather than a quadrupedal branch runner. Thus we must look to the chimp with hope but caution, for the creature that emerged from the forests was of his stamp. Our ancestral adaptations to the woodlands and plains could have been functionally the same as the baboons without the necessity of the same biobehavioral mechanisms. A relatively sharp birth *peak,* for example, could have substituted for seasonal breeding without losing the year-round breeding potential. And as Reynolds suggests, exploratory male bands such as one finds in chimpanzee populations could have become the foraging and hunting units. None of this need have involved the evolution of a one-male group system with its specialized adaptations to extreme arid conditions. This may have been the correct path for nonhunting vegetarians, but to an animal more like a hunting chimpanzee it could have been equally a dead end. This does not mean that the subunits of the protohuman group were not polygynous families. It is highly likely that they were at some point. But the assignment of mates must have been on a very different basis than was the case with the sexually dimorphous, seasonal-breeding, desert baboon. For a start female baboons mature at roughly twice the rate of males which is an excellent way of preserving a polygynous system despite equal sex ratios. Human systems have to try to achieve analogues of this by artificial means, such as lowering the age of marriage of females and raising that of males, if polygyny on any scale is to be attempted.

The trend in human evolution would then have been polygynous and competitive if the Chance theory is correct, but not on the same basis as is found in the desert baboons. The modified chimpanzee model is more attractive, but again this can only give us clues. The important thing about human polygyny is that it required at some point the *assignment* of mates. Men had to work out systems for the allocation and control of women. The motivation to control women for breeding purposes, if we are correct, must have been deep in the creature, but there were no specialized biobehavioral adaptations for "harem formation." Sex ratios being equal, men would have to compete under some set of rules for the available females. It is the transition from the competition without rules to competition with rules that is our concern here, but this transition would not have been necessary had the hominid line developed a highly specialized system like that of the desert baboons. Again, all we need to assume are very *general* primate characteristics for our protohominid ancestors. For in behavior as in anatomy, the strength of our lineage lay in a relatively generalized structure. It was precisely because we did *not* specialize like our baboon cousins that we had to *contrive* solutions involving the control and exchange of females.

3. Any contrivance of this kind however, depended on those capacities to classify and to act according to rules that Lévi-Strauss stresses and that, like the capacity for speech itself, must lie in the brain (Lenneberg 1967). Much of the theory depends on the "rapid" evolution of the forebrain, and this is itself a controversial issue. Caspari, as we see, put this in the very rapid range of evolution, but Count (1964) would argue that man's forebrain is not disproportionately large and that "in exponential terms man's brain is only slightly greater than the ape's. Two more binary fissions of the brain cells would advance the chimpanzee's brain to human size . . ." (p. 156). Holloway (1966) argues persuasively against taking measures of cranial capacity as a sole guide to function. It is the number of components and subsystems that count and not the size per se. That the components have increased is not doubted, but it is impossible to say for fossil man whether this increase was rapid or remarkable since cranial capacity is the only reliable measure we have. However, some authorities like Kotchetkova (1960) detect certain specific differences in the development of areas of the brain between the *Australopithecus* and *Homo erectus* stages. The areas which the latter gained most over the former were those concerned with sound signalling and the analysis of objects by touch. This is the tools and language development that we have already spoken of, and it took place during the crucial breakthrough from ape-size brain to man-size brain. The development of these areas must therefore have been relatively rapid. Whether or not this required a special kind of breeding system is still a moot point of course.

4. A more devastating consideration is whether the kind of breeding system that Chance posits in truth exists. We have already seen that not all baboons have year-round breeding, and that this applies to Baboon 1 as well as Baboon 2 (Lancaster & Lee 1965). Hence one of the main props of the theory, constant sexual provocation, is weakened. This was derived in any case from the work of Zuckerman (1932) on captive hamadryas in the London Zoo under "concentration camp conditions." This view of primate society as based on constant sex warfare is not now thought to be adequate, although Altmann (1967, p. 56) has recently defended it on the grounds that sex-like activity goes on all the time even if actual copulation does not. What is true is that *dominance* quarrels continue and that *status provocation* rather than sexual provocation may be the guiding factor.

However, if constant sexual provocation is out, then we are left with the creation of a breeding elite as the remaining crucial aspect of the theory, since it is through the creation of this elite that sexual selection and shifts in gene frequency toward the more equilibrated end of the scale occur. But is there a breeding elite? The idea has been challenged by Mitchell (1966ab). I can do no better than put it in his own words (personal communication):

> 1. A female reaches sexual maturity earlier (around age 4) and retains reproductive potential over a longer period of time than does a male. Menopause and death coincide and life expectancy upon reaching maturity is about 8 more years.
>
> 2. In the male, "sociological maturity" is delayed perhaps 3 years past physiological maturity. That is, a male will not begin to mate until his entrance into the dominance hierarchy, at perhaps 8, and may continue to be dominant (and thus mate) for perhaps 4 years. During this time his dominance will rise and fall, with concurrent fluctuations in his reproductive contribution.
>
> The difference between such a system, and, say, a system of human monogamy is this: it is as though a man were to cluster his production of offspring in one or two years, by different females rather than to spread it out over many years by the same female. The females, of course, will then in later years be similarly impregnated by other males, during the short reproductive time of those males. In any given year a minority of the males will be doing a majority of the breeding, but at another time another younger, minority will be breeding, and so on. Nearly every normal male will have a chance to contribute to the next generation. In a system of this nature . . . any reproductive inequalities are *not* the result of the mating system.

In coasting back through the literature I have not seen this point made and a lot of the discussion assumes that the system sorts out the "best" genes through the breeding structure. Mitchell would maintain that it does not. Most normal males eventually breed—what Chance and others have ignored is the temporal dimension—but this does not mean they make *equal* contributions to the gene pool or that all their offspring will be either viable or successful.

What remains true is that at any point in time certain males will be doing much *more* of the breeding than others, so that although all males may eventually have an equal chance to breed at all, some will be more equal than others. Even so, DeVore (1965a) concludes that "one should be very cautious in making inferences about selective advantage and dominance status" (p. 287). But in a comment on DeVore's data in Beach (1965), Benson E. Ginsburg says:

> It seems to me there is a genetically important aspect of this system of mating. It is a system in which instead of all the males contributing to the gene pool of the population at once, only a relatively small number of males have their genes tried out with different females over a period of years. Then another group of males moves in, so the gene frequencies in the population keep changing. It could be that this system of mating by itself has a selective

> advantage because it provides a situation where some genes are "tried out" in all different combinations. That is, the most frequent genes come from a small number of males, and these are "tried out" in a variety of combinations with the genes of the larger population of breeding females, and then another cycle of males phases in. This is quite a different population mating structure than if all mature males were mating at once, and this, in itself, may confer some advantage upon the population in a long-term evolutionary sense (p. 287).

Here is a theory which marries long-term evolutionary advantage to the particular kind of mating structure Mitchell envisages. If the long-term advantage were in the direction of increased cortical control, then the breeding structure would still contribute to this, although in a radically different manner from that envisaged by Chance and myself. We saw the system essentially as producing a "breeding elite" with the majority of males being only peripheral breeders or even nonbreeders. But this may be based on a misconception of the breeding system as we have seen. In fact as we now know, males are very migratory and probably end up breeding *somewhere,* as I noted in the 1967 paper. More information is coming in on this now which promises to be very interesting, and it seems species differ in the degree to which this happens. In fact males who leave one group through a failure to achieve a place in the hierarchy can end up as Alpha males in other groups! Mitchell points out that DeVore's material suggests that males who are individually the most dominant do not necessarily make the hierarchy and eventually migrate.

The model that emerges is one in which, in each monkey band, as the 4 year olds come up to challenge for places in the hierarchy, only some make it while the others leave the band altogether (see the beautiful demonstration by Kaufmann 1967). Those who leave may be individually very dominant and may succeed better in other bands, perhaps because they get attention (Chance 1967). This suggests a "lost generation" theory, because it will be the next wave of youngsters who will take over from the aging members of the hierarchy.

However, it is again not all that clear. The work of Vanderbergh (1967) suggests a high death rate among the four-year old males, both from tetanus in wounds inflicted in fights and also infected wounds received while running recklessly about on the edges of the group. The sexually mature but subdominant males tend to be very agitated, to neglect food, to suffer from malnutrition, and to be constantly running to avoid being savaged by the members of the hierarchy. That the death toll among them can rise as high as 80 per cent is not surprising. Not all of them leave to join other bands, and for some isolated groups (as on the open savannas for example) there may be nowhere else to go. The socionomic index remains heavily in favor of males in all known groups. We still need more data on this, but in those cases where we have it, it does appear that some rather savage selection may be going on during the breeding season and that the victims are the maturing males challenging for places in the hierarchy. If this is so, then the sexual selection theory still has a chance. But the objections have to be noted.

5. A serious objection that could be raised has to do with the rate at which the proposed changes took place. The essential leap took place between the late *Australopithecine* stage and the full development of *Homo erectus*, perhaps over a period of half a million years at most. Why would there suddenly, in evolutionary terms, have been such an extraordinary increase in the rate of sexual selection over this period? For that is what is involved. The other higher primates took several million years to achieve their relatively large brains, but with the hominids there was this sudden upsurge. If sexual selection had only been continuing at the old rate, then there is no reason why the brain should have expanded as it did. If sexual selection is the leading factor, then there must have been this tremendous rate of increase. Is this feasible?

One has to consider a number of related factors here. We have made the control functions of the neo-cortex central to the theory, but of course the growth of inhibitory processes, as J. Z. Young has pointed out (1965) is also essential to the development of memory storage, and the large forebrain has to do with memory storage as much as control over sex and aggression. Also, it was the hand and speech areas that grew fastest, which suggests that the best communicators, manipulators and memorizers were being selected for. If these qualities were in the forefront of selection, along with control and effective use of sex and aggression, then the picture painted earlier of the type being selected for has some plausibility. But was the selection sexual? It we assume that the creature was basically primate-like in its competitive and hierarchical tendencies, then the advent of systematic hunting and wielding of weapons, however crude, must have made for a period of fantastic tension in the social relationships within the troop. There is no question that the young baboons of the troop would kill their elders if they got the chance, and the elders do in fact kill the younger ones who challenge them. A great deal of the talk about the ritualization of aggression in animals like baboons misses the point that ritualization only works once it is clear that force won't, or alternatively when force has already established the dominance rank order of the band. Hunting would have completely reorganized the selective pressures at the same time that it put weapons into the hands of the males. (For the effects of hunting on evolution, see Lee & DeVore 1968, parts 5, 6 and 7.) During the transitional "pre-rule" period, it is therefore highly likely that selection was sexual and ruthless, with only the more cortical and aggressive males succeeding in contributing appreciably to the gene pool. Once selection had had the effect of crossing the "culture gap" and producing a brain that could make, communicate and obey rules, then the creature could devise systems to mitigate the conflicts (still inherent) by which this state had been achieved, thus slowing down the rate of ruthless selection. Among these new systems kinship and initiation were the most important. We must of course add the selection pressures favoring neotony (Róheim 1968, Montagu 1965, pp. 167–183) which themselves would produce larger brains, and the physical problems of increasing bipedalism which would tend toward earlier birth because of the narrowing of the pelvis in females. All these factors are related; but the differential growth of certain key areas of the brain noted by Kotchetkova (1960) does suggest that selection not only for size but for *specific abilities,* such as those we have outlined, was taking place. It is not unreasonable therefore to persist in the sexual selection theory, although of course all evidence here is indirect.

That such a form of selection can be very efficacious in rapidly fixing new traits in a small population is confirmed by the work of Suarez and Ackerman (1971). They are concerned with the genetic consequences of breeding based on "social dominance"—the form of breeding we have been concerned with—and they maintain that one of the possible evolutionary consequences of such a system is "the intensity with which sexual selection could operate on autosomal genes associated with male dominance" (p. 221). While acknowledging that dominance is polygenetic, they make the assumption that it is controlled at a single locus with but two alleles. In an inbreeding population, they conclude, "If a beneficial mutation occurs in the most dominant male, the rate at which it spreads through the breeding males in subsequent generations is a function of the number of sexually mature, nonpregnant females in the group. Nevertheless, in groups of any realistic size ($n < 250$) the mutant allele will become fixed in all breeding males by either the fifth or sixth generation" (p. 221). One does not, of course, have to assume that dominance is so controlled, but what this model means is that any of the various features contributing to dominance could be rapidly fixed in this way. The optimal time is six generations, but the optimal conditions for this degree of rapidity will not always be met, and the cumulation of many beneficial mutations would be necessary as the criteria of dominance became more complex. Nevertheless, it seems that sexual selection could indeed be the mechanism responsible for relatively rapid genetic change of the kind we envisage.

Suarex and Ackerman conclude that the most important factor governing the rate of genetic change is the probability of a female being in estrus. "As this parameter increases, the effect of dominance becomes reduced; as it decreases the effect of dominance becomes more pronounced" (p. 222). Which brings us to our next point.

6. There is one problem which I include for its intrinsic interest, and because it has been raised (Etkin 1954) as an objection to the Chance theory: the problem of the evolution of the female neo-cortex. According to Etkin the theory applies only to the male neo-cortex and does nothing

to explain the parallel evolution of the female. This issue is linked to the problem of what happened to the estrous cycle in the human female. Insofar as cortical control grew in relation to hormonal control, the hominid female was freed from either periods of anestrus or periods of sexual mania followed by unreceptivity such as occur during the menstrual cycle of subhuman primates. There is much dispute about the cycling of sexual receptivity in the human female, and evidence is hard to come by since it is largely subjective; there are no obvious external colorations or swellings as in baboons or chimpanzees. Also, the human female does not have obvious periods of mania at the peak of ovulation. One popular theory of relative sexual receptivity in the human female suggests that it is at its height just before and just after menstrual bleeding (Ford & Beach 1952). This, however, may have more to do with cultural factors such as taboos on copulation during menstruation. Michael (1968), comparing his own work on macaques with that of Udry & Morris (1968), found that in terms of copulatory success there was an almost exact correlation between the performance of macaque and human females, with the height of success occurring at ovulation. This makes more sense than the other theory, since it is clearly to the species' advantage to have most sexual activity occurring at ovulation in order to ensure impregnation; ovulation is brief, lasting perhaps only forty-eight hours. Birth control would have been no use to an expanding species. Also, other factors point to the continuity of experience from subhuman to human females despite the growing cortical control. For example, the female sense of smell with regard to odors like musk is fantastically increased (up to 100,000 times) during ovulation (Le Magnen 1953) while their perceptual abilities are diminished during the period just before menstruation, a period also associated with poor motor performance and emotional disturbance (see, for example, Kopell et al. 1969, Hamburg et al. 1968).

All this suggests that the estrous cycle still operates at a very profound level in the human female. Cortical control is there, of course, and helps to even out the responses of the female and allow her to channel and control them; but the basic hormonal changes and their behavioral concomitants still exist. Discussion then of the "disappearance" of the estrous cycle in our species needs to take these facts into account.

The question is whether there is any need for a special theory to account for the growth of the neo-cortex in females. Morris (1967) thinks it has to do with the evolution of pair bonding; Jay (1968) thinks it had to do with the general move towards permanent families and social order which pronounced estrus would disrupt. But she also notes that families of a permanent kind are found among primates which nevertheless have periods of heat. This is essentially a problem that geneticists could help solve, but it seems that if highly cortical males were being selected, then the benefits of this selection would be passed onto female offspring. But it is also possible that females were contributing more actively to this process. We saw that high-ranking mothers gave their sons an unfair advantage in life. If the characteristics of dominance are primarily genetic then it may be that the more cortical male derives his advantages as much from his high-ranking mother as his dominant father. If this were true then it would of course help to speed up the process. (Note that in Kaufmann's study [1967] the only one of the four-year olds who got a regular place in the hierarchy was EY who was the brother of another dominant DW, and both were sons of the highest ranking female 119.) We need more information on the characteristics of high-ranking females. If something other than sexiness is involved in their rank then it may be that they are making a positive contribution to the selection process which would help the speeding-up process that we have envisaged. But it could just be sexiness, because, as we saw in the previous section, an increase in the average length of the period of female sexual receptivity may well have *increased* the dominance factor in mating which in turn would have led to a faster rate of genetic change.

7. This raises a final serious question. The reason the son of a high-ranking mother finds it easier to get into the hierarchy may have nothing to do with genetics. His constant association with a dominant female means that (*a*) he is tolerated for a long time by the dominant males: he is not peripheralized as early as the other males, and he is familiar to the members of the hierarchy, and (*b*) he is constantly the recipient of deference behavior directed towards his mother so that he becomes, like a young nobleman, habituated to this. Since comportment counts for so much in the elaborate bluff of dominance interaction, this demeanor of habitual dominance must stand him in good stead. Also, the other animals will be habituated to defer to him. It may be that his genetics have nothing to do with this. If we add here the work of the Harlows (see summary in Harlow & Harlow 1965), then another dimension is clear: it is the confident and well socialized monkey, that is, the one that has stayed with its mother the longest, that will best be able to treat the world with confidence and perform well sexually.

We can phrase the problem as the conflict between genotypic and phenotypic explanations. On the one hand it is assumed that the characteristics of dominance are inherited, on the other that they are learned. Of course, it is obvious that both factors are involved, but it remains a problem whether the animal that is phenotypically the most dominant differs genotypically from the others. Experiments could be designed, with artificial impregnation, to decide this, but they would be rather elaborate and long-term if done with primates.

The Theory Revised

I will here try to summarize the state of the theory in the light of the objections.

The point of the theory was to link the seemingly obvious fact of the rapid evolution of the brain in the hominids in the early Pleistocene (that is, over the last two million years) with selection pressures for increased cortical control over behavior and to link these to a particular kind of breeding system which provided the mechanism for the rapid development. It was assumed that hunting and its consequences were the most important selection pressures and that these required increased manual dexterity and communicative ability as well as facilitation of the sexual and aggressive drives combined with their finer control. The breeding system involved a hierarchical arrangement in which some males had a breeding privilege and others were excluded. This was a system that would take advantage of any mutations favoring greater cortical development (originally an expansion of the amygdala) by having their bearers take positions of dominance and pass on their genes more or less exclusively to the next generation. In subsequent generations, again, it would be the more cortically developed males who would dominate the breeding process, thus continuing the trend and shifting gene frequencies in the direction of larger and more complex brains.

Let me sum up the difficulties:

1. This does not take account of different possibilities for the type of breeding system, for example, those of Baboon 2 type.
2. The evolving hominids were probably more chimpanzee-like than baboon-like, but the contemporary chimpanzee has the largest relative brain size of all nonhuman primates without having a breeding system like the baboon.
3. The evolution of the brain need not have been remarkable or rapid.
4. The kind of breeding system with a "reproductive monopoly" in the hands of dominant males may not in fact exist.
5. There must have been an implausible intensification of the breeding process in order for the breeding system as such to be the main agent of change.
6. The theory does not account for the growth of the female neo-cortex.
7. Dominance capacity may result from socialization experience not from genetics.

The answers to these objections have been given, but it is obvious that the theory needs some modification, and even more obvious that we lack a great deal of the data needed to answer many of the questions raised.

In my 1967 paper I objected to attempts to pin down the protohominids to any particular form of breeding system, particularly on a direct analogy with savanna baboons. This is to deny to the hominids their most important characteristic: generality and flexibility. Since they occupied many niches they were probably experimenting with many forms. Those in the woodland edges may have been relatively loosely organized, while those in the open savannas must have had a tighter organization. Those that really took to hunting seriously must have tightened up even more, while some probably never have made the leap into hominization. All we need to assume is that the breeding system of the more successful populations was competitive and hierarchical. The relevance of the primate data lies not so much in the models of our early social organization that it provides, as in the information it gives us on the primate biogram, many aspects of which we are heir to. We wove this primate biogram into our own very peculiar path of behavioral evolution and it may be the fact that we were *not* doing the things which seem so adaptive for baboons in their various ecological niches that got us where we are.

Let us hazard the following speculations on the Australopithecine stage during the early Pleistocene. (During the Pliocene, Australopithecine adaptations were probably largely governed by seed-eating (see Jolly 1970).) There must have been many populations of the species living in relatively isolated groups differentially engaged in hunting and gathering activity. The internal structure of these groups we cannot know, and it is highly unlikely that it was uniform from group to group since different niches were involved. It was, however, competitive and hierarchical, and at this stage there were no institutions to cope with aggressive young males or to assign mates according to rules. Each group would therefore inbreed considerably, thus fixing certain characteristics that went with dominance. These were the characteristics of the good hunter previously mentioned, all dependent on an increasingly large amygdala and an expanding neocortex. These were characteristics that natural selection would have favored anyway, but their relatively rapid fixation was facilitated by the breeding system. If young and aggressive males who were not killed, however, left their bands and went off elsewhere in search of breeding success, then a "Sewall Wright" effect would have served to speed up the evolutionary advance of the brain even more (Wright 1939). Migrating males would have provided the necessary hybridization that would have pooled the specializations of the various isolated breeding populations, especially if these migrating males were the most dominant. This method of hybridization, however, was somewhat haphazard, and it may be that local exogamy, with the advent of rules and categories, would have served to systematize the process even more. (See Ginsburg 1968 for a discussion of such a breeding system.) But this was later. The stage envisaged here was pre-institutional, although we can see how the foundations of certain institutions were being laid. It was the stage in which the hominids were, through their newly acquired hunting way of life, adapting to the fluctuating exigencies of the Pleistocene. Given their generalized structure and relative disadvantage in the struggle for existence with the carnivores, their only hope for success lay in the expansion of cultural means of adaptation (such as tools, weapons, shelter, fire, and language) and this in turn depended on the expansion of the cortex, which, as we have seen, took place primarily in the relevant areas. It also depended on keeping up a certain level of aggressiveness. This point is beautifully made by Ardrey (1961), but he fails to emphasize that, as important as the facilitation of aggression was, the all important control, or *inhibition* of aggression that we have been stressing here was just as significant. It was the equilibrating animal that eventually made it to the top and so dominated the genetic structure of the next generation.

This intensification stage, then, was able to take advantage of the breeding system to fix rapidly those characteristics that were necessary for a more effective exploitation of cultural adaptation. If we wish to hold to Chance's version of the theory, then we could maintain that without such a breeding system natural selection could not have operated rapidly enough to effect the spectacular expansion that in fact occurred. The version of the breeding structure proposed above takes account of the natural selection pressures operating, but adds the sexual selection system of hierarchical breeding as part of the mechanism by which the rapid change took place. Once we accept that the breeding populations were not closed but that periodic (or rather episodic) hybridization took place, then the whole scheme has considerable plausibility. It has the right balance of inbreeding and outbreeding to avoid too much inbreeding on the one hand, and too much panmixia on the other.

This then would take us to the point where the essential breakthrough from simian to human cranial capacity and complexity occurred. We have to note, with Geertz (1965), that cultural factors were involved in this breakthrough and that therefore we cannot make a sharp distinction between nature and culture in the way Lévi-Strauss does (although he has retracted his more extreme position; see Lévi-Strauss 1969, pp. xxix–xxx). Cultural factors were in some way *responsible* for the breakthrough since man had committed himself to cultural adaptation and hence to dependency on the neo-cortex.

By the time a cranial capacity of 900–1000 ccs was reached, there was surely enough in the way of cortical control of rage and sex, memory storage, and at least the ability to name and classify in a rudimentary way through sound signalling, for genuine institutions, that is, rule governed activities, to appear. But in the same way that the forebrain does not obviate the activities of the lower brain but amplifies and controls them, so institutions did not abolish old primate patterns, they built on them and, again, controlled them.

The period of intensification had fixed even more rigorously into the pattern of hominid behavior certain primate features such as competition among males, cooperation between males (for hunting), and exclusion of young but sexually mature males from the breeding system until such time as they could work their way back into it. What hunting added in particular was a division of labor between males and females and between the men themselves. The male-female division of labor has to do with vegetable foods which the women gather and animal protein obtained by the men. The trading of these products, essential to the diet of the omnivorous hominid, is probably at the root of a truly human society since it required a quite different set of relationships between men and women than had existed previously. Men no longer needed women for sexual purposes only, and women no longer needed men for protection only, but each had a vested interest in the products of the other's labor. (For the relative contributions of vegetable [female] food, and animal [male] food to the hunter's diet, see Lee 1968). This was a very different situation from the free-for-all food gathering of the prehunting stage. Cooperation and competition among the males also took a different turn, since lone food-gathering was replaced by cooperative hunting, and this meant that men needed allies both within the band and even in other bands. Thus the hunting way radically altered the content of social relationships in the band, even if their general structure remained the same. It is the tension between the old structure and the new content that lies behind much of the "human situation" even as we know it today, in fact more so as we know it today since we have divorced politics from breeding and ruthlessly removed our economic systems from their primitive hunting base.

The crucial organizational change can perhaps best be described by saying that whereas all primates have *ecologies,* only the human primate has an *economy.* The essence of an economy is *property,* that is, *things that can be exchanged.* The most primitive of these exchanges is that of vegetables and meat between the women and the men, a change which forced men to change their relationships with women into something other than a mere 'breeding/dominance' encounter. The next most important exchange was probably that of specialist services among the men. And the third was the exchange of women among the men—again a result of the economy forced upon the hominids by their adaptive pattern and facilitated by their capacity for inhibition, their ability to follow rules, and their ability to categorize and remember genealogies—all of which followed from, and were in reciprocal feedback interaction with, the growth of the neo-cortex, itself a product partly of the system of breeding which determined the shape of the social structure of the early hominid bands.

From Breeding Systems to Kinship Systems

In this section I want to return to the problem of the incest taboo, exogamy and kinship systems, which was our starting point.

As to incest, the human patterns make much more sense when seen as an end product of an hierarchical system than when viewed as adaptive processes within the nuclear family. Females tend to be under the control of older males. A young male does not mate with his mother anyway, for reasons advanced earlier, and will be prevented from mating with his sisters by the older males who have first claim on them. What is more, he is "programmed" to learn sexual avoidances and guilts on this score since this is precisely what equilibration is about, and he has been selected as an equilibrating animal. These are general processes to do with the relationship between older and younger males and females; they are 'focused' on the family since this is where the little human primate has to learn to equilibrate with respect to his own father and his mother and sisters. The young male is a creature that has built into it by several million years of natural selection a readiness to control very rapidly and easily its sexual responses to females and its aggressive responses to older males. These flare up again at puberty, when the control has to be re-asserted by the older males. In the human situation the older males do not kill off or drive away the young males; they initiate them. Initiation is the great human answer to this age-old problem. It is our cortical and symbolic way of dealing with the re-incorporation of the young primate into the hierarchy as a cadet, and of controlling his sexual and aggressive drives and bringing him under the dominance of the older males. Next to kinship it is the most important of the truly human institutions, but my brief is to deal with kinship so initiation will have to be left aside.

With the father-daughter relationship we have more of a problem. The father is a dominant male and the daughter is within his provenance. There is nothing for him to learn here as there is with a growing male. Yet, even though this, as we would expect, is the most common of all consummated incest relationships, restraint usually ensues. The capacity of the father to inhibit his own sexual responses is of course involved here, but it may simply be that a relationship which has been primarily protective is hard to convert to a sexual relationship, in the same way that it seems difficult to convert the asexual brother-sister relationship or the dominant-inferior mother-son relationship. Once one kind of bond is established it seems hard to make it over into a different one. But in the father-daughter case, and to some extent and by extension in the brother-sister, the purposes of inhibition seem more directly related to the exchange of females we have already mentioned.

Here we enter the area where evolutionary studies, primatology and social anthropology meet in earnest. The daughter, like the sister (but only in unusual cases the mother), is a potential mate for another man who is a potential ally. Put more abstractly: the women of the group (whatever the group is) are assets in forming alliances with men of other groups. But, one might ask, why need this be a problem? There are plenty of women to go around, sex ratios are equal. The answer must lie in the fact that the older and more dominant males monopolize the females thus creating scarcity. If this holds true, and in terms of our theory it should, then there will always be many males in the society who are dependent on other males for gifts of women. This only makes sense if a permanent assignment of mates, or at any rate a relatively permanent assignment of mates, is customary; but it builds on the old primate pattern whereby the dominant males take the females and the young males have to work their way back into the breeding system.

That men began to assert regular rights of sexual access over women was a function of the economic system that was described earlier. Not only were a women's vegetable products important, but her offspring also: males as automatic allies recruited by descent and females as the means to further allies (brothers-in-law and sons-in-law, or even nephews as we shall see). Perhaps we should look again at the basic formula for the difference between simian and human breeding systems. The simian formula aims at controlling the females of the group for the sexual purposes of the dominant males; the human formula aims at controlling the females of the group in order to exchange them for females of other groups. The change is from consanguine females as objects of use to consanguine females as objects of exchange.

We can perhaps therefore see the interweaving of all the tendencies in hominid behavioral evolution that we have looked at in the course of this argument:

The tendency to evolve a breeding system based on dominance and dispersion to maximize both the rapid fixation of desirable mutations and the effects of hybridization in the direction of rapid increase in cortical size and complexity.

The tendency of dominant males to monopolize control of the females of the group for mating purposes.

The tendency of younger males both to desire and to avoid the females controlled by the older males.

The tendency of the younger males to challenge the older for places in the hierarchy.

The tendency of the older males to exercise severe control over the younger.

The tendency to develop inhibitions over feelings of sex and aggression in this context.

The tendency to develop improved memory storage and the ability to classify, with the advent of rudimentary language. These are products of neural inhibition.

The tendency to internalize group customs and follow rules, and to feel guilt over transgressions (a product of both language and inhibition).

The tendency of males to seek cooperative relationships inside and outside the group boundaries (intensified with the development of hunting).

The tendency to trade vegetable food for animal protein between men and women.

The tendency for males to demonstrate dominance status through the control of females.

The tendency to utilize females as gifts and counter-gifts in the forging of alliances.

Once the crucial breakthrough to the economy with its necessary exchanges was made, and given the monopolizing tendencies of the older males, some form of regulation had to be evolved which would define who were one's own females on the one hand and who were 'marriageable' females on the other. And the crux of this argument is that the selection process we have posited as necessary for the development of the neo-cortex produced a creature with the appropriate mental and motivational equipment on the one hand, and the social system (itself the breeding system) which demanded kinship regulations on the other.

The first essential was to define own females versus other females, that is, to evolve some theory of consanguinity. Much ink was spilled in the nineteenth century concerning the relative priorities of reckoning consanguinity through males or through females. It is not terribly relevant whether kinship is reckoned through one sex or the other or through both. What really matters is that a definition of own and other exists and that rules apply (*a*) to the assignment of individuals to these categories and (*b*) to the exchange of women between groups so defined. How this happened we do not know, since nonhuman primate groups do not exchange females in this way, so we can only look at human models for examples of possible early exchange systems. The clues we have from nonhuman primates are however interesting. Monkeys and apes do recognize their kin within certain degrees it seems, but these are by necessity maternal kin since fatherhood in anything but a genetic sense does not exist. A baboon or macaque, for example, knows its mother and its siblings, and a male may well therefore recognize its sister's offspring. The basic unit here, is the mother-child group (which is also the basic unit in human society; see Fox 1967a and Count 1967, as well as Bowlby 1969). The subunits of a macaque troop tend to be groups of mothers and their offspring and sometimes the offspring of their daughters as well. That these constitute a unit can be seen not only by their patterns of interaction but also by the astonishing fact that dominance is group determined, that is, all the members of one of these lineages will rank higher than all the members of another and so on down a pecking order of lineages. This is really an extension of the principle that a son of a high-ranking mother will outrank the sons of lower-ranking mothers. In a macaque troop there may be, say, six such units with a peck order 1→2→3→4→5→6. If the group splits, then it will split into 1, 2 & 3 versus 4, 5 & 6. The first group will outrank the second, but as long as they are proximate, males may move between groups (see Koyama 1967, 1970, Furuya 1969). According to Reynolds, chimpanzees recognize kin similarly.

If some such pattern, essentially to do with relative dominance, existed in the early hominids during the transition stage, then the first definition of exogamy may well have been applied to what was essentially a matrilineage. A dominant male could take females from the less dominant lineages, but in return would have given his females to the males of these other lineages. He thus doubly asserts his dominance by taking more than his fair share of women from the pool on the one hand, and by condescending to the other lineages by allowing them to have his women on the other. Also, since the act of exchange sets up a relationship between the exchangers, these lineages would be tied together as partners to the exchange. A male's relative dominance then would be measured by his ability to extract females from other lineages and also by his success in binding males of other lineages to him by giving them females in return. It is easy also to see how this principle can be extended across group boundaries; that is, how it could operate between bands as well as within them. Some writers would want to see all exogamy in its origins as *local* exogamy, that is, males of one local population not mating with females of the population. There is no necessity for this except where local groups are very small indeed. In human society exogamy is rarely purely local, and interband alliances do not depend on this. As long as some marriages are made between different groups then alliances will hold.

It is obvious that this approach raises again all the problems that agitated nineteenth-century thinkers on the origins of kinship institutions. The pattern described here, which is only one of many possible ones and is simply given as an example of a possibility, would have delighted McLennan (1865) and probably have disturbed Maine (1861). I cannot here rehash the entire matriarchy versus patriarchy debate, but its relevance is there. Some of the questions asked by these anthropologists which have been too readily dismissed by their successors, can perhaps now be tackled from another angle with some hope of a successful answer.

The relevance of Freud's arguments in the much abused *Totem and Taboo* are clearly relevant here also, but since I have dealt with them elsewhere I will not pursue the matter (Fox 1967b). It is enough to say that Freud saw quite accurately the enormous importance of the invention of weapons, of the relations of dominance and the tension between the adjacent generations of males, of the renunciation of own women, and of the role of guilt as a controlling mechanism in this process (see also Fox 1966).

Before moving on to look at some patterns of exchange, let us stop to compare the essential change of content that occurred during the transition. Figure 10.1 shows the basic relationships or transactions between the three major blocks of animals in nonhuman primate society. The block of mother-child units gives up males to the periphery whence they return by

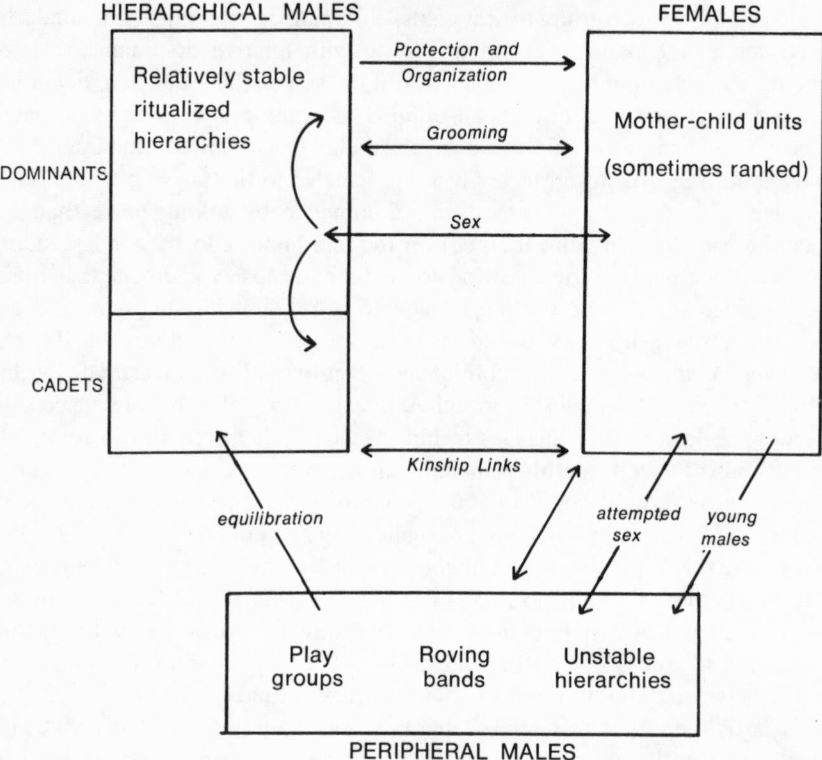

Figure 10.1. Schematic representation of social organization of terrestrial open country primates.

way of challenge and equilibration to the center and the breeding hierarchy. The males primarily provide protection and sex for the females and the females sex for the males. They groom each other. All the animals seek their own food. The control of copulation and hence of breeding is in the hands of the dominant males who either monopolize it totally or share it on their own terms with cadets and apprentices. Some form of kinship recognition, matrilineal in nature, may link older males, females and young males, and may help determine dominance status.

In Figure 10.2 the same structure appears but with the changes in the nature of transactions that followed on the hunting transition and the reformed male-female division of labor. As well as protection and organization, the males now provide animal protein to the mother-child units; the females in turn provide vegetable food and the service of food preparation. Sons still move from the mother-child units and are peripheralized, but they enter the male hierarchy and the breeding system via the process of

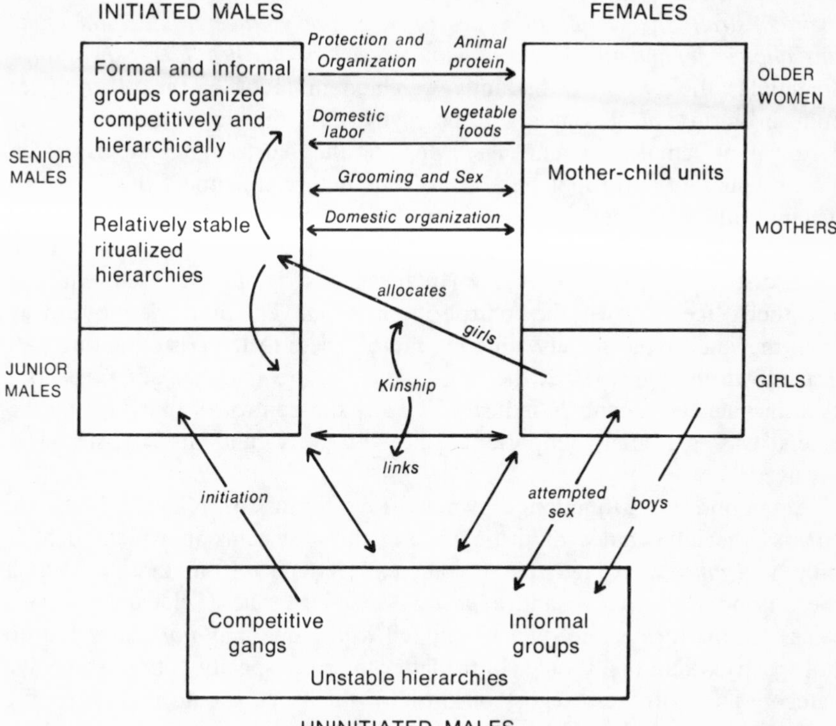

Figure 10.2. Schematic representation of social organization of genus Homo.

initiation. Some form of domestic organization links males and females because of the requirements of food gathering and preparation, and, most importantly, kinship not only *links* individuals together, but its rules act as principles whereby females are *allocated* to the domestic units of various males through formalized mating—or marriage, if we wish to call it that at this stage. Whether this allocation is isomorphic with actual breeding patterns of course depends on how strictly people keep their own rules; but it must be to some extent a determinant of breeding. Again, as with the control of sex among the nonhuman primates, the allocation of mates is in the hands of the older dominant males, and again they either monopolize or share on their own terms with initiated juniors. But the primary aim here is not just reproduction, it is the economic and political control of women. In societies with institutionalized premarital intercourse, for example, many girls will be pregnant before they are assigned. It is the role of the women as labor and as objects of exchange that is important.

This control of women by the older dominant males is probably the clue to all human kinship systems. The rules of these systems do not so much restrict the sheer sexuality of the young males as Freud thought; primarily *they constrain the choice of mates open to the younger males and make this choice dependent on the previous decisions of the older generations.* Sometimes the system is blatantly weighted in favor of the older males both in terms of gerontocratic polygyny and the rules governing the bestowal of females in marriage. Most of the Australian systems which have so puzzled anthropologists are of this nature. In others this is not so blatant, but the sheer mechanics of the system restrict the freedom of choice of the young males. In others an overt freedom of choice exists in terms of the rules, but control over marriages is rigidly exercised, while in yet others, like our own, the controls are minimal. The more we move away from the small-scale society adhering more or less to the basic hunting pattern shown in Figure 10.2, the more likely we are to relax our rules. But even in nineteenth-century industrial society the control of marriage by the elders was extremely important since property and its transfer was involved.

An important distinction drawn by Lévi-Strauss is relevant here. He stresses the importance of distinguishing those systems in which there is only a *negative* marriage rule ("complex" systems) from those in which there is both a negative and a *positive* marriage rule ("elementary" systems). In the former the rules simply tell whom one may *not* marry but do not specify whom one should. In the latter the rules specify both the negative category and also the category of kin into which one should marry. Simply in terms of the rules, elementary systems are more restrictive then than complex systems. Our own system, for example, is complex in that it specifies certain kin whom we may not marry but does not make any pronouncements about a suitable kinship category of spouse. The choice of spouse, then, is not governed by the rules of the system. Compare this with a system in which the rule states that a man may not marry any member of his own kinship group (for example, anyone related to him through females in a matrilineal system or through males in a patrilineal) but that he should marry someone of the kinship group of the parent from whom he does not trace descent (for example, a member of his father's group in a matrilineal system and of his mother's in a patrilineal). Here the choice of spouse is narrowly restricted by the rules.

Elementary systems work in two ways to effect exchange between individuals and groups. Sometimes the exchange is direct in that two groups simply swap women. Thus a society may be divided into two moieties which intermarry. This often disguises a more complex arrangement whereby, for example, the men of each moiety actually exchange amongst themselves their nieces—their sisters' children, who are in the opposite moiety in a patrilineal system (see Maddock 1969). Thus while daughters (or sisters) are passing from the men of one moiety to the men of the other, nieces are circulating among the men of each moiety. Typically in Australian systems of this kind, a man may control the marital destiny of a niece as remote as his sister's daughter's daughter, thus beautifully illustrating the way in which these elaborate systems allow the established males to control females two generations removed, thus preserving the gerontocratic monopoly (Shapiro 1969). And this is preserved by the very nature of the rules. Other direct systems are simpler, and it may simply be the case that families or lineages try to recreate marriage alliances generation after generation and these become enshrined as rules to the effect that he must marry where his father married, or alternatively phrased that he must get a wife from the group his mother came from. Add to this the rule that he must always return a woman where he got one, and we have the simplest formula of direct exchange: A↔B. Whatever the units concerned, families, lineages, moieties, clans, and the like, unit A gives to unit B which in turn gives back women to A and so on. Note here that "gives" does not refer necessarily to corporate action on the part of the unit. The corporate group may not as a body arrange the giving and taking of the women. What is referred to is the functional effect of the rules of marriage which result in women passing from unit to unit in a certain way. A great deal of confusion has been caused in anthropology by a failure to distinguish the rules from their effects. This will come out when we look more closely at some models of Australian type systems later. Thus a rule which has to do with the direct exchange of nieces may have the effect of indirectly exchanging sisters.

But what does indirect mean here? The essence of indirect exchange is that no two units ever exchange women directly. Thus if A gives to B, B must give to C, which in turn may give to A; but B can never give to A having received from A in the first place. Lévi-Strauss argues that such a system makes the units more organically dependent on each other than in a direct exchange system, and hence can handle more units and is more capable of expansion. The interest in the indirect system is in the way it allows for intergroup dominance relationships (as in the macaque example). If, for example, wife-givers are considered superior to wife-takers in the system (or vice-versa), then permanent relationships of dominance and submission can operate; but someone always has to be inferior to someone else since wives have to be received. In principle such systems should be circular on the model A⟶ B⟶ C⟶ (A) (see, for example, Needham 1962, Chap. 4). In a direct system the debt is always paid and the parties are therefore technically equal. Yet other systems seem to arrange for dominance to alternate with one unit giving women in one generation and taking them in another.

In all these systems the effect is to regulate the marriage choice of marriageable males somewhat narrowly in the interests of control by the older males and the perpetuation of intergroup and interindividual alliances. It would be possible to spell out all the other variations but again I have

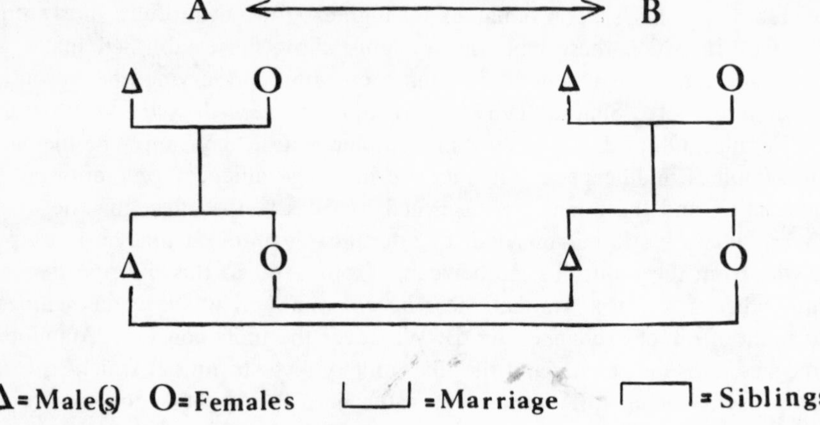

Figure 10.3.

done this elsewhere (Fox 1967a) and the reader who wishes to do so can follow the argument there. Here I will only pause to illustrate why these systems are often phrased in terms of the marriage of cousins, since this is of obvious interest to students of breeding systems.

Typically parallel cousins (father's brother's children; mother's sister's children) are forbidden in marriage, while cross-cousins (father's sister's children; mother's brother's children) are preferred or prescribed. More esoteric relatives are sometimes involved, for example a man may be required to marry a woman who is at once his mother's brother's daughter, his mother's mother's brother's daughter's daughter, and his father's sister's daughter's daughter's daughter. Let us start with perhaps the simplest case, where two men exchange sisters, or alternatively phrased, where two families exchange daughters (see Figure 10.3). If this exchange is carried on over the generations we will get the result illustrated in Figure 10.4.

It will be seen that a man is here marrying someone who is at once his father's sister's daughter and his mother's brother's daughter, but that for the exchange to be effective he cannot marry either of his parallel cousins —since his mother is equated with his mother's sister and his father with his father's brother. If we use the symbols not to signify individuals, but "Men of group A," "Women of group B," and so on, then we can see how this is simply a corollary of the rule that if group A gives to group B then group B must give in return. In genealogical terms the nearest relative to qualify as a marriage partner will be the cross-cousin: the child of the marriage of mother's brother and father's sister.

The structure operates if men exchange not daughters but nieces, their sister's children, by giving the nieces to their sons (Figure 10.5).

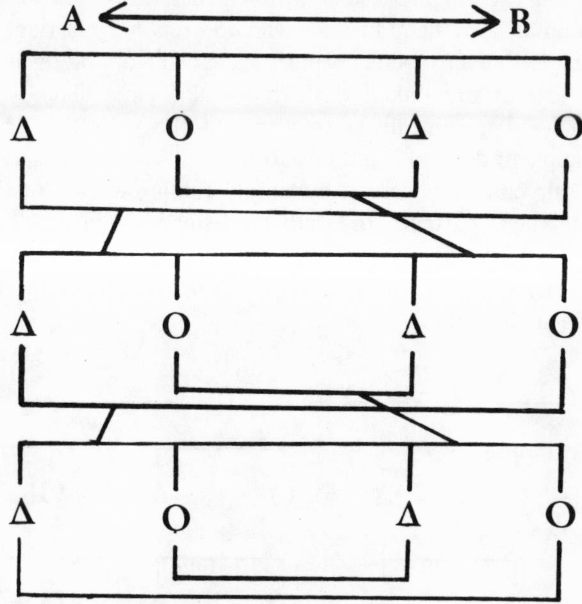

Figure 10.4.

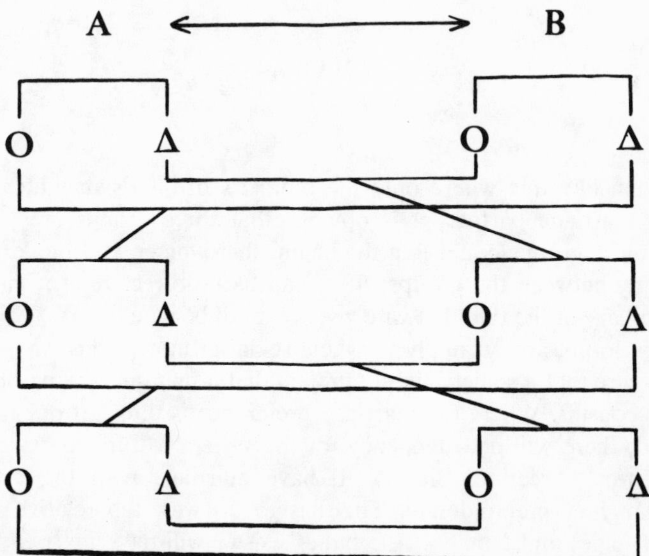

Figure 10.5.

These men are still exchanging sisters within generations, but across generations it is a woman's mother's brother who controls her marriage not her father. The point is that cross-cousin marriage is still operating here even though the generations are linked through females (matrilineally) rather than through males (patrilineally). In terms of the structure of the exchange, the principle of descent is not important.

The indirect rule can be observed by simply ruling out one of the cross cousins as a marriage partner: the father's sister's daughter. The ideal model of such a system as it operates between patrilineal groups is shown on Figure 10.6. The same structure again would operate if the groups were based on matrilineal descent.

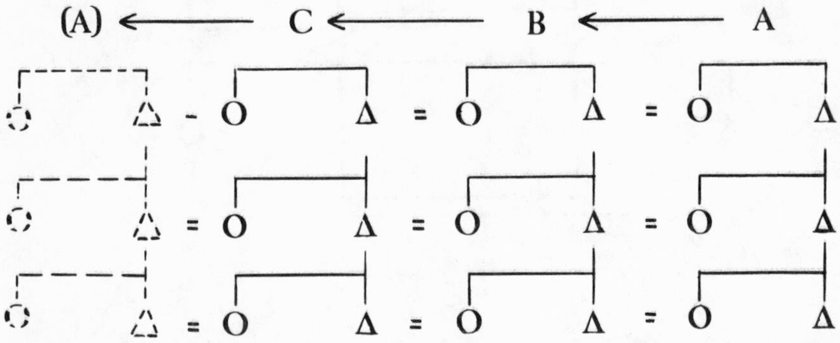

= : marriage

Figure 10.6.

In a system like this where only the mother's brother's daughter is allowed as a marriage partner, it is obvious that three groups are a minimum; that more groups could join the chain; that women will move in one direction only between the groups; there can be no direct return; and that this is a corollary of the rule that wife givers cannot be wife takers.

The rules do not always apply to whole social groups in this way, and it is often the case that a society simply prefers that a man marry one or other of his cross cousins. Where the marriage preference is thus left open, it has been argued, there will be a tendency for the system to turn in an indirect or asymmetrical direction, that is, to have marriage with the mother's brother's daughter preponderate. This has to do with the relative age at marriage of males and females. The father's sister will have married earlier than the mother's brother—women usually marry much earlier than men because of the need for a supply of wives for the older men—and her daughters therefore will tend to be older than her brother's sons who are the prospective marriage partners. Hence they will already have been taken by the time the candidate comes of age to marry. His mother's brother's daughters on the other hand will always tend to be younger than he, and hence suitable marriage partners. Thus, if there is no strict rule of sister exchange, and if he has a choice of cross cousins, he will be forced in the direction of the maternal cousin (see Hajnal 1963, Fox 1965, Rose 1960).

The two tendencies—direct and indirect, symmetrical and asymmetrical—should be viewed as just that: tendencies or processes, not as definitions of opposing types. It is quite possible—indeed it is done by the Australian Aborigines—to combine some of these principles into systems of considerable elaboration, systems which have been baffling to analysts but which in essence are elementary both in the literal and technical use of the term.

We saw earlier that men of two moieties might either exchange women directly with each other, or that sister's daughters might be exchanged among the men of each moiety. The moieties here would be patrilineal, so a man's sister would have married into the opposite moiety and her daughter would belong there by birth. If he, in his role as mother's brother, controlled the marriage destiny of his sister's daughter, he could give her to another man of his own moiety but of another patrilineal clan within that moiety. Let us for simplicity's sake imagine the set of exchange relationships between any four patrilineal subgroups of the moieties which are working this system. We will continue to call the moieties A and B with the subgroups of A being 1 and 2, and the subgroups of B being 3 and 4. The system phrased in terms of the circulation of sisters (daughters) could look like this (Figure 10.7): thus, 1 gives sisters to 3, which gives to 2, which gives to 4, which gives to 1. Women are thus passing symmetrically between A and B, and asymmetrically between 1, 3, 2, and 4. If the system is asymmetrical between these patrilineal units, then it would seem to require the 'mother's brother's daughter' rule as in Figure 10.6. But we saw that it

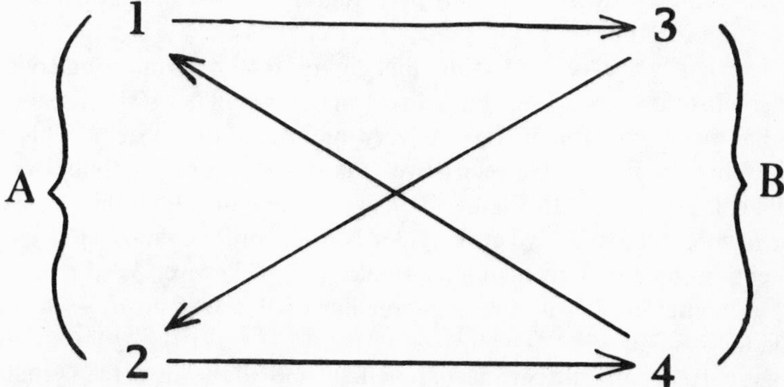

Figure 10.7.

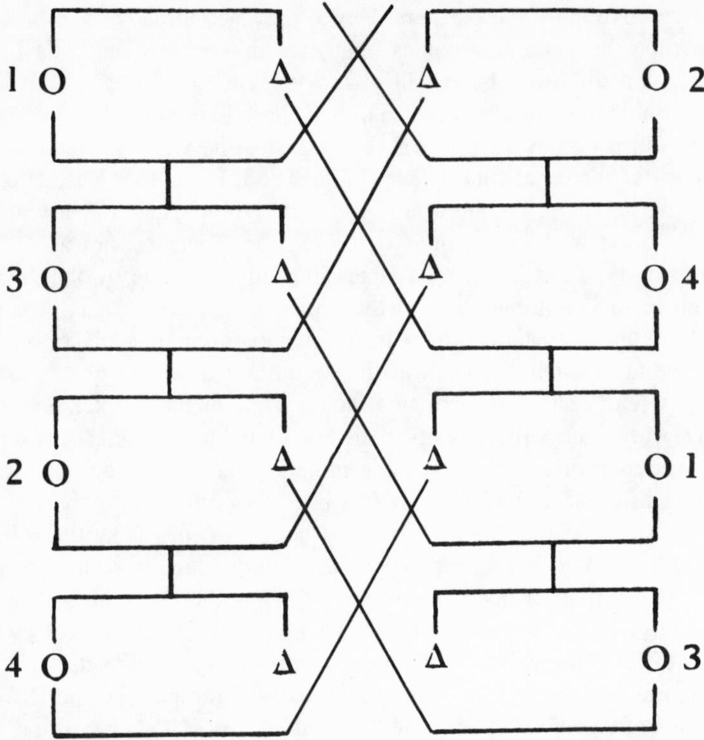

Figure 10.8. Numbers refer forward to the discussion of Figure 10.9.

operated in fact on a rule of niece exchange according to native theory. The niece exchange involved differs somewhat from that on Figure 10.5 in that it is cross-generational; that is, the men do not give their sister's daughters to their own sons, (thus perpetuating sister exchange) but to each other (Figure 10.8).

It can easily be verified from this figure that a man is marrying his mother's brother's daughter, but cannot marry his father's sister's daughter, who has been pre-empted by the very nature of the system. This figure shows the exchange between two matrilineal groups, but ours are patrilineal. If we refer to Figure 10.7 again, we can follow this through. A sister from 1 goes to 3, so her daughter is in 3; this daughter is given by her mother's brother in 1 to his moiety-mate in 2. Likewise, 3, which has just given a women to 2, will give the daughter of this woman to 4, and so on round the system.

Figure 10.9 puts all these facts together, and shows how the system puts them all together.

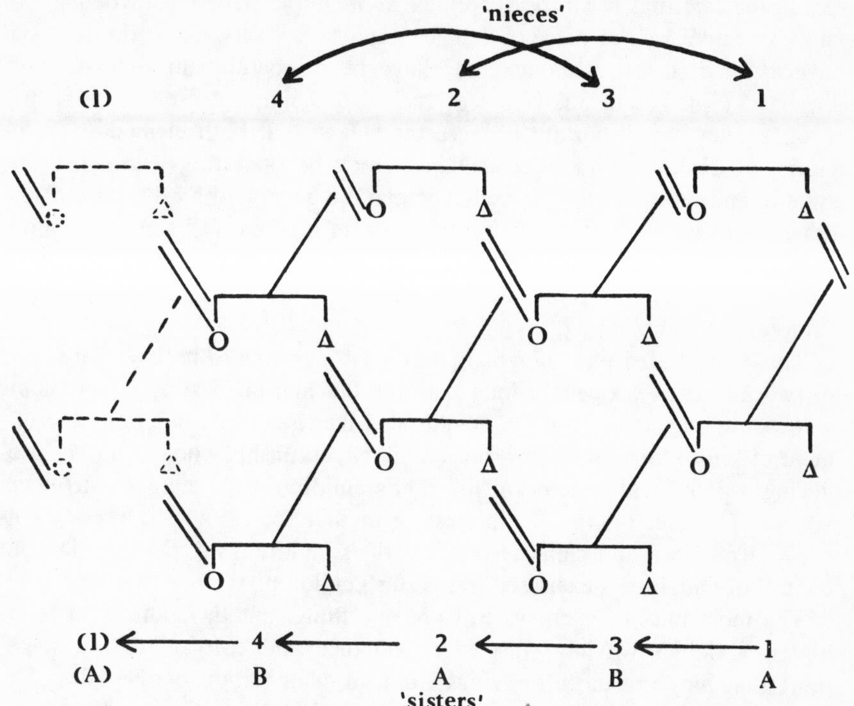

Figure 10.9. The matrilines can be easily followed. If we start with 1: the sister's children of 1 will be in 3; the sister's children of 3 in 2, and so on. Thus the matriline of 1324 is exchanging nieces with its opposite 2413, as in Figure 10.8.

Here we can see how sisters' daughters are passing directly between 1 and 2 and between 3 and 4. Given the two patrilineal moieties divided into exogamous clans, *this is the only rule needed to generate the system.* The consequences are, however, that women in their roles as sisters and daughters pass indirectly from 1 to 3 to 2 to 4 to 1 again; and that women pass directly between the two moieties. By comparing this figure with Figure 10.8 in terms of the numbers used for the subunits, it can also be seen that there is direct exchange involved between the matriline 1324, and the matriline 2413. It can also be verified that a man is marrying not only a woman who is his mother's brother's daughter, but also his mother's mother's brother's daughter's daughter and his father's sister's daughter's daughter's daughter. This seeming anomaly is a very simple outcome of the cross-generational niece-exchange system, and it is the way the natives themselves often describe the rule of marriage.

This is a hypothetical model of a system which could, in terms of the principles of elementary alliance, literally have everything. Its importance lies in the fact that it can be generated by a simple structure involving two moieties and a rule of niece exchange. But systems very like it do exist and have been described although they have been woefully misunderstood in the past. (For recent analyses see Hiatt 1965, Shapiro 1968, Lane 1961, 1962.) They are important because they show that both elementary principles, of direct and indirect exchange, may be operating within the one system, and that one type of exchange may be generated by the rules of the other. In general, also, they serve to illustrate the complex sets of relationships that can be erected on the very simple bases of swapping sisters, daughters, or nieces: principles of operation well within the reach of our protohominid ancestors.

The control of sister's daughters may seem puzzling in itself, but it is one of two alternatives open: a man controls the marital destiny either of his wife's children or of his sister's children. Likewise, in terms of the recruitment of kin to kinship groups, he can either recruit his wife's children, producing a patrilineal system, or his sister's children, producing a matrilineal system. The Australians are interesting in that they generally recruit kin-groups (moieties and clans) from the wife's children; i.e. patrilineally, but control of marriage is exercised over sister's children.

The mechanics of such systems are one thing, but their effects in terms of the variables we have discussed—alliance and constraint—are something that may not be too obvious from an examination of the rules. The alliance-effects and their possible elaborations, even with the observation of fairly simple rules, should be obvious from the foregoing. The ways in which such systems constrain the young, however, need a closer examination.

To take a synthetic example of what happens in Northern Australia we should imagine a tribe where a man has the right to bestow his sister's daughter (for example) as a mother-in-law on another man. That is, he promises the daughters of his niece to this man as brides. There are other variations, but the essence of the matter is that a man has to wait until his mother-in-law, who will be usually younger than he, produces female offspring before he has at least one wife, and then he has to wait until the wife matures before he can have offspring of his own. It is not uncommon for a man of forty to have two mothers-in-law of say 16 and 14, and to be just receiving his first brides. These little girls will grow up in his camp and eventually he will cohabit with them. In the meantime he may have inherited or acquired a couple of old women past childbearing age to start off his domestic establishment. Old men will look out for promising younger men of suitable kinship categories on whom they will bestow their nieces. The young men will then be bound as affines to the old men in an alliance. The younger a man is when he receives his first bestowal the better since that way he starts his household earlier and can collect more wives. Success breeds success and if a young man is favored then several older men will make gifts of mothers-in-law to him. The result is easy to see. Some men monopolize the females, but all men are dependent on the favors of the old and will not have a fully functioning polygynous household until they are quite old themselves. Some men will be cut out of the breeding system altogether, while others of the less successful will contribute less to the gene pool because they only have one wife acquired late in life. A good many men will die before they breed. Thus selection will be operative in a way similar to the basic model (for examples see Hiatt 1965, Meggitt 1962, Hart & Pilling 1960, Lee & DeVore 1968, part 4, Rose 1960, Goodale 1962).

Young men in such systems have to equilibrate for a considerable time. They of course attempt to have sexual relations with the young wives of the older men, and the latter attempt to keep them at bay. It is perhaps not surprising that Australian initiation ceremonies are among the more elaborate known to us, including several genital operations such as circumcision, superincision and subincision (the slitting of the urethra).

This is an extreme example of the constraint element, but the point is that the rules of the exchange system help to perpetuate the gerontocratic monopoly (Hiatt 1967). Other systems are less extreme, but the same *principle* applies. The rules ensure that the marriage choices of the young are constrained by previous decisions of the old.

What is important about these elementary systems is the way they render mechanical or automatic the perpetuation of alliances over time, and the way in which they constrain the marriage choice of the young and render the control of the allocation of females into the hands of the older generations, *by the very nature of their rules.* The direct exchange systems are obviously suited to small-scale societies with a relatively small number of exchanging units, and it thus may be that they are elementary in a chronological as well as a technical sense. It could also be that they are a highly specialized version of something that was in its origins much more simple. However, nothing could be much simpler than the formula A ↔ B which is the basic principle of reciprocity applied to the exchange of women: if we give you one of ours then you must give us one of yours and we will henceforth be bound to repeat this exchange over the generations.

If we put elementary systems of exchange into the context of our hominid hunting society evolving from its primate base, we can see that they are very simple mechanisms for uniting two or more parts of a group that would otherwise simply split up when population pressure increased. If nonhuman primate groups split in this way then they become to all intents and purposes separate groups, but hominid groups after they had reached the stage of being able to categorize, inhibit, and follow rules, could easily maintain a relationship with the other half through such a simple exchange system. Indeed this is the basis of the moiety principle. Another mechanism, dependent again on the ability to memorize and categorize, could work to this end. As the two original groups split up yet again, the new local entities would remember they came from either "A" or "B." This could be done through simple naming, and moieties like clans and other kinship units, usually bear names derived from nature: "Eaglehawk vs. Crow," for example, or "Wolf vs. Raven." Thus the A's would know they were Eaglehawks and that they got their women from Crows (the B's), and vice versa. These two mechanisms: the recognition of common descent, and the definition of exogamy, are the basis of all kinship systems. The elaborations of these systems which occupy so many pages of anthropological literature are basically, as we have seen, to do with the way the systems are geared to the preservation of the control of the older generations.

Where, for various reasons, such a system of exchange would be cumbersome to operate, one gets the development of complex systems (see Lévi-Strauss 1949, chapter 28, Fox 1967a, chapter 8). If the kinship units are still descent groups like clans, for example, then one simply gets a negative rule of exogamy: do not marry a member of your own clan. Which clan you then marry into is a matter of choice. This does not mean it will be the candidate's choice, of course, and it rarely is since his elders will most likely determine it for him; but this control by the elders is no longer built into the system and the system is that much more flexible. Yet again, as with ourselves, there may be no such descent groups and the rules may simply specify degrees of kinship within which marriage cannot take place. In a small-scale system this can still be pretty restrictive. Thus if the rule says that no one within the range of third cousin may be married, the number of potential spouses for any individual may be quite small: and we must remember that we were evolved to live in small-scale systems. Again the choice of spouse in such a system would be constrained by marriages made three generations earlier, and tight control by elders would be common (for example: Ireland, Mediterranean). But even so the system is potentially more flexible and could open up, as ours has done, into one where choice of spouse is almost a matter of personal preference and is determined by proximity, social class, religion, and the like, rather than by the rules of the system. Such a pattern obviously suits a large industrial society where mobility is at a premium.

There is perhaps justification for looking at one type of system that seems to stand half-way between the two types we have discussed. While being technically complex, those systems designated 'Crow-Omaha' found in North America, Central Africa, Melanesia and elsewhere have some of the features of elementary systems. Let us take the Crow instance (named after the Plains Indian tribe). Crow systems are matrilineal, and we can assume one in which there are, say, five matrilineal descent groups or clans. A totally complex rule would simply say that a man should marry outside his own clan. Crow systems often go further, they say that he should not only not marry in his own (mother's) clan, but in his father's clan and even his mother's father's clan. These are both clans to whom his clan has given women (mother and mother's mother) and so he cannot take women back from them. He must take his wives from the remaining two clans. The formula, if we call the man's clan A, his father's B and his mother's father's C, would read (D,E)⟶ A⟶ (B + C). A has given to B and C and so must take from D or E. This looks like the formula for indirect exchange, except that it applies only to the individual and not to his whole clan. Men of clan A whose fathers are not from clan B, can marry into it, for example. Thus women are passing back and forth between the clans. But for any individual, the world must look like it does to someone in an indirect exchange system. There are us, there are wife givers and there are wife takers. Sometimes Crow systems approximate direct exchange by having a positive rule that a man should marry into either his father's father's clan or his mother's father's clan. These systems have been puzzling to anthropologists, perhaps more so than the complicated Australian systems. It is coming to be seen, however, that they may well be various ways in which elementary systems change in a complex direction, which is why they have features of both (see Lévi-Strauss 1965, Fox 1967c, chap. 7, Fox in press).

But the striking feature again for such systems is the way that they seem to conspire to limit the marriage choices of the young males in terms of decisions made by the older generations. Crow systems, while opening up slightly in a complex direction, still tend to cut down the possible categories from which a man might choose a wife. The same elements of exchange and constraint dominate these systems.

Summary

I will try to summarize the argument.

In the last section I was only able to sketch the basic mechanics of exchange and constraint as they operate in human kinship systems. So used are we to our own system that we must often ask why there should be any constraint at all or why elaborate mechanisms of exchange need operate at all. But, as Lévi-Strauss insists, all systems are in fact systems of exchange, differing only in the degree of control they exercise over the direction of exchange. There is constraint in all systems, even our own, represented by the negative taboo on incestuous mating. This enforces exchange in the purely negative sense: it makes us give up our close consanguines and seek mates elsewhere. In our system, to use a crude metaphor, we cast our bread upon the waters; we release our sisters and daughters to the world at large in the expectation of receiving someone else's sister or daughter similarly released. Many other societies (and without doubt most of our recently hominized ancestors) do not leave such things so much to chance. At the opposite end of the scale they narrowly prescribe the kinship category from which a spouse can be taken, and such a prescription inevitably involves the perpetuating of an alliance over the generations between two kinship units. This is not news to anthropologists, but the other factor—the constraint that this imposes on the young males, is a neglected dimension that makes sense in terms of our sexual selection theory.

But what of the theory? Our aim was to tie up the Chance theory of sexual selection and the evolution of the brain with Lévi-Strauss's theory concerning the basic elements of kinship systems: rules, reciprocity and relationships. What I tried to do was to show how the process Chance outlined would have produced, given the selection pressures brought into play by the change to a hunting existence, both a creature equipped for and a social system demanding some form of kinship organization. This organization would have required the ability to inhibit sexuality with close consanguine females, to make and obey rules, and to categorize and classify. The pressures of natural selection speeded up by the sexual selection process would have effected this. The social system in turn was based on a series of transactions between the three blocks which were changed in content by the hunting adaptation and which demanded the organization of exchange, the control of the young males by the older males, the formation of regular alliances between males, and the regulation of mate allocation among the older males (or, by now, the initiated males). (For relationships *within* the block of males, and their implications, see Tiger 1969.) The consequence was the definition of exogamic groups and degrees of relationship, and the development of rules for the passage of women back and forth between these groups. These rules were probably in origin elementary and involved the direct or indirect exchange of women. Indirect exchange was capable of evolving into complex exchange where a narrow prescription of mate choice was lacking. Contemporary human kinship systems illustrate the whole range of these types of exchange system.

The move from breeding system to kinship system then, was in a sense inevitable given the evolving pattern of hominid adaptation. The elements proposed by Lévi-Strauss with their minimum expression in the incest taboo are indeed basic elements, but to these should be added the element of constraint exercised by the older males over the younger. This in itself is a product of the sexual selection mechanism proposed by Chance.

If the theory is correct, then it takes Darwin's ideas on sexual selection far beyond anything he might have envisaged. But ever since Huxley (1914) applied these ideas to the evolution of sexual *behavior* and Chance took them into the study of primate evolution, it has perhaps been inevitable that they should eventually be used in the analysis of human social action. The perspective which sees such social action as the end product of the evolution of social behavior in our species, despite the early insights of Carveth Read (1920) and Freud, is relatively new (Tiger & Fox 1966). It is also immensely difficult since it requires data and analysis from a wide range of sciences, wider than any one scientist can hope to master. But before we can even make the attempt we need some frameworks, some theories, to generate hypotheses and suggest ways to pull together all this disparate knowledge. This essay has been an exercise to this end by a social anthropologist who has realized that his subject is a branch of primatology and ultimately of evolutionary biology. It thus attempts not only to return man to the natural order from which he was untimely ripped by the social sciences in the first half of this century, but it also attempts to place the study of human social action and social systems back into the Darwinian tradition from which they should not have strayed in the first place. If the theory proves inadequate, it matters little; what matters is that the attempt should be made. And ultimately the answer must lie in a better understanding of the evolution of the brain and central nervous system and their role in the regulation of behavior. As Donne put it in *The Funerall:*

> For if that sinewie thread my brain lets fall
> Through every part,
> Can tye those parts, and make me one of all. . . .

then, we might add, therein lies the answer to the whole man: it is in the wiring. All we need to know is *what* got into the wiring, *how* it got there, and *when*. Only then can we write programs with meaningful instructions.

References

Aberle, D. *et al.* 1963. The incest taboo and the mating patterns of animals. *Amer. Anthrop.* 65: 253–65.

Altmann, S. A. 1967. *Social communication among primates.* Chicago: University of Chicago Press.

———. 1965. *Japanese monkeys: a collection of translations.* Atlanta: Altmann.

Ardrey, R. 1961. *African genesis.* London: Collins.

Beach, F., ed. 1965. *Sex and behavior.* New York: Wiley.

Bowlby, J. 1969. *Attachment and loss.* Vol. 1. *Attachment.* International-Psycho-Analytical Library No. 79. London: Hogarth Press and The Institute of Psycho-Analysis.

Campbell, B. G. 1966. *Human evolution: an introduction to man's adaptations,* Chicago: Aldine.

Carpenter, C. R. 1942. Societies of monkeys and apes, *Biol. Symp.* 8: 177–204.

Caspari, E. 1963. Selective forces in the evolution of man. *Am. Nat.* 97 (no. 892): 5–14.

Chance, M. R. A. 1962a. Nature and special features of the instinctive social bond of primates. In *Social life of early man,* ed. S. L. Washburn. London: Methuen.

———. 1962b. Social behaviour and primate evolution. In *Culture and the evolution of man,* ed. M. F. Ashley Montagu. New York: Oxford Univ. Press.

———. 1967. Attention structure as the basis of primate rank orders, *Man* 2: 503–518.

Chance, M. R. A., & A. P. Mead. 1953. Social behaviour and primate evolution. In *Evolution: symposium of the society for experimental biology* 7. London: Jonathan Cape.

Count, E. W. 1958. The biological basis of human sociality. *Amer. Anthrop.* 60: 1049–85.

————. 1964. Comment on *The human revolution* by C. F. Hockett & R. Ascher. *Current Anthrop.* 5: 156.

————. 1967. The lactation complex: a phylogenetic consideration of the mammalian mother-child symbiosis, with special reference to man. *Homo* 18 (no. 1): 38–54.

Crook, J. H., & J. S. Gartlan. 1966. Evolution of primate societies. *Nature, London,* 210: 1200–3.

DeVore, I. 1965a. Male dominance and mating behavior in baboons. In *Sex and Behavior,* ed. F. A. Beach. New York: Wiley.

DeVore, I. ed. 1965b. *Primate behavior: Field studies of monkeys and apes.* New York: Holt, Rinehart and Winston.

Durkheim, E. 1915. *The elementary forms of the religious life,* trans. J. W. Swain. London: Allen and Unwin.

Etkin, W. 1954. Social behavior and the evolution of man's mental capacities. *American Naturalist* 88: 129–42.

Ford, Clellan S., & F. A. Beach. 1952. *Patterns of sexual behavior.* London: Eyre and Spottiswoode.

Fox, R. 1962. Sibling incest. *British Journal of Sociology* 13: 128–50.

————. 1965. Demography and social anthropology. *Man* 65: 86–87.

————. 1966. *Totem and taboo* reconsidered. In *The structural study of myth and totemism,* ed. E. R. Leach. A. S. A. Monographs No. 5. London: Tavistock.

————. 1967a. *Kinship and marriage: an anthropological perspective.* London and Baltimore: Penguin.

————. 1967b. In the beginning: aspects of hominid behavioural evolution. *Man* 2: 415–33.

————. 1967c. *The Keresan Bridge: a problem in pueblo ethnology.* London School of Economics Monographs on Social Anthropology 35. London: Athlone Press.

————. 1970. The cultural animal. (UNESCO) *Information Sur Les Sciences Sociales.* 9 (no. 1) 7–25.

————, in press. Crow-Omaha systems and the elementary-complex continuum: problems for research.

Freud, S. 1952. *Totem and taboo,* trans. J. Strachey. New York: W. W. Norton.

Furuya, Y. 1969. On the fission of troops of Japanese monkeys. II. General view of troop fission of Japanese monkeys. *Primates* 10: 47–69.

Geertz, C. 1965. The transition to humanity. In *Horizons of Anthropology,* ed. Sol Tax. Chicago: Aldine.

Ginsburg, B. E. 1965. Comment on DeVore, I., Male dominance and mating behavior in baboons. In *Sex and behavior,* ed. F. A. Beach, p. 287. New York: Wiley.

————. 1968. Breeding structure and social behavior of mammals: a servomechanism for avoidance of panmixia. In *Genetics,* ed. D. C. Glass. New York: Rockefeller U. P. and Russell Sage Foundation.

Goodale, J. 1962. Marriage contracts among the Tiwi. *Ethnology* 1: 452–65.

Hajnal J, 1963. Concepts of random mating and the frequency of consanguineous marriages. *Proceedings of the Royal Society* 159B: 125–177.

Hamburg, D. A., *et al.* 1968. Studies of distress in the menstrual cycle and the postpartum period. In *Endocrinology and human behaviour,* ed. R. P. Michael. London: Oxford.

Harlow, H. F., & M. K. Harlow. 1965. The affectional systems. In *Behavior of non-human Primates,* ed. A. M. Schrier, H. F. Harlow, & F. Stollnitz. Vol. II. New York: Academic Press.

Hart, C. W. M., & A. R. Pilling. 1960. *The Tiwi of Northern Australia.* New York: Holt, Rinehart and Winston.

Hiatt, L. R. 1965. *Kinship and conflict: a study of an aboriginal community in Northern Arnhem Land.* Canberra: Australian National University.

———. 1967. Authority and reciprocity in Australian aboriginal marriage arrangements. *Mankind* 6 (no. 10): 468–75.

Holloway, R. 1966. Cranial capacity and the evolution of the human brain. *American Anthropologist* 68: 103–21.

Huxley, J. S. 1914. The courtship habits of the great crested Grebe (*Podiceps cristatus*); with an addition to the theory of sexual selection. *Proc. Zool. Soc. London* pp. 491–562.

Imanishi, K. 1965. The origin of the human family: a primatological approach. In *Japanese Monkeys,* ed. S. A. Altmann. Atlanta: Altmann.

Itani, J. 1968. The social organization of chimpanzees. Paper presented at Wenner-Gren Foundation Symposium on Social Organization and Subsistence in Primate Societies, Burg-Wartenstein, Austria, Aug. 1968.

Jay, P. 1968. Primate field studies and human evolution. In *Primates,* ed. Phyllis Jay. New York: Holt, Rinehart & Winston.

Jolly, C. J. 1970. The seed-eaters: a new model of hominid differentiation based on a baboon analogy, *Man* 5: 5–26.

Kaufmann, J. H. 1966. Social relations of infant Rhesus monkeys and their mothers in a free-ranging band. *Zoologica* 51: 17–28.

———. 1967. Social relations of adult males in a free-ranging band of Rhesus monkeys. In *Social communication among Primates,* ed. S. A. Altmann. Chicago: University of Chicago Press.

Kawamura, S. 1965. Matriarchal social ranks in the Minoo-B troop: a study of the rank system of Japanese monkeys. In *Japanese monkeys,* ed. S. A. Altmann. Atlanta: Altmann.

Kluckhohn, C. 1941. Patterning as exemplified in Navaho culture. In *Language, culture and personality,* ed. L. Spier et al. Menasha, Wis.: Banta.

———. 1943. Covert culture and administrative problems. *American Anthropologist* 45: 213–27.

Koford, C. 1963. Rank of mothers and sons in bands of Rhesus monkeys. *Science* 141: 356–357.

Kopell, B. S., *et. al.* 1969. Variations in some measures of arousal during the menstrual cycle, *J. of Nervous and Mental Disease* 148 (no. 2): 180–87.

Kortlandt, A., & M. Kooij. 1963. Protohominid behaviour in Primates. *Symp. Zool. Soc. Lond.* 10: 61–88.

Kotchetkova, V. I. 1960. L'évolution des régions specifiquement humaines de l'écorce cérébrale chez les Hominidés. *Proc. 6th Int. Cong. Anthrop. and Ethnol Sci. Paris* 1: 623–30.

Koyama, N. 1967. On dominance rank and kinship of a wild Japanese monkey troop in Arashiyama. *Primates* 8 (no. 3): 189–216.

———. 1970. Changes in dominance rank and division of a wild Japanese monkey troop in Arashiyama. *Primates* 11 (no. 4): 335–390.

Kummer, H. 1968. *Social organization of Hamadryas baboons. Chicago:* University of Chicago Press.

Lancaster, J. 1968. Primate communication systems and the emergence of human language. In *Primates: studies in adaptation and variability,* ed. Phyllis Jay. New York: Holt, Rinehart and Winston.

Lancaster, J. B., & R. B. Lee. 1965. The annual reproductive cycle in monkeys and apes. In *Primate behavior,* ed. I. DeVore. New York: Holt, Rinehart and Winston.

Lane, B. S. 1961. Structural contrasts between symmetric and asymmetric marriage systems: a fallacy. *Southwestern Journal of Anthropology* 17: 49–55.

———. 1962. Jural authority and affinal exchange. *Southwestern Journal of Anthropology* 18: 184–97.

Lee, R. B. 1968. What hunters do for a living, or how to make out on scarce resources. In *Man the hunter*, ed. R. B. Lee & I. DeVore. Chicago: Aldine.

Lee, R. B., & I. DeVore, eds. 1968. *Man the hunter*. Chicago: Aldine.

Le Magnen, J. 1953. L'olfaction: le fonctionnement olfactif et son intervention dans les régulations psychophysiologiques. *J. Physiol.* (Paris) 45: 285.

Lenneberg, E. H. 1967. *Biological Foundations of Language*. New York: John Wiley.

Lévi-Strauss, C. 1949. *Les structures elémentaires de la parenté*. Paris: Presses Universitaires de France.

———. 1962a. *La pensée sauvage*. Paris: Plon.

———. 1962b. *Le totémisme aujord'hui*. Paris: Presses Universitaires de France.

———. 1965. The future of kinship studies. *Proceedings of the Royal Anthropological Institute, 1965.*

———. 1969. *The elementary structures of kinship*. Trans. by J. H. Bell, J. R. von Sturmer, and Rodney Needham, editor. Boston: Beacon Press.

Maddock, K. 1969. Alliance and entailment in Australian marriage. *Mankind* 7 (no. 1): 19–26.

Maine, Sir. H. 1861. *Ancient law*. London: Murray.

McLennan, J. F. 1865. *Primitive marriage*. London: Black.

Meggitt, M. J. 1962. *Desert people: a study of the Walbiri aborigines of central Australia*. Sidney: Angus & Robertson.

Michael, R. P. 1968. Gonadal hormones and the control of Primate behaviour. Paper presented at Wenner-Gren Foundation Symposium on Social Organization and Subsistence in Primate Societies. Burg-Wartenstein, Austria, Aug. 1968.

Mitchell, J. 1966a. A model for the breeding structure of free-ranging troops of *Papio*. Unpublished Manuscript. Harvard Univ.

———. 1966b. Some proposed anti-inbreeding mechanisms. Manuscript.

Montagu, A. 1965. *The human revolution*. Cleveland: World Pub. Co.

———. 1968. Brains, genes, culture, gestation. In *Culture: man's adaptive dimension,* ed. A. Montagu. New York and Oxford: Oxford University Press.

Morris, D. 1967. *The naked ape*. London: Constable.

Napier, J. R. 1964. The evolution of bipedal walking in the Hominids. *Arch. Biol.* 75 (Suppl.): 673–708.

Needham, R. 1962. *Structure and sentiment,* Chicago: University of Chicago Press.

Read, C. 1920. *The origin of man and his superstitions.* Cambridge: Cambridge University Press.

Reynolds, V. 1966. Open groups in hominid evolution, *Man* 1: 441–52.
———. 1968. Kinship and the family in monkeys, apes and man. *Man* 3: 209–223.
Róheim, Géza. 1968. *Psychoanalysis and anthropology*. New York: International Universities Press.
Rose, F. G. G. 1960. *Classification of kin, age-structure and marriage among the Groote Eylandt aborigines: a study in method and a theory of Australian kinship*. Berlin: Akademie-Verlag; London: Pergamon Press.
Russell, W. M. S. & C. Russell. 1961. *Human Behaviour*. London: André Deutch.
Sade, D. S. 1967. Determinants of dominance in a group of free-ranging Rhesus monkeys. In *Social Communication among Primates,* ed. S. A. Altmann. Chicago: University of Chicago Press.
———. 1965. Some aspects of parent-offspring and sibling relations in a group of Rhesus monkeys, with a discussion of grooming. *Amer. J. Phys. Anthrop*. 23: 1–17.
Shapiro, W. S. 1969. *Miwuyt marriage*. Ph.D. Thesis, Australian National University, Canberra.
———. 1968. The exchange of sister's daughter's daughters in Northeast Arnhem Land. *Southwestern J. of Anthropology* 24: 346–353.
Slater, M. K. 1959. Ecological factors in the origin of incest. *American Anthropologist* 61: 1042–59.
Spuhler, J. N. 1959. Somatic paths to culture. In *The evolution of man's capacity for culture,* ed. J. N. Spuhler. Detroit: Wayne State Univ. Press.
Suarez, D. & D. R. Ackerman. 1971. Social dominance and reproductive behavior in male rhesus monkeys. *Am. J. Phys. Anthrop*. 35: 219–222.
Tiger, L. 1969. *Men in groups*. New York: Random House.
Tiger, L., & R. Fox. 1966. The zoological perspective in social science. *Man:* 1: 75–81.
Udry, J. R., & N. M. Morris. 1968. Distribution of coitus in the menstrual cycle. *Nature: London* 220: 593–596.
Vandenbergh, J. 1967. The development of social structure in free-ranging Rhesus monkeys. *Behaviour* 29: 174–194.
Washburn, S. L. 1959. Speculations on the inter-relations of the history of tools and biological evolution. In *Evolution of man's capacity for culture,* ed. J. N. Spuhler. Detroit: Wayne State Univ. Press.
———. 1960. Tools and human evolution. *Scientific American* Sept. 1960.
———. 1965. An ape's eye view of human evolution. In: *The origin of man.* ed. P. I. DeVore. New York: Wenner-Gren Foundation.
Whiting, J. W. M. 1959. Sorcery, sin and the super-ego: a cross-cultural study of some mechanisms of social control. In *Symposium on Motivation 1959,* ed. M. R. Jones. Nebraska: Univ. of Nebraska Press.
Wright, S. 1939. *Statistical genetics in relation to evolution*. Paris: Hermann.
Young, J. Z. 1965. The organization of the memory system. *Proceedings of the Royal Society* 163 B. 285–320.
Zuckerman, S. 1932. *The social life of monkeys and apes*. London: Routledge and Kegan Paul.

11

ERNST CASPARI
UNIVERSITY OF ROCHESTER

Sexual Selection in Human Evolution

Introduction

The nature and consequences of sexual selection have been thoroughly discussed in the preceding chapters. Even the topic of this chapter, the role which sexual selection may have played in human evolution, has been touched upon from different points of view earlier in this volume. If I attempt in this chapter to focus on the evolution of man, I shall have to refer to many facts and ideas mentioned and covered in the earlier papers. In order to avoid unnecessary redundancy, I shall frequently refer to papers in this volume rather than to the original literature, since much of the material pertinent to this discussion has already been quoted earlier. Only when specific problems are discussed will the original literature be referred to.

I shall start out by discussing sexual selection in the Darwinian sense in its relation to the concept of "components of fitness" developed in modern population genetics. Then the evidence concerning mating patterns in man and in prehominids will be presented and discussed with respect to sexual selection. Finally, the possible roles of selection at the individual and the population level in the evolution of the social characters of man will be given some attention.

Sexual Selection and Components of Fitness

The relation of sexual selection and natural selection has been discussed by Mayr in Chapter 5 of this volume. He points out that the evidence for the existence of sexual selection in the Darwinian sense has become over-

I am grateful to my colleague Dr. Jerram L. Brown for reading the manuscript and making numerous valuable comments and criticisms.

whelming. On the other hand, numerous cases are quoted in which it is not clear whether they should be regarded as examples of natural or of sexual selection. In many cases, the superior vigor of males of one genotype is decisive for their reproductive success, as was shown for *Drosophila* by Sturtevant in 1915; but a role of the female in the choice of the male has been demonstrated in many instances, for example in the "rare male" effect mentioned by Mayr (Chapter 5) and by Ehrman (Chapter 6), again in *Drosophila.* In this organism, reproductive success of individual males may thus be determined both by sexual and by natural selection, and these two components of reproductive fitness are hard to disentangle by observation. Faugères, Petit & Thibout (1971) have shown that in certain crosses of *Drosophila* strains the apparent contribution of the two components depends on the experimental setup chosen. Their experiment distinguishes between "sexual competition," measured in different types of choice experiments, and "sexual vigor" of the males, defined as their "ability . . . to inseminate a given number of females." The latter characteristic would be definitely related to natural selection, while the former would be considered sexual selection.

As Mayr points out (Chapter 5) the distinction between natural and sexual selection depends on the concept of fitness, and the concept of fitness is indeed basic for all evolutionary considerations. Many definitions of fitness have been proposed (see Kempthorne & Pollak 1970), and Haldane's (1949) definition is frequently used: "The fitness of a genotype in a Darwinian sense is measured by means of numbers of its progeny, different generations being counted at the same stage of the life cycle." This definition does not appear to me to differ from Darwin's own concept, as given by Mayr (Chapter 5). According to this definition, fitness is a phenotypic character of genotypes or individuals. Furthermore, it is a quantitative character, and the definition contains a method by which it can be measured. This definition of fitness, and other similar ones have led on to an extension of the concept of fitness. Fisher and Wright have started to use its derivatives as a measure of the fitness of populations. This extension is completely in agreement with the concept of Darwin that natural selection leads to fitter, that is, better adapted populations. But the concept of fitness of populations has been further extended. Thoday (1953) argued that fitness of populations can only be described with respect to units of evolution, "the unit comprising all the contemporary individuals that will have common descendants." He defines the fitness of such a unit as "its probability of leaving descendants after a given long period of time." Thoday's units are obviously collections of individuals, a population, a species or even more than one species. Contrary to the definitions of population fitness proposed by Wright and by Fisher, Thoday's definition contains no reference to the individual fitness at any one time. It refers to the evolutionary future of any group, and the components of fitness to which

Thoday refers are therefore properties of populations or units, such as adaptedness, genetic stability, and genetic and phenotypic flexibility.

Other workers have divided individual fitness into components which make up fitness in the sense in which Darwin and Haldane used the word. Three components are frequently distinguished: viability, fecundity (the average number of eggs produced by an individual or a genotype) and fertility (the probability of an individual or a genotype of leaving any adult offspring). Prout (1971), in discussing fitness in *Drosophila,* has refined these definitions. He distinguishes between a larval and an adult component of fitness. The larval component consists of the probability of survival to adulthood. The adult component is again subdivided into a male and a female component. The female component includes viability as an adult as well as fecundity since these two determine the number of eggs laid by an individual female. It is assumed here that all females are inseminated. The male component is called virility, and mating ability is the most important if not the only component of virility. It will be obvious that virility in the sense of Prout is very similar, and will in many cases be identical with sexual selection in the Darwinian sense. It is regarded here as a component of fitness; in other words, it is assumed that there is no difference in principle between natural, and the two types of sexual, selection. It may be suggested that the difference depends primarily on the point of view of the observer. If the observer is primarily interested in the transmission of genes, there is indeed no difference. But if the emphasis is on the origin of ecological adaptations, there is a vast difference since the virility component, besides genes affecting general vigor, will increase the contribution of genes which have an influence on the behavioral interaction between the individuals of a species with each other, rather than on adaptation to the environment.

A number of other components of individual fitness have been pointed out by population geneticists. They are mostly further subdivisions of the general components of fitness described above. But one additional component should be mentioned here since it raises a serious problem with regard to human evolution. Cole (1954) and Lewontin (1965) pointed out that developmental rate, that is, the reciprocal of the time needed for development to maturity, can be a strong component of fitness, which under certain ecological situations will become of high importance. In general terms, this idea is very attractive. If, in the baboon examples cited by Fox, a young male were to grow faster and mature earlier than his contemporaries, the vulnerable time of adolescence would be shortened; he could challenge the adult males at an earlier age, and possibly himself acquire dominance earlier. Even though the idea is intuitively convincing, the extent of the increase in fitness due to earlier maturity, as calculated by Lewontin, is surprising. He calculated that in *Drosophila* a reduction in developmental time from 8.6 to 7.5 days is equivalent, in its effect on the intrinsic rate of increase of the population, to a doubling of the total fecundity, for example, from 5,000 to 10,000 offspring. It may also be mentioned that early maturity is much more effective in increasing the rate of population growth than an extension of the life span at the other end, namely, reduced adult mortality.

In the last paragraph, a comparison has been made concerning the effectiveness of different components of fitness in contributing to overall fitness. A few further words on this topic appear necessary since it is often assumed that sexual selection, or the virility component of fitness according to Prout, is quantitatively a minor component compared to natural selection, that is, survival and number of offspring produced. Population experiments have shown that this assumption is not always true. The classical experiment of Bateman (1948) in *Drosophila,* described extensively in Chapter 7 by Trivers shows that male mating behavior is a very important component of overall fitness. Cotter (1963) in a population experiment with the moth *Ephestia,* studied the elimination of a mutant gene from the population on a uniform genetic background. He found that only 25 per cent of the rate of elimination could be accounted for by the reduced survival of the mutant, while 45 per cent must be ascribed to the lower success in mating of the homozygous mutant males. The remaining 30 per cent are not explained, but may be accounted for in part by a slower developmental rate of the mutant. The number of population experiments, particularly in *Drosophila,* in which male mating behavior of a genotype turns out to be a major or even the decisive component of fitness could be increased by further examples. It should, however, be kept in mind that experiments with artificial populations may give a biased picture of the working of natural selection since one component of survival, predation, has been systematically excluded. The role of predation in natural selection has been a matter of considerable discussion in the past. Some anti-Darwinian authors in the beginning of the century, for example, Wolff (1933), pointed out that in many organisms (such as plankton) survival of predation is essentially random and thus does not depend on the fitness of the organism. On the other hand, the importance of the avoidance of predation as a component of survival and its dependence on individual characters has been demonstrated in many cases, and many structures and color patterns, such as mimicry, protective coloration, and warning coloration can be confidently interpreted as consequences of selection for avoidance of predation.

The point brought out by the previous discussion is that the relative roles of different components of fitness and of natural and sexual selection are dependent on the specific ecological conditions under which a particular species lives. It is therefore impossible to make general statements which apply to all groups of organisms or to all species. It is even conceivable that the relative roles of different components of fitness may vary at different times in the evolutionary history of a species. Thus it may be possible to assign to sexual selection a particular role at a particular time in the evolution of man, but it may have changed in its importance and its consequences at different stages in the evolutionary process.

The Evolution of the Mating Pattern of Man

The occurrence of sexual selection depends on the mating pattern of the evolutionary unit (species or population) involved. Sexual selection cannot take place if all of the following conditions prevail: (1) The sex ratio at the time of mating is 1:1. (2) The mating system is monogamous. (3) All or almost all individuals in a population get paired. The latter condition prevails in some human populations, such as contemporary rural Turkey, but not in others, such as Western European societies (Demeny 1968). If any one of these conditions is not fulfilled (as in polygamous groups, or in monogamous societies in which a considerable proportion of the individuals do not mate) the possibility of sexual selection exists. Monogamous mating systems in which some individuals, both male and female, do not mate occur not only in human populations but also in monogamous birds. Brown (1970) has shown that in flocks of the Mexican jay only some of the adults form breeding pairs, while the unmated adults and yearlings participate in the feeding of the young. The existence of all the preconditions for sexual selection does not imply that sexual selection actually occurs in the particular species. But the question of the mating system of a species is basic for the discussion of the role of sexual selection in evolution.

For this reason the mating system in prehominids has been discussed in several articles in this volume, particularly in Chapters 9 and 10. The actual point of interest is the mating pattern which prevailed in human ancestors and that of present-day man. For the former problem, some remarks on the methods of verifying phylogenetic relations are necessary.

Fundamentally, all conclusions regarding phylogeny are based on comparisons, between living forms, and of living forms with fossil remains. The importance of the latter resides in the fact that it can contradict certain possibilities which might be assumed on the basis of recent material and thus falsify them. For example, the remains of australopithecines and *Homo erectus* from the Early and Middle Pleistocene show clearly that the hominid brain size, as indicated by the cranial capacity, increased strongly during this time, while at the beginning of the period the hominid line had already evolved bipedal gait, an essentially human type of dentition, and a greater reliance on a meat diet. In other words, the fossil record indicates the sequence in time at which certain changes in human evolution have taken place. The fossil findings exclude the theory of Weidenreich (1946) that the increase in human cranial capacity is a direct consequence of the bending of the base of the skull associated with the change to the upright position, for, under Weidenreich's hypothesis one would expect that the two changes had proceeded concomitantly. Furthermore, the existence in the human ancestry of organisms combining an essentially Pongid jaw with human cranial capacity can be excluded. While this possibility is now regarded as obviously wrong, it must have been accepted by the forger of the Piltdown skull and those scholars who regarded it as genuine; in other words, in the beginning of the twentieth century it appeared a reasonable way to arrange the facts known at the time.

At this place some remarks may be made concerning the evolution of human cranial capacity which has been discussed by Fox (Chapter 10). It was pointed out by Caspari (1963) that the rate of increase in cranial capacity in the hominid line proceeded very fast during the middle Pleistocene, if the long generation time of the hominids is taken into consideration. It indicates that strong selective pressures must have favored increased cranial size during this time, and it has been suggested that the profound behavioral changes characteristic of man, particularly tool making which goes on concomitantly with the increase in brain size, may have been one of the factors favoring selection for increased brain size.

This conclusion has been questioned by Count (1958) and Holloway (1966) for a variety of reasons. There is great variability in human brain size without any demonstrable effect on mental functioning. A similar variation has been found for different inbred mouse strains. It should therefore be pointed out that the relative brain size of present-day man falls out of the usual range found in higher vertebrates. Jerison (1969) described the relation of brain size to body weight in different vertebrates on a logarithmic plot, and found a definite distinction between higher (birds and mammals) and lower (fish and reptiles) vertebrates. The mean square lines of the two groups are parallel and quite distinct, so that no overlap occurs between the two groups. Within the mammals, a shift to relatively higher cranial capacity can be observed from Paleocene-Eocene over Oligocene to Recent. The Primates belong to the animals with relatively large brain sizes, and *Australopithecus* is clearly still within the range of the mammals. Modern man, however, is far removed from the line of mean squares, and far out on the outer margin of the distribution. The fact that cranial capacity provides only an upper limit for brain size does not detract from the fact that the main morphological evolutionary trend in the line *Australopithecus—Homo erectus—H. sapiens* has been a marked increase in brain size. The only remaining question at the level of brain structure is the temporal relationship between shifts in the cytoarchitecture of the cortex and the increase in brain size—whether one preceded the other, or whether they went on at the same time. This question cannot be decided on the basis of the available evidence.

If a physical character like cranial capacity offers such difficulties of interpretation, the same will be true to an even larger extent in a characteristic like mating pattern where we have no paleontological evidence and have to rely completely on the comparison of living forms. The two approaches used in this volume are comparisons of the mating patterns of different Primates, and of different human societies.

A first impression of the mating patterns of different Primate species as given by Crook (Chapter 9) is that of great variability. Practically all conceivable mating patterns occur among the Old World monkeys: promiscuity, polygyny and monogamy. The most frequent are polygynous mating systems which are divided by Crook (pp. 254–255) into "one male/all male group systems" (Sociotype A) and "multi-male group systems" (Sociotype B). Even between closely related species, differences in mating patterns are found. Fox's (p. 293) Baboon 1 system corresponds to Crook's Sociotype B, Baboon 2 to Sociotype A. Crook points out that even within the same species, such as *Colobus* species, both Sociotype A and Sociotype B may occur. A similar variability of mating patterns has been suggested by Fox for the ancestral chimpanzee, in pointing out that not all chimpanzee groups may be completely promiscuous. The choice of any mating pattern for the human ancestors appears at first sight completely arbitrary.

There are, however, aspects of the problem which may permit some conclusions. As Crook points out, the mating pattern of any species of Primates is dependent on its social organization. The social organization, in turn, is dependent on ecological factors, such as availability of food and other resources, defendability of territory, and size of the group. He distinguishes consequently between direct environmental selection ("natural selection") and selective forces dependent on social organization ("social selection"). Four different types of social selection are distinguished. Sexual selection in the sense of Darwin, that is, competition for mates, corresponds to Crook's social selection type *b*. Fox, in agreement with the theory of Chance (1962) assumes that selection of type *b* was the most important factor in the evolution of Primate behavior, while Crook puts particular emphasis on types *c* and *d,* that is, competition for access to resources necessary for the rearing of offspring and selection for the ability to cooperate in establishing an effective social group. There may thus be differences in the evaluation of the relative importance of different types of selection, particularly if it is considered that they are not independent of each other.

Our knowledge of the mating patterns of Primates is derived from observations of animals in the wild and in captivity. This method of observation does not give us unambiguous information on several aspects which are necessary for a full understanding of the genetic consequences of the mating system. We do not know, for instance, how much migration occurs between different established groups, how long in a multimale system an individual male retains his dominance, and how many of the progeny produced in a group are actually the offspring of the alpha male, as compared to other males participating in reproduction. Evidence concerning these questions could be obtained by the use of genetic methods, as has been done successfully in the house mouse and *Peromyscus* (Selander 1970). The study of enzyme polymorphisms (Selander & Yang 1969) and of histocompatibility genes (Klein & Bailey 1971) has given important and unexpected information on the population structure of the species involved. Similar techniques, applied to Primates, would give interesting results.

Any suggestions made for a presumptive mating pattern of ancestral man must be based on assumptions concerning his social structure, and this in turn would be dependent on his ecology (Orians 1969). For a social predator living in the open savanna, the relatively tight social organization necessary for cooperative hunting may be assumed. The size of the social unit was probably small, as long as the prehominids hunted small prey, because this particular food resource was hard to obtain and not reliable in supply. However, human ancestors seem to have progressed early, even at the *Australopithecus* stage, to the hunting of larger animals, even elephants, which necessitates a larger number of hunters. The role of territoriality at this early stage may be doubted, as in most savanna-inhabiting primates. For defense against predators, larger groups might have been advantageous, but as soon as tools became available, they may have been used successfully against the relatively small number of predators able to attack a prey the size of man. These considerations do not give information on the actual mating system, since they are compatible with a system in which all males of the group mate, or in which only one or a few males produce all the offspring. An added factor may be that in hominids the male participates in the procurement of food, not only for himself, but also for the females and the young. In other words, the male investment in the young is higher than in other primates. This problem has been discussed thoroughly in Chapter 7. According to Trivers' arguments, a change in male parental investment during evolution may involve a change in the sexual strategies of the two sexes. The suggestion may be made that there would be a consequent trend towards monogamy. But this argument is not convincing since the existence of helper males, analogous to the Mexican jay described by Brown (1970), may also have prevailed. Finally, it should be emphasized that there is no need to ascribe a specific mating system and social structure to ancestral man. Indeed, it seems likely that they may have undergone a certain number of changes in time, depending on ecological conditions. In view of the present behavior of Primates, including man, it cannot even be assumed that there existed a consistent pattern for all hominid groups at any one time.

A comparison of present-day human mating systems also shows great variability. Monogamy and polygyny are frequent, and polyandry occurs occasionally. In particular societies, any one of these or a mixture may be found.

A general characteristic of all human mating systems is the absence of close inbreeding, as indicated by the avoidance of incest. This aspect has been thoroughly discussed in Chapter 10. Fox emphasizes that an avoidance of mother-son mating has been observed to occur in nonhuman Primates, while the prohibition of father-daughter and of brother-sister mating seems to be exclusively human. In addition, other types of matings may be prohibited in some but not all societies, indicating that the prohibition of certain mating types is based on social rather than biological considerations.

However, the inhibition of close inbreeding in human societies may be of selective advantage since there seem to exist in modern human societies a relatively large number of harmful recessive genes. Incest may therefore lead to a high probability of such genes becoming homozygous. Adams & Neel (1967) described the offspring from 18 cases of father-daughter and brother-sister matings, and found that six of these had either died or showed severe defects at the age of 6 months. Among 18 matched control babies, only one had severe physical abnormalities at the same age. There is thus good evidence for a high probability of actual biological damage due to incestuous matings.

It is frequently mentioned in this connection that under certain historical circumstances incestuous marriages have been continued in certain families, mostly dynasties, for prolonged periods of time without apparent damage. This is perfectly possible, since in the data of Adams & Neel some of the children appeared perfectly normal; but the historical evidence is mostly anecdotal and may not stand up under critical inquiry. The Egyptian dynasty of the Ptolemies who ruled Egypt for almost 300 years (10 generations) is a case in point. While Egyptian Kings were supposed to reproduce by brother-sister mating, Ptolemy V Epiphanes is the first product of such a union in the dynasty. Previously, there had only been one brother-sister mating, that of Ptolemy II Philadelphus and his sister. This mating produced no offspring, even though both spouses had been fertile in previous marriages. Their "children" mentioned in official records are actually the children of the husband from a previous marriage which the couple had adopted. Extensive brother-sister matings occur in the sixth and seventh generations, and these matings gave rise to several children who survived to adult age without recorded abnormalities. These incestuous matings occurred at a time of political upheaval where pretenders to the throne tried to bolster their claims by marriage to a sister. The dynasty became extinct in the direct line with generation eight. The two remaining cases of "incest" were the marriages of Cleopatra to her two brothers, both childless and probably not consummated, since the husbands were children at the time of the wedding and the spouses did not live together through most of their married lives.

This digression has been introduced because the claim that Egyptian dynasties reproduced for long periods by close incest is frequently made.

In addition the facts lend support to the contention of Fox (Chapter 10) that there exist both unconscious and institutional inhibitions against incestuous matings. The mating pattern found in the Ptolemies suggests that the unconscious inhibitions may be effective even where the institutional prohibitions are removed unless particular political situations arise.

While human societies avoid extreme inbreeding, they do not in general tend towards extreme exogamy. This may in turn be due to the fact that extreme exogamy or random mating is not compatible with a stable social organization. The numerically large societies of Western civilization tend to favor positive assortative mating. This has been thoroughly discussed by

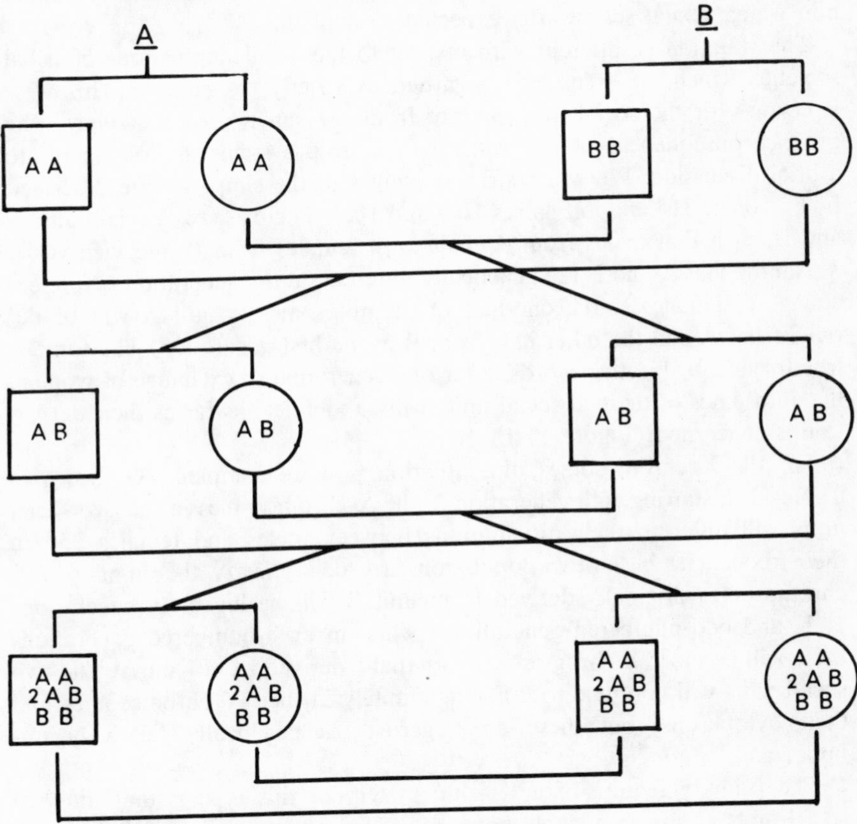

Figure 11.1. Distribution of autosomes in two social units engaged in the type of cross-cousin mating represented in Figure 10.4. It is assumed that the two social units, A *and* B*, have originally different autosomal sets. Two homologous autosomes derived from social units* A *and* B *are designated as* A *and* B*, respectively, and enclosed in the squares and circles symbolizing males and females, respectively. The figure follows these autosome sets in a diagram analogous to Figure 10.4.*

Ehrman (Chapter 6), who shows that mating preferences extend not only to national origin and socio-economic and educational status (see Eckland 1968) but also to clearly genetic characters such as deafness. Different types of assortative matings frequently show different fertilities, and these may affect the genotypic constitution of the population. Even though assortative mating may involve a choice of the sexual partner, and differential fertility results in selection, this complex of factors does not constitute sexual selection in the sense of Darwin, but is a case of natural selection. As Mayr points out, sexual selection in Darwin's sense implies competition for reproduction by one sex only, and choice of mates by the other sex. This situation can give rise to sexual dimorphism, the phenomenon which sexual selection is expected to explain.

The situation is different with respect to the small populations of tribal societies which are frequently regarded as strictly exogamous. This view is correct for the social unit but not from the genetic point of view. The genetic consequences of the Australian kinship systems deserve therefore a brief discussion. We will restrict ourselves to the simplest case described by Fox on p. 315 and in Figures 10.3 and 10.4. There are two social units, A and B, such that males from A mate with females from B and vice versa. Assuming that A and B are genetically different, in the generation before exchange of females starts, one-half of the autosomes in unit A will be derived from A and the other half from B in the first generation. The same is true for unit B. In other words, after one generation of exchange of women, the autosomes of the two social units will be identical as far as their derivation is concerned (Figure 11.1).

For the X chromosomes, the situation is more complex. As shown in Table 11.1, starting with generation 3, the X-chromosomes in the two social units will differ in their distributions between males and females and in their frequencies in the two populations. In social unit A, the number of X chromosomes originally derived from unit B will be higher in generations 1, 2, and odd-numbered generations, while in even-numbered generations there will be more X chromosomes originally derived from Unit A. The two social units will continue to differ indefinitely in their Y chromosomes and their cytoplasms; but these are regarded as genetically relatively unimportant.

The primary feature of a Kinship system of this type is that the two social units approach a single population in the genetic sense. While it appears that in the higher Primates social unit and mating population are identical, the human kinship pattern assures that the gene pool may comprise several social units. Such a population structure may be advantageous where for ecological reasons the social units are small, and the effective breeding population becomes reduced to such a degree that chance fixation of genes becomes likely. Similar considerations may be applied to

Table 11.1. Distribution of the sex chromosomes in two social units engaged in "cross-cousin mating".

Generation	Social unit A ♂	Social unit A ♀	Social unit B ♂	Social unit B ♀
0	$X^A Y^A$	$X^A X^A$	$X^B Y^B$	$X^B X^B$
1	$X^B Y^A$	$X^A X^B$	$X^A Y^B$	$X^A X^B$
2	$X^A Y^A$ 1/2 $X^B Y^A$ 1/2	$X^A X^B$ 1/2 $X^B X^B$ 1/2	$X^A Y^B$ 1/2 $X^B Y^B$ 1/2	$X^A X^A$ 1/2 $X^A X^B$ 1/2
3	$X^A Y^A$ 3/4 $X^B Y^A$ 1/4	$X^A X^A$ 3/8 $X^A X^B$ 4/8 $X^B X^B$ 1/8	$X^A Y^B$ 1/4 $X^B Y^B$ 3/4	$X^A X^A$ 1/8 $X^A X^B$ 4/8 $X^B X^B$ 3/8
4	$X^A Y^A$ 3/8 $X^B Y^A$ 5/8	$X^A X^A$ 3/16 $X^A X^B$ 8/16 $X^B X^B$ 5/16	$X^A Y^B$ 5/8 $X^B Y^B$ 3/8	$X^A X^A$ 5/16 $X^A X^B$ 8/16 $X^B X^B$ 3/16

X^A and X^B: X-chromosomes derived originally from social units A and B respectively.

Y^A and Y^B: Y-chromosomes derived originally from social units A and B, respectively.

the more complex mating patterns discussed by Fox, in which more than two social units are involved in a common gene pool.

The equalizing tendencies of a cross-cousin mating system may be counteracted by polygyny. Polygyny, genetically speaking, may be regarded as a form of inbreeding, since a large proportion of the genes in a particular generation are derived from a few individuals of the preceding generation. For instance, in two villages of the primitive South American Xavantes, one quarter of the individuals were descendants of two males (Chapter 4).

The question arises, how far the mating patterns in so-called primitive societies can give us any information about the mating pattern of ancestral man. Societies are regarded as primitive if they do not use metal tools and practice little or no agriculture, so that their subsistence is mainly derived from hunting and gathering. In addition, the social units are numerically small and organized according to "tribal" lines. These characters are of course interrelated. A further character of modern "primitive" societies is that they are adapted to life in specialized habitats, for example, heavy forest, desert or arctic conditions. For every cultural or biological trait of such a society the question may be raised whether it is truly "primitive" in the sense of similar to ancestral characters or a special adaptation to the particular living conditions. A parallel question is of course well known from comparative morphology of animals where the specially adaptive characters of primitive organisms have always constituted a difficulty. In view of the fact that different so-called primitive societies show considerable variation in mating patterns, their value in determining the ancestral mating pattern of man is limited, and they must be used with great care.

Finally, the question should be repeated as to how long a particular mating pattern remains in force. Our knowledge of changes in mating patterns in primitive societies is limited by the time they have been under observation, and by the impact of their contact with Western civilizations. Only in societies with written tradition can it be shown that mating patterns have indeed changed over time. One example would be the gradual reduction and disappearance of polygyny in the Near East in the last 4,000 years. While polygyny seems to have been widespread about 2,000 B.C., it gradually became restricted to the very powerful and wealthy, and finally disappeared in one society after the other. This progress of monogamy is not based on religious sanctions, since none of the great Near Eastern religions forbids polygamy. In Western Europe, a change from arranged matings to choice of mating partners has taken place in the last few centuries. Furthermore, European populations have changed from a pattern of early and universal marriage in which fertility is not controlled to a pattern of relatively late marriage in which many persons remained unmarried (Hajnal 1965). Fertility control apparently spread gradually in the last four centuries. The latest change in Western civilization seems to be a change from monogamy to a pattern called "serial polygamy" (both polygyny and polyandry) in which an individual may have several mates at different times (Eckland 1968). These instances are mentioned because they indicate changes in mating and reproductive patterns which may affect both natural and sexual selection. They also indicate that important changes may occur over time, a possibility already suggested in our consideration of nonhuman primates.

Thus we are not in a position to propose any mating system for ancestral man and may even doubt whether a general solution to this problem exists. We may, however, propose a number of possibilities for an early hunting stage where hunting was still inefficient, and the social units presumably small. We may assume, in analogy to present-day nonhuman Primates as well as human societies, that some kind of dominance order existed among the males. We can then, on the basis of an assumed equality in number of males and females, conceive the following possibilities: (1) monogamy: all males produce offspring, with one particular female each; (2) polygyny: one or very few males produce offspring; the remaining males do not reproduce but participate in hunting, similar to the helpers in the Mexican jay (Brown 1970); (3) an intermediate pattern in which all the males compete for all the females without the establishment of a permanent bond between males and females. Possibilities (2) and (3) would permit the occurrence of sexual selection, while possibility (1) would not. These schemes do not specify whether males and females are derived from the same social unit, or whether exchange of females had already occurred at this stage.

Sexual Selection in the Evolution of Man

The present chapter will summarize the evidence on the occurrence of sexual selection in nonhuman primates and in modern human societies. It will then consider to what extent we can make assumptions on sexual selection in human ancestors. Finally, the consequences of sexual selection in human evolution will be considered, with respect to sexual dimorphism.

In present-day nonhuman primates, the conditions for sexual selection are given. In most species, some of the males produce most of the offspring, while others are excluded from reproduction or mate only occasionally. One factor mentioned by Darwin (Chapter 5) is assumed to be missing in nonhuman primates; female choice. Reproductive success is based on social interactions between males. But the possibility that the females, at least in some species, can express preferences cannot be dismissed. It is rather characteristic of the present state of primate behavior studies that new and unexpected observations are frequently made.

In present-day human populations, conditions for sexual selection exist in some but not in all societies. In societies permitting polygyny, sexual selection occurs, as pointed out by Dobzhansky (Chapter 4) with respect to the South American Xavantes and Yanomama. On the other hand, in monogamous populations in which everybody marries, sexual selection cannot be assumed to play a large role. It might be expressed in illegitimate reproduction or in multiple marriages, but in general it will be safe to assume that reproductive success will depend on the fecundity and fertility of the marriage partners, that is, on natural selection. In monogamous societies in which not everybody marries, sexual selection is possible if the individuals excluded from marriage have genetic features in common. As Dobzhansky points out, no evidence on this question exists at the present time. In modern Western societies, choice of mates results primarily in positive assortative matings as mentioned earlier, and different types of these matings may have different average fertilities. The genetic consequences of such a system resemble in some respects sexual selection, but they differ from it by the fact that equal numbers of individuals from both sexes will be excluded from reproduction. It seems therefore preferable not to regard this situation as sexual selection.

The consequences of sexual selection appear clear for the nonhuman primates. Many of the characters involved in sexual dimorphism (Chapter 9) such as the larger body size and muscular development of males or the strong development of their canine teeth particularly pronounced in the baboons and the Pongidae can be understood as consequences of the establishment of social dominance. It should be mentioned that these characters would be secondarily reinforced by natural selection since they also serve in the defense against predators. It is harder to envisage the role of sexual selection in characters of the female, such as shape of the human breast (Chapter 9) and the sexual skin development in nonhuman Primates (Table 9.1).

The nature of the problem can best be seen in the objection of Etkin (1954) to Chance's hypothesis that sexual selection is involved in the evolution of the intellectual capacities of man (Chapter 10). He argues that sexual selection acting on the male should not have brought about a parallel evolutionary trend in the female. This is not necessarily the case. If there are in a population additive genes affecting a character, selection for this character in one sex would lead to accumulation of the genes in the population. Selection in one sex only is less effective than selection in both sexes, as can be seen easily from the extensive literature on selection for milk yield in cattle. Nevertheless, if genes having a particular effect on the male are selected, it is not necessary that these same genes have no effect on the female. They may be assumed to either have a parallel effect in the female, or a special effect different from that in the male.

This consideration shows that in the evolution of sexual dimorphism factors beyond sexual selection must be considered. The investigations of Stern and his collaborators (1950) show this with respect to the sex comb on the tarsi of the first leg of *Drosophila* males. In this case, study of sexual mosaics has shown that in both sexes there exists a prepattern, a particular arrangement of the cells in the developing leg, such that a certain area of the leg is distinct from all others. Male cells react on this prepattern by forming sex combs in the distinct area, while genetically female cells do not. In vertebrates, this situation is complicated by the addition of an intermediate level of control, the sex hormones. It appears that all characters involved in sexual dimorphism in mammals are characters which depend for their development on the presence of the appropriate sex hormones. Sexual selection for a character dependent on sex hormones would result in sexual dimorphism; if the character subjected to sexual selection is not dependent on sex hormones, it would affect both sexes equally.

It becomes clear that for an estimation of the action of sexual selection knowledge of the genes selected is important. Unfortunately, little material exists on the genetic basis of secondary sex characters in man and primates. Material could be obtained since many characters, such as development of facial hair in humans, show intrapopulation and racial variation. The best investigated case seems to be pattern baldness in humans (Harris 1946). The genetic basis of this condition appears to be more complex than was originally assumed, but the evidence still supports the hypothesis that certain genotypes react on male sex hormone with a reduction in the size of the hair follicles in a particular area of the head. The prepattern would be brought into evidence only in the presence of the male sex hormone. This character, in its own right, has apparently not been subjected to sexual selection. There is no evidence that in any society bald men have a reproductive advantage or disadvantage. At the present time, it appears to be one of the large number of characters which are affected by genetic polymorphism, a situation present in all populations and at present a matter of much discussion and experimentation. A situation could be conceived in which baldness would become an object of sexual selection, in which case the genes controlling it would become prevalent in the population. Reduction of hair in certain areas of the body (for example, the bare chest of the gelada) is mentioned prominently in the list of sexual dimorphisms in Primates given by Crook.

If it is assumed that sexual selection played a role in the evolution of man, the characters leading to reproductive advantage should be known. If it is assumed that at some stage of evolution polygyny existed in human ancestors and that the socially dominant males were favored in reproduction, the characters involved in the acquisition of social dominance are most important. There is one piece of evidence which should be pointed out in this context. The Dryopithecines who are supposed to be close to the branching point of the Hominid and Pongid lines had increased canines, though they were not increased to the degree they are in present-day Pongidae. If we ascribe the increase in canines in the Pongidae to sexual selection, more specifically to the use of the teeth in the confrontation between individual males in the fight for dominance, it must be concluded that in the Hominid line a different way of establishing dominance must have been used. Furthermore, this difference between the two Primate lines must have arisen early since the process of reduction of the canines was already well advanced in the earliest Pleistocene and possibly even in the Miocene *Ramapithecus*. If we want to speculate further, we may point out that the maintenance of enlarged canines might have been of advantage in the defense against predators and in the consumption of meat in a hunting organism. All this points to a very early change in the mechanism of establishing dominance in the human ancestral line.

What this change was we cannot guess, and it is unlikely that it was the same throughout the long period of time which we must assume for this process. But three possibilities may be briefly mentioned. The possibility that sexual selection favored psychological rather than physical characters has been pointed out by Fox who suggests that skill in equilibrating aggressive tendencies with caution in challenging dominant males may have been involved. Several authors (see Alexander 1971) have suggested that organized warfare may have been a major factor in human evolution. This question will be mentioned again later; here only its possible effect on sexual selection will be mentioned. Since only males are involved in warfare, the possibility of sexual selection arises. The selective process in this case would have two aspects: avoidance of death and increased social standing as a result of success. Both consequences might result in higher reproductive success in polygynous societies. The latter aspect might be prominent in more primitive conditions where weapons are inefficient and the probability of death, low. With more sophisticated weapons, the first aspect might gain in importance. The characters selected at the early stage would be similar to those discussed by Fox: physical strength and motor coordination, as well as a balance between aggressiveness and caution.

Another possibility is suggested by present-day primitive societies such as the Xavantes. As Dobzhansky points out, some individuals contribute disproportionately to the next generation, and these are village chiefs, the holders of political power. Neel et al. (1964) point out that at the death of a chief his function is not necessarily transmitted to his direct descendants. Furthermore, in discussing the political structure of the society, they point to the high role of oratorical ability in procuring social status and power. This high social esteem of rhetoric appears to be widespread in both primitive and advanced societies. If this social esteem of oratory goes further back in the human ancestry than is usually believed, an important role for sexual selection in the evolution of human language might be assumed.

Another possible method of establishing social dominance in early human societies without the use of enlarged canine teeth might be the use of weapons. The characters favored by this type of selection would be similar to those involved in warfare. It appears to me, however, that present evidence contradicts the use of weapons in the establishment of dominance in prehominid societies. The canines of Australopithecines were already strongly reduced at the beginning of the Pleistocene, and probably even in the Pliocene, while pebble tools are to my knowledge found only in Pleistocene contexts. Reduction of canines in the Hominid line appears on the basis of present knowledge to have preceded the production of weapons. Furthermore, the canine teeth of *Australopithecus robustus* are more reduced than those of modern man, and these organisms are supposed to have been vegetarian and not to have used weapons.

All these suggestions are arbitrary and not susceptible to proof or falsification. There is no reason to reject the notion that some or all of them may have been effective at some time in human evolution. There is also every possibility that additional factors may have been involved. I would, however, like to stress the opinion that the divergent evolution of the dentition in the Hominid and the Pongid lines indicates a very early differentiation in the mechanism of sexual selection in these two groups.

Darwinian Fitness and Population Fitness in Human Evolution

In considering the evolution of man, some characters must be considered which do not affect the reproductive success of the individual but which are advantageous for the survival of the social unit of which it is a member. Such characters are not restricted to man but occur rather widely in social organisms. The nonreproducing workers of the social insects are the most extreme example, but cases in vertebrates are not unknown. The helper birds in the Mexican jay mentioned earlier are a well documented instance (Brown 1970). Emerson (1960) and Wynne-Edwards (1962) cite a number of cases, for instance the cooperation of individuals in a social unit, regulation of the size of populations, and death of old individuals. They conclude that the origin of such characters cannot be accounted for by selection acting on individuals but can only be explained on the basis of selection at the population level. In other words, it is maintained that populations of a species compete with each other for resources, and that some populations will become extinct, while others increase in size and may split up, filling the empty ecological niches.

Such characters which do not confer an advantage to the individual but to the population of which it is a member have been called "altruistic" by Haldane (1932). The theory of selection for altruistic characters has been investigated by Hamilton (1964). His main point is that the genes belonging to an individual can be favored by selection, even if the individual itself does not transmit its genes, if its characters enable its relatives who have the same or a similar genetic constitution to be more successful in reproduction. In other words for the transmission of a gene or a constellation of genes, it is immaterial in which individual they occur, and an overall reproductive advantage for genes may be obtained even if some carriers of these genes have reduced fertility at the expense of others. The maternal care of offspring is a simple, obvious example which will clarify the argument. Hamilton has given the conditions, in mathematical terms, under which this type of selection (called selection at the kinship level by Maynard Smith [1964]) will hold. In the same way, the different types of "social selection" mentioned by Crook are regarded as the result of selection at the individual level. He states: "Social selection then is that process leading to the evolutionary enhancement of morphological allaesthetic and behavioral characteristics that function within a social system to provide biological advantages *to the individual* in relation to survival prior to reproduction, the formation of zygotes and the birth and rearing to maturity of young or the progeny of close kin" (p. 264; emphasis mine). This applies even to his social selection type *d* which involves selection for cooperative behavior within the group.

This type of social selection involves not only selection for characters of the individual but also selection for characters of its environment, that is, the other individuals that make up the group. This point can be seen clearly in considering Crook's social selection type *b*, identical with Darwinian sexual selection. If advantage due to sexual selection depends on social dominance alone, as is usually assumed for Primates, it selects simply for characters of the males, and is in this way similar to simple social selection. But if a choice on the part of the female is involved, sexual selection may act on the male, the female or on both. As long as all the females in a population react identically to male characters, female choice can of course be neglected. But if there are differences in the reactions of the females, sexual selection may act on both the male characters and the preferences of the female. Selection for female choice behavior was first considered by Fisher (1929) and the theory has been worked out by O'Donald (1962). He found that if both male and female choice behavior is subject to selection linkage of genes influencing the two behavioral characters will result. The population consequences of selective mating have been investigated by Kalmus & Maynard Smith (1966) and by Seiger (1967) for the specific case that mating preferences in birds may be determined by imprinting so that a bird (male or female) will mate preferentially with animals showing the same phenotype and consequently the same or similar genotype as its parents. The authors showed that this situation will lead to disruptive selection, so that in extreme cases the population would break up into two groups which do not mate with each other and are thus genetically isolated. An example of selection for female choice has been found in Drosophila (Bastock 1956). The sex-linked gene *y* induces in hemizygote males a reduction in virility (Prout 1971) and *y*-males are usually at a mating disadvantage because the females prefer wild-type males. But in a strain which had been homozygous for *y* for many generations the choice mechanism of the females became changed in such a way that they accepted wild-type and *y*-males indiscriminately.

Social selection may therefore differ from simple natural selection by the fact that it acts differently on individual group members; it may therefore be more complex to analyze. Nevertheless, all the examples of social selection mentioned involve selection at the level of individuals.

The assumption of Emerson, Wynne-Edwards and others that selection at the population level is necessary to account for certain characters which have arisen in evolution is therefore not accepted by many biologists. Williams (1966) discusses the argument in detail and comes to the conclusion that most of the characters mentioned by Emerson and Wynne-Edwards can be explained as the result of kin selection in the sense of Hamilton, while others may be spurious. Furthermore, Lewontin (1970) points out that selection for population fitness will be slow compared to selection acting on individuals, and therefore relatively ineffective.

Thus there appears to be no need to assume the existence of selection at the population level. There is, however, some evidence that it may, at least occasionally, occur. Genes have been found which increase the fitness of their carriers, but under some circumstances reduce the fitness of the population. Dawson (1969) described an eye color mutant which arose in his cultures of the beetle *Tribolium castaneum* which increased at the expense of its normal allele in his populations, indicating superior individual fitness. At the same time, the population became extinct in competition with the closely related species *T. confusum,* while in the absence of the mutant, *T. confusum* would become extinct in all replicates. This observation demonstrates undeniably that superior fitness in interindividual competition does not necessarily lead to increased fitness of the population.

Lewontin (1970) gives two examples which show that selection at the population level does indeed occur. The first involves parasites which are dependent for their transmission on the survival of the host. (He uses the myxoma virus of the rabbit as an example.) In this case, longer survival of the host favors transmission of the virus, that is, the establishment of new populations, and lower virulence of the parasite is thus of selective advantage and is actually selected for. His second case concerns the house mouse. The house mouse lives in small (less than 12 animals) inbreeding social units consisting of one or two dominant males, several females, possibly some subordinate males, and the young. (For evidence, see Selander 1970.) Migration between these social units is very low or nonexistent, due to the territorial behavior of the dominant males. In wild populations of the mouse, *t* alleles are frequently found. These genes have no morphological effects except in the heterozygote with the mutant allele *T*. In homozygous condition, the *t* alleles are either embryonic lethals, or they induce male sterility. These unfavorable effects are counteracted by preferential transmission of the *t* allele in the sperm of heterozygous $+/t$ males. In a population containing a sterilizing *t* allele it may thus occur by chance that the dominant male is homozygous for *t,* in which case the local population would become extinct.

Both cases show some of the conditions under which selection at the population level may become important. First of all, there must be relatively well-defined local populations with little or no genetic exchange with other populations. The small size of the effective breeding population may be important, since it increases the probability of unfavorable genes becoming established by chance and leading to extinction of the population.

It is doubtful whether in either case these local populations should be regarded as lineage groups (kinship groups) or as local populations in the sense of Brown (1966). They are certainly lineage groups insofar as they are genetically closely related—an inbreeding family in the mouse, and an asexual clone in the myxoma virus. On the other hand, both are allopatric, and thus defined, local populations of the species. The important fact is that selection in these cases affects the whole group, with the possibility of extinction, rather than individuals within the group.

In human beings, the matter of population selection becomes difficult because the survival of populations in a genetic sense is frequently confused with the survival of social units as defined by conscious identification of the members, and by cultural and linguistic characters. Social groups, such as tribes or nations, have certainly disappeared in the course of history, but whether this involved genetic extinction is doubtful, or at least not clear from one instance to the next.

In analogy to the mouse example it may be suggested that selection at the population level was involved at early evolutionary stages when groups were small and inbreeding strong. It is doubtful whether a small human population could survive prolonged inbreeding if it contained recessive deleterious genes. It may be pointed out here that the mouse is unique among the animals used in genetics in its tolerance to inbreeding. All the numerous pure mouse strains used in laboratories have been estabished by long continued individual brother-sister matings, a procedure which is not used in any other organism, and leads to physical deterioration in some, such as the chicken. In view of the findings of Adams & Neel (1967), it may be supposed that in man, a close inbreeding system like that found in the mouse would frequently lead to extinction of a small population. Extreme outbreeding on the other hand would not be compatible with efficient social organization. The mating patterns found in all human societies are similar in that they avoid both extreme inbreeding and widespread exogamy. Genetic polymorphism, as indicated by morphological variation and by investigation of single gene dependent characters, seems to be of similar magnitude in the small populations of the primitive Xavantes and the inhabitants of the large modern city of Hamburg (Neel et al. 1964). What is suggested here is that the mating patterns found in man have indeed been established on the basis of social considerations, but that biological consequences made some populations more efficient in the production of surviving offspring than others.

Alexander (1971) makes a strong point for the importance of warfare in human evolution, which may have led to selection at the population level. This depends, of course, on the time in human evolution at which organized warfare arose. He assumes that it arose very early (*Australopithecus*), on the basis of evidence for cannibalism, which he believes to have been closely connected with the origin of warfare. The evidence for the occurrence of cannibalism is indeed very strong in *Homo sapiens* in the upper Pleistocene, but becomes less certain when earlier periods are considered. Other authors have pointed out that many (though not all) recent "primitive" peoples do not know organized warfare and that therefore it must have arisen very late in human history. This argument is not convincing because this behavior may have been lost in adaptation to the specific habitats in which they live. This seems indeed the case for the Eskimo, since in prehistoric context body armor has been found (Bandi 1969), and body armor is unlikely to have had any other uses. Be that as it may, even if the argument for an early origin of war is accepted, it is unlikely that it has led directly to the extinction of populations by killing and cannibalism as proposed by Alexander. More likely is the possibility that defeated populations retired into less favorable environments in which they had to restrict the size of the population for lack of resources.

A particular problem is posed by the evolutionary trend in the Hominid line towards a longer period of development to maturity. As pointed out earlier in this paper, this character must have arisen against the strong evolutionary pressures for early reproduction. It may be pointed out that in primitive human societies in which old men have control of most of the females (see Chapter 10), early attainment of sexual maturity may be of lesser selective value than it would be otherwise. Nevertheless, some advantage of slow maturation must be assumed to account for this evolutionary trend, and it is frequently suspected that the advantage may have been the longer time available for learning and acculturation. This is a plausible argument if it is considered that social adaptation in Primates depends to a high degree on learning, and that this will take more time in man with his complex and varied social interactions. It should be considered that even for the modern child it takes several years to attain command of the language. It is therefore conceivable that a prolonged period of immaturity may have permitted more and better learning and therefore closer and more efficient integration of the social activities of the group. In this case, group selection appears thus more likely than individual selection. A difficulty arises, however, from the fact that an extension of the immature period, though not as extreme as in man, is found in the Pongidae. This evolutionary trend must therefore have arisen independently in the Pongidae for which the argument for social selection would hardly apply. Or it must be a very early trend which was well started when the Hominid and Pongid lines became separated. For the present time, the increase in period of immaturity in human evolution may best be regarded as a vexing problem for which no answer can be given.

The strongest argument for the importance of population selection in human evolution has been made by Lewontin (1965, 1970). He points out that although population selection may be rare under most ecological circumstances, it may be expected to play a large role in colonization. In colonization, very few organisms, possibly only one inseminated or pregnant female, may start a new population. This is Mayr's founder principle (1963). Most attempts at colonization will be unsuccessful, that is, the whole colonizing population will become extinct. Only few attempts of establishing colonies will be successful, and these will be dependent on the genetic constitution of the founders. This principle is of importance since man has been a very successful colonizing species. *Australopithecus,* as far as we know, was restricted to Eastern and Southern Africa, but *Homo erectus* had occupied the whole Asian-European land mass, and immigration into the American continent took place in the late Pleistocene. In other words, all inhabitable places on the earth had been occupied by man in prehistoric times. At least part of this spreading of the species took place in relatively short periods of time. Lewontin's argument would lead to the conclusion that at least during the occupation of new areas selection at the population level may well have played a role.

The last few paragraphs have led away from the topic of this book, sexual selection. But it appeared worthwhile to point out some related questions whose consideration may clarify the complex factors which played a role in human evolution. The arguments put forth in the book point to the conclusion that sexual selection in the sense of Darwin probably was one of these factors, that it may have had great importance in the evolution of the specific human behavior, and that it continues to be effective in some, though not in all, human societies. New evidence may be confidently expected from a more thorough study of human populations, as well as a continued behavioral study of different nonhuman Primates, particularly if it can be complemented by population genetic investigations of these organisms. Our greatest limitation in meaningful speculations at the present time is the almost complete lack of fossil prehominid material from the early Pliocene and Miocene. It can be hoped that this material will help to clarify many of the problems raised in this chapter.

References

Adams, M. S., & J. V. Neel. 1967. Children of incest. *Pediatrics* 40: 55–62.

Alexander, R. D. 1971. The search for an evolutionary philosophy of man. *Proc. Royal Soc. Vict.* 84 (part 1): 99–120.

Bandi, M. G. 1969. *Eskimo prehistory*. Translated by A. E. Keap. Alaska: Alaska Press.

Bastock, M. 1956. A gene mutation which changes a behavior pattern. *Evolution* 10: 421–439.

Bateman, A. J. 1948. Intrasexual selection in Drosophila. *Heredity* 2: 349–368.

Brown, J. L. 1966. Types of group selection. *Nature* 211: 870.

———. 1970. Cooperative breeding and altruistic behavior in the Mexican jay *Aphelocoma ultramarina. Animal Behaviour* 18: 366–378.

Caspari, E. 1963. Selective forces in the evolution of man. *Amer. Naturalist* 97: 5–14.

Chance, M. R. A. 1962. Nature and special features of the instinctive social bond of Primates. In *Social life of early man,* ed. S. L. Washburn, pp. 17–33. Viking Fund Publications in Anthropology, vol. 31. New York: Wenner-Gren Foundation.

Cole, L. 1954. The population consequences of life history phenomena. *Quart. Rev. Biol.* 29: 103–137.

Cotter, W. B. 1963. Population genetic studies at the *a*+ locus in *Ephestia kühniella. Evolution* 17: 233–248.

Count, E. W. 1958. The biological basis of human sociality. *Amer. Anthropologist* 60: 1049–1085.

Dawson, P. S. 1969. A conflict between Darwinian fitness and population fitness in *Tribolium* competition experiments. *Genetics* 62: 413–419.

Demeny, P. 1968. Early fertility decline in Austria-Hungary: a lesson in demographic transition. Historical Population Studies: *Daedalus,* Spring 1968. 502–522.

Eckland, B. K. 1968. Theories of mate selection. *Eugenics Quart.* 15: 71–84.

Emerson, A. E. 1960. The evolution of adaptation in population systems.In *Evolution after Darwin,* ed. S. Tax, 1: 307–348. Chicago: Univ. of Chicago Press.

Etkin, W. 1954. Social behavior and the evolution of man's mental capacities. *Amer. Naturalist* 88: 129–142.

Faugères, A., C. Petit & E. Thibout. 1971. The components of sexual selection. *Evolution* 25: 265–275.

Fisher, R. A. 1929. *The genetical theory of natural selection.* Oxford: Clarendon Press.

Hajnal, J. 1965. European marriage patterns in historical perspective. In *Population in history,* ed. D. V. Glass and D. E. C. Eversley, pp. 101–143. Chicago: Aldine.

Haldane, J. B. S. 1932. *The causes of evolution.* London: Edward Arnold. New York: Harper & Row.

———. 1949. Parental and fraternal correlations for fitness. *Ann. Eugenics* 14: 288-292.

Hamilton, W. D. 1964. The genetical evolution of social behavior. *J. Theoret. Biol.* 7: 1–16 and 17–52.

Harris, H. 1946. The inheritance of premature baldness in men. *Ann. Eugenics* 13: 172–181.

Holloway, R. 1966. Cranial capacity and the evolution of the human brain. *Amer. Anthropologist* 68: 103–121.

Jerison, H. J. 1969. Brain evolution and dinosaur brains. *Amer. Naturalist* 103: 578–588.

Kalmus, H. & S. Maynard Smith. 1966. Some evolutionary consequences of pegmatypic mating systems. *Amer. Naturalist* 100: 619–636.

Kempthorne, O., & E. Pollak. 1970. Concepts of fitness in Mendelian populations. *Genetics* 64: 125–145.

Klein, J., & D. W. Bailey 1971. Histocompatibility differences in wild mice: further evidence for the existence of deme structure in natural populations of house mouse. *Genetics* 68: 287–297.

Lewontin, R. C. 1965. Selection for colonizing ability. In *The genetics of colonizing species,* ed. H. G. Baker & G. L. Stebbins, pp. 77–91. New York: Academic Press.

———. 1970. The units of selection. *Annual Rev. Ecol. Systematics* 1: 1–18.

Maynard Smith, S. 1964. Group selection and kin selection. *Nature* 201: 1145–1147.

Mayr, E. 1963. *Animal species and evolution.* Cambridge: Harvard Univ. Press.

Neel, J. V., F. M. Salzano, P. C. Junqueira, F. Keiter, & D. Maybury-Lewis. 1964. Studies on the Xavante Indians of the Brazilian Matto Grosso. *Amer. J. Human Genet.* 16: 52–140.

O'Donald, P. 1962. The theory of sexual selection. *Heredity* 17: 541–552.

Orians, G. H. 1969. On the evolution of mating systems in birds and mammals. *Amer. Naturalist* 103: 589–603.

Prout, T. 1971. The relation between fitness components and population prediction in *Drosophila.* I: The estimation of fitness components. *Genetics* 68: 127–149.

Seiger, M. B. 1967. A computer simulation study of the influence of imprinting on population structure. *Amer. Naturalist* 101: 47–57.

Selander, R. K. 1970. Biochemical polymorphism in populations of the house mouse and old-field mouse. *Symp. Zool. Soc. London* 26: 73–91.

Selander, R. K., & S. Y. Yang. 1969. Protein polymorphism and genic heterozygosity in a wild population of the house mouse (*Mus musculus*). *Genetics* 63: 653–667.

Stern, C., & A. M. Hannah. 1950. The sex combs in gynanders of *Drosophila melanogaster*. *Portugaliae Acta Biol.* Ser. A. Vol. R. B. Goldschmidt: 798–812.

Sturtevant, A. H. 1915. Experiment on sex recognition and the problem of sexual selection in *Drosphila*. *J. Animal Behav.* 5: 351–366.

Thoday, J. M. 1953. Components of fitness. *Symp. Soc. Exptl. Biol.* 7: 96–113.

Weidenreich, F. 1946. *Apes, giants and man.* Chicago: Univ. of Chicago Press.

Williams, G. C. 1966. *Adaptation and Natural Selection*. Princeton: Princeton Univ. Press.

Wolff, G. 1933. *Leben und Erkennen*. Munich: Reinhard.

Wynne-Edwards, V. C. 1962. *Animal dispersion in relation to social behavior.* Edinburgh: Oliver and Boyd.

Index